# EDUCATION
# FROM THE HEART

## A Jungian Symbolic Perspective

To Manisha Roy

with Admiration

Carl Bijingh

Montreal August 23ʳᵈ,

2010

*Other books by the author:*


JUNGIAN SYMBOLIC PSYCHOLOGY

THE LATIN AMERICAN IDENTITY: AN INTRODUCTION TO SYMBOLIC ANTHROPOLOGY

THE ALTERITY ARCHETYPE AND THE SYMBOLIC RICHNESS OF SOCCER

THE ARCHETYPE OF LIFE AND DEATH

THE ALTERITY ARCHETYPE AND THE HUMANIZATION PROCESS IN LATIN AMERICA

CREATIVE ENVY: THE RESCUE OF ONE OF CIVILIZATION'S MAJOR FORCES

CARLOS AMADEU BOTELHO BYINGTON

# EDUCATION FROM THE HEART

A Jungian Symbolic Perspective

———

*Translation by Carlos Byington*
*Revision by Siobhan Drummond*

Chiron Publications
Wilmette, Illinois

© 2010 by Carlos Amadeu Botelho Byington

Cover design by Vera Rosenthal
Book design: Ione Pereira / Vinicius de Souza
Printed in Brazil by Linear B Ed.

Byington, Carlos Amadeu Botelho.
Education from the heart: a jungian symbolic perspective. / Carlos Amadeu Botelho Byington. Translation by Carlos Byington.
Revision by Siobhan Drummond. — São Paulo: Linear B, 2010.

356p. il.

Originally published as A construção amorosa do saber: O fundamento e a finalidade da Pedagogia Simbólica Junguiana. © 2003 by Carlos Amadeu BotelhoByington. Published by W11 Editores Ltda.

B997

Library of Congress Cataloging-in-Publication Data
ISBN - 978-1-888602-48-7 (pbk.)
1. Education. 2. Educational Psychology. 3. Symbolic Psychology.
4. Consciousness. 5. Theory of Knowledge. 6. Constructivism. 7. Jung, Carl Gustav (1875 - 1961). I. Title. II. Byington, Carlos, Translation. III. Drummond, Siobhan, Revision.

Cataloging prepared by Wanda Lucia Schmidt - CRB-8-1922

The illustration on the cover was made by Gustave Doré for Tennyson's Iddylls of the King.

## Thanks

To Elisa, Rita, Olívia and Bianca
for my initiation followed
by countless lessons on fatherhood.

To Maria Helena,
my tireless teacher of companionship and love.

# TABLE OF CONTENTS

# Preface

As legend goes, two dragons met in the end of the sixth century B.C. in China. Both were famous for their wisdom. Confucius was the younger and Lao Tsu the elder. They were asked by their followers for a message, in one word, that would serve to improve mankind. The two geniuses concentrated for three days, during which their followers exchanged their philosophies. At the end of the third day, the words were brought in sandalwood boxes by a couple of adolescents to be opened in the middle of the congress.

When the boxes were opened, the two words were revealed to be one and the same: education.

Although the presentation of a general theory of education may seem at first sight a most difficult proposition, the concept of the archetype has very much helped to face this task.

The theme of symbolic education within Jung's theory of the individuation process is of such importance that it deserves the effort to incorporate it into the general theory of humanism.

May 2010.

*Carlos Byington*

# Introduction

# THE FUNDAMENTALS
# OF SYMBOLIC EDUCATION

Jungian symbolic education is a pedagogic method that can be described as:

Based on the symbolic development of the personality and of culture, coordinated by archetypes, which includes all dimensions of life: body, nature, society, idea, image, emotion, word, number, sound, silence, and behavior.

Centered in experience rather than abstraction and which daily summons forth the imagination of students and educators to reunite the objective and the subjective within the symbolic dimension, activated by the most varied expressive techniques in order to experience learning through symbolic elaboration.

Trying always to be emotional, comic and dramatic, attractive, springing from the loving transference relationship between student, class, and teacher.

Employing the interactive features of apprenticeship and useful labor, while at the same time symbolically relating the material being taught to the totality of life, thus opening education up to a permanent psychodynamic dialogue with health and culture, interrelating the normal and the pathological in the search for wisdom.

Centered in the ecosystem of the human body within its environment, in the emotional, cognitive, and existential processes of the individual, culture, our planet, and the cosmos.

Meaningfully relating the five archetypal positions of the ego-other polarity in consciousness.

Identifying fixation and defensive symbols, complexes, and functions in learning and elaborating them significantly to avoid shadow formation.

Paying special attention to including the ethical function in symbolic elaboration so as to experience it inseparably from learning.

Subordinating learning to wisdom and to the ideology of symbolic humanism, having in mind the development of the psychological potential directed toward the welfare of the individual and of society.

Although this book was originally written in Portuguese and soon translated in Spanish keeping in mind the type of education practiced mainly in Brazil and the Latin American countries, it refers also in many respects to traditional Western methods of education.

The cultural matrix found here takes root in the works of C. G. Jung, Erich Neumann, Piaget, Freud, Melanie Klein, Heidegger, and Teilhard de Chardin. Heidegger's concept of being—which is equivalent to my concept of psyche and which permeates this book—is that being (*Sein*) which in its humanity (*Dasein*) is not separate from the world (*Welt*) because, in principle, being is being-in-the-world (*Dasein ist in-der-Welt-sein*). Heidegger's concept of *Dasein* is equivalent to the concept of symbol, which reunites the subjective and objective dimensions and is the theoretical center of Jungian symbolic psychology. Teilhard de Chardin's concept of humanization, which scientifically and evolutionarily complements Heidegger's ontology (in the collective dimension) and Jung's individuation process (in the individual dimension), states that the matter of the universe was differentiated until it generated life and the biosphere of the planet. Through the differentiation of the nervous system during evolution the biosphere generated the noosphere, the phenomenon of human consciousness, which is considered the aim of the process of symbolic elaboration.

This book deals with symbolic humanism, a method of education, and the teaching of it. I went to high school in Baltimore, Maryland, graduated from college in medicine and psychiatry in Rio de Janeiro, studied and trained in psychoanalysis, and then went to Zürich where I trained to become a Jungian analyst at the C. G. Jung Institute. I have always been a teacher; it was as though my development depended on the transmission of knowledge to people around me, starting with my schoolmates and then with my university colleagues and patients (children, adolescents individually or in groups, adults, couples, and families). My analytical training took place alongside clinical practice while I developed my own creativity in supervisions, lectures, and publications. For ten years, I was involved in the weekly supervision of teachers of elementary and high school in a private institution with approximately four hundred students.

Jungian symbolic education stems from Jungian symbolic psychology (Byington 2008), and both study individual and collective development of the psychological archetypal potential. It follows the old ideal of humanism: that humankind benefits by transforming people through culture in search of a higher consciousness. It is inspired by the great systems dedicated to improving life through knowledge and ethics, for instance, Confucianism in China (approximately 551–479 B.C.) and the *paideia* in ancient Greece. Although centuries have passed, the idealistic essence of these great systems is still alive. An important characteristic of this traditional search for wholeness is the reunion of the subjective and the objective dimensions—learning about things together with emotions and ethics. A contribution to this tradition by modern education is the correlation between the psychological and philosophical formation of consciousness with learning, a true *gnôthe s'autón*, the Delphic Oracle's injunction to know thyself, which includes knowing the world inseparably from life.

I see a close relation between Piaget's constructivism, which influences all modern teaching, and what I call the initiatory method of pedagogic symbolic elaboration. I shall attempt to associate Piaget's findings in the formation of intelligence to the overall emotional development of consciousness. The main theoretical difference lies in the fact that Piaget's pedagogy concentrates on cognitive psychology with an emphasis on extraverted thinking and sensation functions, whereas Jungian symbolic pedagogy emerges from and develops in keeping with the archetypal development of the whole personality during the individuation process.

One cannot teach only by thinking, sensation, and extraversion without leaving behind a large part of the psychic potential in learning. The functions of consciousness, according to Jung, are thinking, feeling, sensation, and intuition, and the two attitudes are extraversion and introversion. Making an association between Piaget's theory of the formation of intelligence and the Jungian archetypal perspective is difficult to accomplish because Piaget's work is centered on consciousness, while Jung's focuses on the collective unconscious. I have come up with five archetypal positions in consciousness to bridge the two theories within the concept of symbolic constructivism.

The main message of Jungian symbolic pedagogy is based on emotion and experience and on the concept of the normal symbolic development of the psyche applied to the affectionate teacher-student transference. Those who experience learning emotionally apprehend by molding the identity of the ego and of the other. By "other", I mean all that is not ego in consciousness, be it a living or a non-living entity. Those who learn without experience absorb the material only on the rational level and soon forget it. For many years, I have delved into the practice of expressive techniques to transform theory into experience, including drawing, painting, and clay techniques, musical and body techniques, dramatic techniques such as sand play and use of "marionettes of the self" (Byington 1993a), meditative and imaginative techniques (active imagination, written and drawn), and oracular techniques such as the tarot, *I Ching,* and runes. Recently, I have become increasingly interested in the fascination that children have for videogames. These games are expressive techniques that develop the imagination and have a brilliant future if employed within the symbolic perspective of imagination in teaching all subjects in the curriculum.

I have always been impressed by the importance of early childhood experiences in the formation of the ego, which I consider to be Freud's greatest discovery. In my teaching, I have applied this same notion to the formation of the ego and of the other in consciousness. Through observation and reflection, I have come to the conclusion that, in consciousness and in the whole psyche, the identity of the ego is formed together with the identity of the other through the elaboration (the experience and differentiation) of symbols. Jungian symbolic psychology conceives the formation of consciousness by endless ego-other and other-other polarities, which represent the identities of the subject and of the object in the mind. It seems to me that the preference given to identity formation of the ego in primary and secondary narcissism, leaving the identity of the other in second place, is a cultural, defensive, narcissistic distortion originating in the Western cult of individuality and not a natural, psychological reality. In this perspective, we have the ego and the other in the center of consciousness as well as the other associated with another, forming the other-other polarity. For example, when I speak of my love for my mother, I am referring to the ego-other polarity, but when I speak of the tenderness between my parents, I am referring to the other-other polarity. When a teacher speaks of his disciples, we have the presence of the ego-other polarity in his consciousness, but when two students talk in class, the teacher registers their chat as the other-other polarity in his consciousness and in his memory.

I have applied pedagogical and psychological symbolic theories in the classroom and in the consultation office and have verified that rational learning often remains on superficial levels. This explains the high degree to which we forget what we learn: we spend twelve years in school and perhaps a few more years in college and graduate school. At age forty-five, when we reach our full maturity in using what we have learned, what is left of our schooling? In most cases, a small percentage of what we were taught. We urgently need statistical studies to quantify this forgetfulness, whether constructivist or not, in so-called Western culture. I estimate that as a result of such studies, this immense forgetfulness will denounce the limitations of the almost exclusively rational teaching we still practice. I think that the lack of studies measuring the end results of such teaching is a defense, an emotional resistance to proving the bankruptcy of dominantly rational education and its giant waste of time and resources.

Due to my experience in psychology, education, and creative processes, I have arrived at the conclusion that everything can become a source of learning and play a role in the development of the personality. The experiential model of identity formation in early life, based on experiences and primary emotional relations, can be seen as the most fertile model of learning throughout life. What has always caught my attention in clinical practice is the resistance to change exhibited by defenses and symptoms formed in early childhood. Instead of attributing this resistance simply to the intensity of the fixations themselves, I realized that it was mainly due to the fact that these fixations occurred mostly in the insular position of consciousness (see chapter 7), which Piaget describes as the sensory-motor phase of intelligence formation and which Jung calls unconscious identity or *participation mystique*. In keeping with the fact that children learn many things—such as languages and videogames—much faster than adults, I concluded that in this position education is much more productive than in the phase of conceptual intelligence.

The archetypal root of the insular matriarchal position means that it is present not only in early childhood but throughout life and, consequently, it can be reproduced ritually in expressive techniques and in the emotion of the student-teacher transference relationship.

Jung's concept of archetype allows us to take symbolic elaboration from its roots in the development of intelligence in childhood and apply it for life. It is the realization of this model on the existential level that opens the path of learning to question dominantly rational teaching and to amplify the concept of symbol to encompass the emotional dimension together with the objective dimension. As this model is the natural path to human learning, I was interested in understanding how it had become so limited in Western culture. In this case, the comparative anthropological study is striking. The vast majority of cultures adopt the experiential model until they undergo the influence of the materialist science of Western culture. In chapter 2, I shall examine this question in detail.

## The Initiatory Aim of Symbolic Education

As in the rest of our modern culture, pedagogy suffers the traumatic consequences of the separation between science and religion that took place at the end of the eighteenth century. In that separation, the objective was equated to truth while the subjective was equated to error, an absurdity that only psychopathology can explain, as we will see ahead. There are pedagogical trends that pass on subjective moral precepts parallel to objective learning, but unfortunately they exclude the subjective-objective and the construction of ethics within existential and cosmic totality from teaching. Symbolic pedagogy seeks to rescue and reunite them. Its place is in science, but in symbolic science, which includes the subject-object interrelation. It deals with moral precepts, but instead of subordinating them to moral tradition, it inserts them within the symbolic development of the personality as the structuring function of ethics. This search is directed by the scientific method, which becomes initiatory when it includes experience. The concept of initiation used here is inspired by the rituals of tribal societies where knowledge is learned and apprehended through experience.

Symbolic education proposes an initiatory knowledge, obtained by the elaboration of symbols within the parameters of symbolic science: knowledge of the whole by experiencing its parts as structuring symbols. The method assigns to the teacher the responsibility of developing his or her creativity in order to present the facts to be taught as experiences, that is, as structuring symbols that form and differentiate the ego-other relationship in consciousness. In this case, it is up to the teacher not only to purge the claim to absolute objectivity but to associate the subjective and objective dimensions creatively in the structuring symbol, thereby making the experience alive, fascinating, thrilling, and touching to the students (Byington 1987a, 1987b). This involves transforming the transfer of knowledge into a dramatic process as exciting as life itself when lived in a courageous, detached, and creative way. Thus, in accordance with Piaget's school and its followers, we may speak about constructive teaching, yet to make it initiatory, we need to use the rational and the irrational, the conscious and the unconscious, the subjective and the objective, equally within the symbolic perspective. In this way, constructivism becomes symbolic constructivism because it is practiced according to symbols within the individuation process of teachers and students.

Symbolic education is based on experience, primordially centered in neither the ego nor the other, and neither in the subject who learns nor in the object learned. Both are relative and secondary. What is primordial is the relationship of ego and other within the Self through the experience of symbols. The Jungian concept of Self includes the dynamic interaction of all conscious and unconscious structures of personality such as ego, other, shadow, and all symbols and archetypes on the individual and collective levels. I have separated it from the main arquetype which I refer to as the central arquetype to avoid ambiguity. I have amplified the concept of the individual Self to include any systemic dimension of totality, such as school activities (pedagogic Self), therapy (therapeutic Self), family (family Self), society (cultural Self), the life of the planet (planetary Self) and the cosmos (cosmic Self). This is, therefore, a pedagogy of relationships expressing the transformation of individual, cultural, planetary, and cosmic being (Self). From individual Self to cosmic Self, symbolic learning deals with the differentiation of cosmic consciousness through matter, as Teilhard de Chardin (1947) so well described in his theory of the humanization process.

To build this knowledge of the Self, Jungian symbolic education is practiced by means of symbols, complexes, functions, and structuring systems, which encompass all the dimensions of being: body, nature, society, idea, image, emotion, word, number, sound, silence, and behavior (Byington 1988a). These dimensions are inseparable but I have listed them to call attention to their nature. From this point of view, we see clearly how rational education is limited and imprisoned: students, whose bodies are usually immobilized on chairs, are told about things they frequently cannot see, touch, smell, listen to, taste, love, or hate. They listen to exclusively logical explanations without emotion, pleasure, humor, or existential involvement. There is no pedagogic group interaction among themselves nor with the teacher. They are far away from nature, isolated in rational thought, with their heads separated from their bodies, floating in the air like a blimp, full of words and concepts. This type of learning is almost exclusively evaluated by verbal-logical testing weeks after it occurred. It makes a methodological point of excluding whole life from its method and of ignoring its evaluation by the greater or lesser capacity of students and teachers to insert what is learned meaningfully in the existential process.

## Memory and Intelligence in Symbolic Learning

According to the point of view described above, it comes as no surprise that the memory of the Self has difficulty retaining and even resists and rejects exclusively rational knowledge. Taking into account all basic components of symbols, complexes, functions, and structuring systems, we realize that predominantly rational education lays claim to teaching mostly by the sole use of the thinking function, which is but one of the four functions of consciousness. This method still pervades most teaching from lower school to graduate school and college,whether based on constructivism or not. How is it that we have come to such a distortion of the natural method of symbolic elaboration inherent in the development of consciousness? If symbols are experienced in all human dimensions, why expect to teach life mainly through ideas? The symbolic perspective transcends rational intelligence, which is often transformed into the IQ tyranny used in selection tests. This perspective remits us to the concept of existential intelligence, which encompasses Goleman's emotional intelligence, the evaluation of which is tested by the capacity to apply existentially the content of teaching to any dimension of the Self through both the cognitive and the emotional dimensions (Gardner 1983; Goleman 1995)

Thus, Jungian symbolic education is offered as a practice of knowledge for the understanding cognition of life and for the use of this comprehension as early as possible in society, through activities at the sources of production. Symbolic education allows for the ongoing experience of knowledge as a result of differentiation of the whole, which in turn promotes an increasingly conscious approximation to this same whole. It is a circular apprenticeship in which by getting to know the new, we also know the old, because the new is inseparable from the old, from which we originate and to which we return to continue differentiating endlessly through the humanization process.

We seek knowledge of being rather than simply knowledge of things because we do not remain in the rational concatenation of facts. We try to perceive what things do to the ego and what the ego does to them, recording these experiences in existential memory. Whether in the pedagogic, individual, conjugal, family, cultural, planetary or cosmic Self, we cultivate knowledge to dedicate it in our daily work to the most productive of all these dimensions. While erudite knowledge suffers from chronic narcissism and places the ego as an autonomous entity in life, symbolic knowledge roots the ego, the other, and their interrelationship in the cosmos by archetypal symbolic elaboration of things lived in experiences. This involves a being that, knowing life and things as parts of the cosmos (Heidegger 1927), begins to perceive learning affectionately as a manifestation of the creative urge within, which includes eternity and infinity.

This attitude toward teaching reduces the difference between ordinary teaching and so-called professional teaching. Because symbolic teaching is perceived as applied—to be used in life and, as often as possible, at the sources of production—it is always highly professional in its orientation. To learn things symbolically is to know what they are good for, educating students from their first encounter with knowledge to discuss its use with experts.

For teachers to evaluate their efficiency in applying this teaching, they must always ask themselves:

Is this application important in our lives, in the lives of the students, and in life in general?

This way, teachers constantly evaluate the content of their teaching and the work they transmit to the existential intelligence and memory of their students. This is of value for all levels of teaching, from preschool to postgraduate study. Brazilian educator Paulo Freire recommends (apart from the ideology of the oppressed) that even teaching to read and write should have a pragmatic purpose in the student's daily universe (Freire 1970). The teacher should bear in mind that teaching things that are alien to the students' practical context is like introducing a functional island in the students' brains which sucks memory and intelligence into itself, withdrawing them from life. The transmission of useless teaching favors alienation and the waste of existential intelligence of the student, the teacher, and the school, as well as of the family income and social resources.

## The Religious, Political, Artistic, and Philosophic Aspects of Education

The philosophy of symbolic education is essentially humanistic and scientific, and therefore it does not profess any religious or political creed, although, being archetypal and ontological, it naturally experiences both religiosity and a connection to society, to the *polis*. This cannot be avoided, for teaching with structuring symbols, complexes, functions, and systems keeps the notion of transcendence of the part and its connection to the cultural and universal whole. Very probably this is why Jung called the psychic symbolizing function the transcendent function. This transcendence of the part and its meaningful connection to the whole introduces the concepts of initiation and sacredness in teaching. Learning only about things keeps us on the level of the literal and profane. Learning the meaning of things connected to the individual, cultural, and cosmic whole enables us to cultivate transcendence, which leads to the experience of the sacred through symbolic dimension. Here the dimension of the sacred does not refer to any sort of religious cult but solely to the connection of the part with the cosmic whole through the countless meanings already present in every part.

As might be expected, symbolic education is also artistic. Its science is the already accumulated knowledge of being, and especially the scientific method of understanding it. Its art lies in the emotional creativity aimed at reuniting the subjective to the objective in its teaching. It is political and sociocultural because it constantly interrelates student-teacher-class-school-family-culture and it roots knowledge in the interdisciplinary and cultural Self, preventing its alienation by transcending islands of fragmented knowledge. Its knowledge does not lie in abstraction. It is an emotional knowledge engaged in application, in work, in the productive change of life. This makes teacher and labor a permanently interrelated cultural polarity whose value links, exalts, and dignifies work and knowledge, learning, making, and living.

Finally, symbolic education is philosophical and expresses symbolic science and symbolic humanism in so far as it uses the path of knowledge to make being conscious and to affectionately elaborate that it is in the world, *in-der-Welt-sein,* as Heidegger (1927) described it. Thus its goal is not to know things in themselves but to know emotionally the revealed things as transforming and differentiating symbols of cosmic being through human dramatization within the individuation process.

The scientific points of reference of symbolic education are not those of materialistic and positivist science, solely centered in the object, but those of symbolic science (Byington 1987b), which reunites the objective and the subjective in the symbolic dimension and differentiates them by symbolic elaboration. Thus, symbolic education equally admits and studies exoteric experiences, such as geography and chemistry, basically oriented by the characteristics of objects, as well as esoteric experiences, such as dreams and myths, basically oriented by the subjective fantasy of reality. Yet, it is most careful to avoid the esoteric bias of upholding subjective symbolic perception as being objective.

Reality is always symbolic. Whether perceived through special states of consciousness, such as through a medium, psychography, fantasy, dreams, poetry, or any other imaginative form, it always needs to be submitted to symbolic elaboration to decode the subjective from the objective. In this way, symbolic education avoids two great reductive attitudes that mutilate reality and knowledge. First, it avoids positivism and materialism, which imprison knowledge in dehumanized, aseptic objective knowledge. This is true for those who only accept as knowledge what they can see, touch, measure, and weigh. Second, it avoids objectified esotericism that has neglected to differentiate subjective from objective perception in the imagination, as for instance when people believe that human beings live concretely inside the earth because they imagine it to be so. In the epistemology of this symbolic theory of knowledge, one seeks to profit from exoteric and esoteric knowledge through symbolic elaboration. The identity of ego and other and of the subject-object in consciousness emerge from symbols, and it is their elaboration and separation as proposed by Descartes in his genial, although frequently misunderstood, *Discourse on the Method* (1637) that laid the foundations of modern science.

Symbolic education seeks to teach the natural way we learn in childhood, a method of learning whose model is the process of identity formation of ego and other in consciousness through the emotional experience and elaboration of structuring symbols, complexes, functions, and systems. In this model of symbolic formation of the ego, we are in the presence of the passive-active polarity. At first the ego relates to the other primarily in the passive and afterward primarily in the active position to elaborate and integrate the meaning of the symbol at issue. A hungry baby at first only cries and opens its mouth. But in the next moment it sucks. Then, in response to satisfaction and frustration, it invents a pacifier with its fingers and then elects other transitional objects from breast to life (Winnicott 1965). Thus it becomes more and more active in the elaboration of symbols within the structuring function of nourishment, until one day, it proudly holds knife and fork and, at the postgraduate level, even a napkin. The timing of the passive-active interaction of educator and of the student in symbolic elaboration is an essential part of the art of teaching. First it is necessary to feed and only long afterward teach how to plant and harvest.

This method coordinates, in its way, four great trends in education. First, the genetic, developmental, psychological trend inherent, for instance, in Piaget's school. It is distinguished by its archetypal and symbolic points of reference, which do not privilege the rational nor reduce development to the evolutionary stages of intelligence, for it also always recognizes the stage archetypically, which can return in later circumstances. In second place is the social psychology trend of Vygotsky, because of its archetypal view of pedagogic transference. Third comes thematic education, which selects certain themes according to their importance within the cultural Self. The fourth is teaching the moral and religious trend of the path of wisdom, to be achieved by the emotional and rational knowledge of life in the world through the individuation and humanization processes.

## When the Symbol Appears in the Psyche of the Child

The notion of when a symbol becomes active in the psyche is crucial here. Usually, we consider symbolic activity to be a cognitive acquisition of the development of the ego's intelligence. This is ego psychology, which tends to create a rational education, practiced by the teacher's ego and directed to the student's ego. Centered in the development stages of the ego, traditional education and psychology tend to reduce symbolization to a progressive process. In this way, we fail to realize that long before the ego actively practices symbolization at the age of five the structuring symbol is already expressing the central archetype and sponsoring the formation and differentiation of the identity of ego and other, starting from nondifferentiation and following

Piaget's sensory-perceptive intelligence or the insular matriarchal position of consciousness. When we are aware of the archetypal trans-egoic component of the symbol, we conclude that teaching does not need to be exclusively delimited by the cognitive development of the ego and of rational intelligence. It can also be oriented by symbolic roots, which naturally originate and provide the ego's development, with all the existential forms of intelligence, of which cognitive intelligence is the consequence.

## The Symbol Appears with the Psyche

The perception of the psychological dimension through the perspective of the ego has led many researchers to the conception that infantile concreteness is not symbolic. In such a case, we wrongly condition the acquisition of the symbolic capacity to ego development and conclude that the first significant symbolic experience occurs through the transitional object, the security blanket or the teddy bear, which the child sucks and hugs to replace the breast and the mother (Winnicott 1965). In this case, the initial mother figure would not be symbolic.

From the point of view of the ego, this is true. The child initially is attached exclusively to those who care for it, and as it develops it relates progressively with transitional objects, which substitute primary relationships. From this point of view, primary relationship would not be symbolic, and symbols would only appear with transitional objects. But, from the point of view of the Self, this is not so.

The concreteness of the breast, which makes it "the part for the whole" (*pars pro toto*), and of the mother herself is highly symbolic. She expresses the Self with so many meanings that her loss, between the baby's third and seventh month, may lead to mortal anaclitic depression (Spitz and Codliner 1966). In this case, the child dies because it has been deprived of the immense number of symbolic meanings that its mother represents in this stage of life. The psyche does not live on things, but on their meanings. It is precisely the symbolic strength of that concreteness of mother and father, and of the characteristics of the marriage bond between them that make the parental complex one of the main structuring symbols in the formation of ego and other identity. It is mainly the existential and concrete truthfulness of the symbol that will allow us to amplify it by imagination and insert it in the existential drama by experience. When we realize that the symbol forms the ego, we place the acquisition of symbolization by the ego at a later stage of its development. It is preceded by the structuring activity of the Self, consciously and unconsciously coordinated by archetypal patterns to form and transform the identity of the ego and of the other. This trans-egoic symbolic activity lasts throughout life, expresses the essence of the central archetype, and, therefore, is the heart of Jungian symbolic education.

This intimacy with daily life, provided by experience, makes teaching existential and pragmatic and inserts it into the workforce, which allows for an early association between school and labor. The youngster stimulates the forces of production with innocence, curiosity, idealism, and questioning, and industry offers youth the path to socialization through work. Nothing justifies teaching what a society is and how it works in a cloistered school, which speaks about culture but does not live it. In this sense the forbiddance of child labor in developing societies is necessary to allow them to attend school, but from high school onward, it should not exclude school life from society.

In the present situation, most noticeably in underdeveloped countries, not only adolescents but also college students often have four months per year of idle vacation, which is a cultural distortion with serious consequences (Byington 1988b). The less favored social classes have neither adolescence nor vacations. The more favored have an extended adolescence and too many vacations, which favors marginal and risk behaviors and social pathology because their vitality is not being productively used. In this case, the school functions parallel to the real life of the adolescents, becoming an institution that excludes pleasure and cultivates mostly duty without students knowing exactly why. The reaction is long vacations, centered solely in pleasure. This makes both vacations and school time artificial.

Rational and abstract teaching favors this alienation because, not being based on experience, it makes it difficult to relate youths to the pragmatism of the workforce. Precious human power, which remains idle to the detriment of education, of society, and of the youths themselves, is wasted. The result is that this unused apprenticeship is forgotten much quicker. One significant cause of lack of interest in studying is the fact that students (and often teachers, too) do not know how to explain where, how, and when they will apply what they learn (and teach). Separation between teaching and its application to life and work is one of the great limitations of our traditional teaching system. Schools are not expected and teachers are not trained to channel apprenticeship into social production during high school years. This is perhaps even more intense in Latin countries, where the Iberian tradition passed on to the young people of the modern bourgeoisie is that of the compulsory idleness of nobility. Absurdly enough, work came to have a status inferior to that of a diploma. In this context, work tends to become isolated from theory and knowledge in general. Historically, this dichotomy is rooted in the nobility-serfdom polarity characteristic of feudalism, which resisted the institutionalization of the bourgeoisie and the proletariat, mainly in developing countries. In our days, this tradition has been inherited by parasites—corrupt, smart-minded speculators—who exploit the productive working classes.

Symbolic education encourages the formation of a resource library in each school, in which teachers' contributions with ideas and expressive techniques culled from the daily creativity of teaching are stored as digital files. Saved in computers, these resources serve as consulting material to inspire other teachers in the school and beyond. This dynamic archive of the teachers' creativity stimulates and rescues their creativity from the isolation and abandonment in which it finds itself today. When we realize how little the students' creativity is used, we also perceive that in rational teaching, the creativity of many teachers is also not being put to good use. To a great extent it is still encrusted, waiting for integral teaching to let it burgeon. This happens when the teachers' training and development follow the vocation of affectionately transmitting knowledge with all its existential emotion and creativity.

The digital recordings of the paths of creativity to transform objective material into experience may also play a role at meetings and in national and international libraries (a format for which already exists—the Internet). This educational creativity will certainly attract artists interested in combining fantasy, playfulness, and teaching in movies, cartoons, and videogames so as to dramatize learning more and more. Nowadays there is a discrepancy between the interest in cartoons and videogames and in the content of school teaching, which can only be explained by the subject-object dissociation present in our cultural pathology. It is not by chance that the artistic class is so distant from education. In a country as vast as Brazil, united by a single language, what a surprising educational effect the appearance of our actors would have in educational videogames! I am not speaking of objective education, but of education on all levels, presented in an emotional and dramatic way. This does not imply subordinating artistic creativity to collective ideals. What I suggest is the inclusion of the pedagogic method as one of countless means of expression of artistic creativity. What I support is the summoning of artists, sportsmen, journalists, scientists, politicians, and other public figures to imagine education in all fields of knowledge and transform society through youth using expressive techniques.

If education is open to art through symbolic pedagogy, there will be reciprocity for the cultural Self to work systemically as a multiple feedback system. The fact that soap operas and live audience programs on television have a scant pedagogic element and are thus of doubtful cultural value can be ascribed to their mentors but also indirectly to teachers who practice such emotionless and lifeless education.

Insofar as educational methods are boring, without love, emotion, and pleasure, identified exclusively with duty, and alienated from life, they cannot be expected to be included in entertainment and leisure programs. But as soon as education is methodologically open to animation, creativity, and dramatization, the media will also open up to include it in their live audience programs. Just as commercial merchandising is already present in many programs, together with a playful competitions with cultural tests, education can likewise find a place there. Emotionally motivated knowledge can become one of the most appreciated of human activities. If education opens to emotion and calls the artists, the media will also open itself and do their part. The main thing is to realize that apprenticeship in itself is not boring and can even be very entertaining, including games and all human activities. What made it aseptic and sterilized was the rational method and the exclusion of the subjective. One of the central teachings of symbolic education is the restoration of existential drama to learning.

It is likely the absence of creativity, due to the block access to the subjective dimension, that has led educators to the rationalization that learning is one thing and entertaining another. It is as though humorous, imaginal, dramatic, attractive, amusing, and even fascinating teaching could not be efficient, serious, or profound. This attitude has led to frustration in many teachers, a result of the repetitive apathy in their work. They tend to use exams as a form of correction and grades as control and punishment, since to them the very nature of teaching has become coercive. This imprisoned vitality is often expressed in a rarely affectionate and spontaneous attitude in the classroom, which reinforces emotional repression and the maintenance of evaluation by a system of rigid concepts, school reports, punishments, exams, and grades applied unilaterally to students. All this disguises the indifference, boredom, frustration, and aggression that this method of teaching arouses. Exclusion of this creative and emotional wholeness may lead teachers, even those with constructivist orientation, to a repetitive and "de-spirited" teaching; as the years go by they become, unwillingly, transmitters of disaffection for knowledge.

Symbolic knowledge, within the various dimensions of the Self, attempts to relate dramatic teaching to the historic functioning of individual, cultural, planetary, and cosmic life. To do so, it is fundamental to have objective and emotional experiences of the body inserted systematically into education. The student's emotions must be, whenever possible, transferentially related to the teacher and the family in the Self of class, school, and culture. This was the case of the nine-year-old boy who showed his father a drawing he had made of the alveoli of his lungs and pleaded with great emotion: "Daddy, please stop smoking or you will irritate and destroy your alveoli. I don't want you to have emphysema or lung cancer." Another example comes from a small town in the interior of Brazil where the mayor decided to cut down the trees of the central square "to open up space." Children from the local public school were shocked, and when the day came and the machines arrived to cut down the trees, they found them packed with children who had climbed up into the trees at dawn and were there to save them. And so they did, and they celebrated proudly with a parade the following Saturday.

In Latin American countries, there is a lot of discussion today about increasing the efficiency of education and its importance in individual and social development. Yet it is difficult to find public authorities who have the knowledge and the courage to promote teaching better-fed students with better-paid and better-prepared teachers together with education useful to students and their families in everyday life. We see great proposals to improve education materially that do not even touch on the subject of changing the method or the content of teaching.

The disfiguration of knowledge in the Western tradition has been taking place since the Enlightenment, when science took over teaching. The gravity of separating teaching from the subjective was not perceived and began to be practiced with pride as the one and only truth. Thus, dominantly rational and objective teaching became absurd and monstrous in its waste of life, intelligence, time, and money. As in Ionesco's play *The Rhinoceros*, the animal began to be seen among human beings. Many noticed it but did not have the courage to say so. Time went by and humans began to feel more and more like the rhinoceros without noticing it. The concept of the symbol in education is the mirror, which allows the pedagogic rhinoceros to perceive that it is also the unicorn. If beautiful knowledge, turned into a horrible pachyderm overcome by boredom, looks at itself in the mirror of symbol, it may find its fascinating beauty once more in the paths of imagination and love.

# Chapter 1

# BASIC CONCEPTS

## SYMBOLIC PSYCHOLOGY, ANALYTICAL PSYCHOLOGY, PSYCHOANALYSIS, BEHAVIORISM, AND SYSTEMIC THEORY

The difference Jung proposed between ego and Self is fundamental for the understanding of this pedagogic perspective. For Jung, ego is the center of consciousness and Self is the whole personality, including the ego. Jungian symbolic education operates through symbols and complexes, which interrelate the ego with the totality of the Self (a complex is here defined as a meaningful group of symbols). Therefore, it is rational but also emotional, existential, and cultural.

The Self is the sum of all psychic contents, including the identities of ego and other in consciousness and in the unconscious, symbols, complexes, and functions, the shadow, and the archetypes. Following Freud (1909), I consider the ego-other and other-other polarities in the shadow as the part of structuring symbols and functions that was cast aside and repressed into the unconscious. I have amplified the Jungian concept of individual Self to all dimensions of being which have a dynamism of totality extending from the atomic Self and the cell Self to the cosmic Self. Within these dimensions of totality, the group Self, first formulated by Erich Neumann (1949), expresses the totality of conscious and unconscious forces, objective and subjective, which act in a group and are coordinated by the same archetypes as the individual Self. Besides the archetypes, all dimensions of the Self have symbols as a common operational denominators. Based on the concepts of individual Self and group Self, I was able to understand that, whether on the individual or the collective level, dominantly rational education is based on the transmission of knowledge exclusively on the conscious level, without global participation of the Self. In addition to this reduction to consciousness, there is another reduction within consciousness itself.

When we consider the four functions of consciousness described by Jung (1921)— thinking, feeling, intuition, and sensation—and the two attitudes—extraversion and introversion—we see that dominantly objective education favors extraverted thinking and sensation, limiting the functions of feeling and intuition and the introverted attitude. From this we can infer that dominantly objective teaching is emotionless, more specifically, it lacks the feeling function. It is a way of teaching that methodologically excludes love. This alone expresses its aberration. Jung once wrote, "Where love reigns, there is no will to power; and when the will to power is paramount, love is lacking" (Jung 1943, par. 78). Teaching dominated by duty subordinates it to power and excludes the affectionate relationship to knowledge. In this manner, teachers can teach and students can learn many things, mainly through competition, inspired mostly by the power principle, but the main thing—a loving relationship to learning and culture—is irreparably damaged. A power attitude toward knowledge, subordinating it to grades and diplomas, exaggerated to the point of excluding love, pollutes the creative relation to knowledge and may even forever condemn it to disinterest (Guggenbühl-Craig 1971). The teacher's participation in this condemnation is a crime against the student's relationship to learning. Teachers, even if they are scholars, are not immune to providing this distortion. In my view, this is the chief explanation for the aversion to studying that is affecting an ever-greater portion of youth. This may also explain why so many young people study to get a diploma merely for the status it confers and for the power to compete for jobs.

Jungian symbolic education, proposed here, is a pedagogy of Self that includes both attitudes and all four functions of consciousness, where dominantly objective education is a pedagogy of only part of the ego. Learning by experience is the essence of the education of the Self. Why refer to experiential pedagogy of the Self as symbolic pedagogy? By amplifying the concept of symbol, it forms a permanent bridge between all psychic representations and the whole through meaning. In this view, every symbol is simultaneously the expression of archetypes and the root of the identities of ego and other in the conscious and unconscious. In this context, all things and experiences are symbols, including the Jungian concepts of archetypal image and complex. The perception of the part as symbol remits it to the whole. Conceived in this way, symbol is the cell of psyche (Saiz Laureiro 1989). Teaching through symbols, therefore, is an experience that situates the part inseparably from the whole.

These observations on the learning process also lead to the conclusion that consciousness is incapable of full objectivity, or what Kant (1724–1804) called "pure reason" (Kant 1781). When we root this philosophy of knowledge in the development of personality, we also ground it psychologically. The ego is differentiated in the Self and goes on forming ego-other polarities, which constitute the fields of consciousness and shadow (conscious and unconscious). Yet, this is never a full differentiation. No one can think to be totally separated from something and claim to know it objectively. This is not possible because ego and other have common archetypal roots in the symbols of the Self, where they are formed and permanently transformed. They cannot exist in a pure and totally differentiated form because they have a symbolic and archetypal common denominator, which roots and contains them. It is this fact that psychologically grounds the impossibility of pure reason.

Kant postulated time and space as absolute categories (*an sich*), which could be intuitively known but not conceived of rationally. Following Einstein's perception of time as the fourth dimension of space, the space-time dimension can be seen as a paradigm within which the ego and other differentiate. Thus, fourfold space is one of the great structuring functions of the cosmic Self. It is inside the Self that the ego and the other are differentiated in consciousness through symbolic elaboration. Developmental psychology shows us that ego and other are relatively separate entities only in consciousness and shadow. As far as the Self is concerned, ego and other are part of a whole, coordinated by the central archetype that permanently encompasses, transcends, forms, and transforms them.

## The Extended Concept of Archetype

The concept of archetype as conceived by Jung and here extended to encompass the objective in the symbolic dimension is the most important concept of Jungian symbolic psychology and of Jungian symbolic education; it allows us to transcend the reduced use of the symbol concept and cornect it to the totality of individual, planetary, cultural, and cosmic Self. Without this extended concept of archetype, we invariably fall back to reduction, to a person, childhood, nature, power, pathology, body, society, or other specific instance. This extended concept of archetype pervades this book and should therefore be better explained. Jung, in *The Archetypes and the Collective Unconscious* (CW, vol. 9i), described archetypes as matrices of the collective unconscious of the human species. The images or archetypal themes, such as hero, mother, father, child, master, disciple, the search for the treasure, fighting the dragon, are thus considered as typical of our species as our biological behavior of eating, sleeping, and mating.

I have amplified the concept of archetype to encompass not only unconscious and subjective symbols but also consciousness through the description of five archetypal positions of the ego-other relationship. Therefore, in this book, the concept of archetype is not limited to the collective unconscious but includes the whole psyche with its conscious and unconscious characteristics, as well as personal and collective and subjective and objective ones. This extension permits us to teach the individuation process and to conceive of symbolic education and symbolic constructivism.

Archetypes express, through symbols, the roots of ego and other identity. Archetypes are always bipolar or multipolar. Parental complexes that are intensely archetypal encompass filiation and parenthood, that is, the way in which we are children and parents. The hero archetype is expressed by the symbols of the hero and the dragon, which will be differentiated in ego-other polarity in consciousness in the same way that the archetype of teaching includes the teacher and the student. This differentiation of the archetypal matrices happens through the experience of symbols.

Although he gave central importance to polarities, Jung described the functioning of archetypes only in the unconscious and mostly in the second half of life. During a great part of his work, he left the formation of ego in early life to psychoanalysis. After the 1950s, many followers of Jung realized that the archetypes are present from the beginning of life to coordinate the formation of the ego in consciousness and in the shadow. The formation of both ego and other identities whether in consciousness or the unconscious always happen through symbolic elaboration coordinated by archetypes. Following the concepts of fixation and of the repressed unconscious from psychoanalysis, shadow formation is here attributed to fixation and defensive expression of normal symbolic elaboration. As it frequently happens in the treatment of addiction, symbols of the shadow can also become conscious. Therefore, the identity of ego and other, whether in consciousness or in shadow, is inseparable from symbols and archetypes within a systemic whole. The concepts of the ego, consciousness, shadow, and archetypes are distorted whenever they are used as entities acting separately.

## The Ego and the Other

The ego is the representation of the subjective dimension and the other is the representation of the objective dimension. The erudite objective knowledge characterizing an ego that knows a great deal about "things," that is, about "others," in reality does not know any other to the extent that it claims to. The great pretension of such an ego to know the other totally is a narcissistic illusion, an omnipotent wish capable of inflating the ego and making it feel as great as the Self.

The ego's knowledge is always partial. Since the development of the computer, even the ego's capacity to memorize has become so limited that arrogant claims of erudition are demoralized. It is the end of the glorious erudites who quoted by heart the content of the pages of famous authors. In this way, technology favors abandoning the cult of encyclopedic knowledge, saving energy to cultivate the creativity of being, which no machine can give us. In this manner, the computer, besides being a marvelous machine to store erudition, has become a faithful shield-bearer in the heroic journey to free wisdom from erudition.

Ego and other, or subjective and objective identities, are differentiated starting from the endless cosmic Self that roots and encompasses them. The knowledge of the ego about the other is very relative, for the basic dimensions of life are common to both, for instance, the space-time continuum as well as all archetypes. The differentiation of ego and other impels them to know their differences more and more, but always in a relative way, because in absolute terms both are always the expression of the whole. Differentiation of ego and other coordinated by the central archetype expresses the development of the Self, and one day, through wisdom, they may also discover their equality in the expression of being (Heidegger 1927).

## The Central Archetype

The ideological heart of this book is the notion of the creative vitality of the Self and its central archetype, which coordinates and tends to integrate all other archetypes through existential happenings, therefore making them structuring symbols, complexes, functions, and systems of the Self. To avoid ambiguity, I reserve the term Self for the conscious and unconscious totality of the psyche and have chosen the term central archetype for the main archetype of the Self. The main archetype is the genius formulation, described and experienced by Jung, of a virtual regulating, totalizing center of the psyche. It is so important that the primary images that express it in the cultural and cosmic Self are the religious image of God or the scientific image of cosmos, with the common theme of omnipresence. It is the integrating action of this archetype that tends to interrelate significantly all the good and evil that happens to us in life and thereby coordinates the unique process of each being, which Jung (1935) called the individuation process. It is complemented by Teilhard de Chardin's concept of the humanizing process of the cosmos (1950).

My approach to the symbolic dimension in education refers to the relation of everything that affects our senses, in one way or the other, with the integrating activity of the central archetype. This activity makes everything symbolic and each thing we experience a symbol of the Self. Accordingly, truth is the most vital and reality the most profound symbol in life.

This centralizing and integrating capacity of the central archetype not only operates in keeping with the great cosmic whole, it forms a totalizing psychological field in any event and can be perceived by the ego as regular and systemic relationships between the phenomena. From this, I have formulated the concepts of Self in individual, family, pedagogic, therapeutic, institutional, cultural, planetary, and cosmic dimensions, all interacting within cosmic totality. Thanks to the totalizing notion of the central archetype, one may perceive the gestalt of the class functioning as a systemic whole (pedagogic Self) within the school (institutional Self), society (cultural Self), environment (planetary Self), and finally within the great cosmic Self.

I chose the designation of symbolic education as the pedagogic discipline based on symbolic psychology and symbolic humanism, precisely that existential philosophy which senses in each experience the involvement of the totality of being through the central archetype (Byington 1987a). The concepts of the Self and of the central archetype, equally present in the individual and in the group, allow us to elaborate any teaching situation simultaneously in the Self of student, class, school, family, culture, planet, and universe. This approach enables us, for instance, to identify the main learning difficulty of grade school, high school, and college in the method and content of teaching and also take into consideration the social, family, and nutritional problems of the students as well as the teachers' competence and pay. In highly emotional, erotic, and mystical societies, such as we have in Latin America, the dominantly objective teaching—fragmented and abstract—is not harmonious with the culture and therefore cannot produce satisfactory results. The repression of the erotic, matriarchal cultural pattern becomes the greatest limitation when the Western teaching tradition is applied to cultures in developing countries.

## Psychic Reality

The greatest difficulty in understanding Jungian symbolic psychology, on which Jungian symbolic pedagogy is based, comes from the concept of psychic reality, here defined as the human experience of the world. In this context, the concept of psyche coincides with the concept of being as formulated by Heidegger in his ontology (1927). The psyche-nature and psyche-body dichotomies do not exist here because psyche also includes the symbolic representations of mind and of nature, as well as mind and body as polar opposites within unity. Teilhard de Chardin contributed much to this perspective when he described consciousness formation through the progressive differentiation of matter.

Exclusively objective teaching, which ignores the subjective connotation of what is being taught, is nonetheless incapable of eliminating it. Even when dissociated and repressed, these subjective characteristics, although distorted, survive. Where it is unilaterally practiced, this kind of teaching enhances and perpetuates the dissociation of being in culture and the growth of shadow.

Psychic reality, seen as the world containing subjective and objective phenomena, fundamentally affects the notion of objective reality and of scientific truth, modifying the theory of knowledge itself, that is, epistemology. When the symbol is considered the psychic unity, it becomes the main concept of human truth that permanently expresses the objective and the subjective dimensions. In this case, the aim of teaching is not ego amplification and erudition but rather the development of consciousness and wisdom. Such an overall concept of psychic reality is the essential framework of Jungian symbolic education.

The wisdom of humanity, expressed since time immemorial through creeds, myths, and religions, has always had a common denominator: the human being is inferior to God. In the philosophical dimension, great thinkers express this fact when they say that human reason is incapable of knowing the essence of reality. Whether through Plato's cave, where the reality to which we have access is formed by shadows on the inner wall of a cavern created by objects never seen, or through Kant's *Critique of Pure Reason* (1781), or through the limitations of the method of researching atomic particles described by Heisenberg, this admission of the limits of human reason is a characteristic of mythical traditions and of many of humanity's great scientific minds.

However, the complete reversal in *Weltanschauung* caused by the discovery of the heliocentric system, and followed by so many other extraordinary discoveries by modern science, misled many to believe that science was capable of perceiving the truths of the universe, which were equated with absolute truth beyond the apparent reality perceived by our senses. It is often thought and taught that objective science operates with the essence of reality, and objectivity is frequently mistaken for truth. Rather, it should be said that science elaborates a symbolic reality that blends subject and object and unveils them in relation to each other during differentiation. Thus, we will elaborate forever the nature of fundamental archetypes of cosmos such as space, time, matter, electromagnetism, energy, light, and gravity. The fact that we deal with these by means of mathematical equations misleads many into thinking that we know and can explain their essence. By doing so, we do not perceive the very nature of mathematics as a function of relationship between beings and things, that is, as a kind of language, like Portuguese or English or any other means of communication Mathematics is the most abstract of sciences, but this does not make it a science that can explain the essence of things; rather, it expresses—in the concept of equation—the relationship of things.

It seems to me that as we draw closer to the essence of these dimensions of the universe, we approach our very nature as participant-observers. Since our psyche is the representation of the universe itself, we reach the methodological phenomenon of the observer who observes him/herself. How can our ego, with all its limitations, observe a much greater whole as an other when this other also forms and encompasses our ego? We need only to consider the symbol for infinity— $\infty$ —and the impossibility of our imagining infinity, to have an idea of how distant we are from the capacity to perceive the space-time dimension in itself, objectively separated from our ego. When we then follow modern physics and consider that one of our limitations results from the difficulty we have imagining that the space-time dimension is curved, then indeed we have some idea of what epistemology is.

Therefore, we have to admit that the knowledge of reality and the teaching of it are always relative and that the subject-object fusion, which expresses deep reality, limits and guides our quest for truth during its symbolic elaboration in the formation of consciousness. We have to accept humbly our condition as microscopic passengers in the eternal and infinite journey of the universe. Our quest is to describe this vast journey—our experience as passengers—without any omnipotent pretensions of positioning ourselves outside the whole.

By using the concept of symbol unifying duality and plurality within psychic reality, understood as the human reality of the world, I elected it as the transformer that is capable of separating subject from object and of revealing the truth of the world to us through our existential experience. The symbolic method of knowing thus becomes the experience of permanent revelation of mystery; it is always subjectively and objectively the universal whole to which we belong and which, when it is shown to us, also reveals who we are. By doing so, we detach ourselves from the omnipotent objective perspective of world-controlling erudite knowledge and dedicate ourselves to the symbolic trail of wisdom in which we study, research, and work in order to know, contemplate, admire, hate, and love the work of creation. In this manner we get to know many forms of intelligence, typologies, and ways of coming to and seeing the world. Little by little, we realize that all of them, whether in mythical or in scientific thought, lead us to the understanding of a creative force as the intelligence behind life and the universe. In this case, religions continue to be ethical expression of cultures but religiosity becomes the permanent structuring function to search to find ways to relate to this creative force of the universe.

## The Extended Concept of Symbol

Theories of knowledge have used the concept of symbol in many different ways, but always to associate different things. I use the concept of symbol to express meanings, including the subjective-objective, healthy-sick, virtuous-sinful, legal-illegal, as well as the conscious-unconscious, mind-body, and mind-matter polarities within the process of development of the totality of the Self. Therefore, in order to perceive the symbolic meanings of things and of experiences, we must consciously participate in the process of symbolic elaboration by which symbols differentiate into ego-other and other-other polarities through projection and introjection to structure consciousness. From this perspective the concepts of structuring symbol, complexes, function, system, and symbolic elaboration emerge; these express the capacity of the central archetype to produce a symbolic net that forms the ego-other and other-other polarities in consciousness (Byington 1990a). The snake is a structuring symbol. Our fear of it is a structuring function that helps us to form the identities of the ego and the other in relationship to the snake symbol and complex so that every time I think of a snake, I will have an attitude (identity of the ego) which expresses my judgment of snakes (identity of the other). The elaboration of many symbols of animals and of many structuring functions dealing with them will form a structuring system in the Self to deal with them in an adequate way. Rain is a structuring symbol. The structuring functions of wind, drought, and storm make up the structuring system of climate, which guides us in elaborating and knowing the various regions of the earth. And so on. This conceptual perspective of symbolic systems forming a symbolic net allows us to see the process of symbolic elaboration as the common denominator between symbolic pedagogy and the existential development of the Self that form the basis of symbolic constructivism.

Conceiving psychic reality as the human reality of the world influences this concept of symbol by modifying its traditional meaning which excludes concreteness from the symbolic dimension. This definition of symbol, which is the core of Jungian symbolic psychology and Jungian symbolic education, includes concreteness. Thus, the difference between a rhinoceros and a unicorn or a lion and a dragon is not that the rhinoceros and the lion are actual animals and the unicorn and dragon symbolic animals. All four are symbolic. They differ in that the unicorn and the dragon are fantastic and lack concreteness, while the rhinoceros and the lion possess concreteness but may also have fantastic characteristics, such as the Nemean lion of Greek mythology and the totemic rhinoceros of certain African cultures. This concept of symbol, which includes subject and object and functions as the structuring cell of consciousness, is the main paradigm of symbolic science and allows us to include chemistry, physics, and mathematics within psychic reality in the acquisition of knowledge. Although Jung reduced the concept of archetype to the collective unconscious, he often considered the symbol as encompassing the conscious and unconscious polarity, for instance, when he wrote in the commentary to *The Secret of the Golden Flower* that "the symbol is the primitive expression of the unconscious, but at the same time it is also an idea corresponding to the highest intuition produced by consciousness" (Jung 1957, par. 44).

## The Ego and the Other in Shadow
## Normal and Defensive Symbolic Elaboration:
## Creative and Defensive Structuring Functions

The fifth amplified concept—in addition to Self, archetype, psychic reality, and symbol—used in Jungian symbolic education is the concept of shadow. According to Jung, the shadow is that part of the psyche which remained unconscious the same gender of the ego (Jung 1950). Jung further includes Freud's repressed unconscious as well all the archetypes of the collective unconscious in the concept of the shadow. I have modified Jung's concept of the shadow to include symbols from both genders and to exclude the normal collective unconscious. In this manner, I have equated the shadow with Freud's repressed unconscious, whose contents are here considered always personal, archetypal and pathological. In this way, I propose to integrate analytical psychology and psychoanalysis in the normal ethical and pathological development of the personality. The shadow is thus seen as a dysfunction of the process of symbolic elaboration through which structuring symbols, complexes, functions and systems become fixated and are inadequately expressed through the ego-other polarity (Byington 1988c). The structuring function of ethics coordinates the elaboration of the good-evil polarity. Its normal expression forms consciousness and its fixation is the origin of evil (symptoms, sin and crime) and forms the shadow. The shadow is circumstantial or chronic depending on the degree of fixation. The circumstantial shadow is formed by symbols primarily unconscious, which can be confronted by the conscious ego because the defenses, which express them, are recent and fragile. The chronic shadow contains symbols blocked by the long-term conditioning of resistance and defenses, which cause it to resist elaboration even when quite conscious (Byington 2006a).

The differentiation by the educator of normal structuring functions, which form consciousness, from fixated structuring functions, which form the shadow, has a central importance in Jungian symbolic education.

A student, age twelve, was being teased and had become very shy and limited in his normally high learning capacity in class because he had fallen in love with a classmate. After a few weeks of teasing and suffering, he recovered his self-control and was able to express himself again (circumstantial shadow). Another student, the same age, was very shy and suffered such an inhibition complex that every time he was asked to stand up and address his class, he had to rush to the bathroom for fear of wetting his pants. The situation became so serious that he needed psychotherapy (chronic shadow).

The ability to identify and differentiate shadow-structuring symbols, complexes, functions, and systems is very important in the areas of education and mental health; while the circumstantial shadow generally predominates in the classroom, the chronic shadow is more familiar in the consulting office. However, the chronic shadow frequently begins as circumstantial shadow in front of teachers and parents, who therefore are those most able to prevent chronic shadow and neurosis formation. On that account, I want to emphasize that in Jungian symbolic education, the main professional role of preventing mental disease belongs to teachers and parents. The social function of education can become even more important when the school has direct contact with the student's family. The younger a student, the more fixations in his/her individual Self are directly related to fixations simultaneously operating in the shadow of the family Self. Symbolic perception of pupils' anxious or depressive reactions enables the sensitive teacher to relate them to the class or to their family and coordinate expert counseling to help them. This becomes even more productive when the psychological coordinator of the school has access to the interaction between the individual and the family Self. It is quite impressive how frequently students act out symbols from their family shadow in school, both circumstantial and chronic (Wickes 1927). Jungian symbolic education proposes the education of family and society through children just as much as the other way around. Symbolic knowledge and the teacher's open-mindedness can contribute greatly to preventing psychopathology, together with the creative development of the individual, the family, and society.

Due to the weakening of institutions in modern society—including the family—school has acquired more and more importance over the past decades as a means to identify psychological problems and prevent the formation of future neurosis of many students. The function of the pedagogic coordinator, who supervises the content of learning, and of the psychological coordinator, who elaborates the student-family relationship, is increasingly important in the development of the personality of students and in the orientation of their families' dynamics. Unfortunately, the psychological training of teachers has not kept pace with this growing need, at least in Latin America.

The student-teacher-school-family quaternity has become increasingly important, and its creative efficacy depends heavily on the ability to reason symbolically and systemically. Two aspects of the quaternity are important here: first, the student-teacher polarity, where direct learning of content takes place; and second, the student-family polarity, which strongly influences personality formation and becomes closely associated with its student-teacher counterpart. Both polarities are essential in education, which is why two professionals are needed in Jungian symbolic education; one specialized in the school curriculum (pedagogic coordinator) and the other in psychological development (psychological coordinator). Both, however, must be trained to reason systemically and symbolically in a dialectic relationship of multiple feedback circuits within the individual, the family, and the school Self. Every therapist today needs to know the fundamentals of family therapy. It is very limiting to separate the individual self in childhood from the family Self. Any consideration of learning problems should take into account the pupil's family dynamics. It is absurd to recommend child or adolescent psychotherapy without knowledge of the family's psychodynamics.

I strongly recommend that case studies of children be carried out in relationship to their families and that written reports on children's problems not be shared with parents and teachers. It is astonishing how often such written reports are manipulated by parents and the school to cast the shadow side of learning exclusively onto the student while covering up the shadows of the parents and the school. Rather, case studies of children and adolescents should include the family and the school in joint work, coordinated by the psychological coordinator or by a psychotherapist without written reports.

The concept of structuring functions includes two very important ideas: the defense mechanism, from psychoanalysis, and archetypal creativity, from analytical psychology. Their common archetypal denominator, conceived by Jungian symbolic psychology, allows us to see structuring functions as operating productively (normal structuring functions) or pathologically (defensive structuring functions) in the individual and collective self. Normal structuring functions express and elaborate symbols in all existential situations and include learning. A boy who admires his father's erudition can identify creatively with him through the structuring functions of projection, introjection, idealization, and competition and come to enjoy reading and studying to know as much as his father, possibly even surpassing him. On the other hand, defensive structuring functions are formed whenever symbolic elaboration suffers frustration and fixation. In this case, instead of expressing the meaning of symbols creatively to expand the ego-other identity in consciousness, structuring functions become fixated, coalesce in the shadow, and affect learning. As Freud described, these defenses present repetition-compulsion and resistance to further elaboration and integration in consciousness. A boy who suffers paternal rejection, abandonment, or repression may—through the same structuring functions of projection, introjection, idealization, and competition now become defensive—feel a failure or an outcast and develop serious difficulties in studying and learning. The importance of recognizing the normal-defensive polarity for teaching is that it includes the normal and pathological characteristics of all life situations. This polarity expresses the very important fact that normality and pathology are not expressed by radically different functions but by the same structuring functions, which may operate normally or defensively. In this perspective, education and mental health can and should be intelligently perceived and interrelated by parents, educators, and therapists (Byington 1990b).

It is not necessary for an educator to have a degree in psychology to recognize the formation of a neurotic defense. It suffices to be familiar with how normal structuring functions operate in the personality, and in the class as a whole, to be able to identify the appearance of defensive structuring functions acting circumstantially or chronically in the shadow. Normal structuring functions carry out symbolic elaboration productively and satisfactorily and integrate it systemically but when they become fixated and display repetition-compulsion, the pupil's personality or the class as a whole becomes impoverished, loses harmony, and becomes resistant to learning and subject to repetition-compulsive and/or dysfunctional behavior. The river either overflows or turns into a lake. The student either becomes anxious and disrupts the classroom or withdraws. A normal structuring function is life structuring with all its capacity toward health, self-fulfillment, adequacy, and good, while a defensive structuring function is prone to error, inadequate behavior, disease, evil, and destructivity. By recognizing defensive structuring functions operating in the circumstantial shadow, the educator can help the student and contribute decisively toward reverting them to normal structuring functions. An attitude of understanding, emotional empathy, and direct symbolic elaboration with the student (and occasionally also with his/her family) can be decisive in reverting defensive reactions to creative ones and thus avoid chronic shadow formation, which is the basis of a future neurosis. When educators learn to recognize the interaction of normal and defensive structuring functions in education, they not only are able to transcend exclusive objective teaching but also to recognize good and evil—that is, normality and shadow—within the intimate area of being where the personality is formed (Byington 2008).

All psychic functions are structuring functions: fear, admiration, intelligence, curiosity, teasing, competition, intuition, thinking, feeling, sensation, voluntary silence, speech, calculation, envy, communication, courage, anxiety, cowardice, meditation, jealousy, sleep, creativity, dreaming, projection, introjection, sadness, aggression, hate, tenderness, sexuality, idealization, imitation, lying, cheating, walking, eating, breathing, digesting, honesty, dignity, shame, pride, and so on, and all of them can operate either normally or defensively (Byington 2002a).

A twelve-year-old boy was afraid of failing and isolated himself from his classmates. This strategic withdrawal helped him in his studies, resulting in very good normal elaboration: the structuring function of fear helped to elaborate his anxiety creatively. Another student, age eleven, began to study math but was afraid of not being able to understand it. His older brother terrified him with descriptions of the difficulties of the curriculum. As his fear increased, he became unable to pay attention in class. From the tension in his body, his teacher noticed that something was wrong. When class was over, the teacher went over the situation with the boy and clarified his doubts, which helped to calm him down. The boy became aware that his fear was also associated with being separated from his former teacher, whom he loved and missed very much, and with the increasing complexity of the curriculum. From then on, through constant dedication, he was able to control his fear and cope well with math (circumstantial shadow). In a third case, a fourteen-year-old boy displayed deep anxiety in Spanish class, which his teacher noticed because the student was sweating from his armpits. The teacher discussed this anxiety with the student, and the boy told her that his father had lived in South America and often spoke Spanish with him, mocking his accent and grammatical mistakes. An interview by the psychological coordinator with the student's parents revealed an atmosphere of intense competition at home.

The father showed a strong inferiority complex, which he acted out on his son (reactive formation), varying from ridicule to physical aggression (chronic shadow). The mother said she could not interfere because the one time she had done so, she also received a beating. It became evident that in this case the structuring function of fear and aggression had become defensive, fixated, and chronic in the individual and family Self. The psychological coordinator, seeing that she could go no further, recommended family therapy.

Let us now consider briefly the structuring function of admiration. A third-form Brazilian student admired her Portuguese teacher very much. Formerly, the girl had not liked to read, but now she became a very enthusiastic reader of novels, wrote essays, and even changed her voice and began talking like her teacher. It was evident that the structuring function of literary creativity had been intensively activated and was being expressed through admiration within a normal transference reaction between teacher and student with excellent results. Admiration, however, like all other structuring functions is not always normal and can also become defensive. In another case, an art student greatly admired her teacher, who was a well-known painter. The student had drawn since childhood and was admired in her family for her artistic talent. After two semesters, however, she became increasingly inhibited and her output diminished substantially. Her teacher informed the psychological coordinator who interviewed the student and worked through her inhibition until both of them came to the conclusion that her admiration for her teacher had formed a fixated learning complex. The teacher's drawing was clean, with many angles, clearly Gothic, whereas the student's style was the opposite: rounded, baroque, overdecorated, almost rococo. She began to feel that her teacher would never admire her if she kept her style, and therein lay the cause of her inhibition. Her structuring function of admiration had become progressively defensive within the pedagogic transference and had been fixated in a circumstantial shadow. The elaboration with the psychological coordinator, plus a gift from her teacher of a book of paintings by Rubens with his warm, round figures, so full of feeling and vitality, were sufficient to liberate the complex and lead her to regain her exuberant creativity, including the return of her normal structuring function of admiration.

A third case presented a much more complex situation. At the beginning of tenth grade, an outstanding student, who up to that year had excelled at writing essays, experienced a severe creative block and became incapable of writing a single line with no idea of what was happening to her. The teaching coordinator interviewed her and was told an impressive story. The girl was a precocious writer, admired by her family and her teachers. Her mother, who was artistically endowed but who had never expressed herself, began to show her daughter's writings to her friends. At first, the daughter felt flattered and stimulated by the admiration of her mother's friends. As time passed, however, she became increasingly uncomfortable and her mother's admiration began to bother her. Her mother regularly took her daughter's writings to meetings with her friends and read them aloud for the group with great pride and success. The girl felt her mother was becoming more and more like a vampire who fed on her creativity. This made her feel guilty. She became shy and sensitive to any remark about her creativity, a reaction that included her teacher, and a defensive complex with a creative block paralyzed her. In tears, the girl told these feelings to the psychological coordinator and begged her not to tell her teacher and mother. It became evident that the structuring function of admiration had become fixated and defensive in a chronic shadow. Due to the entanglement of the individual and family Self, the situation was carefully handled by the psychological coordinator in an interview with the mother, and family counseling was indicated with a focus on the mother-daughter relationship.

Jungian symbolic education, being focused on symbolic elaboration through normal and defensive structuring functions and systems, gives the educator a new way to deal with normal and problematic learning. The problems of learning are rooted in the same structuring functions that the educator employs daily for symbolic elaboration of current rational teaching. Further, structuring functions, both normal and defensive, belong to the symbolic development of the personality together with learning. With time and practice, the educator grows accustomed to the association of the symbolic dimension of teaching with personality development, of health with disease, of individual with family and society, of learning with work, of production with value, of good with evil, that is, with duality and plurality within unity (Byington 1965).

## Systemic Holistic Teaching and Symbolic Education

The holistic movement (*holos* in Greek means totality), with its intention to reunite all areas of knowledge, is nowadays an important cultural movement worldwide. As a cultural trend in the new millennium, it counteracts fragmentation of knowledge in order to recover an interdisciplinary relationship among all the activities and afflictions of humanity.

The concept of archetype allows us to transcend individual, national, and cultural differences within the perspective of the planetary Self. One expression of this is the Gaia theory, wherein Mother Earth is seen with her joys and sorrows while caring for her children—a systemic movement to form a planetary community (Lovelock 1979). By developing holistic consciousness, we tend to acquire supraconsciousness, which encompasses consciousness and shadow, good and evil, and subordinates planetary consciousness to cosmic consciousness with its characteristics of eternity and infinity. Inseparable from physics and its universal laws, from religions (especially the ancient religions of China, Japan, India, and Tibet), from biology and cybernetics, and from the global movement, holism in this new millennium is a religious and scientific humanism directed toward the totality of all things and of the cosmos. The appearance of holism in culture is directly related to an effort to preserve the human phenomenon, threatened by its Frankenstein shadow in the labyrinth of existential alienation brought on by the compartmentalization and specialization of knowledge, which dissociates the part from the whole.

The most significant contribution of symbolic humanism to holism is expressed in the concepts of structuring symbols, complexes, functions, and systems relating the part to the whole, which allows for individual and collective construction of knowledge of life and the world through symbolic elaboration. This proposal reveals the archetypal nature of all symbols and renders human experiences sacred by transcending materialism permanently through the countless meanings that link daily events to wholeness. However, without the concepts of structuring symbols, complexes, functions, systems, and of symbolic elaboration, which by definition link every part to the whole, and can operate normally or become defensive, holism remains a worthy and idealistic intention that lacks the means to relate consciousness to totality in daily life.

## Symbolic Education and Behaviorism, Expressive Techniques and Symbolic Elaboration

The dissociation between subjective and objective, internal and external world, and mind and body was accompanied by the unilateral development of two great trends in modern psychology: dynamic psychology, centered in unconscious subjective processes, and behavioral psychology, centered in conscious behavior. From the latter emerged cognitive psychology, which permeates Piaget's pedagogic constructivism: predominantly conscious, rational, and directed toward adaptation to external reality.

Expanding the concept of archetype to include subjective and objective, conscious and unconscious, is one of the main contributions of Jungian symbolic psychology toward building a conceptual bridge to reunite dynamic psychology and behavioral psychology. A second contribution is the amplification of the concept of symbol to unite the ego and the other, consciousness and archetype, the subjective and the objective, conscious and unconscious, individual and society, internal and external, and consequently also mind and body, mind and matter, thought and conduct. The concept of the symbolic body relates the body and behavior in the objective physiological dimension to the imaginary subjective dimension. If we compare the body to a computer, the physiological functions are the hardware and meaning is the software accumulated by civilization (Byington 2002b). The symbolic body includes all anatomical and physiological aspects and, at the same time, their metaphorical meanings, starting with symbolism above and below the waist, front and back, right and left, inside and outside the body, as well as countless other meanings related to every sense, organ, function, and movement.

This amplification of the concept of symbol allows us to join dynamic psychology and behavioral psychology, and also speech, thought, and imagination, that is, the conscious-unconscious motivation processes behind behavior. Herein lies the importance of expressive techniques such as drawing, painting, sculpture, singing, dancing, poetry, dramatics, meditation, letter writing, conscious dreaming (Désoille 1961), active imagination (Jung 1958), family photos, and videogames in teaching. These and many other forms of symbolic elaboration invite our whole being to participate in the psychic process of development common to psychology and education (Byington 1993a).

Everything in life is symbolic because our brain functions through the meaning of events and is not capable of dealing with them only literally. Therefore, all life events form structuring symbols, complexes, functions, and systems, acting through the process of elaboration to form the ego-other identity and relationship in consciousness.

The most important relation of cognitive behavior to Jungian symbolic education is the analogy between Piaget's sensory-motor stage of intelligence development and the insular matriarchal position of symbolic elaboration. Their great divergence resides in the emphasis Piaget gives to the importance of the development of conceptual intelligence in learning, while Jungian symbolic psychology emphasizes the primacy of maintaining sensory-motor intelligence in education and in life, so as to make learning an animated relationship of the ego to other and not exclusively rational. In this respect, the animation brought about by expressive techniques in teaching is related to the religious phenomenon of animism in tribal cultures, through which all animals, plants, and natural phenomena are mystically, that is, symbolically, related. This association of sensory-motor intelligence with the insular position of consciousness is meaningful because both are rooted in the matriarchal archetype and its insular position of the ego-other relationship, which will be seen in detail in chapter 7.

# Chapter 2

# THE HISTORIC ROOT OF THE SYMBOLIC QUESTION

The bringing together of the subjective and objective dimensions in symbolic theory and method evokes in the scientific world vision the nightmare of religion, occultism, sorcery, irrationality, superstition and, above all, the Inquisition. Against these menaces, nineteenth-century science entrenched education in the rational and objective dimensions, reinforcing agnostic, positivistic, and materialistic philosophy.

The reactions to Jungian symbolic education—its propositions and its roots in symbolic archetypal psychology—are often highly contradictory. On one hand, it is seen as "modern," excellent, natural, already thought out and progressing well in culture. On the other hand, it is seen as utopian, alternative, religious, moralist, esoteric, and immediately associated with other idealistic methods already used to integrate subjectivity in teaching and which, more often than not, have remained on the ideal level without any practical application. Underlying these pro and con reactions, I see cultural factors at work which transcend them. These reactions confirm that the problems of education in Western culture are not generally discussed in the deep, archetypal dimension of the cultural Self. The best way to reach this depth is to dive symbolically into the mythical roots of cultural tradition, for myths are the fountains from which much of cultural life originates. Science is no exception, for, as I conceived in my archetypal theory of history, the extraverted scientific method, which separates truth from error, originated in the introverted monastic "examination of consciousness", which over the centuries practiced the separation between virtue and sin (Byington 2008).

The magical-mythical vision of the world, rooted in the insular matriarchal pattern, has traditionally been seen as the greatest opponent to scientific vision. On one side, we have the subjective emotion and motivation, which sees the world through imaginal projection. Its roots have been expressed from the beginning of civilization through animism: "The world is as I feel and imagine it." On the other side stands critical rational analysis (the polarized patriarchal position), which thinks about the world based on the scientific mentality of practical observation and experience, also present in greater or lesser degree in all cultures since time immemorial (Lévi-Strauss 1962).

The opposition of these two worldviews is an undeniable reality. However, as with all opposites, they form an archetypal polarity, reunited within symbols, which is inherent in the nature of being and of teaching in the development of individual and cultural consciousness.

*Cum granum salis*, as Jung liked to say, the magic-mythic worldview can be associated to Piaget's sensory-motor intelligence, to Levy Brühl's *participation mystique*, to animism, to Jung's unconscious identity, to Freud's primary process or pleasure principle, and to Jungian symbolic psychology's insular matriarchal position.

On the other hand, perhaps with a pound of salt, the scientific and positivistic worldview can be associated to Piaget's conceptual intelligence, to Freud's secondary process or reality principle, and to Jungian symbolic psychology's polarized patriarchal position (see chapter 8). Whereas Piaget and Freud tend to separate these worldviews radically as succeeding stages of development, Jungian symbolic psychology recognizes their differences but conceives them as archetypal and therefore describes their expression in consciousness during every symbolic elaboration throughout life (Byington 2008).

This is a very important fact in psychology and in education, because if one stage is completely separated from the other and reduced to stages of development, an archetypal dissociation is established. However, when these stages are always seen in succession, during symbolic elaboration, they are not prevented from being also meaningfully associated . This is important because it is exactly what we must do in Jungian symbolic education: to "animate" teaching through expressive techniques with the sensory-motor intelligence from the insular matriarchal position inseparably from the scientific paradigm.

To place animism exclusively in the past and objective reasoning in the present is, in my view, a huge methodological mistake, because these two different structures of thinking—the mythical and the scientific—are in fact two consecutive stages of every symbolic elaboration, which can also function very productively side by side.

There is unquestionably a polarity between mythical and scientific mentality if we oppose one to the other. However, this opposition should not determine the exclusion of one for the practice of the other, for such exclusion creates an archetypal dissociation. Was Socrates a champion of philosophical reflection, victimized by its incompatibility with mythical tradition? Or was he condemned for the political use he made of philosophical reflection, turning youth against the government of Athens? Or did the government use this polarity as an excuse to repress his revolutionary ideas?

For James Frazer (1890), a pioneer of classical anthropology in the early twentieth century, magic was the bastard science of "primitives" who did not know how to think. Decades later, direct studies of tribal cultures showed Claude Lévi-Strauss (1962) that scientific and magic thought can live together side by side in these societies; that is, they are conflicting opposites and at times clearly complementary but are not mutually exclusive.

I can confirm Lévi-Strauss's position, having observed the warriors of a Xavante Brazilian Indian tribe preparing to hunt a jaguar. It would be unthinkable for them to set out without a propitiatory magic ritual, consisting of flinging spears and arrows at the jaguar's image drawn on sand, while dancing and singing the anticipated victory. Is this magic? Of course it is. But it does not prevent the warriors from moving silently into the wind to the place near where they know the jaguar to be. Is this science? Absolutely. So magic and science, methodologically opposed, are daily used creatively and productively side-by-side, both correct and useful. Magic acts on the emotional side, stimulating and reassuring the hunters. Science provides objective data about the direction of the wind and the behavior of the animal that favor its capture, as they explained to me.

> A samurai tells his disciple that
> he must meditate before a fight.
> "What for, master?"
> "In order to take from your head the will to win."
> "And then what will happen, master?"

"Then your blows will come from within your being and will
be much more suitable to each moment of the fight."

This passage illustrates the idea that the rational mind must not be the sole commander of action. Put aside, it allows for the correct balance of behavior. This is also the meaning of *wu wei,* the practice of nonaction in Taoism.

The work upon the subjective is only incompatible with the work upon the objective if they are not correctly differentiated and one is mistaken for the other. Together, they complement each other and make action much more integrated and efficient.

Applying the model of natural development of the personality to Jungian symbolic education, the same thing happens. Don't we need the emotional magic for our subjectivity to bring forth our objectivity? Don't we sway the whole time between magic and scientific thought? I do not mean "magic" in the sense of fantastic wishes, such as lighting a candle in order to win the lottery. That is only one type of magic. I refer to the magic way of thinking applied to everyday life, which reinforces and reassures the emotional to engage the objective. I refer to the magic of love, of cheering, of optimism, of expressing the wish to make the objective performance come out to one's heart's content: "God protect you, my son. Mother will be praying for you to pass your examination." It is the magic the teacher can develop in the transference relationship of symbolic pedagogy: "I am not teaching you this equation only so that you learn physics, but because it will be important to your life", he might say. Its fruitful results are undeniable.

The great resistance of rational education to symbolic education, as I see it, stems from the traditional reluctance of scientific thought to acknowledge the magic-mythical dimension expressed in any subjective, emotional, or irrational manifestation. Part of this defensive cultural complex is due to European ethnocentrism, deeply influenced by Darwin's theory of evolution, which so strongly permeated the nineteenth century. According to prejudiced ethnocentrism, which unduly misused Darwin's theory of evolution, animism was labeled primitive and left in the past or in so-called undeveloped tribal cultures in the present.

I believe that the resistance to magical thinking is rooted in the historic separation that pathologically dissociated the subjective from the objective in the European cultural Self at the end of the eighteenth century. One of the consequences of this dissociation was the veto of scientific thought on animistic or esoteric magic-mythical thought, radically eliminating the subjective dimension from education. This attitude seems to me a prejudiced, reactionary, dogmatic, and sectarian reaction, which indicates the presence of a defensive structuring function that formed a cultural complex that pathologically limits the cultural Self.

All this is necessary in order to understand the resistance to symbolic education, for this resistance is rooted in the historical phase marked by the French Revolution and the period that followed it. It seems undeniable that the difficulties of present-day teaching, which we propose to transcend, are rooted in nineteenth-century university teaching, established during the Enlightenment when science seized power in the university.

For many historians of science, mainly of the materialistic trend present in nineteenth century and in the first half of twentieth century, it is as if the lights of science dispelled the darkness of the Inquisition. Intolerance and ideological persecution would have been followed by openness and full acceptance of creativity; the cult of prejudice by that of revelation through freedom of research. In short, it is as if science freed research and brought liberty of teaching to the university. Yes and no!

Yes, because once free from religious intolerance, the scientific method could be practiced in the university without the coercion of religious dogmatism and prejudice. No, because truth became identified with the objective by the unilateral and exclusive emphasis on the extraverted thinking and sensation functions, and radically dissociated subjectivity, introversion, intuition, feeling, and ethics, which from then on were censored and excluded. Science did not exorcise or repair the Christ-Devil dissociation that had made the European cultural Self spiritually insane in the Middle Ages. Instead of curing this huge wound, science dislocated it defensively to an intense subjective-objective dissociation, which threw the European cultural Self into the madness of materialism and rationalism in the nineteenth century. The sociopolitical consequences of dialectical materialism in the twentieth century were incomparably more costly in lives than those which occurred during the previous fourteen centuries of religious oppression.

The verbalism of words without experience that permeates present teaching is much more than the re-edition of the nominalism of the Middle Ages, which sought to deal with things only by their name. This present-day exaggerated rationalism comes from the same materialism without subjective support that predominated in the nineteenth century and stemmed from the subject-object dissociation that occurred at the end of the eighteenth century.

Only with the intense destructiveness of Hiroshima and Nagasaki did we begin to awaken to the fact that objective rationalism does not bring common sense and wisdom to the planet. This illusion, celebrated in the Enlightenment, brought about the unilateral crowning of reason in the seventeenth and eighteenth centuries. With the atomic holocaust of the twentieth century, we began to realize that unless we submit the objective neutrality of scientific truth to the feeling function and to the ethics of humanism, it can lead to the destruction of our species. Along with the terrible evidence of the destructiveness of modern weaponry, we are amassing countless reports of climate disturbances, of the exhaustion of natural reserves, of pollution and environmental devastation, of exaggerated consumption, of the frightening increase of drug traffic, in the midst of corruption and the dissolution of spiritual values by unbridled consumerism, all covered up by the growing dependence on medical psychoactive drugs and the alienated conception of progress and happiness (Worldwatch Institute 2010).

Yet, in spite of the growing perception of the subjective-objective dissociation, its mythological roots in the Christ-Devil dichotomy in the Middle Ages have not been duly recognized and elaborated. The philosophy of science has not yet clearly linked the scientific paranoid defensive relationship to the subjective with the wound caused by three centuries of persecution by the Inquisition and, therefore, continues to act defensively.

The subjective-objective dissociation of the cultural Self and the resulting disciplinary fragmentation are still explained by many students of our culture as something exclusively inherent to the nature of scientific, mathematical, and technological machinelike development (Capra 1982). Thus, one remains embedded in rationalism and positivism even when denouncing and wishing to avoid them. It seems to me that an understanding of the above-mentioned emotional and mythical factors imprisoned in defensive structures is essential in order to redeem a subjective-objective reunion within a total (holistic and systemic) symbolic perspective.

The subject-object dissociation has had countless consequences. The most serious from the psychological perspective are the loss of intuition, feeling, ethics, and the reference of totality through faith. It is important to realize, however, that science does not have to go back to religion to redeem these. They can be rescued from this dissociation by conceiving them as structuring functions of symbolic elaboration coordinated by the central archetype of the Self. The proposition of Jungian symbolic education is to transcend the philosophy of materialistic science—not exchanging it for a religious worldview but for the humanism of symbolic science.

Nowadays one hears a lot about systemic and holistic integration. This shows awareness of the cultural dissociation and fragmentation in which we live and marks an effort to attain reintegration. However, speaking about the whole is not enough to avoid rationalism and to live holistically in everyday life. For that, it is necessary to experience the symbolic transcendence of reality, beginning with its perception in consciousness as well as in the shadow. This is the symbolic paradigm, according to which each experience is elaborated as structuring symbol, complex, function, and system related to the whole and constantly forming and transforming the ego-other polarities in consciousness. The recycling of each family's trash, for instance, is, on the subjective and objective level, just as symbolic to the experience of wholeness as the necessity of disposing of radioactive material in an ecological manner.

When experiences are perceived as symbolically related to the wholeness of the Self, it is crucial to differentiate whether they are being expressed by normal or defensive structuring functions, that is, whether they are acting in consciousness, in the circumstantial shadow, or in the chronic shadow. If individual or collective experiences are being expressed by defensive structuring functions—in chronic shadow—it is not enough to simply identify the problems. One has to amplify the problems and elaborate on their historic archetypal roots, as we are doing with the subjective-objective dissociation in order to rid them of their conditioning.

This materialistic and rationalist dissociation of the cultural Self is deeply pathological, and its structuring symbols occupy a great part of the chronic shadow of our European cultural tradition. If we only mention the symbols and do not repeatedly elaborate their mythological and archetypal roots and the traditional ways in which they are experienced, we will not be able to rid them of their defenses and reintegrate these symbols in collective consciousness. When we merely identify these defenses and do not elaborate on them, we are actually reinforcing them by defensive rationalization, and instead of solving the fixation we simply improve our ability to hide and to avoid facing them in the shadow.

Together with the loss of the experience of totality and alienation from the process of transcendence, the subjective-objective dissociation in the European cultural tradition has brought about a vast array of knowledge in specialized islands, creating a real cultural Babel. Specialists who speak of the same things using different labels prevent us from recognizing that the same knowledge is being gained in different fields. This situation is made worse by the fact that some fields of knowledge are treated with defensive resistance, for instance, when they are concerned mainly with intuition, feeling, sexuality, aggression, or mysticism, which obscures the shadow confrontation and integration into the cultural Self. The educator must be familiar with these aspects when teaching structuring symbols that include them.

The feeling function has been especially affected because it belongs primarily to subjectivity. Sexuality, intuition, and imagination have all been strongly affected both by scientific subjective-objective dissociation and by the religious Christ-Devil dissociation that preceded it. Sexuality was repressed by religious Christian Puritanism. Intuition and imagination were restrained because they favored the creation of noncanonic variants, which led to their being defensively considered dangerous sources of heresy and evil during the religious era and expressions of esotericism during the scientific era.

Many readers who are not used to dealing with defensive structures operating in the individual Self, and even more so in the cultural Self, may find it exaggerated that such an old problem can still affect the teacher-student relationship. They may also find it incomprehensible that, once identified, these dissociations have not been since long overcome.

Here we rely on the genius of Freud, who discovered defenses and identified among them repetition-compulsion and defensive resistance. However, resistance is not always defensive; emotional resistance, for instance, may perform a creative structuring function of great importance in one's psychic life and in an apprenticeship. Thus, resistance in teaching is not necessarily defensive. In a classroom situation where there are two drowsy students, three absent-minded ones, and four who are chatting, the teacher must not simply reprehend the class for its lack of attention. He or she must consider (that is, elaborate on) what is being taught and how he or she is teaching it, for the students' resistance may be justified and creative, and the teacher may be the one who needs to adjust. But when a defensive structure is involved, resistance is at the service of defenses, which render the structuring symbols inaccessible to consciousness. This was the case of a class that was absent-minded and very resistant to studying following the tragic death of a schoolmate (circumstantial shadow). Instead of rejecting the students' attitude, the teacher dedicated the class to elaborating symbols expressing death, and in the next class the defensive behavior subsided.

In these cases, defensive resistance must be considered together with teaching; otherwise resistance to the symbols taught will probably not allow them to be learned. This is precisely the case with many symbols, complexes, functions, and systems that Jungian symbolic education wishes to integrate in its theory and practice. This is the reason why the historically defensive resistance to the symbolic dimension has to be elaborated together with its creative potential. The teaching of history must identify and elaborate traditional defenses still present in the cultural Self. The resistance of today's youth to compartmentalized, alienated, and rational teaching may be an expression of creative resistance. On the other hand, the resistance many teachers display toward integrating emotions and pragmatism into the students' everyday lives may be expressing a defensive structuring function and cultural complex rooted in this historical dissociation.

The nonelaboration of these defenses in individual, institutional, and cultural Selves has probably been a large part of the reason for the failure of many progressive educators who attempted to teach with a more integrated subjective dimension. The tragedy portrayed in the film *Dead Poets' Society* (1989), which had a great impact on the educational *milieu* some years ago, illustrates well what I mean.

Therapists with long experience in dealing with defenses will have no difficulties in understanding their actions within the cultural Self, especially those couple, family, and institutional therapists who are used to dealing with defensive prejudices and complexes that are generations old. We have only to think of prejudices against social classes, ethnic groups, the body, homosexuality, and the feminine-masculine dynamic, for instance, to realize how defenses can remain in action consciously and unconsciously for centuries and millenia. This web of customs in the cultural Self leads us to defensive attitudes in the individual Self for which we know no apparent justifications.

Regarding the subjective-objective dissociation which occurred at the end of the eighteenth century, two defensive structures and cultural complexes were set up which deserve full attention: defensive projection on the subjective and the defensive idealization and rationalization of objective truth. These two defenses, as always happens in the same dissociation of the Self, began to operate jointly.

Subjectivity was equated with error to such an extent that any sign of it was considered a contaminator of scientific truth, like an infectious microbe during surgery. Also defensively equated with the subjective, as its essential characteristics, were the negative qualities of subjectivity, such as inconsistency, prejudice, frivolity, irresponsibility, incompetence, dishonesty, manipulation, mendacity, histrionic dramatization, and many other types of crookedness. Meanwhile, all human virtues were defensively idealized and projected onto objectivity, such as seriousness, profoundness, intelligence, consistency, honesty, and even harmony, which is something objectivity without subjectivity cannot have.

The problem worsens when we realize that not only are the defensive structures and cultural complexes archetypal but they can also be very large and encompass great archetypal zones, forming huge defensive systems. In these cases, a true war of archetypes may occur. An analysis of these conflicts must be undertaken on the archetypal level at the risk of not being able to elaborate the problem in its real amplitude. Let us consider, for instance, the case of the structuring function of sexuality.

It is well known that Freud was so impressed by the importance of the structuring function of sexuality that he made it the center of his psychology. Now when we examine the cultural repression of sexuality during the religious era from a symbolic and archetypal viewpoint, we see that it was repressed together with many other functions of being.

Why do we require students to remain in their chairs during class? Why is it that a subject being studied is rarely seen, touched, smelled, heard, tasted, recited, danced, acted, or sung? Why does teaching remain generally on an abstract verbal level? Why are there rarely animals in schools, not even familiar dogs and cats in the classroom, and often not even a single fruit tree in an otherwise beautiful campus garden? Why was subjectivity excluded together with intuition, love, ethics, emotion, drama, and group intimacy? Why have women been the target of sexual repression while men have been instigated to promiscuous sexual performance? If one reduces all this exclusively to "repression of sexuality" and Victorian Puritanism, one does not perceive the problem in its symbolic and archetypal extension in the cultural Self.

When we realize the huge variety of complexes or structuring symbols and functions involved, we must search for an archetypal pattern that encompasses them, without reducing them to one single drive as happened with Freudian psychoanalysis. When we apply the symbolic archetypal method to our cultural tradition, we find, underneath the subjective-objective dissociation, nothing less than the matriarchal archetype brutally wounded by the extraordinarily defensive repressive dominance of the patriarchal archetype.

What these archetypes and their patterns mean, that is, their ways of functioning, will be explored in the following chapters. Illustrated by Freud's reduction of many psychological functions to sexuality, we can clearly see how the lack of the archetypal perspective seriously limits the understanding and the systemic elaboration of the fixations and dysfunctions of the Western cultural Self.

Freud did not take into consideration that the sexual repression of the Victorian Era (rooted in the Middle Ages) was not the same for everybody but significantly stronger for women than for men. The repression of sexuality was accompanied by the repression of many other complexes or structuring symbols and functions, coordinated by the sensuality of the matriarchal archetype, which formed the dissociated shadow, symbols, complexes, and functions expressed in hysteria.

The matriarchal pattern is one of sensuality, fertility, and survival. It operates through the intimacy of the ego-other relationship and of all polarities, including the conscious-unconscious polarity. It is a pattern in which sexuality is but one aspect of the exuberance of the senses and of life in general. In this human and psychic connection of people and functions, the erotic, pictorial, intuitive, dramatic, visionary, fanciful, affectionate, humorous, and visceral elements are abundant. In culmination, woman was the great depositary of the matriarchal archetype in cultures with strong patriarchal dominance like ours, not because of her nature exclusively, but because she was the protagonist of erotic attraction, pregnancy, and nursing, hence her biblical repression in our cultural origins. The traditional archetypal social roles of men and women during historical patriarchal dominance explain the differences in their cultural repression, rather than the mere repression of sexuality.

Here we can draw two important conclusions: the first is that the subjective-objective dissociation of the late eightteenth century showed specific symbolic and archetypal components due to the historical condition in which it occurred. The second, which is interrelated, is that it is useless to try to redeem a structuring function like sexuality separate from the archetypal systemic dynamics of Self.

We now understand what happened to Freud by concentrating on the elaboration of sexuality, rather than on the repressive patriarchal-matriarchal relationship within the history of the cultural Self. The failure of psychoanalysis to free the matriarchal archetype from repression is well illustrated, among other issues by the couch, which, when systematically used, paralyses the body and prevents the use of any other expressive technique, by symbolic elaboration established exclusively on verbal expression, and by the very limited creative interaction between patient and analyst. If we compare the couch and the free association method of psychoanalysis with the whole array of expressive techniques that we nowadays have at our disposal for symbolic elaboration including active imagination, it becomes clear that talking about sex with the body imprisoned in the couch could never bring about sufficient elaboration of the wounded matriarchal dynamism or provide creative conditions for symbolic elaboration of the matriarchal archetype in all its exuberance.

The situation of the classroom is astonishingly similar: students whose bodies are prisoners of chairs, studying subjects mostly on an abstract verbal level and with a minimal experiential component, both in learning and in applying knowledge: animal and vegetable nature "hygienically" excluded from schools and teaching methods, together with aspects of feeling and intuition, and unpasteurized emotions, such as aggression, sensuality, fantasy, and pleasure. Teaching is overburdened by specialists who overextend their areas, indifferent to the demands imposed by others. The syllabus is typically significantly exaggerated, fragmented, cut off from experience and utility in the students' everyday lives, and therefore to a great extent condemned to oblivion. Even worse, this system tends to evaluate only the students, by means of simple exams, grades, and school reports, rather than that which also needs it, that is, the system itself, the teachers, the methods of teaching, and the contents of programs.

One realizes, then, that the understanding and practice of Jungian symbolic education calls for the understanding of the fixations and defensive formations present in our archetypal and historical roots. Considering this reality, we will now specifically focus on the theoretical and practical pillars of Jungian symbolic education, applying its concepts to our present reality whenever possible.

# Chapter 3

# PEDAGOGIC SYMBOLIC ELABORATION AND PEDAGOGIC TRANSFERENCE

In the development of personality, the process of symbolic elaboration coordinates through archetypes the energy of symbols and the structuring functions for the formation and transformation of ego and other in consciousness and in shadow, whether circumstantial or chronic. The process of symbolic elaboration is the center of psychic activity in Jungian symbolic psychology, and thus in Jungian symbolic education.

The notion of transformation of consciousness during apprenticeship is based on the idea that the new often interacts with the old to originate new syntheses, which are new states of consciousness. This may generate confusion during apprenticeship but it is a creative confusion, which Piaget called indiscrimination or deconstruction. It is an important and inseparable part of the creation of knowledge, and it is all the more intense the greater the transformation of the Self brought about by the new knowledge. We might even make the generalization that when there is no indiscrimination in consciousness, it is a sign that the new symbols at stake did not existentially affect the ego-other relationship. In this case, the new symbols were likely memorized exclusively by the ego as others and were not rooted in being, which explains why they are so easily forgotten.

As Freud did not have the concept of archetype and tied psychological development primarily to the adult-child polarity, he tended to equate any ego indiscrimination with a regression to the infantile unconscious. The method of psychoanalytic treatment itself remained based on regression to infantile symbols of an unresolved Oedipus complex.

Erich Neumann's formulation of the concept of centroversion is important in differentiating indiscrimination from regression (1955). When we study something that fills us with enthusiasm and is experienced as indiscriminate, confounding everything we knew before, we are not necessarily in a state of regression. We can be engaged in centroversion, moved by the archetypal roots of consciousness in the central archetype. Neumann's centroversion is closely related to the structuring function, which Jung called transcendent function (1958). It is inherent in all symbolic activity of the archetypal components of ego and other. Regression to the past is a form of indiscrimination that can involve the symbols of the shadow (defensive regression), and it should not be taken as the explanation for every kind of indiscrimination. If this were so, the whole spiritual life of many cultures— those that include meditation, often accompanied by indiscrimination of consciousness—would be reduced to regression. The indiscrimination that occurs naturally during meditation has its origin in centroversion. It happens through detachment of the ego from adaptation and existential attachment and is directed toward its archetypal transcendence, which normally harmonizes and spiritually enriches the personalities of those who practice it.

The value of clarity and the demonstrative logic of the subject being taught are important but not fundamental, while indiscrimination is essential to the initiatory symbolic method. Ready-made teaching should be avoided together with exclusively logical teaching which makes it difficult for the student to achieve emotional engagement, even when it is practiced in a constructivist way. Experiencing knowledge emotionally by "chewing it before swallowing" is equivalent to initiation in constructivist symbolic elaboration. The teacher or student presents the subject according to what is being studied. As soon as possible, symbolic elaboration begins as a collaborative effort. In this sense, the more mediocre the teacher, the more he or she tends to present the subject in a literal and exclusively rational form, devoid of metaphors, symbolic amplification, emotional context, and indiscrimination.

A good parallel to symbolic constructivism is the *koan* of Zen Buddhist teaching methods which favors centroversion. The *koan* indiscriminates, that is, confuses consciousness to the point where one can barely reason, but this is its function, since only in this way can the conditioned state of the mind be disrupted to reveal the depth of being. This is what Piaget describes as deconstruction, which accompanies the construction of learning. Jungian symbolic education also teaches us how very different the intelligence of the ego is from the intelligence of the Self, as in the following example.

A disciple was very dependent on the master, and this delayed the development of his apprenticeship. The master called his attention to this limiting dependence. The disciple understood the logic of his words but not their deeper meaning. The disciple was brilliant and capable of the most complex and abstract reasoning, but for all his conceptual intelligence he failed to reach the existential wisdom that the master wanted to convey.

Master and disciple were staying at a monastery during a journey and in the middle of the night went together to the restroom. While they stood urinating side by side, the master suddenly sighed and exclaimed: "This is an activity which I will never be able to do for you". Unexpectedly, Zen happened! In a flash, the stunned disciple realized the whole problem of teacher-student dependency and its relationship to apprenticeship. He went to bed bewildered and could not sleep. He thought about this symbol over and over, like someone who looks at a print every day on the living-room wall and finds it always has something to say. In turn, he became a master. He taught for many years. He never forgot that experience.

What happened to the disciple was the reactivation of sensory-motor intelligence by concentrating in the physiological act of urinating, which transcended the abstraction of conceptual intelligence and permitted the occurrence of Zen, that is, the psychic state of whole being. The monumental educational psychology of the Piaget school, which formulated the constructivism largely prevalent in Western teaching today, although conceived in the dialectic ego-other interaction of the alterity archetype, could not overcome the subject-object dissociation and remained mostly in the extraverted thinking-sensation dimension. When we practice symbolic constructivism, we must not center education on conceptual abstract intelligence because, as in Zen Buddhism, when we deconstruct, that is, indiscriminate consciousness through centroversion, we are reuniting conceptual and sensory-motor intelligence to elaborate symbols at an existential level, that is, beyond the rational.

Many exercises of hatha yoga include sensory-motor practices in meditation to enrich the rational mind by rooting it in the body. Let us not forget that *yoga* means union. Sit in the lotus position and enter the vegetative rhythm following your breathing. Inhale, exhale. Once you feel detached and your mind begins to empty, touch the soft palate of your mouth with the tip of your tongue. Remain quiet and concentrate on your sense perception. This and countless other positions in yoga help to reunite the abstract mind with the body.

A good example of this problem has been richly expressed in the movie *Forrest Gump* (1994), in which a young American with an IQ of seventy-five (below normal) demonstrates existential wisdom inspired by love. It is difficult to imagine a more eloquent example of a cultural revolution in progress against the alienated and alienating tyranny of traditional, exclusively cognitional IQ. Indeed, therapists see countless cases of patients with very high IQ who have little common sense and are incapable of love.

The main thing to be redeemed is the symbolic experience of teaching that transmits the wholeness of being together with apprenticeship. In the symbolic process, transcendence of the subject taught is experienced naturally, for the experience inserts itself through symbols into the totality of the Self. Knowing is one thing. Teaching is something very different. Important for the transmission of symbolic teaching are the educator's authenticity and existential wholeness, which stem from intellectual, emotional, and professional commitment. Together with the subject taught comes the formation of the student's and the teacher's characters and personalities.

To this end, the teacher needs to maintain the tension of the discrimination-indiscrimination polarity in the elaboration of symbols during teaching. Too much discrimination, that is, too much abstraction emerging from conceptual intelligence, disturbs and even prevents the emotional engagement of the students. Too much discrimination occurs when a teacher presents a completely finished subject, without emotional and rational participation of the students in its construction. Symbolic constructivism aims to teach by stimulating the whole nervous system in a balanced way, including the left and right brain hemispheres, with conceptual and sensory-motor intelligence. It therefore takes into account thinking, sensation, feeling, and intuition, extraversion and introversion, as well as the literal and the abstract, word and image, active expression and silence, body, emotion, and fantasy, together with the entire range of human reactions, all of which are here considered different forms of intelligence.

Too much indiscrimination generates great confusion from too much sensory-motor intelligence and may unleash resistance in the student. When the teacher starts one subject on top of another, without adequate timing, he may cause confusion and resistance, which can increase to the point of saturation. In this case, there is the risk of resistance becoming defensive. This circumstance is very serious, for it can lead to the feared aversive emotional reaction, a defense formed during teaching, which must be avoided at all costs. This is a permanent difficulty in assimilation, which may turn the student away from the subject. "I cannot stand mathematics", "I have no gift for languages", "I have not the least interest in history" can be examples of expressions of the shadow of teaching found in the aversive emotional reaction.

It is important to admit, then, that indiscrimination is part of symbolic elaboration and that excessively clear teaching is to be avoided. Indiscrimination is especially important in teaching because it affords the activation of sensory-motor intelligence amidst conceptual intelligence and signals the need to use expressive techniques to elaborate symbols rich in sensory-motor characteristics and in this manner integrate new meanings into conceptual intelligence. Sensory-motor intelligence is used here as part of the concept of the insular matriarchal position, which will be described in chapter 7.

It is very important for the teacher to recognize how indiscrimination is expressed by students in order to become aware of their learning dynamics. It is also important for the teacher to recognize indiscrimination as normal and to open space for it to be accepted and experienced in class not as something bad but rather as a necessary stage of apprenticeship, like the cloud that brings rain and then gives way to a blue sky.

## Parrot Learning as a Disturbance of Pedagogic Symbolic Elaboration

Rational teaching dissociated from experience favors superficial learning, which may be quickly forgotten or memorized and applied later in life but without creative intelligence. This limited learning diminishes creativity and, when carried throughout life, gives rise to stereotyped thinking.

Parrot learning is the opposite of constructive and dialectical learning. It is a one-way learning in which teachers utter truths and students swallow them without due elaboration. They are swallowed raw, so to speak. Teachers that pose narcissistically as the owners of truth and do not ask or care for student participation in creative interaction tend to favor such superficial learning quite unwillingly and unconsciously.

Parrot learning is a defensive form of learning by rote due to lack of deep symbolic elaboration. The teacher's ego-other discriminations in consciousness are imitated automatically by the student's ego, which will repeat them unquestioningly.

The defensive vanity of a teacher may lead him or her into this shadow temptation and become very satisfied and even proud of it. Every creative, intelligent, honest, and capable teacher must abhor on moral grounds his or her participation in the formation of parrot students. It is commonly known that Jung was glad not to be a Jungian...

Parrot learning may be productive when it is present in the very first phase of learning. At that moment, it may be creative, but if it does not pass on to constructive learning, it will become defensive.

The best way to avoid the formation of defensive parrot learning is by stimulating symbolic elaboration of the subject in question, which can be done by asking students to participate creatively and to apply intelligently expressive techniques to animate those symbols which are being taught.

## Equal Participation of Projection and Introjection in Symbolic Elaboration

Projection is a structuring function that deposits contents of symbols to form the identity of other, while introjection deposits the meaning of symbols to form ego identity. Projection and introjection complement each other, as do all structuring functions through their polarities. When projection exaggerates and attributes to the other what belongs to the ego, introjection corrects it and vice versa through the structuring function of evaluation. This is a very particular way of using the concepts of projection and introjection because it considers the identity formation of the ego and of the other as a simultaneous and common dialectical process. These concepts of introjection and projection as complementary structuring functions differ from Klein's projective identification, which includes all ego identity formation and in which introjective identification is not considered as a complementary function.

In Jungian symbolic psychology, the outside and inside separation exists for the ego and for the other, but not for the symbol or for the Self. This fact makes the structuring functions of projection and introjection operationally equal in importance. In projection, we basically elaborate the blend of symbolic ingredients that include the ego and the other, in keeping with the other. It is not the ego but rather the central archetype that coordinates projection. It includes the ego but is much more than it. In introjection, we essentially elaborate the blend of symbolic ingredients in keeping with the formation of ego identity, and again, it is not the ego that introjects but rather the central archetype.

Jungian symbolic education consciously uses the structuring functions of projection and introjection in teaching, especially when employing expressive techniques. In learning, balancing the participation of the ego and the other through the introjection-projection relation is one of the arts of symbolic teaching.

"Now you are the people in the French Revolution", a history teacher could say to the class (the teacher projects, the students introject), "and I am Napoleon" (the teacher introjects, the class projects). "Let us talk about whether you want me crowned emperor or not" (symbolic elaboration of the crowning of Napoleon, with psychodramatic expressive technique) (Moccio 1980).

## Transference Dynamics in Education

When we speak about the social dimension of the Self as the symbolic interaction of parts among themselves and with the whole, vis-à-vis the student-teacher relationship, we are speaking about transference dynamics. Hence, the mere mention of the pedagogic Self, which involves the conscious-unconscious whole of the teacher-student relationship, already invokes the pedagogic transference. Like all structuring functions, transference too can be normal or defensive (Byington 1984).

Vygotsky is considered one of the pioneers of modern education due to the importance he gave to the interpersonal dimension in learning:

> All functions in child development appear twice: first on the social level and then on the individual level. First between people (interpsychological) and then in the child's interior (intrapsychological). This applies equally to voluntary attention, logical memory, and formation of concepts. All superior functions originate in real relationships between human beings. (Vygotsky 1960, p. 64)

Interpersonal dynamics were introduced into psychodynamic psychology by the concept of transference. We know how Freud (1917, p. 503) brilliantly discovered transference and considered the neurotic transference as the main defense in the psychotherapeutic relationship. According to him, neurotic transference consists of the projection of the nonsublimated Oedipus complex by the patient. When the Oedipus complex is well sublimated to form the superego, the patient sees the analyst simply as a person and does not transfer defensively. If the therapist transfers something to the patient, Freud called it countertransference. Therefore, Freud treated transference mostly as a defensive reaction in the therapeutic relationship.

It is also known that, unlike Freud, Jung emphasized the importance of transference as a creative archetypal phenomenon of relationship. According to him, transference involvement between people who are intimately related is unavoidable. To Jung the analyst's transference is as archetypal, normal, and inevitable as the patient's. Both are part of the creativity of the Self in the individuation process (Jung 1946).

Thus two forms of transference have been emphasized: the defensive transference, mostly by Freud, and the creative transference, mostly by Jung. In my view, these two forms of transference operate permanently side by side in both psychotherapy and teaching. The concept of transference in symbolic Jungian psychology includes the perspective of psychoanalysis, as defensive transference, and that of analytic psychology, as normal transference, within the concept of the therapeutic Self. It encompasses a transference quaternio, which expresses the interaction of the normal and defensive structures of the analyst and of the patient. The concept of the therapeutic Self is here differentiated from the concept of the therapeutic vessel that Jung brought to psychotherapy from alchemy. The therapeutic Self encompasses all experiences in therapy, while the therapeutic vessel refers specifically to the relationship built between therapist and patient (Byington 1984). These concepts were transposed from Jungian symbolic psychology into education and applied to the teacher-student relationship within the pedagogic Self. Iraci Galiás (1989) had already introduced the concept of the pedagogic vessel in teaching. The pedagogic Self is the totality of psychic reactions of the ensemble represented by teacher and students. The pedagogic vessel is the teaching relation rationally and emotionally built during the teacher-student school year, through which structuring symbols and functions of the pedagogic Self are elaborated.

Like all other human groups, the pedagogic group has the same transference quaternary structure as the therapeutic Self and, therefore, students and teachers may present normal and defensive transference reactions

(Byington 1984). Naturally, in each group situation we deal with this quaternio in a certain way. In the therapeutic Self, the examination of transference falls predominantly upon the patient's defensive structures, which are mainly responsible for the symptoms and sufferings of psychodynamic syndromes. But in the pedagogic Self, the focus of transference analysis falls basically upon normal transference structures of students and teacher. It goes without saying that throughout symbolic elaboration, all four structures of the transference quaternio are experienced to a greater or lesser degree in the elaboration of transference situations, as Maria Zelia Alvarenga described in her article "Transference Relationship and Structuring of Consciousness" (1991).

When dealing with a subject, it is up to the educator to animate the pedagogic Self by choosing the content and the adequate mobilization techniques to teach it, always paying attention to the four transference-structuring functions. Naturally, this demands a minimum of self-knowledge; the teacher needs a basic understanding of his or her own emotional structure and of the usual pattern of relation between the normal and defensive structures in his or her individual Self. This degree of self-knowledge is necessary in teaching in order to apply it to the pedagogic Self of the class, students, school, and culture.

It is important for the teacher to know the main defenses present in his or her shadow and to be willing to recognize and confront them when they are constellated. There are teachers who react defensively to students' bad behavior with depression (defensive introjection); others react with abnormal anxiety and aggression (paranoid defensive projection); and many find it difficult to deal with the students' competition with them (defensive competition). Some teachers tend to speak too much and leave little room for the students to construct their learning (defensive exhibitionism and narcissism); others feel overly shy and scare their pupils by their remoteness (defensive shyness), unlike those who speak loud and are authoritarian because of insecurity (defensive self-affirmation). We must not forget that teachers and students are in asymmetric positions in a hierarchy regarding authority, legal footing, and financial conditions. Pedagogic transference, even when unnoticed, always includes this asymmetry. When it is disregarded and not responsibly considered, the pedagogic field is prone to form a pedagogic shadow.

The more knowledgeable a teacher is about his or her weak points in the pedagogic relationship, the easier it will be to elaborate the transference situations in the classroom by identifying and separating the students' transferences from his or her own. To gain this knowledge, the best method is to undergo analysis. However, even without analysis, a good pedagogic orientation or coaching in nontherapeutic groups of professional training may be of great help in the teacher's self-knowledge. The greater emotional and creative participation of teachers and students in symbolic constructivism makes the knowledge and elaboration of transference situations one of its main points.

Abstractly, this theoretical approach may seem difficult to practice, but in day-to-day teaching this is not so. If there is a democratic and affectionate attitude that provides an atmosphere of intimacy and humanistic opening in school, the various dimensions of the Self, of students, classes, teachers, parents, tutors, directors, and employees may interact and help each other systemically to elaborate problems symbolically. The fact that this theoretical approach encompasses reality in its multiple aspects seems very complex. In its practical experience, however, it is greatly simplified, for its very basis is the normally creative and affectionate development of the individual and the group.

Because of the enormous importance of transference in every human relationship as formulated by Jung, it holds a central position in the elaboration of any situation within the pedagogic Self. I will deal briefly here with some of the most important structuring functions, which creatively or defensively affect the transference relationship.

## Normal-Defensive, Harmonious-Conflicting and Constructive-Destructive Polarities

Before going into the concept of structuring functions in the transference relationship, it is necessary to separate out three polarities: normal-defensive, positive-negative (or harmonious-conflicting) and constructive-destructive. Regarding the normal-defensive polarity, we have seen that the fixation of structuring functions and symbols turns them defensive and forms the shadow. In the circumstantial shadow, defenses are activated in a present context. In the chronic shadow, defenses have been structured in the past and have become autonomous complexes.

The harmonious-conflicting polarity refers to the affectionate or aggressive relationship between teacher and student. It is not a synonym for normal-defensive polarity since both structures, affection and aggression, can be normal or defensive. It is important not to identify aggression and conflict either with pathology or with destructiveness, since they can be quite constructive and creative when normally handled. Aggression frequently is born of frustration. It is the structuring function that says no to anything that hampers life. To say "no" creatively calls for honesty, courage, integrity and symbolic elaboration capacity. The teacher needs sufficient emotional maturity to withstand defensive aggression from students; it is most important to teach them to channel it into a creative "no," which they frequently do not know how to do. When the teacher is not mature enough, he or she may receive the students' "no" defensively and repress it. In such cases, the student either submits or rebels, damaging the pedagogic relationship. To deal properly and creatively with the harmonious-conflicting polarity is one of the great secrets in the art of teaching symbolically. There are teachers with defensive authority, who inhibit their students' aggression and feel successful when they mold their students into sheep or parrots. They believe that submission, passivity, good manners, and respect are synonyms. They have not learned that creativity, dignity, transgression, and aggression operate together in the healthy development of the personality.

The constructive-destructive polarity refers to the consequences of our actions in the existential process, whether in the individual or the social dimension. An educator needs to know this polarity well to be able to evaluate both his or her own and the students' behavior. The use of this concept is difficult and delicate since often something may seem destructive in the short run but turns out to be constructive in the long run, and vice versa. As usual, appearances can be very misleading. After I graduated from medical school, I started my first analysis. At that time, I was teaching and doing research at the university and felt an intense vocation to undertake a university career. I had just presented a paper at an international congress on Chagas disease and was very proud of it. I went to sleep delighted by the presentation and had a terrible nightmare, which influenced my whole professional life. I dreamed that the foundation that sponsored the congress, which was where I taught and did the research, was poisoned by a lethal gas. It was heavier than air and accumulated first on the ground. No one could escape. Children were already dying because of their low stature. Adults would be next. I entered a restroom, stepped on a toilet bowl, jumped over the wall, and escaped. During that analysis, I submitted my resignation and abandoned my university career. At that time, many colleagues told me I was committing professional suicide and doing something very neurotic and destructive; and there were times when I believed this might be true and felt anxious and afraid because of that decision to run away through the back door. Now, decades later, I see that it was the most constructive thing I could have done. The corrupt, stupid, humiliating, bureaucratic compromises many colleagues were forced to accept in order to "build" an academic career, which often led to the prostitution of their creativity, honesty and initiative, would probably have mutilated my creativity. The ethical criterion of what is constructive or destructive must be established by the development of the Self and not by collective appearances and the immediate conveniences of the ego (Neumann 1948).

Associating the harmonious-conflicting polarity with the constructive-destructive polarity, there are cases where relationships are very affectionate and apparently productive but in reality are not, like, for instance, the attitude of the overprotective mother or teacher who subdues and weakens the son or student with overflowing affection and stimulates them to hide the shadow. On the other hand, aggression can be very healthy and constructive, as in the case of the mother dog who bites and repels her puppy when it still wants to suck in spite of being too grown up to do so.

The separation of these three polarities is important in the student-teacher-school-family relationship in helping us to avoid preconceived moralism by equating student-teacher conflict and aggression with destructive behavior and a harmonious relationship with a constructive one. This discrimination is also important in situations that are out of control for lack of limits, when educators imprudently accept the acting out of destructive behavior, which may precipitate dangerous overacting.

Here we enter the important field of limits and discipline in education. The educator has to create the conditions that allow the student to engage as many structuring functions as possible. After all, the essence of education is the formation of the personality, not its repression. In fact, it is with all the ingredients of soul that the existential whole is built. All functions of life are necessary for the structuring of consciousness, including those normally rejected by culture, such as aggression, shame, dissimulation, lying, treason, contempt, envy, and cowardice. They are structuring functions of the Self and have a pedagogical role proportionate to their capacity for psychic mobilization. Therefore, adequate evaluation of experiences through these functions is essential for the teacher-student relationship. This does not mean accepting them as they come, but rather always taking their meaning into consideration and at the same time elaborating them and separating the normal from the defensive aspects.

Jung described the persona as the mask we wear for social adaptation. I have amplified this concept to define persona as the structuring function that uses anything, but especially culture, for symbolic elaboration in the social dimension and at the same time helps to form the identity of the ego and of the other (Byington 2008). Language, habits, customs, and traditions are aspects of the persona that the child uses to elaborate symbols and form identity. The educator's skill consists of teaching how to build the persona, of employing appropriate channels to experience structuring functions in an adequate and constructive way, even if these functions are intensely aggressive and conflicting.

The educator's skill and flexibility when providing creative aspects of the persona for inadequate and even destructive situations can transform extremely difficult transference situations into experiences of high pedagogic meaning (Bustos et al. 1980). We must not forget that iron is cast only at high temperature. Transference crisis can do more for the relation of the teacher with the class than many tedious sermons. In this situation, we have to value the teacher's capacity to identify limits and act to elaborate them creatively before they get out of control, by using expressive techniques. Before scolding the class or expelling a student, for instance, it can be very profitable to try to channel the energy of the individual and group Self toward a pedagogical activity that dramatically and creatively expresses frustration, aggression, absentmindedness, hatred, envy, competition, or captiousness, whatever the case may be. To simply repress bad behavior is to waste golden opportunities to learn how to deal creatively with transgression in the structuring of character.

## The Structuring Function of Aggression

Let us suppose there is a conflict between students and teacher or vice versa. Although the situation is difficult and painful, it must not be covered up or repressed. Precisely because of its emotional charge, it provides a good opportunity to go deeply into the experience and draw from it various meanings for the student and for the class (Kaufman 1991).

As a structuring function, aggression is very important in life, and we cannot do without it. Affection teaches the ego to say "yes", while aggression teaches it to say "no". Both are equally important in ego development. Jungian symbolic psychology proposes teaching through the symbolic loving transference bond. For this purpose, it is indispensable to know that love includes both affection and aggression. The more the human being is tame as a lamb, the more he or she produces a savage, mutilated, or perverse wolf in his or her shadow. That is why wolf and lamb must be practiced and integrated on the conscious level as much as possible. The problem is how, where, and when. If we can manage to experience aggression in a creative way by arranging a context and the means to express it, we are not only teaching how to elaborate one of the most problematic structuring functions of the individual and of society but also contributing to the effort to avoid individual and collective shadow formation.

The structuring functions of aggression and affection are equally important for the development of consciousness. In the first half of the twentieth century, Freud discovered infantile sexuality, which allowed the teaching of sexuality to be included in the normal curriculum. It seems to me that the equivalent discovery in the second half of that century was that the structuring function of aggression is also normal and fundamental to the structuring of consciousness. The creative use of normal aggression in pedagogic transference relationship and avoiding its destructiveness is one of the great skills desired for the teaching profession in Jungian symbolic education.

Affection brings the ego and the other close together. Aggression separates them. Both are fundamental in the process of symbolic elaboration, in which symbolic contents are brought together and separated in order to achieve their differentiation. The adequate incorporation of "yes" and "no" into socialization is one of the most important and fundamental lessons to be learned in life.

Coercive patriarchal measures, such as imposition of silence, giving low marks for bad behavior, expelling or suspension from class, must be considered coarse, extreme, radical impositions of limits with little structuring capacity, because they do not elaborate and integrate normal aggression on the level of its multiple meanings. The educator can make use of these measures but must bear in mind their pedagogic inadequacy. When someone lets the end of a cigarette fall in the middle of a lively conversation and the sofa suddenly catches fire, we may have to throw the ice bucket on it or even resort to using a guest's jacket hanging on the nearby chair to beat out the flames. Yet we must admit this is not the best way to put out small fires. Expelling from class and suspension should be acknowledged as extreme resorts, which educators practice when they have exhausted their capacity for creative elaboration of the aggressive function and thus feel compelled to attempt elaboration in a radical patriarchal way. The students transgress and the teachers, incapable of elaborating aggression creatively and intelligently, act out their impotence through repressive measures backed up by the patriarchal hierarchy of the institution. In acting it out in this way, the educator should experience this as a moment of pedagogic failure and frustration. Punitive directive measures are patriarchal, as is all directive, nonconstructed teaching. In order to elaborate emotional structuring functions, exclusively rational constructivism becomes impotent and often resorts to the directive, nonconstructivist patriarchal pattern. We commonly see teachers who profess constructivism become directive and nonconstructivist in situations that demand constructive elaboration of emotions, particularly when it comes to insubordination and aggression. They simply resort to merely punitive measures. I do not mean to say that punitive measures are never used. We expel, we suspend at times, and we even feel tempted to resort to physical aggression, but this is a confession of pedagogic impotence rather than a description of efficiency.

The first condition in dealing with the structuring function of aggression is to admit that it is necessary and indispensable to life. Without aggression there is no transgression, and without transgression creativity cannot exist. Without elaboration, aggression remains hidden and raw. It cannot be denied that many sadists and torturers live normally until they are led by "a superior" to act out their aggression which had remained hidden and not differentiated in their shadow.

The second condition for elaborating aggression is to start working with it in frustration, which is its root. Frustration is burgeoning aggression. In order to elaborate it, a pedagogic vessel sufficient to contain it has to be built with the class. In the same way that love cannot be great if it does not include experiences of hatred, there is no deep pedagogic transference without a sufficiently ample vessel for the elaboration of frustration and aggression. The perception of the class group Self, for instance, cannot dynamically exclude the last row where the shadow is usually lodged. It is there that the rowdiest students generally sit, but these are often also the most creative. Transgression and creativity are inseparable structuring functions. It is up to the teacher to articulate them productively.

At the first signs of frustration, signaled by restlessness, inattention, or poor discipline, the teacher begins an elaboration in order to find out if the frustration is individual or of the group, normal or defensive. Based on experience, one can quickly find out the originating focus of frustration and perceive whether it is normal or defensive. Often the focus is on the content of teaching, which is either too difficult or too abstract or both and therefore hard to understand or has no apparent usefulness whatsoever. The focus may be that the content lacks interest not only for the student but also for the teacher, who shows apathy. The focus may lie also on the teacher's weariness or on a specific psychological state of one or more students. Once frustration is identified, it is important to know that its elaboration, rather than its repression, will show the way to understanding and assimilating its symbolic content for the maturation of personality.

The teacher who knows that frustration is the key to understanding the structuring function of aggression and has a minimum experience in symbolic constructivism does not wait for the extreme situations of a "blackboard jungle" to interfere. He or she is alert to any sign of smoke to elaborate the fire and, in so doing, opens space for expressions of frustration. In the same way that a doctor can take the pulse while listening to a patient's complaints, so the educator evaluates students by observing their reactions in class and by asking about their feelings at the beginning and at the end of every class. This should include frustrations and reactions to the contents of the subject, to the teacher, and to the class performance during the previous and present lessons.

The elaboration of frustration or aggression is as important as that of affection in pedagogic transference in order to turn the emotional bond between teacher and student into the great condition for learning to love knowledge in Jungian symbolic education. The film *Freedom Writers* (2007) presents many examples of how a teacher can confront the aggressive shadow of students and transform it into normal and productive aggression through acceptance, understanding, and finding an adequate persona for its creative expression.

The ability to elaborate frustrations is one of the great teachings in life. When the teacher elaborates aggression with the class frequently within the teacher-student emotional bond, he or she teaches how to do it. This is true symbolic constructive teaching. Here, besides teaching, the teacher contributes to the formation of the character of students, and may uncover the beginning of a character neurosis in certain cases.

Once it is clinically structured, character fixation, which I call psychopathic defense, is one of the most difficult defenses to treat, especially since, peculiar to these cases, it is their belief that they do not need treatment because they have the right to have and act out their symptoms. At the heart of this disturbance is the incapacity to elaborate frustrations which then search for direct satisfaction through aggression when necessary. These students did not have a space to learn to express frustrations and elaborate their complaints. They thus subtly find out how relationships and institutions work in order to act out their shadow without elaborating their frustrations. They are hungry wolves who study the best ways of donning sheep's clothing in order to attack. It is in elaborating the class's frustrations that the teacher detects those students incapable of the elaboration of frustration and who are headed toward forming a character pathology. If the educator is able to help these students learn to complain and to elaborate their frustrations creatively, which contributes to diminishing the formation of the character defense, in this alone the educator will be making a huge contribution to the creative formation of the student's personality and to the community he or she will live in.

In puritan and repressive societies, hysteria and obsessive-compulsive neuroses were predominant. Nowadays, as society becomes more democratic and permissive, corruption and demagogy increase, and with them, character pathology, also called psychopathic behavior. It is an educator's great social contribution to individual students and to society to identify this defense and revert it to normal expression early on.

## The Structuring Functions of Affection, Competition, and Companionship

We have seen the role of aggression in the formation of the personality. Affection is just as important. Affection is one of the main structuring functions within the teacher-student transference relationship for the practice of symbolic elaboration. Feeling creates universes. In Jungian typology, together with aggression, affection corresponds to the feeling function, one of the four structuring functions of consciousness. When a teacher or a student has a dominant feeling function in their typology (see the next chapter), this function becomes correspondingly more important in teaching.

School being the second family, it is obvious that students will relive and elaborate with their teachers and classmates the model and complexes of their own family Self. This means that teachers will receive projections concerning the relation to parents, aunts and uncles, grandparents, brothers and sisters, and so on. On the other hand, teachers are also subject to experiencing in themselves parental transference with students, which can express their shadow when they project onto students the defensive complexes they formed with their parents, siblings, or children. For them, too, the experience of continuity of the family Self in school life is very strong. This underscores the importance of affection in the pedagogic transference relationship, and it is up to the teacher to consider this and make good use of it in the dynamics of the classroom and teaching. It is advisable for the teacher to seek an individual relationship and a minimal degree of intimacy with each student in the class. A few words once a week, a glance, a smile, a personal comment, an affectionate demand for better behavior or performance can help build an individualized relationship.

Here the family model is instructive. Very often we observe that parents relate to their children *en masse*. They address them in the plural even when the child is alone. Swapping of one child's name for another is also common. As fathers tend to be with their children more on weekends, their interactions are often with all the children together, but mothers can also commit this lack of differentiation. Overburdened by the general functions of feeding, health care, education, clothing, and housework, they sometimes neglect their children's individuality by treating them as a collective duty to be fulfilled rather than as separate persons. When this happens, frequently it is because the mother herself has turned into a maternal machine and stopped functioning as a person. In these cases, the children commonly express feelings of rejection and lack of consideration and understanding which at first is hard to identify where they came from. Or else their histories reveal deeply happy memories they keep of the rare situations in which they experienced and related to their father or mother directly as persons. Perhaps the worst consequence of these undifferentiated family relationships is the failure to learn an individual, intimate, and profound model of relationship. Such children become adults who may live a whole life without being able to experience and enjoy the richness of intimacy in human relations. Often the teacher can also become a machine for the transmission of education programs and forget to relate to his or her students individually. Such teachers always refer to the class as a whole or divide it into good and bad students, forgetting that each one is a person, an infinite individual and unknown world.

Very often the teacher is the offspring of a family that lacks the model of intimate and individual relationship. In this case, the difficulty in being intimate and relating to the students individually may be the consequence of childhood experiences. Nevertheless, if this limitation is a function of a circumstantial shadow without intense defenses, making it conscious and training can differentiate the feeling function in a short time. If the teacher is dedicated to doing so, significant progress can soon be achieved. In these cases, the students' satisfaction and the improvement in their performances may become a source of incentive to teachers, not to mention the improvement in the quality of the relationship within their own family, with their spouse and with their own children, since the pedagogic Self and family Self of teachers are also in close conscious and unconscious interaction. Hence, the creative effort demanded by Jungian symbolic education to reunite the subjective to the objective is highly rewarding not only for students but also for teachers, because it allows for a permanent development of the educator's personality in and out of school. The humanization practiced through symbolic teaching is reflected permanently in the growing humanization of the teacher as well as in his or her own family. This is a method of teaching that is never repetitive or dull since it is rooted in the richness of life and develops not only the personality of students but also of teachers.

The intense transference experience of the feeling function in education as well as in the family Self plays a significant role in activating the structuring functions of envy, jealousy, and competition between parents, students, and siblings. This fact must be realized and worked out very carefully since it often generates many personality disturbances and difficulties in learning. For this very reason, its intelligent elaboration can provide substantial pedagogic improvement.

The system of evaluation based on report cards, written examinations, and grades stimulates the competitive function and often directs the student through the power drive more toward finishing a task and getting through the examination than toward loving to learn. As the culmination of the apprenticeship, grades and examinations can imprison students and teachers in the competitive function and cause them to deviate from the essence of knowledge and learning within the affectionate transference bond. The teacher must follow an instructional program and the student must get through examinations, but if teaching remains subordinated exclusively to performance, learning is bound to be absorbed by competition and by the principles of *status* and power only to be forgotten after the examinations. The lack of affection in the pedagogic transference jeopardizes the establishment of a loving relationship to the subject being taught. In this case, teacher and student can live a defensive transference in which the structuring function of competition tends to act out the shadow of teaching. The goal of school, in this case, has been distorted since it places exaggerated emphasis on results rather than the pleasure and the love for learning.

It is important to acknowledge that the system of evaluating learning essentially through grades may be not only inefficient but also highly damaging. The instructional program can be taught and the student can get high grades on the examination, but with little intimate, practical, and affectionate experience, that learning ends up as a mere instrument of power. In this situation, the danger is the reduction of learning to a status. Such a teaching system can turn away creative and enterprising students, who may be perceived as bad students because they do not adapt to it. If we were to evaluate present-day teaching by the development of love for knowledge, few students, teachers, and schools would escape failure.

Symbolic education evaluates teaching mostly based on the cooperative alliance of students and teachers. In the exceptional circumstances where there is a test, it should be done by a teacher from outside the class or by another institution and never by the teacher of the class. After the test is done it should be elaborated and evaluated jointly by teacher and students, for both of them have been tested. The grades bestowed on students must also be seen as grades on the performance of the teacher-student dyad, for better or for worse. It is fundamental that teachers consider and refer to students' grades as "our" grades and not only "your", that is, the students' grades. In this way the class becomes a team and the teacher its coach. In this approach to evaluation, grades become a symbol of the relationship.

In general, teaching must be practiced and integrated in such a way that its evaluation is perceived by the teacher on the spot in class. Think of a cooking class, during which teacher and students try recipes, tasting the food during its preparation. Evaluation done monthly or every two months through tests is grotesquely artificial, whereas evaluation by practical and immediate experience is much more efficient and significant. Such evaluation is equally impressive for teachers and students because it is constructed within the learning relationship. Teachers should always refer to students' evaluation as an evaluation of "our" work to stimulate companionship and teamwork. In this manner, evaluation becomes the permanent reflection of the students' and the teacher's performance. Stimulating competition and cooperation at the same time is very useful for identifying limitations in learning. It is important for teachers to learn how to favor teamwork and use competition affectionately, for instance, by challenging students who know more to help those who know less, whereby the success of learning will be shared by the whole class.

When examinations and grades are given by the class teacher, they create an atmosphere of competition and persecution in the teaching relationship. This negatively affects the competition-cooperation polarity of the class and the whole transference relationship in teaching. When the teacher gives exams and grades, the constellation of cowardice and betrayal is favored. In this way, teachers distort the constructivist method which they profess by betraying the trust of students in the transference bond; if the teacher-student bond is really emotionally constructed, it is not conceivable that only students should be tested, and by their own teacher at that. Only substitution of love for power in the pedagogic bond can explain the incapacity to detect infidelity and treason in dominant patriarchal methods of evaluation, which unashamedly consider themselves democratic and constructive and omit evaluating teachers, the teaching method, and the school together with the evaluation of students.

In symbolic constructivism, evaluation must be included as part of learning in which teachers and students reflect upon the productivity of their relation. It is very important to evaluate whether teaching is increasing or diminishing the interest and love for the subject. Even when constructivism is practiced exclusively on the cognitive level, it is already essential for evaluation to include both teacher and student. After all, if the proposition is that knowledge should emerge from the dialectic relation between the two, how is it possible to evaluate its efficiency if the teacher is excluded from it? In symbolic constructivism, it becomes very clear how evaluation, when reduced to the students alone and handled by the teacher of the class, contaminates the pedagogic transference bond with ambiguity, rejection, betrayal, and cowardice. If the pedagogic transference bond unites students and teachers emotionally and rationally for the construction of teaching, it is not morally acceptable to blame only students for bad results. When used in this way, isn't such testing clear evidence of the betrayal and distortion of the constructivist method?

One argument that is sometimes put forward is that life is full of tests and therefore to test the students prepares them for future competitions and tests. I fully agree that learning should be tested and that teaching should prepare students for life, but my hope is that in facing the tests of life, students will be able to rely on the images of teachers who were their coaches and faithful companions and cheered for them in all circumstances and not be frightened, harassed, or weakened by the introjected image of a teacher who betrayed their alliance by becoming an examiner. Teachers and students in being tested together will strengthen students for the tests of life, whereas in the classical method of testing students form an internal judge that will undermine the role of teaching because of its treacherous and persecuting attitude. The symbolism of testing is completely modified when an outside teacher administers tests because this reinforces solidarity, loyalty, affection, and cheering through teamwork within the class.

Within the perspective of Jungian symbolic education, the structuring function of competition is activated along with the feeling function of pedagogic transference directed toward action. Ideally, competition should take place during teaching and before final examinations. As symbolic teaching is experimental and thus inseparable from doing, checking what has been learned during class work is inherent to teaching. A teacher may ask: "How is it possible to evaluate whether a student knows a math equation or a certain mountain system in Asia or the wars of the Middle Ages without an examination?" The teacher who asks this question does not evaluate students during class and therefore has not yet discovered how much teaching and evaluation form a lively process of interaction. Such a teacher has not reunited the objective and the subjective in existential symbolism nor inserted this experience pragmatically in the Self. Symbolic constructivism summons teachers and students to construct the knowledge of being and creatively include in it the evaluation inseparable from their affectionate alliance in the teaching process. In this way, teachers will not be remembered only as transmitters of knowledge but also as images of the archetype of the coach or of fidelity of the older friend, brother, or sister.

## The Structuring Functions of Curiosity and Shame

By working with the subjective dimension, symbolic education endeavors to develop a series of structuring functions that are specific to learning, one of them being curiosity. This does not involve using subterfuges, tricks, or falsely artificial means that increase the curiosity but weaken the authenticity of being. The deliberately astute subliminal advertising that fosters curiosity together with ignorance and alienation in the affluent society is bad enough. All expressive techniques, starting from the natural characteristics of the personality, can be used to try to root teaching in what is most archetypal in it, that is, peculiar to its creative way of being. In this way, curiosity will be activated in keeping with the knowledge of our being-in-the-world, directed toward the truth of the thing in itself and to its role in our lives. When we use curiosity this way, we cannot dissociate subjects that we may consider more difficult, such as math, physics, chemistry, and psychology, from the study of history, geography, and languages. In order to bring forth a real curiosity for the mountains of Asia, one has to convey their connection with the ego of the student, and this is done through the Self rather than directly through the ego. Will the students not feel more curious about the mountains of India if they see a video of many wise men meditating in the lotus position in their ashrams? "Let us do a meditation in the lotus position in order to foster truth and love in the world as so many wise men are doing right now in the Himalayas", the teacher may suggest. Curiosity will operate on the existential level of being-in-the-world if the truth of being is always fully put at its disposal from the beginning. As it is true for love, there can be no half-truths for knowledge.

In the past, it was believed that a child should first crawl, then walk, then run, and only after it had good coordination would it be able to learn how to swim, until the day someone tried teaching children how to swim while they were still crawling, and it worked. The model of structuring curricula according to the degree of complexity usually does not take into account the archetypal nature of human activities; it is a programmatic model of the patriarchal ego rather than of the Self as a whole. Everything we live is symbolic and can be perceived within the whole. If we symbolize things sufficiently we will soon transcend their appearances and experience their archetypal and universal aspects; in the example above, crawling and swimming have common archetypal roots. There is not the least existential reason for physics, chemistry, and biology to be taught only in high school. They are already present within us when we are born and therefore the study of them does not have to wait for high school. Intimacy with science in lower school should prepare the foundation for scientific abstraction later. The fragmentation of predominantly rational teaching hinders the structuring function of curiosity in its most archetypal, natural, and existential root, which remits it to the whole.

Exactly like children who play computer and video games with curiosity and pleasure, learning the essence of the natural sciences while still very close to sensory-motor or insular matriarchal intelligence can be very productive for later high school learning. Teaching the natural sciences to small children who are learning to read and write, for example, by showing them videos of the astronauts, is a way to teach not the facts of science but its essence within the process of thinking and living. Another example: teach the physics of rain that is falling outside; the physics and chemistry of tea with cookies prepared by the class; the digestion process from the production of saliva until the cookies become excrement; the tea, which has turned into urine, filtered by the kidneys and becoming part of the ecosystem; the filtering system of the kidneys and the pollution in the local river and nearest dam; the water reserves of the planet. There is no reason to separate these topics. Why not dramatize the relation of the rain with the wind, lightning, and thunder, the nearest mountain range, and the rivers? When teaching evolution in primary school, why not make up a story of the first fish born, which, before meeting a girlfriend, fell in love with a crustacean whose family was against the marriage because they were more traditional among living beings?

Here we are reminded of the famous Brazilian educator Monteiro Lobato's imaginal method, in which teaching is inserted into the framework of a story. Through his fertile imagination, Lobato developed a whole family of people, animals, and figures, which animate geography, history, math, and all subjects. They are so poetical and peculiar that they have become part of Brazilian folklore (Penteado 1997). Mystical, esoteric, and animistic forms of thought are by no means against science. We have wrongly turned them into enemies of knowledge. When they are used to complement rational, objective, and exoteric teaching, their association is in accord with life and learning. And it is the imagination that unites them. The ego may not be imaginative, but the Self is always a fantastic animal. The central archetype is a poet, and that is why it never stops dreaming and symbolizing; when it does, it is because it is fixated and sick.

By reanimating the objective dimension through the imagination, we reunite science and magic; body, society, and nature; image, idea, emotion, sound, word, and number. We again insert the whole being into education and experience curiosity for it. Direct activation of the central archetype summons the structuring functions to carry out their actions. In this way curiosity also functions in keeping with the whole. It is one thing to know that rain forms rivers that descend from the mountains into the sea; it is another to remember that life initiated in that water, preserved in the ecosystem to the present day, and that human beings can protect the waters or poison or exhaust them and create deserts.

Shame and curiosity are complementary structuring functions. Both need to be known by the educator. Through curiosity, being is expanded in the boldness of knowing. Through shame, being hides and renounces knowing to avoid suffering and humiliation, in particular on the social level, in front of the class. After the family, school is the most important socializing institution. Shame is one of the great structuring functions of the socializing transference relationship to build self-esteem (Jacoby 1991). Its consideration in the student-teacher emotional bond has a direct effect in education.

Symbolic learning is an expansive movement of being from which there is no return. Adam and Eve left paradise because they learned; their conscience was expanded, and it no longer fit into the previous state. This version of the expulsion myth is a patriarchal one that manipulates the structuring function of curiosity and knowledge in order to control it. It proposes knowledge as forbidden for some, a privilege for others. It punishes the trespassers and keeps them always constrained through guilt. This version of the myth of knowledge expresses the patriarchal pattern with all its dogmatic, organizing, elitist, and domineering delimitation of curiosity and shame.

The consequences of increased consciousness include the detachment or sacrifice of previous positions, which had relatively secured adaptation, to assume new positions, which are home to unknown and dangerous regions. Insecure, anguishing, and even threatening regions promise new and fascinating privileges. The structuring function of fascination speeds up curiosity. Fear makes us retreat. Here the structuring function of fear is practiced within the pedagogic Self and the transference relationship with teachers and students, and the greatest fear is failure in conquering these new challenges. Therefore fear is regulated by the structuring function of the student's shame in front of the teacher, colleagues, school, and family.

The institutional Self of the school propitiates initiation rites of the ego, parallel to the family Self, in the process of socialization. Pedagogic transference includes the structuring functions of affection, envy, jealousy, and competition that strongly activate the experience of approval or rejection. As the school Self moves around knowledge and learning, maladjustment and failure are expressed by the disgrace of making a mistake in front of the class, getting bad grades, or failing exams. Shame controls this fear. Its polar opposite is curiosity and the affectionate reassurance of the family, teacher, and class.

Shame is the regulating function of the opening of being in the social dimension, and it can be normal or defensive. This is why Adam and Eve covered their genitals when they discovered good and evil; in doing so, they established the normal separation between intimacy and social relationship. Within the pedagogic Self, shame can become defensive and close doors that will never open again. Many teachers are aware of this power of shame and use it in the pedagogic transference to intimidate difficult students, humiliating them through irony and ridicule to preserve discipline in class. This is an arrogant, cowardly, and vile practice, which may severely harm the learning capacity of many students. Consequently, defensive shame is one of the main constituents of the aversive reaction to studying.

The teacher must be aware of the archetypal power inherent in the capacity to approve, accept, and ratify or disapprove, reject, and discourage. The figure of the teacher receives projections equivalent to those of father and mother and more. The teacher symbolically retains knowledge and, even more so, the capacity to transmit knowledge, representing the archetype of wisdom. The educator is often the representation of the central archetype in the pedagogic Self. With the power of these projections, a teacher can foster or mow down the vitality of students' development. Being conscious of this is the essential ethical condition in realizing the function of responsibility and being aware of the limits of power in the teaching profession (Guggenbühl-Craig 1971). The careful transference usage of these structuring functions symbolically elaborated in teaching can be highly productive for learning, individual maturation, and acquisition of the creative and affectionate capacity to deal with success and failure in society.

## The Structuring Function of Precocity

The educator must learn to recognize precocity in order to deal with it properly. To identify the different capacities of students and to continue to treat them adequately requires science and art. Many overly clever students should be transferred to more advanced classes and in certain cases receive individual instruction. However, in such cases, special attention must be paid to the emotional development of the personality to avoid overcharging which may be welcome at the cognitive level but harmful on the emotional level. Each case must be carefully evaluated and attended to, in order to correctly orient the student's direction. A twelve-year-old student can have the cognitive age of eighteen, but the emotional age of eight.

Precocity is a structuring function, and therefore it can function normally or defensively. Defensive precocity identifies brilliant intelligence with the persona and may repress emotional immaturity. It may also lead parents to practice exhibitionistic exposure. Had Mozart been protected from exhibitionistic exposure and emotional overcharging by his father, Leopold, his fate might not have been so tragic (Byington 2002a).

As psychoanalysis has so fully demonstrated, ego development occurs together with diminishing omnipotent symbiosis with the parental image. Nondifferentiation from the central archetype favors grandiose fantasies in childhood, which propitiates magic identification with the dimension of heroes and dragons. This omnipotence of the ego in childhood makes it feel immune to danger and even death. Fixations during this phase of development cause personality damage, which may be accompanied by grandiose feelings, as described by Kohut (1988). An archetypal perspective of fixation allows us to see appearance of the grandiose ego in any moment of life, a phenomenon Jung called inflation and psychoanalysis referred to as omnipotence.

The main problem of the precocious child is the danger of being overexposed (over exhibited) by the parents. Prevented from showing emotional weakness, the child may have its omnipotence fixated and become incapable of coping with normal frustration. In this case, the ego can only operate with permanent admiration, which makes it liable to depression and aggressive responses. With this type of emotional handicap, precocious children rarely escape failure. Teaching them to deal with frustration is the main condition to successfully develop the gifted structuring function with which they were born.

## Defensive Precocity and Consumerism

The artificial stimulation of precocity in the younger generation has become a very profitable way to expand consumerism and create new markets. The padded bra for preadolescent girls is an example of how precocity can be explored through well-organized marketing campaigns that are specifically aimed to tempt young minds. I recently accompanied the case of a street-raised boy in São Paulo who murdered a student to steal his tennis shoes. Arrested and cross-examined, he confessed to the crime and justified it by saying he had seen the tennis shoes advertised on television with such glamour that it became an obsession—obtaining them became the required condition for him to feel happy.

World consciousness is becoming increasingly aware of the social problem of street kids in large cities and the relationship of abandonment to character dysfunction, delinquency, use of drugs, and prostitution. It is also becoming quite evident that the artificial conditioning of precocity to increase market expansion tends to propitiate the fixation of omnipotence and jeopardize character formation. Many parents, educators, and public authorities are not sufficiently aware of this disturbance in youth brought about by consumerism. Government planning is still generally oriented toward economic growth, material welfare, and improvement of employment rates. Parents, conditioned by the same media and marketing which fascinate youngsters and induce precocity, also favor their consumerism, believing that the more goods their children have, the happier they will be. Historically conditioned to fear hunger and famine, which is now recognized in eating disorders, humanity is waking up to another equally serious feeding disorder, obesity. Symbolically this disease dramatically expresses the overfeeding of consumerism.

It is hard to realize that the multi-million-dollar market campaign launched on television for tennis shoes, the rich boy who purchased them, and his parents who gladly bought them all have the same marketing-conditioned fascination as the poor boy who murdered their son for the shoes. All of them have the same scale of values, which expresses the inhuman materialistic ideology of consumerism that permeates modern society and induces youngsters to consume precociously and compulsively.

Undergoing this immense alienating pressure to explore precocity in youth at the expense of character formation, educators are called to the task of preserving humanism through the values and ideas, which they live and teach.

## The Structuring Function of Symbiosis

It is the first day in kindergarten. The child goes with its mother but does not want to stay without her. It is reluctant, going back and forth between curiosity and fear, until one day, it stays. It is an important step when the ego begins to transcend the shelter of the family Self, a real initiation ritual to step into the cultural Self. Other rituals will follow: primary school, lower school, high school, college entrance exams, college, post-graduate school, and tests for employment, each one more differentiated and demanding more individuality of consciousness in the ego and other identity.

Schooling is accompanied by a progressive differentiation of the individual Self, and teachers are its coordinator and the bridge toward the cultural Self through the pedagogic transference relationship. As they bring in new subjects of knowledge each year, they are offering a new phase of differentiation for the student's being.

The development of the student's individual Self within the pedagogic Self through symbolic transference elaboration is the continuation of the process of identity formation that starts in the family Self, at birth and before. We consider identity formation before birth for two reasons: first, today we conceive an intrauterine corporeal ego; second, before we are born and sometimes even generations before we are conceived, we receive projections of our future parents, grandparents and great-grandparents, which contribute to form our identity. "In my family no one will be an artist", "I would rather die than have a homosexual son or daughter", "to bear a boy is a mother's greatest blessing"—these and similar affirmations are made by parents, grandparents, and great-grandparents frequently before the child is even conceived. "If I ever have a child, I will do everything the opposite of what is being done to me!", predicts an adolescent. "If one day I have a daughter, I want her to do everything I could never do!", wishes another adolescent. In the search for our deep individuality, we always need to elaborate what other generations have programmed consciously and unconsciously for us.

This process of differentiation occurs through symbolic elaboration, starting from a state of nondifferentiation in which the individual Self is agglutinated within the family Self. This differentiation is done by experiencing the symbols, complexes, functions, and structuring systems that differentiate the Self and the ego-other and other-other polarities in consciousness. These experiences, which are the essence of symbolic elaboration, take place within relationships where there initially exists a fusion between subject and object that little by little becomes differentiated. Symbiosis is what we call this state of fusion. The symbiotic function is differentiated throughout life via the other structuring functions. Its greatest dysfunction is fixation, which characterizes organic autism and also psychodynamic defensive autism. Organic autism is a neurological disease, which must be diagnosed and treated by specialists in infancy, whereas defensive psychodynamic autism is a fixation that can occur in any stage of life and can be dealt with by parents, teachers, and therapists.

When symbiosis becomes defensive, the process of symbolic elaboration is paralyzed at that point and the symbols at issue are expressed through defenses in the shadow. This is the phenomenon of fixation described by Freud. All of us have many fixated experiences, which become the pathological complexes that form our shadow. They are resistant to creative human relationship and learning. The teacher has to have a certain clinical eye in order to subdivide learning difficulties into two main groups. The first one involves lack of studying due to various circumstantial situations frequently accompanied by a circumstantial shadow. A good anamnesis of the student's existential and schooling situations, with incentive to diligence and motivation, helps in teaching how to study. Positive reinforcement of results and recapitulation of the subjects in which the student feels lost are of great help. The second group involves chronic defenses and shadow, which block learning and include defensive resistance that must be elaborated with family help and, if necessary, with psychotherapy. It is absurd to indicate therapy for a student before elaborating his or her learning difficulty within the school and the family. Only after identification of a chronic psychopathological condition resistant to elaboration in the student-teacher-family-school quaternio should a specialized psychological family evaluation be indicated, and only after that, individual psychotherapy, which must be carried out always in relationship to the student's family.

Although the study of ego archetypal formation was only discovered by Jung's followers in the 1950s, he always stressed the great influence of parent's unconscious problems on their children. Frances Wickes, who was the first Jungian child therapist, met Jung in the 1920s and was supervised by him in her clinical work with children for almost thirty years. In her book, *The Life of Childhood*, and in Jung's preface to it, we see clearly how much importance they gave to the relationship of children's shadows to their family dynamics, and how much they stressed that therapy should consider this symbiotic defense and elaborate it within the child-family relationship as much as possible (Wickes 1927). This approach is worlds apart from the psychoanalytic model of child psychotherapy adopted primarily by Melanie Klein and her followers, wherein children should be treated separately from their family mainly through the transference relationship with the therapist. When we realize fully the degree of symbiosis that exists between children and parents, in early childhood continuing in adolescence and throughout the whole life, we easily admit that it is much more productive to treat children within their parental transference rather than within a fresh transference formed with the therapist. To deal with this problem, I recommend periodic analytical sessions with the parents in child psychotherapy, including some sessions with both parents and children.

The symbiotic structuring function never disappears, because, as all structuring functions, it is archetypal. However much we differentiate ourselves from our parents, siblings, and other primary relationships, we will never separate from them in the same degree to which we separate from later relations during life. The symbiotic function operates in various degrees during the individuation process. Properly elaborated, working through attachment and detachment, which will be repeated in all-important emotional involvements, the ego's and the other's identities will become more and more firmly established. However, new relationships tend again to be symbiotically nondiscriminated and, in order to become differentiated, need to be lived through. This is especially the case in new creative work and love relationships.

The fact that the identities of the ego and the other are progressively strengthened does not mean that they no longer become nondifferentiated. On the contrary! The more we grow and are strengthened, the more capable we are of keeping one part differentiated and, with another part, plunge into great indiscrimination and nondifferentiation, mainly in vigorous and creative personalities. Only those who have an ego strengthened through the capacity to integrate frustration and aggression and who have confronted their shadows in meaningful battles are capable of dealing with intense creativity, which isolates one from the traditional knowledge of one's social group. Growth crises are inherent to deep personality development.

Changing teachers always brings about a state of indiscrimination and nondifferentiation, mainly in childhood and adolescence, due to a new symbiotic learning relationship, which will have to be elaborated in the course of a whole school year or more. It must be remembered that indiscrimination is the state of confusion, which accompanies the ego during elaboration, whereas nondifferentiation refers to the first stage of the ego-other polarity in symbolic elaboration.

Even though the pedagogic transference process is basically rooted in the student-teacher-school-family of the social dimension, symbolic elaboration through it must include the characteristics of symbols in all other dimensions. The presence of various animals in school, to which students become affectionately related, of trees (especially fruit trees), of workshops including culinary, biological, physical, chemical, artistic, imaginative and corporeal experiences are essential. It is important to experience each dimension as much as possible and associate it to the others through imagination and expressive techniques. Only thus shall we understand that the differentiation of the symbiotic function of being is done fully within the world throughout life, and learning must take this into account.

The structuring functions discussed in this chapter are examples and do not diminish the importance of many others, which for lack of space have not been mentioned. Functions like envy (Byington 2002a) and jealousy (Byington 2006b) are very important within transference. Creativity deserves a book all to itself. Ambition, pride, dedication, and will power are also very important, along with countless others. One of the most important structuring functions of symbolic elaboration in the initiatory teaching method, intimately related to the differentiation of symbiosis, is the transcendent function of the imagination expressed through attachment-detachment polarity. Because of its importance, we need to consider its characteristics when coordinated by each of the four ruling archetypes, and therefore, I will include a discussion of it in chapter 6, which deals with the ruling archetypal quaternio and the pedagogic Self. There we shall also see the five possible positions of the ego-other relation during the process of symbolic elaboration.

## Pedagogic Transference and Family Transference

One of the major signs that the learning process corresponds to the development of the personality can be seen in the continuum between parental and family transference and pedagogic transference. Classmates and teachers form a new family within the cultural Self, which continues the symbolic elaboration of the main structuring symbols, complexes, functions, and systems activated in the original family. The continuity is such that, during teaching, a symbolic dialectical relationship forms between family life and the school, in the personality of students and teachers. That which was learned and is being learned at home continues to be creatively or defensively lived out in school, and vice versa. This interaction needs to be understood within the concept of the teaching profession and its role in the relationship of students, teachers, family, and society (Novoa et al. 1991) and within the process of individuation and humanization.

Just as I cannot conceive of an analyst who ignores the psychodynamics of the family Self and its structuring function in the development of consciousness, I believe that an educator needs to know the interrelationship of the psychodynamics of the individual, family, pedagogic, and cultural Self. The growing trend in the psychology of teaching is to train educators to perceive normal education and its problems within the interaction of these various levels. However, it is a pity that the reduction of symbolic life to childhood and pathology already rooted in psychology is contaminating our understanding of education. The symbolic archetypal perspective is capable of diminishing the reduction to childhood and pathology by conceiving the meaning of symbols prospectively during normal adult life.

Reduction is a natural tendency of the ego to explain something greater exclusively through something smaller. The importance of this stage should not be diminished. It is the function of every scientist, artist, educator, and student to value the smaller part of the picture with which they work. However, in order to value the part we do not have to asphyxiate its relationship to the whole. Defensive reduction can become a real cancer of knowledge when we exaggerate the value of the part to the extent that it swallows the whole. To identify normality and pathology in the problems of learning is part of the reunion between education and mental health, one of the most fruitful marriages of modern scientific development. To reduce systematically the problems of family and pedagogic transference to immaturity and pathology, however, is to practice an asphyxiating reduction. It is like buying a computer with a virus that will diminish its capacity (Byington 1990b). We may thus conclude by saying that, in Jungian symbolic education, reduction is the greatest enemy of symbolic elaboration within the holistic, transference, and archetypal perspectives of the pedagogic Self in its development toward wholeness.

# Chapter 4

# JUNGIAN TYPOLOGY AND THE PEDAGOGIC SELF

We acknowledge more and more the importance of manifold intelligences in learning (Gardner 1983; Goleman 1995). To teach and learn, teachers and students make use of many channels, some better than others according to each person. Psychological types are also channels of manifold intelligences, which can and should be identified in teachers and students.

Jung's great contribution to the study of typology lies in the fact that the psychological functions that characterize the types he described are archetypal structuring functions; they exist in everybody, although each individual has certain functions more developed than others (Jung 1921). This means that, from birth, we have characteristic ways of elaborating our symbols that we can complement throughout life. This is important in education, for it leads us to the fact that each person has peculiar ways of learning, of studying, and of teaching. Therefore the study of Jungian typology in education, as described by Grimaldi Moreira (1986), is of the utmost importance for the evaluation of a student or a class and to enrich the understanding of transference in the pedagogic Self. As the structuring functions are also active in the collective consciousness of the cultural Self, typology is very useful for understanding and elaborating historic difficulties, which restrain teaching activities.

Within the perspective of the symbolic development of the Self, enriched by the concept of shadow formation through the notions of fixations and defense from psychoanalysis, the four functions of consciousness (feeling, thinking, intuition, and sensation) and the two attitudes (extraversion and introversion) are structuring functions that act creatively or defensively in the process of elaborating structuring symbols. We have typical ways of learning and also of expressing our psychic pathology. For better or for worse, when we organize our learning or when our defenses are constellated, each person elaborates experiences in one of a number of typical ways. This does not mean that our less differentiated functions do not participate in learning or in the organization of pathology. Often they are the ones that command decisive episodes. If we observe a right-handed man playing soccer, we will see that his habitual way of dribbling and positioning himself on the field is related to his physical typology. He also kicks with his left foot but in an accessory way. His right-sided physical typology clearly stands out when he kicks the ball toward the goal. The same is true for the psychological functions. Life is a forest which the individual and the collective travel through by the paths they have at their disposal. Some of these paths are better known and are kept as desired routes. Others are more tortuous, sometimes misleading, but they are all part of the journey and always have characteristic patterns that can be typological.

Typological structuring functions, like all the other structuring functions, are strategies of symbolic elaboration and of being in the world. They are archetypal, which means that everybody has all the functions. This is one of the qualities of Jungian typology. One type always also includes the functions of the other. It is characteristic of types to have more or less skillful functions. People tend to associate themselves with opposite types in order to complement their development. We hardly ever see a young couple in which both have the same typology. Generally one of the ingredients of passion is that the archetypes of anima and animus search for the opposite type. As the years go by and we develop our less skillful functions, we tend to have intimate relationships with people whose typology is more similar to ours. This is sure evidence that the creative symbiosis with people of opposite types has brought about a good result during the individuation process.

We frequently see classmates of the same gender and opposite typology who develop inseparable friendships. In their symbiosis, one performs the functions in which the other is less skillful, as Don Quixote and Sancho Panza in the famous tale by Cervantes, for instance. These relationships in adolescence can vary from a creative symbiosis to a defensive one. In such cases, the two less-differentiated functions and the less-developed attitude are projected on the other, become fixated, and are not introjected. Projection becomes defensive and the other becomes the exclusive depositary of the capacity to express intelligently the typological function at issue. In this case, the creative and healthy function of symbiotic attraction, which is the close companionship with the opposite type and the learning and integration of what is most skillful in him or her is benumbed and paralyzed. One feels incapable of performing certain functions, feels dependent or even enslaved, believing that only the other is capable of doing them. Once fixated, the symbiotic function generates uneasiness, possessiveness, defensive envy, and aggression, because it no longer contributes to the integration of the envied symbol. From then on, bickering and quarreling are sure to follow. The paradise of friendship turns into the hell of neurotic dependence and, not rarely, of sadomasochism. A defensive symbiosis with defensive dependence has formed, which can sometimes be very quarrelsome and even aggressive because of the frustration brought about by fixation. In other cases of defensive symbiosis, people may become dependent, submissive, and obedient, but that also contributes to slowing down development. Defensive conflict gives way to defensive accommodation. All this can happen to classmates and affect learning. The teacher should pay attention to the learning transference of good students who idealized the teacher very much and who suddenly develop misbehavior and lack of interest. These may be cases of defensive symbiosis that have formed within the pedagogic transference relationship because of a typological problem.

Let us consider now how the typological functions elaborate symbols. Let us choose a symbol, for instance, the school visited by father and mother whose child is to start kindergarten, and make a circle around it. If we now situate feeling, thinking, intuition, and sensation on the four cardinal points of the circle, we will see that the functions complement one another extraordinarily well in the elaboration of the symbol. Thinking may define the school as a private institution with a good reputation, which educates students from kindergarten to high school. Intuition may tell you that the school will provide excellent objective and moral education to your child together with classmates who may one day become helpful colleagues. Feeling may show you that the school atmosphere is cozy, the teachers charming, and the director upright and understanding. Finally, sensation can signal that the school is near home, its classrooms are adequate, there are not too many students, the courtyard is spacious and well cared for, and the tuition is compatible with the family budget. Extraversion will conclude that the school will provide many good opportunities to develop important social relationships, and introversion will add that your child, in keeping with its sensibility, will certainly feel well in this atmosphere.

The four cardinal points orient the navigator about the situation of any point on the planet. The four typological functions situate symbols on the map of life. The two attitudes set the elaborated situation according to the subject (introversion) or the object (extraversion). The four functions and the two attitudes are ways in which the intelligence perceives and analyzes reality. In this manner, meanings of symbols are worked through in consciousness and integrated into the identity of the ego-other polarity. Obviously the symbolic elaboration, in our example, of the meaning of the school in the life of the child and of its parents will not end. This is just a beginning. The rest will follow. Once the child begins to attend the school, countless symbols, complexes, and structuring functions will be activated. It is the teaching process underway. The typological structuring functions will also continue their work in elaboration. They are archetypal, and in each new situation they will operate again. They are structures and functions like sight and hearing.

Nevertheless, as we have already seen, as is the case with manual skills, all psychological functions are not equally differentiated in every individual Self, hence the typologies. We all have two hands, apparently equal. Someone opens a door or greets a friend or starts writing, and the typological difference appears, right- or left-handed. Psychologically the same happens when you talk to someone.

In the case of the couple who visited school, the functions operate according to their typology: the father comments at the gate, "This is a school for the rich. I don't know if I can afford it" (thinking-sensation); the mother catches his arm tenderly and says, "Calm down, honey! I am loving it. I'm sure it will work out right" (feeling-intuition).

We notice something curious here. Two functions are already in opposite positions, like north and south, both logical but examining reality in opposite ways. Thinking is using its abstract and generalizing logic. It is the intelligence of the head. Feeling is using the intelligence of the heart, always intimate, immediate, and particular. The sensation-intuition polarity has also taken position in a secondary form, equally complementary like east and west, sensation registering the obvious and intuition imagining the future possibilities.

During the interview and after the director's initial explanations, the mother asks if they notify the parents at once if something happens with the children and, should she be late to fetch her child, if a teacher would stay overtime to look after the children. Once she is reassured, the father intervenes by saying that he does not understand why the index of readjustment applied to matriculation is different from the index applied to the first monthly fee. Further, he wants to know the interest rate charged in case of delayed payment. Then he asks how many students and teachers the school has and what is the criterion for the selection of teachers. And thus the interview goes on, the director and the teacher doubling their efforts to change their typological intelligence as fast as possible to please the complementary typological polarities of the parents. In the end, they conclude that they have satisfied both parents in spite of the couple's different reactions. The mother takes leave with a kiss followed by a cheery, "I loved meeting you", and the father with a laconic handshake, mumbling a clumsy "farewell, my ladies".

The four typological functions form a pair of opposites, two by two. Feeling and thinking are in opposition to each other rationally by abstract logic and by intimate affectionate logic. Intuition and sensation are irrational and opposed. Intuition is expressed through the wings of the imagination. Sensation is the obvious reality of facts. Intuition extracts from the structuring symbol what it could have been or what it may become. Sensation underlines and calls consciousness to realize what facts literally already are. The most skillful function has as its pair the fourth, least skillful function, and therefore the one that is most subject to inadequacies. The other pair holds the second and third positions in the scale of skill. In the couple in our example, she is the extraverted feeling-intuition type and he is the introverted thinking-sensation type. Typological complementarity can be very useful in a normal symbiosis, or very troublesome when it becomes defensive.

After the interview is over, the teacher, whose typology is extraverted feeling-intuition, comments: "The mother is charming but how could she marry such a boring man?" But the director, with all the rationality and pragmatism of the introverted thinking-sensation type, adds: "He seemed to be very intelligent. In my evaluation he is extremely competent. A very consistent person." Without realizing that they have both typologically praised themselves, they go for tea.

This polarization between thinking-feeling and intuition-sensation acts jointly in the Self, such that in the case of thinking being the most skillful function, feeling will be the least skillful and vice versa. This is true to the point that one can diagnose which is the most skillful function of a person by the perception of his or her least skillful one (von Franz and Hillman 1971). We can define the least skillful fourth function, also called inferior function as the one responsible for many of the shameful situations we have been through, the memory of which is capable of making us blush even in the dark under the blankets before falling asleep.

But the visit of the typological couple who comes to see the school is not yet finished. When they leave, the wife pinches the husband and exclaims: "My God, how different we are! How could you ask those questions about money and then at the end let out that formal 'farewell, my ladies'?" He is indignant and attacks her with: "My dear, how can you say such a thing? To start with, I am the one who earns the money and that is why I have to know how much things cost." "You have to humiliate me", she exclaims, already in tears. He, resentful: "I said what I think." She: "But they must have found you ridiculous!" He, pale with hatred: "And what I think does not matter? Why do you attach so much importance to what other people think?" She, losing control: "Because other people are everything, don't you understand? My goodness, how selfish you are, you see only yourself!" The anger was so strong that only later, when they were leaving the movies in the late afternoon, did they hold hands again.

The difficulty of complementary typology in the experience of the creative symbiotic function of the marriage or the pedagogic Self is that the ego usually perceives the limitation of the fourth function of the other much better than the contribution of the other to his or her own fourth function. The more immature we are, the more we concern ourselves with valuing in the first place what frustrates us, and treating what we receive and enjoy in a matter-of-fact way.

One part of teachers' training should be to identify their typology and learn to identify that of the students. With this capability, a teacher can realize at once that a fair part of the positive and negative transferences they get from students or even from a class as a whole is related to their typology. There are many learning problems that are due to the awkwardness of the less skillful function and to the difficulty of adapting the more skillful function of the teacher to the less skilled functions of students. These are clearly difficult cases of complementary transference typology.

The teacher who is conscious of the importance of typology will identify the students in class who have an opposite typology and pay particular attention to them before learning problems arise, because this will help these students with the difficulties they might encounter as a result of having a different typology from the teacher. In teaching, one cannot simply let oneself go. To do so is to imply that one is teaching only students of the same typology. We have seen in great detail that teaching blossoms or not depending on a transference relationship. It is often the case that consciousness of typology is essential for understanding the harmony and the dysfunctions of teaching and learning.

Expressive techniques in teaching are very useful for fostering symbolic elaboration in learning through all typological functions. Fanciful and imaginative techniques favor intuitive expression. Explanatory techniques stimulate the thinking function. Corporeal and graphic techniques favor sensation, whereas musical, poetic, and interpersonal techniques favor feeling. As we tend to find the first function easy and have difficulty with the fourth, the second and third functions serve as intermediary steps from the first to the fourth, like a staircase. It is common for the second and third functions to alternate serving as the second and third steps according to different situations. One thing is certain: symbolic constructivism is existential and therefore always depends on the four functions to really integrate the symbols in life. The privileged activation of one function does not prevent the others from also being activated and exercised. Dramatic techniques, however, can activate all four functions along with emotion.

The teacher's attention should follow two opposite and complementary paths: on one hand to perceive and watch his or her own fourth function and assure its performance in teaching. But not the "farewell, my ladies" type, please. Some people of the introverted thinking type learn a few extraverted affectionate stereotypes to help the inadequacy of their extraverted feeling function. They collect a few funny sayings and half a dozen jokes, which they repeat throughout life. The remedy is worse than the disease. Soon the half-hearted smiles begin to crop up in the class. I knew one teacher who used to tell three jokes about how a girl in his hometown managed to get married. Then one day, a lady and her granddaughter were chatting, and the grandmother found out that her granddaughter was a pupil of her old teacher and that the jokes were still the same. Forty years with the same repertoire. What an inadequate feeling function!

Worse than this are those thinking type doctors who have some affectionate stereotypes in store for their patients. I remember an orthopedist who always said to his patients that he wanted them to recover quickly to dance and make love once more. One day he exaggerated. The case was an eighty-four-year-old woman, a widow and the mother-in-law of a colleague, who had been run over by a car and hospitalized with eight fractures. The room was full of visitors. The doctor came in and automatically repeated his usual joke. In the midst of a few half-hearted smiles the voice of the woman resounded from within her plaster casts and bandages: "You indecent rascal!" There was a general explosion of laughter, which made that typological inadequacy unforgettable in the history of the hospital.

Another technique that teachers should employ is to tone down their most differentiated typological function so that the students of the opposite type can follow their teaching better. This can be done mainly by making use of the intermediary second and third functions through examples, which will act as a bridge in elaboration. In the case of an introverted thinking type, for instance, instead of resorting to dull, affective stereotypes, the teacher would be better off if he or she intermediates feeling through intuition and sensation. The teacher accomplishes this by filling the exposition with examples about the possible usage of what is being taught (intuition) or with concrete cases of its daily usage (sensation) or by asking the students how they feel about the subject and the way it is being taught (feeling). In this last example, the teacher is asking the students for help with the fourth function (feeling). This procedure is very creative because it allows the students of the opposite type (extraverted feeling) to manifest themselves, stand out, and avoid an inferior position in class. Usually, the students who are less articulate with the teacher are those who have an opposite typology. The understanding of typological functions as forms of intelligence can change a teacher's perception about the students' intelligence. The adaptive change of typology can radically influence the teacher-student transference relationship and the productivity of its constructivism.

## Jungian Typology and Christian Mythology in Teaching

Jungian typology is also applicable to collective consciousness, which helps us to understand the historical problem of the implantation of symbolic education in the cultural Self as we saw in chapter 2.

As I described in my archetypal theory of history (Byington 1982a, 1983, 2008), the first millennium of elaboration of the Christian myth in the Western cultural Self privileged the introverted feeling-intuition typology. In fact, the mythical nature of the Passion, culminating in the themes of excruciating suffering, death, and resurrection elaborated in the intimacy of the monasteries required that typology. Augustinian introversion, rooted in the ideal of love and Neoplatonic intuition, is a good example of that typological intelligence.

The second millennium of the myth saw the beginning of its extraverted thinking-sensation typological elaboration, profusely expressed in the *Summa Theologica* of Saint Thomas Aquinas (1225–1274), based on Aristotle. In his *Psychological Types*, Jung dedicated many pages to characterizing Plato's work as introverted in counterpoint to the extraverted typology of his disciple, Aristotle. It is not by chance, then, that Saint Augustine (354–430) turned toward Plato and Saint Thomas, toward Aristotle. In this respect, one can also understand the introverted monastic dominance in the elaboration of the Christian myth in the first millennium and the extraverted dominance in the second, which gave birth to the universities and to modern science.

The monastic introversion of the Middle Ages gave way during the Renaissance to an exuberant extraversion. Almost five centuries of science have followed the Renaissance, during which thinking and sensation have been extraordinarily differentiated through this extraversion. It is curious to observe how the philosophical thought of the Middle Ages arises so intensely from intuition, while in the philosophy of science, consolidated around the experimental method, sensation became the main source of extraverted thinking. The intensely unilateral aspect of the first and second millennia of symbolic elaboration of the myth occurred in a typically complementary way. The intuition of the meaning of the mystery of Christ's Passion was elaborated through introversion and love. The application of the myth to the knowledge of life and the world, which gave birth to the natural sciences, to the formation of the European nations, and to the progressive implantation of democracy, occurred through extraverted thinking and sensation. The unilateral aspect of the Middle Ages was compensated by the typological shift of the Renaissance and modernity. This change would have brought about the well-balanced elaboration of the myth within the cultural Self were it not for the subjective-objective dissociation that occurred at the end of the eighteenth century, as a reaction to centuries of repression by the Inquisition.

Rebelling against the religious intolerance of the Holy Office and seizing power in the university at the end of the eighteenth century, science identified truth, the experimental method, and objectivity with extraverted thinking-sensation and banished, together with the dogmatic intolerance of the Church, intuition, feeling, introversion, and all forms of subjectivity, including irrational imagination, as sources of error incompatible with science. The serious dissociation of the cultural Self, which defensively separated the subjective and objective dimensions, split thinking from feeling, intuition from sensation and extraversion from introversion (Byington 2008).

The explanation given by many historians for the cultural dehumanization of the West by the mechanization of scientific ideology as expressed in the thinking of Newton and Descartes (Capra 1982) fails to take into account the fifteen centuries of the myth prior to science in which that dehumanization is rooted. This dissociation sprang first from the Christ-devil polarization of the Middle Ages, which progressively dissociated good and evil within the European cultural Self, and continued in the end of the eighteenth century when science seized power in the university and dissociated the objective from the subjective dimension. Modern materialism can only be deeply understood when seen in the light of the two thousand years of the Christian myth. The three-centuries-old rationalism and materialism of the West is such a defensive and ingrained structure that it can only be transcended, in my view, by being elaborated within the psychopathology of the Christian myth, where it developed.

Reread typologically, the sentence ascribed to physicist Robert J. Oppenheimer (1904–1967), one of the fathers of the atomic arsenal — "In the twentieth century no one has known sin as much as the nuclear physicists"— means that after the tragedies of Hiroshima and Nagasaki, scientists began to see that the rationalism which denied feeling, intuition, and introversion generated a genocidal shadow that endangers the survival of the species. The scientific community, compelled to face its chronic shadow by the guilt of genocide, began to realize that it had been separated at some point in history from the ethical responsibility for the future consequences of technological industrial implantation upon humanity itself. By relegating the feeling and intuition functions dissociated together with subjectivity, scientists, although usually full of ideals and good intentions, contributed to form a huge chronic shadow in the planetary cultural Self. Hiroshima and Nagasaki mark the tragic end of the Enlightenment, which enhanced materialism and enthroned the idolatry of reason. This dissociation was illustrated in literature through the monstrous image of Frankenstein to point out the shadow side of scientific development.

Unfortunately, this humanistic consideration of the symbolic and archetypal levels of the cultural Self has not yet fully reached academic teaching, which continues to act out the typological dissociation throughout most of its teaching system. The chances to redeem the banished subjectivity of the symbolic body, emotions, feeling, pleasure, playfulness, intuition, imagination and faith, together with objective creativity, in education are merely starting and in a very hesitant way. When one wants to rescue these banished functions, as in the case of the old teacher and the orthopedist, it is often difficult to integrate them coherently in the whole.

This great typological reintegration, indispensable for the teaching practice of symbolic education, has already begun more clearly at the level of the early grades. The students participate more because they are still near the insular matriarchal sources or sensory-motor intelligence of the Self and have not yet gone through years of dissociated teaching. Because of the young age of the students, the direct overlapping of the pedagogic and parental functions allows the teachers to practice playful, imaginative, and affectionate activities. Another explanation for why preschool and primary school teachers are allowed to be freer on the subjective, intuitive, and affectionate levels is that these stages of teaching are mostly taught by women who are traditionally more open to the insular matriarchal position in teaching. It is regrettable but unfortunately true that teaching of adults is still strongly identified with the polarized patriarchal pattern and the dissociated rationalist teaching, even when it assumes the constructive method, as we shall explain further in the following chapters.

Many high school and college teachers in Latin American countries, although they understand and practice constructivism and are open to new methods, still cling to the predominantly rational and objective system of teaching. They do not want to take the risk of facing and surpassing the taboos that seclude the traditional method. Here and there, however, we see attitudes and methods tentatively appearing at different points on the planet with novelties to make teaching more participatory. If we pay attention to the symbolism of these new creative paths, we will notice that they are usually characterized by two currents: the denunciation of the limitations of the rational objective method and the proposition to integrate corporeal, social, natural, emotional, subjective, intuitive, imaginal, affectionate, and existential elements within a participant-observer and constructivist student-teacher relationship. It is important to absorb all these new methods into a symbolic, archetypal transference relationship within the teaching Self so that we do not limit ourselves to partial innovation.

There are two other typological references to which I attach great importance in the process of elaboration, and I will explain them in detail further on. The first is based on the typological predominance of one of the four archetypal patterns (matriarchal, patriarchal, alterity, and totality) over the others. The second is the narcissism-echoism typology with two complementary types, one with narcissistic dominance and the other with echoist dominance (Montellano 1996). This last typology is explicated using the characteristics of Narcissus and Echo in the Greek myth (Stein 1976; Berry 1984) and is especially important for the study of the teacher-student transference relationship in the process of learning.

A fourth typology, also based on mythological figures, was described by Jean Shinoda Bolen in *Goddesses in Everywoman* (1984) through the characteristics of seven Greek goddesses. Although reductive to the feminin, it describes the dominant aspects in women's personalities . A fifth typology is formed by the active (*yang*) and passive (*yin*) polarity present in every symbolic elaboration and also in psychological types.

These typological perspectives involving the ego-other relationship are very important for understanding the typical intelligence with which people approach learning, with better or worse results. These typologies are also useful for the teacher's awareness of the unilaterality with which teaching approaches knowledge, so that we can prevent many methodological distortions. We also saw in the previous chapter the importance of typology in forming the pedagogic transference bond for a better understanding of both its good and bad functioning. Some functions are complementary to others, which makes each typological ensemble a complete structuring system for perceiving and acting in reality.

These typologies must become part of school programs in order to be implemented in the practice and evaluation of learning. Their study can occur within multidisciplinary aspects of the curriculum. In geography, for instance, it can be seen in the variation of cultures due to climate, illustrated by the typical introversion of northern European people, who have long severe winters, as opposed to the extraversion dominant in Mediterranean cultures, where a temperate climate prevails. In history, we can apply the typological paradigm in relation to cultural implantation of the experimental method of modern sciences or with different approaches to reality in tribal culture. Umberto Eco's *The Name of the Rose* (1980) is a resourceful illustration of the greater pragmatic capacity of extraverted thinking-sensation functions, represented by the English detective-monk, in contrast with the fanciful imaginal introverted intuition-feeling expressed by the Italian monks. In mythology, in literature, and in the arts, we can apply typology in the understanding of important works and authors. It is also useful in comparing the differences between authors and works, as Jung did with Aristotle and Plato and as I will do with Piaget, Freud, and Jung in chapter 11. The best aspect of this study is that it can be and should be applied in the classroom directly between teachers and students, as long as it is done with sufficient sensibility to avoid hierarchies of one psychological type over another. Fundamentally, the functions of a typological system are complementary and therefore all are necessary for the understanding of reality. Within a typological system, no one function is better than any other, just as in the human body there is no single organ better than another. Each function is indicated for a certain situation, but all are necessary to life. These typological considerations in education should be used primarily by teachers without necessarily being revealed to students.

Unfortunately, distorted use of the typologies often occurs mainly because our cultural typological perspective can prejudicially identify, for instance, thinking with computerized intelligence, intuition with reverie and disorganization, feeling with sentimentalism, and sensation with dullness and lack of imagination. Consequently, it is important to notice that these typologies, inspired by Jung, are conceived within the systemic notion of the Self, according to which the person (or culture) who is of a certain type plods through the relationships of life to develop and integrate the functions of the opposite type, which are by definition underdeveloped and act in a limited way in the personality and in collective life. For example, it is foolish for a thinking type to despise a feeling type, considering him less intelligent, because the thinking type will find out during the individuation process that his acquisition of wisdom will depend to a great extent upon the integration of the opposites in the personality, among which, in his case, will be the feeling function . . . underdeveloped, inadequate, and, frequently defensive, of course. As one progresses, not in erudition, but in wisdom, the thinking type will discover that the intelligence of thinking brings distinction and admiration rather than profound integration, peace, and happiness. More and more he or she will discover that the plenitude of being depends, in their case, very much on discovering the intelligence of the heart. And more important, the thinking type also discovers that unilaterality, through which the persona of "genius of abstract logic" was built, filled the shadow with complexes formed by badly elaborated, unfit, immature, insecure, and destitute experiences derived from the despised (and consequently underdeveloped and hurt) feeling function, which eventually has to be faced and integrated. No matter our typology, we go through life to fulfill our personality by integrating and developing the opposite typological functions. This fact allows for humility and encourages us to draw in our horns and put aside omnipotence, for we are always underdeveloped and inadequate when it comes to the opposite functions that destiny defies us to confront and integrate in the construction of the existential peace of wisdom.

# Chapter 5

# THE MASTER-APPRENTICE ARCHETYPE

The vocation to transmit knowledge, to disclose and share it with other people is profoundly archetypal. A lesson is potentially a moment of *agape*, a spark of the communion of the world's intelligence with the light of individual consciousness within love. To experience that magic moment in which teacher and student build knowledge through the teacher's enthusiasm, and the shine in the students' eyes confirming the transcendence of the ego is fascinating. It is not merely Miss Miller teaching another chapter of the history of the Middle Ages. It is more: the shine in her students' eyes and their concentration upon her words is an experience that transcends the immediate and is rooted in the world of archetypes, specifically in the archetype of the master-apprentice, which coordinates the elaboration of the structuring symbols that transfer knowledge in the teacher-student relationship (Villares de Freitas 1990).

An archetype is a pattern that coordinates processes of relationship and therefore includes polarities. It can be good or bad, constructive or destructive, beautiful or horrible, according to the conditions of the process of symbolic elaboration: the fairy or the witch mother; the engineer who builds or destroys bridges; the physician who researches the cure and the expert in bacteriological warfare. In the archetype of the master-apprentice, it can be the teacher who teaches how to love studying and the one who enhances aversion to learning.

Among the countless bipolarities of the archetypes is the giving-receiving or active-passive polarity in the ego-other relation within the process of symbolic elaboration. To define the archetype of the teacher only as agent, as the one who knows and passes on knowledge independent of the student, is to take its role literally without perceiving its dialectic experience with the students within the pedagogic Self.

The archetype of the teacher, like all archetypes, includes a relation pattern of the ego with the other, of the giver and the receiver, the active and the passive. The archetype of the teacher is the archetype of the teacher-student, of the master-disciple relationship.

Without the shine in the student's eyes accompanied by fascinated concentration, the spirit disappears from the teacher's words. Charisma in teaching depends on the activation of the archetype, what the Greeks called the presence of the *daimon,* which demands a true initiation in teaching in order to animate the process of the teacher-student relationship. The fascination that reveals the activation of the archetype of teaching refers to the process of transmitting and receiving knowledge. It requires a transmitter and a receptor, a teacher and a student. Without these two poles of the transmission of knowledge, especially when dialectically related, the current of psychic energy does not circulate and ignite the light of symbolic constructivism through archetypal learning.

An important aspect of the development of the Self in symbolic constructivism is that the ego and the other experience the polarities of the archetypes. We saw how in the symbiotic structuring function, the identification of the ego with one pole and the other with the opposite pole is creative in the beginning but, if they remain exclusively in opposition, leads to the fixation of symbolic elaboration and propitiates the activation of the defensive symbiotic structure. The ideal in this process is that, even admitting and expressing the dominance of one pole of a polarity, the ego remains open to express the complementary pole so that the two poles express and integrate in the ego, in the other and in the Self, as much as possible, the archetypal potential at issue (Byington 1965). The oracle of the *I Ching,* the millenary book of Chinese wisdom, teaches us that the *yin* and *yang* polarity expresses all polarities conceivable in individual, cultural, planetary, and cosmic life. The poles are inseparable and complementary. Together they express wholeness. We shall understand better the dialectical relation of polarities when we study the archetype of alterity, which is the archetype of constructive teaching (chapter 9).

This means that in view of the polar nature, common to all archetypes, of the archetype of the master-apprentice, the teacher who identifies exclusively with the pole of the one who knows and assigns the pole of not knowing on the student will be adopting the polarized position of the patriarchal archetype in teaching, which will eliminate any constructivist intention he/she may have. The same goes for the elaboration of the symbols of all other archetypes during the existential process. Many authors have called attention to the archetype of the wounded healer in therapy (Garcia 1983). Guggenbühl-Craig (1971) signals the danger of the helping professional depositing the wanting pole exclusively on the needy. By doing that, therapists and teachers may feel omnipotent and become dissociated from their shortcomings, favoring fixation and defensive expression through the shadow.

I briefly described in the preceding chapter the complementary typological division between a husband and wife in a marriage. If the couple identifies with the polarities of the marriage roles and does not exchange functions, as time goes by, the integration of the archetype of *coniunctio* will be paralyzed and the amorous relationship will decline toward stagnation and boredom (Byington 2008). The archetype of *coniunctio* rules the union and separation of the polarities within a dialectical interaction (Jung 1955–56).

It is the gradual integration of the master-apprentice archetype that demands that the teacher also be a student. Thereupon, the humility and wisdom of the teacher appear together with the search to exert teaching also as a student in the constructivist relationship. This fact, should not confuse us as to the individual and social identities of the teacher and the student. Both have roles, rights, and duties. Their identities have been elaborated and discriminated by the tradition of generations. They belong to different social roles and, like all complementary social opposites, they appeal and repel, fraternize and antagonize each other. In short, their roles, rights, duties, and responsibilities are different. Teachers who act as if they are "part of the gang" forget these differences, generate great indiscrimination in the pedagogic Self, and allow for inadequate, potentially dangerous and destructive acting-out, so well illustrated in the film *Dead Poets' Society*.

The challenge of the teacher's profession, considering the bipolarity of the archetype of the master-apprentice, is to perform a professional role with its attributes and responsibilities and, at the same time, be open to experiencing the bipolarity of the archetype in the dynamics of teaching. This role is quite different in two situations: in the institutional dimension, which includes school, colleagues, parents, and students, the teacher should maintain the dominant unilateral role within the patriarchal archetypal dimension (chapter 8), while the students should perform the complementary unilateral role, each with its intrinsic characteristics and responsibilities; when it comes to the practice of teaching in the pedagogic Self (constructivism, strictly speaking), the two roles interplay and interchange whenever possible, and open to performing the complementary polarities of the archetype of the master-apprentice in a dialectical relationship.

This will be much clearer later when we get to know the difference between the patriarchal and the alterity patterns of relationship with their corresponding polarized and dialectical positions. Traditional teaching presents a patriarchal dominance in which teacher and student tend to perform opposite poles of the archetype of the master-apprentice (polarized position). The teacher knows and the student is ignorant. The teacher speaks and the student listens, and in exams, the successful student demonstrates that he or she can repeat the teacher's words. In contrast, symbolic constructivism proposes a dialectical practice at the pedagogic level, with a participant relation in the teacher-student dynamic. This relationship, in which both experience democratically the two poles of the archetype, is basically different from the patriarchal pattern and characterizes the alterity archetypal pattern.

## The Narcissism-Echoism Typology

A polarity that I have already described as typological (Byington 1988b), which is very useful for workshops with educators (Byington 1993b) as well as students, is the narcissism-echoism polarity expressed in the myth of Narcissus and Echo, as told by Ovid in the *Metamorphosis*. Narcissus represents, among many other things, the *yang*, the agent, the one who shines, who innovates, who wants everything for himself, the focus of attention (Stein 1976). Echo, on the contrary, is mostly receptive, *yin*, pale, abnegated; she doesn't create, she only echoes (Berry 1984). Some people have predominantly narcissistic characteristics, others clearly are predominantly echoist. Couples tend to exhibit this polarity, and it is usually easy to see who expresses each role. But as usual, because they are archetypal, we all have both poles. Those who are predominantly narcissistic have to open themselves to their echoist pole; they must allow echo to develop and vice versa (Montellano 1996).

In teaching, the narcissism-echoism polarity is a very useful typology for examining the way in which each teacher experiences the bipolarity of the master-apprentice archetype. There are teachers with such a dominant narcissistic typology that they project the echoist polarity onto their students en masse, corralling them into it and forcing them to perform it. Without realizing it, they concentrate the shining, the creativity, the initiative of teaching, in short, the *yang* side of the archetype upon themselves. They tend to eclipse their students and prevent them from actively participating. These are the teachers who grade exams and judge their students according to how much they echoed them. They greatly improve as teachers when they become aware of their pronounced typological unilaterality and open up to develop the echoist pole. Without that awareness, their constructivist capacity remains very limited and tends to become fixated and to function defensively and inadequately in the shadow.

Teachers with this narcissistic typology are frequently found in universities in which researchers often teach as an obligation of their research contracts rather than by vocation. These cases are illustrative of how knowledge is one thing and teaching quite another. Certain researchers may know a lot but, due to their narcissistic typology, have great difficulty teaching their students; they often don't recognize creative persons and end up unwillingly training copycats. Their students feel it is not enough to understand in their own way; rather, it is necessary to express the content in the same way as the teacher did. Those students who have echoist typology are delighted and accentuate their unilaterality; those with narcissistic typology either rebel or submit reluctantly. The most unilateral case of this type, which already borders the defensive structure, is that of the teacher who at heart would rather not be teaching but doing research and creating instead. In fact, a researcher teaching within an intense narcissistic typology will have a strong tendency to lecture to himself or herself and will have difficulty practicing symbolic constructivism, although intending otherwise.

The echoist type in teaching tends to repeat what he or she learned and to be very open to the students' creativity. These are the cases that, when exaggerated, may sound like broken records. Year after year, they say the same thing. Even the examples are the same, which can turn them into great sponsors of rote memorization. Their constructivist limitation may become significant when their echoism turns defensive and they become incapable of sharing creative participation. When creative, however, echoist teachers can be marvelous nests, where their students find the loving acceptance and dedication to develop their individuality. A good exercise for an educators' workshop with the myth of Echo and Narcissus is for each participant to identify and work with this typology and then reverse it, using the psychodramatic technique of role-playing.

Knowledge of the archetype of the master-apprentice is important for the teacher to open toward symbolic constructivism in the pedagogic Self. It is awareness of the function of this archetype that allows the teacher to perceive when to be *yang* or *yin*, Narcissus or Echo. For those who teach, it is sometimes less important to know the subject than to feel the right moment to echo or to take a narcissistic role, in keeping with a student or the class as a whole. Initiation into the polarity of the master-apprentice archetype helps the educator transcend the traditional unilaterality of the role and, at the end of this important lesson, to be able to discern when he or she acted dominantly as teacher or as student. This dialectical experience of teaching is essential for the perception that, in Jungian symbolic education, the primary intention is not to fill the students' mind with things but, instead, to propitiate the intellectual, emotional, and existential formation of human beings. The knowledge of the phenomenology of the archetype of the master-apprentice is fundamental for the passage proposed herein, from exclusively rational to symbolic constructivism. In fact, the same archetypal foundation, for the teacher's and student's personalities in the relationship with knowledge, works as a bridge to express the transference relationship of teaching within the individuation process and for understanding better why symbolic teaching is the education of being.

Archetypally perceived, the teacher-student relationship allows us to subordinate the archetype of the master-apprentice to the archetype of *coniunctio*, which rules the union and separation of opposites. In light of the archetype of *coniunctio*, teacher and student build knowledge through a complementary interaction of opposite functions that fertilize each other dialectically and bring forth learning. The alchemists understood the interaction of opposites as what they called the alchemical *opus*, which included objective and subjective characteristics, the goal of which was to generate the philosophical stone, the philosopher's son, at the same time object and emotion, erudition and wisdom. The symbolic constructivism of alchemist and matter transformed the laboratory into a factory of goods and, at the same time, a transformer of personality. Together with the transformation of chemical substrates, alchemists cultivated structuring functions that developed the whole personality: dedication, affection, abstract intelligence, patience, reverence, humility, excellence, willpower, coherence, discipline, honesty, love, respect for creativity and truth, religiosity, faith, and team work. The development of these subjective and objective structuring functions turned them alchemists, scientists, artists, priests, and above all, humanists. In Jungian symbolic education, the archetype of the master-apprentice subordinated to the archetype of *coniunctio* allows us to see both teacher and student as alchemists and their affectionate and intellectual transference relationship as a "labor-oratorium", a teaching vessel capable of bringing about symbolic learning that is objective and subjective at the same time.

## The Archetype of the Guru

In developing a theory of teaching in Jungian symbolic education that relates emotion and cognitive knowledge through the student-teacher transference relationship, we introduce the affectionate function in the relationship through which we can better understand the nature of the sacred teaching method in India. The great spiritual masters of India become revered *gurus* who are followed by many disciples throughout generations. They are living examples of what they teach, and this wisdom continues after they die.

Due to the subjective-objective dissociation in Western education, the tendency is to teach the ideas of the great geniuses separated from their personalities. We all know the main ideas of Galileo, Newton, and Descartes, and we may have seen their pictures, but we typically have not the least knowledge of their childhood experiences, their married life or intimate relationships, their ideologies, their hopes and sufferings, their relationships with their children, with animals and nature, their feelings and emotions, and therefore, although we admire them immensely, we cannot love them. Because of this, although we are thankful to them for the scientific treasures which we have inherited, they cannot become our gurus, teachers of wisdom who we can follow with devotion.

I have a friend, a professor of physics, who is very affectionate. While I was pondering these ideas, I asked him one day whether he loved Einstein. He stared at me for some time, silent, and then blushed, while tears flowed down his cheeks. He was very ashamed of his reaction and scolded me for asking such "absurd questions". His answer through the symbolic body, which included the meaning of his silence, showed me dramatically the degree to which his scientific mind did not have a normal persona to express his feelings verbally, and also how they could only be shown intensely through a defensive persona in the shadow.

This flaw in Western humanism greatly impoverishes our education, for we spend many years benefiting from the work and lifelong dedication of these geniuses, but because of the subjective-objective dissociation, we cannot have rituals to praise and love them. In this manner, they will never become our gurus and guide us in the path of wisdom. This is why Jungian symbolic education employs animation in teaching and includes in it the emotional lives of our teachers from the past. Whenever pioneers in any given field are mentioned in class, their pictures are shown and that which they discovered is associated with their historical context and their personal lives and dramatized by teachers and students in "artificial dreaming" (Désoille 1961) or active imagination (Jung 1958).

When we have a very important teacher for a long time, we undergo a symbiotic relationship with him or her and become emotionally involved, conscious and unconsciously, with his or her personality. This experience in time may reveal to us that, although Westerners, we can also have a guru, a master of wisdom, an expression of the divine.

While writing this book, during which I used dreams, ideas, emotions, and active imagination to elaborate my feelings toward Jung, I became aware that our relationship was that of a disciple with a guru. This showed me that the guru is an expression of the master-apprentice archetype when this teaching is elaborated symbolically in the individuation process. This insight instructed me also about the symbolic meaning of the theory of metempsychosis or reincarnation, in which great masters, long after their deaths, continue to relate to disciples. As Plato observed, learning is remembering. In the beginning, he says, you learn through the words of the master; then, you learn just by sitting in the same room, and finally, just by being in the same house. Wisdom is archetypal. It is present in all of us from time immemorial because it is the soul of being. Original sin can be seen as a primary symbol of this forgotten wisdom, whose teaching the great masters have remembered and have helped their disciples to remember.

## Jung and Symbolic Education

My analyst and Jung's lifelong *soror mistica*, Marie-Louise von Franz, told me that Jung at first did not agree to found an institute to train analysts. According to her, he believed analysts had to be called they had to look for their own development and initiation and could not learn through academic training. Due to academic pressure, according to von Franz, he finally gave in. The C. G. Jung Institute was founded in 1948, and candidates came to train. Naturally, a selection process was necessary, and Jung was a member of the selection committee. The first candidate came and Jung asked him to imagine a talk with his gardener, who had seen a book cover with the word *archetype* and wanted to know its meaning. The candidate, a professor of philosophy, explained that the archetype was a pattern of the collective unconscious that expresses itself through archetypal images.

Jung failed him and asked the next candidate to come in. She was a doctor in biology. Jung asked her to imagine she had a cook who had seen the word *archetype* on a book cover and wanted to know its meaning. She explained that the archetype was similar to a pattern of animal behavior repeated instinctively through generations without learning. Jung also failed her. As these two candidates were very mature and highly educated, they were accepted by the other members of the selection committee, and Jung, for many years, did not come back to the Institute (von Franz personal account).

This tale is interesting for what it allows us to imagine about Jung's relationship to teaching. I would guess that he wanted the first candidate to teach the meaning of *archetype* to the gardener through the image of the seed that lives to become a tree. Regarding the doctor in biology, we can imagine that Jung wanted her to explain the meaning of *archetype* to the cook using a parallel between alchemy and the cooking vessel which prepares a miraculous jewel as the food of the soul. We can imagine that Jung could be testing the candidates for their capacity to express symbolic education, which constructs learning through symbols within the living participation of students and teachers.

In any case, through active imagination, I consulted Jung as a guru many times in the elaboration of symbolic education, and he participated in it always helped greatly.

# Chapter 6

# THE FIVE ARCHETYPAL POSITIONS OF THE EGO-OTHER POLARITY

At this point, we reach the heart of symbolic elaboration. Around the central archetype, which is the grand star of the archetypes, I will describe a constellation formed by four secondary stars, which play a considerable part in the process of elaborating symbols. Even when they do not play an active part in elaboration, they are in some way affected by it. I have grouped these four pillars of symbolic elaboration and designated them the ruling archetypal quaternio. Just as the four typological functions cover symbolic elaboration according to four different perspectives toward examining and understanding a symbol, the four ruling archetypes, with the central archetype, cover five typical ways of coordinating, expressing, and elaborating structuring symbols, functions, complexes, and systems of the Self. We can therefore view these as the five major archetypes of human intelligence, four which express and understand psychic life, coordinated by the central archetype as the creative and systemic intelligence of the Self.

Matriarchal and patriarchal patterns are exemplified in historical and anthropological works as defining the forms and customs of family life, marriage, heritage, religious cults, and social rights, under such terms as matriarchate and patriarchate (Bachofen 1967, Neumann 1949) or matrilinear and patrilinear (Lévi-Strauss 1958), but here they are conceived as something similar and, at the same time, very different. The main difference in this perspective is that the matriarchal and patriarchal archetypes are conceived as being bi-gendered, present equally in the psyches of man and woman as archetypal patterns of ego-other relationship.

The enlargement of the concept of the archetype to embrace, in addition to the expressiveness typical of images, the pattern of the ego-other relation in consciousness is particularly important in the ruling archetypal quaternio. In applying this concept to the four ruling archetypes and to the central archetype, we realize that each of them has its own characteristic intelligence, that is, a typical position in relating the ego to the other. It is this characteristic of the ruling quaternio and the central archetype that links the functioning of consciousness with the collective unconscious and renders them inseparable in every symbolic elaboration within the individual Self and the cultural Self.

The matriarchal archetype is expressed in consciousness through the insular position within this extended concept of the archetype; the patriarchal archetype is expressed through the polarized position; the archetype of alterity (which embraces both the anima and animus archetypes) is expressed through the dialectic position; and the archetype of totality is expressed through the contemplative position. In this chapter, I shall offer a brief description of each of them and afterward, in individual chapters, enumerate their characteristics and relationship in greater detail.

The participation of the central archetype and the ruling archetypal quaternio in all individual and cultural symbolic elaboration of the life process encourages us to ponder their functioning in the historical development of the psyche and how they apply to education. As they are the pillars of psychic elaboration, it is obvious that they also function as the mainstays of teaching.

It is quite revealing to compare archetypes to genetic material, even though the comparison is relative and should be made with all due care. Both are inborn, that is, they are already present at birth and express their potential during life. In both, these features remain virtual and do not appear until they are expressed through events, here considered as symbols. The notion of the gene and that of the archetype require considerable abstraction or transcendence of the characteristics expressed, which obliges us to undertake a long journey of the imagination. Both are central while their manifestations are peripheral, which gives them the connotation of matrices. Both fit into the global coordination of being, which lends them the connotation of integration and creative operation as a function of the whole. The primary difference lies in the fact that the actualization of genes is somewhat less related to culture than that of the archetypes. The genetic material that imparts the senses, for instance, is relatively independent of culture in its actualization in individuals. On the other hand, the patriarchal archetype in a tribe living in the Neolithic age encounters great limitations in coordinating the storing of foodstuff in lean times, whereas in modern times, the patriarchal archetype can easily coordinate the calculations to fly a spacecraft, and find out how many seconds it will take a rocket to reach a far-off target. The same archetype is at work in both cases. In one culture, the result of its functions of abstraction, coordination, organization, and prediction is ten, in another culture, ten million.

Let us imagine the gene of the posterior lobe of the pituitary. What a distance exists between the coordination of the posterior lobe of the hypophysis, which secretes the pituitary hormone and induces the reabsorption of approximately two hundred liters of water a day in the kidneys' glomeruli, and that gene, that specific protein that is present in every cell in the body! To get from the one to the other, it is necessary to transcend the mere reabsorption of water and travel many biochemical paths, a journey during which it is also necessary to interact with numerous other factors, such as the amount of water ingested, the amount of sweat excreted in the regulation of the body temperature, the needs of urinary volume, and any possible deviation of water to other parts of the body. Above all, it is necessary to coordinate the general functioning of the organism. The archetype functions in a similar way, except that, due to its capacity for symbolic expression of adaptation and historical transmission, its capacity for variation is many times greater than the genes throughout individual and collective history.

The integrated functioning of the body strongly suggests the existence of centralizing genetic mechanisms, similar to what we conceive as the central archetype. An image of this archetype as a mandala of the symbolic body is the Vitruvian man with open arms and legs inside a circle, which became famous due to Leonardo da Vinci's drawing. This circular image of the human body, with a center and a periphery connected to a circle by radii, is an archetypal image of the Self expressed through the symbolic body. This is especially so when we place the human body in the center of the ecosystem and the individual Self in the center of the cultural Self and the cosmic Self. And why not link this to the model of cell and atom, the model of the solar system, the galaxies, and the universe?

In the parallel models of the gene and of archetype, we find the important principle of a multiple biofeedback system. This communicating system, originally derived from biology (von Bertalanffy 1968) and cybernetics, claims that in all living systems the emission of a stimulus by any source triggers a multiple reaction that comes from other parts of the system and affects many parts, like boomerangs (Watzlawick, Bavelas, and Jackson 1967). The notion of the archetype, like that of the gene, cannot be considered outside the systemic concept that includes multiple feedback operation.

When we join the concept of the gene and the archetype to the principle of multiple biofeedback, we see that their abstract, timeless, and universal potential is inserted, molded, and considerably affected by the historical context of the here-and-now in the realm of archetypes and herein lies the great difference between genes and archetypes: genetic changes require mutation and acquired characteristics are not genetically transmitted to subsequent generations, whereas archetypal expressions modify history and these changes are passed on to other generations through culture and the ecosystem without mutation. This is the case of the increase in the predominance of the patriarchal pattern through history, which has caused such deep harm to the matriarchal pattern in our traditions. The chronic social repression of the matriarchal archetype over the millennia fosters the formation of a legion of hysterics and psychosomatics that make up around 70 percent of the planet's medical consultations, alongside the wounds of Gaia— the pollution of her rivers, depletion of her reserves, and the poisoning of her atmosphere. However, in spite of the extraordinary change in their collective expression, each one of us is born with archetypes that are relatively and potentially the same as they have always been.

Let us take a brief look at the main features of the four ruling archetypes. All four are coordinating principles to express structuring symbols, complexes, functions, and systems together with a typical position of ego-other relationship. What follows offers an overall view of this quaternio, so that we can realize how it expresses totality through four immense, complex, yet simple intelligence matrices. The central archetype constellates symbols in every new situation and coordinates the function of all archetypes in the symbolic elaboration during the whole process of development.

The matriarchal archetype is the archetype of sensuality; it tends to express intimately and naturally the elaboration of countless symbols of fertility, desire and survival. The patriarchal archetype is the archetype of organization; it tends to rule the elaboration of experiences characterized by order, obedience, duty, planning, and execution. The archetype of alterity is the archetype of dialectical encounter (Guerra 1988); it elaborates the polarities of symbols that have characteristics of search, creativity, and dialectic interrelationship as a systemic function of totality. Finally, the archetype of totality propitiates the synthesis of symbolic working through the existential process by contemplating wholeness systemically at the end of every symbolic elaboration, and in the end of life.

In the general coordination by the central archetype, the ego and the other are expressed by an undifferentiated or uroboric position in the beginning of every symbolic elaboration.

In the matriarchal pattern, the ego and the other relate in the insular position, historically expressed in animism, *participation mystique,* or in the magical-mythical world view; the relationship of the ego and the other is very intimate and symbiotic. It has many characteristics of Piaget's sensory-motor intelligence, Freud's oral phase, and Melanie Klein's paranoid-schizoid position. In the insular position, psychic polarities are not yet firmly established, and the ego relates to one pole of a future polarity independently of what shall later become its counterpole. The hungry baby yells with rage and minutes later expresses total satisfaction after eating. This pattern forms islands of desire and emotion with their own logic, which do not have to match one another rationally they are the *scintilla* of archery. The islands of consciousness are surrounded by unconsciousness. They interact with each other and with the central archetype mostly through unconscious imagination.

In the patriarchal pattern, polarities are clearly formed and organized; the ego and the other, including the conscious-unconscious polarity operate in a polarized position, which is an abstract, hierarchic way that forms great coherent, logical-rational systems. This controlling, delimiting tension between the ego and the other establishes a dominating-dominated pattern of relationship that is imposed with perfectionism and guilt, with the challenge of tasks and obligations, which tends to become very coherent, repetitive and traditional. This position is related to Piaget's conceptual intelligence and Melanie Klein's depressive position. The big difference between the concepts of the insular matriarchal and polarized patriarchal positions compared to most traditional theories of personality development is that the polarized position follows the insular position in early childhood and later on in all symbolic elaboration, but the insular matriarchal position is never extinguished or left out. On the contrary, due to its archetypal nature, it continually strives to express itself even under the most desperate situations of strict patriarchal dominance.

The insular matriarchal position is frequently repressed and injured by the polarized patriarchal position, but even fixated and deformed in the shadow through neurotic, psychopathic, borderline, or psychotic symptoms, it continues its structuring function (Wahba 1996).

These characteristics alone enable us to see that the matriarchal and patriarchal patterns, due to the diametrically opposed nature of their intelligence, are liable to be in immense conflict in disputing the space of symbolic elaboration. Their productive articulation, however, stands among the great manifestations of human wisdom, on individual and cultural levels, coordinated by the dialectical position of the archetype of alterity in life and in teaching.

It is in this very tense field created by the extreme polarity of matriarchal and patriarchal patterns that the third ruling archetype, the archetype of alterity, operates. I have named it so because, in its pattern, the main goal of the ego is to respect and consider the other so as to establish with it a dialectic, democratic, and constantly interchangeable rapport as a function of the experience of totality mostly through undestanding and compassion.

Alterity does not pursue equality of parts but rather equal rights and opportunities for their differences to express themselves and interact. Only the considerably dialectic and creative nature of the archetype of alterity is capable of seeking the democratic interaction of the matriarchal-patriarchal polarity along with all the other polarities. The alterity pattern of relationship coordinates equal rights of opposites, including their differences and their equality. It encompasses the anima and animus archetypes.

It is also in this field, addressed differently by the functioning of the insular, polarized, and dialectic positions of the countless ego-other polarities, that the synthesizing intelligence of the archetype of totality functions in the contemplative position. It seeks the permanent experience of wholeness abstracting from the creativity, conflicts, frustrations, wounds, mutilations, and accomplishments of the elaboration of structuring symbols, functions, complexes, and systems that interact in the process of fulfilling the potential of being coordinated by all other archetypes. In this position, the ego and the other detach from all polarities so that their difference disappears in contemplation of reality.

It is important to consider the contrast between the patterns of alterity and totality on a very different plane from the tension between the matriarchal and patriarchal patterns. Although alterity detaches partially from matriarchal sensuality and patriarchal power, it is deeply engaged in the attempt to interact democratically with significant parts of these archetypes to express wholeness. The totality pattern, on the other hand, stands for an enormous archetypal capacity of the ego and other to detach from all parts in order to contemplate the process of elaboration.

## Symbolic Elaboration, the Transcendent Function of Imagination, and the Attachment-Detachment Polarity

The transcendent function was described by Jung in 1916 (Jung 1958). In 1902, he recorded in his medical thesis, titled "On Occult *Phenomena*", possession states of spiritualism he had witnessed in his maternal cousin, Hélène Preiswerk (Helly) at his maternal grandmother's home. After 1913, having separated from the psychoanalytic movement, he went through a very creative phase of isolation and introversion in which he had deep experiences which lasted from 1913 until 1930. They were registered in drafts he named "black books," later reunited in his famous *Red Book* (Jung 2009). They included the *Septem Sermones ad Mortuos* in 1916 ("Seven Sermons to the Dead", Jung 1961). He wrote them in three nights during a week of great tension, when the atmosphere of his home presented strange parapsychological phenomena. All this played a significant role in his continuing to develop his capacity to detach from the literal meaning of things and conceive symbolic life within the theory of archetypes (Bair 2003).

Jung took forty years to publish "*The Transcendent Function*"—four decades during which he conceived and applied the theory of archetypes that enabled him to explain by means of the scientific model the experience of the transcendence of the ego which he had had in the esoteric dimension (experience without rational understanding). From this work onward, the transcendent function has been acknowledged as the function that links the ego and consciousness to the archetypes. From the acknowledgment of the formation of the identity of the ego and the other coordinated by archetypes through structuring symbols, complexes, functions, and systems, the transcendent function takes on a central role in the process of symbolic elaboration. This is what allows us to conceive the symbolic experience that forms and transforms consciousness, coordinated by the central archetype and the other archetypes.

Jungian symbolic psychology understands the transcendent function as the structuring transcendent function of the imagination because it recognizes the imagination as the essence of the symbolic dimension. The symbol fascinates us by its archetypal content, which forces the identities of the ego and the other to detach from and transcend their previous states within symbolic elaboration to form a new ego and a new other. Fascination and detachment are the poles of the transcendent function of the imagination in the experience of symbols, which lead us to an understanding of the phenomenon of sacrifice as an archetypal structuring function that coordinates the change from what has passed to what is to come. There is no transformation without fascination, detachment, and sacrifice. In symbolic teaching we experience these functions when we detach from the old to receive the new. Deconstruction and reconstruction are inseparable within constructivist teaching. Insofar as the teacher activates the structuring function of fascination with charisma and use of expressive techniques, it is necessary at the same time to sacrifice the position of the one who knows and detach from the power over knowing to build up knowledge democratically and affectionately.

## The Five Ego-Other Positions in Symbolic Elaboration

The ego-other relationship presents itself in consciousness in five characteristic ways with which the educator has to be familiar. These are the five positions of the ego-other polarity, namely: the undifferentiated position (central archetype), the insular position (matriarchal archetype), the polarized position (patriarchal archetype), the dialectic position (alterity archetype), and the contemplative position (totality archetype). Anything that is experienced and thus becomes a structuring symbol necessarily passes through these five positions during the symbolic elaboration that will integrate its meanings into the knowledge of being by forming and transforming the identity of the ego and the other in consciousness. When parts of the fixated ego-other polarity are relegated to the shadow, this is due to the fact that one or more of these positions has been fixated and formed defenses. The phenomenon of fixation was discovered by Freud and is here described archetypally. Psychoanalysis considered fixation to be a historical paralysis of development, mostly in childhood. The archetypal perspective allows us to see fixation as an archetypal wound, which may fix the coordinating function of a regent archetype and of symbolic elaboration in any difficult situation in the life of the individual or of the cultural Self.

Comments were made above on indiscrimination, nondifferentiation, and symbiosis. Any of the five archetypal positions of consciousness may represent confusion in consciousness caused by indiscrimination of the ego-other relationship. Elaboration in a certain position does not mean that the ego-other polarity is already discriminated in this position. Elaboration may be a long process depending on the content of the symbol. Parents, for instance, are symbols so full of meanings that their elaboration is a lifelong process that continues after their deaths.

To my knowledge, Neumann (1955) was the first Jungian author to describe ego archetypal positions when he mentioned ego characteristics in matriarchal and patriarchal patterns. The undifferentiated position, Erich Neumann's uroboric stage, occurs when the symbol activated for elaboration is largely unknown to consciousness and is mostly immersed in the psychic nondifferentiation of unconsciousness. Parts of the symbol become conscious and parts remain unconscious. The parts of symbolic elaboration which suffer fixation and form the shadow can have conscious and unconscious characteristics in varying degrees.

In the undifferentiated position, there occurs a greater or lesser involvement with the elaboration of the activated symbol. With the passing of the years and with psychological knowledge, we learn that our ego cannot immediately know the importance of a newly activated symbol. We often have symbols activated in our dreams and fantasies, where they remain for years apart from our central existential attention and occupations. Sometimes, they are such important symbols that they potentially hold the very essence of our ontological identity, the profound identity of our being, and yet we fail to recognize their value. There is a legend whose archetypal meaning may relate to this fact: every seven years, a treasure rises from the bottom of the earth. It comes to the surface and remains there for seven days. Its value is not apparent. If it stays undiscovered and unrecognized by anyone, it submerges again for another seven years. Taking the symbolic use of the number seven, four plus three, as process (Jung 1948), we may associate this legend to the activation of very important symbols in the existential process. If they do not receive proper commitment and elaboration, these symbols fail to go beyond the undifferentiated position and are once again deactivated.

The undifferentiated position is closely associated to the archaic essence of the central archetype, which embraces and coordinates all symbolic activation from the start. The other positions are also coordinated by the central archetype, but each presents a much more specific elaborating function, which expresses the regent archetype to which it corresponds.

In drawing up a curriculum, the educator's responsibility lies in activating structuring symbols and functions and triggering their elaboration in the pedagogic Self. We must remember the legend and only activate what we can consider treasures for the future life of the pupils. Will these contents be important enough in the life of the pupils for them to spend their existential energy studying them? Perusing the school curriculum, I see that current learning is overloaded with specialized contents and often wasted in a pile of facts, many of which are of no importance whatsoever to anyone's life. At the same time, many other facts, generally psychological and artistic—and real treasures of life and culture—are not activated in teaching and do not feature in curricula. An extraterrestrial examining most curricula from kindergarten to post-graduation might conclude that our species is born already knowing many themes of central importance in life and so does not have to study them. Can one imagine a sixteen-year curriculum in which there is not a single class on love or on the difficulties of relationship between people, between husband and wife, between parents and children, not a single class on the existential meanings of learning or on coping with frustrations, mainly those of unhappiness, sickness, and death? A curriculum has to be enormously limited for that to happen, and yet that is the rule, which does not prevent us from proudly graduating doctors and embarking on postgraduate studies in all the areas of learning. Can a university call itself a temple of knowledge when it does not teach its graduates how to love, to have peace, and to die?

It is important to relate these limitations to the subjective-objective dissociation of Western culture already mentioned. To be thoroughly convinced of the validity of this thesis, one has but to learn about the education based on the mythologies of other cultures. Among all those which I have studied, not a single one is so limited as to exclude these fundamental existential themes, which are absent in the curricula of our schools and universities. This is a strong argument to relate the subject-object dissociation of Western culture to the loss of its roots in the Christian myth, when science triumphed over the Inquisition and defensively separated truth from faith and myth from objective reality.

When I mention faith in this context, I am referring to the archetypal structuring function of faith, which does not necessarily operate within the dimension of institutionalized religion. Faith is basically related to the psychological dimension of emotion, which is a dimension frequently beyond rational understanding but which, nonetheless, deeply affirms the nature of being. Although mostly irrational and unpredictable in their origins, emotions have a convincing nature in their manifestation, which we call faith. When I love someone, I have faith that cultivating this affection will be good for me, whereas when I hate someone, I am sure (faith) that this person's existence brings harm to me. Of course, reason can reassure or question faith one way or another, mainly regarding feelings, but its primary root lies beyond reason. To convince yourself of this, it is enough to try to like someone you dislike or to feel one single moment of aversion for someone you like on the team you cheer for.

To heal this shadow present in the subject-object dissociation, we first have to admit that it is still today the main root which feeds the resistance against the symbolic perspective when it proposes to reunite the subjective and the objective within our cultural Self.

In the insular position, the ego and the other live in great intimacy with psychological functions that have not grouped themselves as polarities. This is a type of consciousness that resembles islands linked by sea currents that connect their flora and fauna in a peculiar way. There are islands with hatred, others with love, some with admiration, and others with scorn, with no logical, systematic concatenation among them, except through a dominantly unconscious undercurrent, which meaningfully interrelates these islands according to the sensuous needs and desires of the life process. It is interesting to correlate this position as it manifests itself in early childhood to the six phases described in Piaget's concept of sensory-motor intelligence development, which characterizes the ego function dominantly until two years of age (Piaget 1963).

The insular position of the matriarchal archetype should not be confused with splits or pathological complexes, because, although islands are set apart, they communicate mainly unconsciously and very creatively among themselves. This relationship can be perceived by intuition, which includes ESP (extrasensory perception). Surprisingly to the conscious mind these islands produce reactions that frequently express totality in a very meaningful and creative manner, even though their logic remains incomprehensible. One island can even present a volcanic emotional eruption and circumstantially dominate all others, as happens with the structuring function of possession, which, as all structuring functions, can be normal or defensive.

Although characteristic of the matriarchal pattern inherent in the infant's relationships in early life, the insular position should not be reduced to childhood; to do so enormously impoverishes the understanding of the functioning of the matriarchal pattern in adult life, including teaching. As mentioned before, centroversion is not synonymous with regression, but rather brings indiscrimination to all new symbolic elaboration. Allowing elaboration in the insular position is indispensable, since only in this way do we gain sensuous familiarity with the meanings of the new symbol, so that elaboration can be performed within the psychic time of maturation. The insular position allows consciousness to become sensually familiar with the contents of symbols. A good example is the seven days of Genesis, the biblical creation myth in which the elements are first formed and then named, or the famous philosophical saying of the Middle Ages: "Nothing is in the intellect which has not passed through the senses."

When the learning process is speeded up and the matriarchal phase is skipped, the future price paid is artificiality. In such cases people can say many names without really knowing what they are talking about. It is very impressive how much the abstraction of the patriarchal discourse can build up thoughts devoid of any deep meaning.

Psychic processes are rooted not only in the motivational nervous system, which moves a muscle at the moment that the will so decides, but also in the vegetative and limbic nervous system, which can take days to digest food, synthesize a certain hormone, or act in integrated fashion within the metabolism. Only the insular position, by maintaining experiences and emotions separated and focused in intimacy, can ensure the hatching and growth of symbols in the time necessary for their ripening. This notion is essential in education; the educator must not hamper the curriculum by presenting one new concept on top of another without giving the pupil time for matriarchal sensuality to look, smell, taste, chew, and swallow the initial concept. When learning is precociously submitted to abstraction and its absorption is artificialized, it remains superficial and removed from the deep sensuality of the Self and therefore condemned to oblivion.

The need for the insular position is clearly shown at the start of symbolic elaboration in exuberant structuring functions like sexuality. Although children begin to learn rationally and superficially about sexuality very early now, true learning is kept secretly in their own bodies and develops gradually through masturbatory activity and sexual games. Like a plant that grows in a nursery, protected from the rain, wind, and strong sunshine and is then transplanted to the garden, the elaboration of sexuality is clearly very slow and takes years to develop in the insular matriarchal position. Even in late adolescence, the young often experience sexuality in a still rather insular form before entering its fully existential experience. The early activation of the insular position of sexuality, generally due to fashion and pressure from the social group, exemplifies the artificiality and alienation of the experience for lack of proper time taken in maturing. One sixteen-year-old adolescent girl confided to her mother: "I hated my birthday this year, because now all my friends think I've got to screw my boyfriend."

The insular position is host to conflicting situations on different islands. This is not dissociation but rather a way of living. The child can love its father, mother, siblings, and friends one moment and hate them the next without experiencing the least logical need to face the two conflicting situations and feel obliged to consider, decide, and act coherently by framing the conflict in a single attitude. Many matriarchally-dominated experiences, personalities, and cultures work this way.

Like all structuring functions and archetypes, each position of the ego-other relationship is more important than all others when we consider one specific context. When the insular position is not properly lived through sensory-motor intelligence in teaching history, geography, languages, science, arts, or mathematics, these subjects may become a foreign and unfamiliar experience to students, although they may "study" them afterward for many years in the conceptual intelligence of the polarized patriarchal position.

The phenomenon of creative possession, for instance, present in many cultures with matriarchal dominance, expresses the normal circumstantial intense dominance of one island over all the others. Normal possession was taken for hysteria in many traditional anthropological studies of tribal cultures. Hysterical possession may occur when one island suffers fixation or dissociation and takes command of the others autonomously.

During life, especially at the beginnings of very new situations, the insular position is highly important to ensure a healthy, integrated symbolic elaboration. Introducing the concepts of languages, history, geography, mathematics, chemistry, and physics, the educator has to exercise the insular position in all its pertinence and fundamental importance. However, in so doing, it is necessary to resist pressure from the patriarchal dominance of culture and traditional teaching that tends to abstract teaching and rush ahead with the program and submit learning to tests. Being constructivist helps but does not resolve things because rationalism frequently rushes over sensory-motor intelligence to reach precociously conceptual intelligence. This hinders the experience of the nature of things because it does not take emotional timing into account in the ripening of the learning process (Saiz Laureiro 1986). In this respect, it is important to consider that Piaget's theory of the formation of conceptual intelligence in childhood may mislead the educator to approach the education of adolescents, college students, and adults through rational constructivism reduced to conceptual intelligence. In the perspective of Jungian symbolic education, however, any symbolic elaboration of something really new in the learning process, independent of age or instruction level, must be undertaken within the sensory-motor or insular matriarchal position, before going on to the conceptual intelligence of the polarized patriarchal position to avoid alienated learning.

When it assumes an important role in consciousness in the individual or cultural Self, the insular position operates in the magical-mythical mentality of animism and magic causality frequently without the objective rational coherence of the polarized patriarchal position. My desires, my emotions, and my imagination conceive my worldview. My land, my family, my friends, and the team I cheer for are much better than others (simply because they are mine). Of course, if elaboration suffers fixation in this position, the scope of consciousness presents many limitations, such as those of superstition, defensive narcissism, and fanaticism, but this does not justify denying the insular position its due importance in teaching and in the process of individuation in general.

The result of rushing, skipping, or aborting the insular position in symbolic elaboration is artificiality and empty discourse, of life and of apprenticeship, which leads to cultural alienation and oblivion regarding what has been learned. This is one of the main causes of the inability of students to employ learned subjects existentially and creatively. In these cases, people and cultures never really know what they are talking about. They have heard about certain things and repeat what they heard, but they do not know how to operate them coherently and creatively within the whole because they have swallowed them without duly chewing and experiencing their taste. When the patriarchal predominance precociously leads to abstracting, analyzing, cataloging, and explaining experiences in the polarized position, it may establish a reduction that asphyxiates the full dimension of things.

Modern psychology has done this exuberantly in the twentieth century, creating a conceptual reduction of many matriarchal functions to childhood, to pathology, and to "the unconscious", which makes it difficult to recognize the immensity and depth of psychic reality and creativity. Limits have been frequently equated with repression, emotional exuberance with hysteria, control and organization with obsession, the pursuit of love in adult life with immaturity, affection with dependence, meditation with regression, tenderness with childhood and weakness, doubt with ambiguity, normal with pathologic depression, enthusiasm with mania, creativity with transgression, dreams and the imagination with "the unconscious", and so on.

I carried out some research on the dimension of dreams that much impressed me. Two groups of educators met weekly for eight weeks in two-hour sessions. They presented their dreams, and we experienced them rather than analyzing or interpreting them. The experiences could be dramatization, imagination, or simply accounts of how they experienced their own dreams and those of the others. It was a bit difficult at first, chiefly because nearly everyone had undergone some type of analysis and so was mostly conditioned to interpret dreams rather than to experience them. Little by little we managed to fulfill the purpose of the research, which was to experience the dimensions of the dreams. To this end, we had to contradict the historical reduction of psychodynamic psychology, which equated the essence of dreams with "the unconscious". We learned to open to the conscious experience of the oneiric dimension. To our surprise and delight, we realized that dreams differ from the usual conscious state not because they are unconscious, but rather because the dream dimension has everything in common with the dimensions of poetry, myth, fantasy, the right brain hemisphere, and with the insular matriarchal position. The expression of dreams through metaphorical images capable of evoking the most varied emotions and nuances of the soul's sensitivity without the obligation to explain anything make dreams the night poetry of the Self (Byington 1991b). The result of this research shocked me as an analyst. I had practiced psychotherapy for decades, including dream interpretation, and I had never grasped so profoundly the essence of the oneiric dimension. I soothed my frustration with a vast professional company. It became clear that my training lacked the experience of dreams in the matriarchal insular position. Right from the start, I had skipped their conscious poetic sensuality and had experienced them as the "royal road to the unconscious", which radically separates conscious from unconscious characteristics as though the latter were a place and not an attribute of symbols. I learned from psychoanalysis and from analytical psychology that dreams had to be interpreted. It is true that Jung painted and sculpted many of his dreams in order that he might live with their images daily, but I had understood this to be of secondary importance to interpretation. The Jungian method of active imagination showed itself to be one of the most productive to experience dreams in the insular and dialectical positions.

Worst of all is that when the educator, parents, or analysts remain in the insular position along with their pupils, children, or patients, they often feel guilty of not doing anything and yet, the growth of the personality and formation of identity often have their crucial moments deeply rooted in the intimate, full, generous, and protective experience of the matriarchal insular position. Endless times, I have accompanied cases in which the key to learning was my remaining as container of the student or patient in the insular position; without analyzing or explaining anything, I just stayed there and echoed in cases of discovery of true vocation, blocked aggression, deep affection, deliverance of creativity or sexuality, discovery of intimacy, self-esteem, and even the wisdom of death. Many times, years after elaborating defenses, all of a sudden there appears the free, creative structuring function. There is no point in rushing to see immediate results. The insular position is necessary for the Self to become familiar with the experience of the new, grow mature, and accommodate to the change inherent to its arrival, before handing it over to the automatic pilot of daily life as something already known. Once I asked a woman in what way pregnancy had changed her life. "Hardly at all", was her answer. "I go on working like before. I just feel a bit sick and at night I sleep on my side. I don't drink coffee because of the heartburn, and now and again I cuddle my belly and chat with my baby, so that we can get to know and get used to one another." One day a colleague of mine said, in jest, that if the patriarchal pattern were in control of gestation, children would soon be born without pregnancy.

It is difficult to exaggerate the importance of the insular matriarchal position in symbolic education, because it is something that cannot be rationally taught. Rather, it must be experienced, and yet, I really think that it is the essential part of learning. It is the sensuous basis of true knowledge, indispensable to later abstractions with all the conceptual intelligence that will follow. Without it, later teaching, full of programs that generally include a huge amount of abstract learning, becomes alienated and artificial, something that can be repeated and applied superficially but not used creatively.

Students who begin to learn a certain subject need first of all to learn to "breathe" the essence of the subject, before learning the abc's of its content. In swimming lessons, for instance, before learning how to swim, it is importance to learn just to stay in the water, playing around until one feels intimacy with it. What this means and how to apply it in every subject taught has to be learned by teachers through empathy, because it cannot be rationally understood. This is the reason for starting to teach the natural sciences and humanities in primary school, because there the mind is very much open to learning through the sensory-motor intelligence of the insular matriarchal position. Much more important than learning things is the subliminal experience of the nature of things which is only conditioned through intimacy.

An engineer had five children and could not afford to pay servants to help his wife take care of them. So, year after year, they took their children along daily on his regular visits to the building that he was supervising during construction. When the children grew up, all five had enormous facility for understanding mathematics and physics. As they explained to me: "Whenever we come across mathematical calculations and thinking related to mechanics, we associate them to all those sheets of paper filled with numbers which daddy took around with us during our childhood." It is impressive how such early experiences condition intimacy not only with the exact sciences but also with the humanities. The intimate experience of music, mechanics, literature, painting, handwork, nature, and sports through imitation in early childhood strongly conditions students with many aspects of their symbolic meanings, including familiarity and affection, which will strongly influence studying and expressing them later in life.

The imitative structuring function is the most profound and productive function in forming identity in early life through the phenomenon of imprint. Ally this notion to the concept that the main desire in the individuation process in childhood is to become an adult and we understand the importance of the examples of adults in education. The way parents deal with other people's shadows and with their own, the way they live, talk, dress, eat, listen to music, take care of their health, caress each other, quarrel and make or do not make peace, deal with aggression, and take pleasure in science, art, politics, and sports strongly conditions the education of children and their identity formation. Much more effective than what parents say, the sermons they preach, and the punishments they give is what they feel and do—the living example of who they are—the main values, principles and abilities with they will teach to their children.

The insular position is followed by the polarized position of the patriarchal archetype that tends to abstract, organize, and articulate the ego-other and other-other polarities within logical and rational coherent systems, well described by Piaget in the conceptual intelligence beginning after the child's second year. I have called it polarized because polarities are now firmly organized in opposition, traditionally and hierarchically cultivated, refined, and coherently maintained. The principle of rational causality is dominant here, guiding people and symbolic elaboration so that everything is abstracted, foreseeable, deductible, organized, and reassured, which strengthens consciousness significantly and increases its power exuberantly in the world. This position allows for transversal knowledge forming large logical systems. It is related mainly to objective reality, which is different from the magical causality of the sensory-motor intelligence of the insular matriarchal position in which the subjectivity of desire prevails. Objective causality is the platform on which scientific knowledge was and is built. The forest is green not because it is animated with spirits, but because all trees and other plants have chlorophyll. Sodium and chlorine combine to form salt due to the complementary number of valence electrons in their outer shells. Diabetes is a disease in which insulin secretion by the Langerhans islands in the pancreas is diminished, which causes hyperglycemia.

The organization inherent in the polarized position establishes causality to regulate the ego-other relationship in space and time, delimiting their role and territory and laying down specific characteristics for their responsibility and behavior. Every function so polarized complements others and generates systems, which form a logical psychic whole. This coherence may be, and generally is, ensured by the formulation of two opposite and mutually exclusive principles treated as, such as the life and death drives postulated by Freud. In this case, one causally explains constructive events and the other explains destructive ones. There is no dialectic relation between the poles. Memory maintains the identity of the poles so that they do not get mixed up in order to sustain the rational and perfect logical coherence of the system.

The polarized position is far more organized than the insular. This is made possible by abstraction, which forms psychological representations that make the ego and the other clearly separated and systemically interrelated as polar opposites. Cozy intimacy, animism, participation mystique, and magic causality cease. There is a weakening of the erotic binding that relates things with no condition other than the being-with that we find in the insular position. The relation of the ego and the other is now conditioned to well-established stereotypes. For example, man is strong, sexually promiscuous, and *yang*, while woman is fragile, chaste, and *yin*. Anyone who steps out of this role is liable to be labeled pejoratively as wimp, queer, dike, or whore. Children listen and obey; adults talk and give orders. Children are irresponsible, old men weak. Men who do not earn money are losers. This has been the dominant orientation of consciousness for thousands of years and still prevails in many aspects of social life, varying from culture to culture. Patriarcally dominated teaching aims at repetition of tradition.

This polarized position generates countless immutable concepts that in time become tradition and sometimes become fixations, which turns them into prejudice and even fanaticism. Nonetheless, precisely because they are abstract and do not consider details in symbolic elaboration, this becomes the strongest and most productive position from which to control nature, emotion, body, and society and the one most capable of organizing and planning existential reality. Its planned strategies strengthen and reassure the ego in such a way that it is hard to relinquish. This reassurance makes the ego submit to the law, trusting that when the other is in its place in the same situation, it will do exactly the same. So it is not a matter of a circumstantial privilege of the ego or the other, but rather of an existential code of truth and behavior that submits the ego and the other to a transcendental, asymmetrical reality of power, authority, and task fulfillment reinforced strongly by a sense of duty and guilt. Each oppressor has a victim within because what oppresses the victim is the polarized patriarchal archetypal pattern and not merely a person.

The remarkable organizational power of the polarized position allows the energy of symbols to be foreseen and planned as in no other position. Mass vaccination against different diseases at different ages, for example, would be impossible without this position, as would numerous other situations in big cities. The polarized position is the basic position of the computer system that dominates so much of today's technological life and more so every day. The functioning of a hospital, banking system, library, museum, airport, telephone, or television is impossible without it. Its absence leads any institution to chaos or bankruptcy in no time at all.

The polarized position is the most convenient one for the performance of the patriarchal pattern and its incompatibility with the insular position in general is related to the conflicts that the patriarchal and matriarchal patterns have with one another. The attachment of the ego to the intimacy of the insular position and to abstract power in the polarized position makes it difficult to transcend them and deal with symbolic elaboration in the dialectic position.

Two great attachments that educators have toward the polarized position are first expressed in the content of teaching by the objectivity of the curriculum, and second in assessing learning by means of tests given by the class teacher.

Constructivism is essentially exercised by the dialectic position, and it requires relative detachment from the insular position and from the polarized position. That is why many educators defend non-constructivist education with such ferocity in order to preserve assymetry in teaching.

The dialectic position of symbolic constructivism requires detachment from exclusive objectivity and demands modifying the content of teaching programs and giving secondary importance to the assessment of learning by means of examinations and grades given by the teacher of the class. Systemic symbolic constructivist evaluation of teaching emerges from the student-teacher relationship during the learning process, and when tests are given, these should be carried out by a teacher outside the class so that students, teacher, and learning are all evaluated together.

The higher capacity of organization, responsibility, and the rational, conceptual, and logical-deductive scope of symbolic elaboration by the polarized position is characteristic of the patriarchal archetype and is unquestionably accompanied by a loss of erotic involvement in the ego-other relation of spontaneity, joy, pleasure, and sensuality of living inherent to the insular position typical of the matriarchal archetype. Not to realize this in due fashion was perhaps the greatest limitation and drawback in the evolutionary scheme of Piaget's work, where he conceived the development of intelligence in childhood. However great the individual's capacity for abstraction and conceptual intelligence, if we disregard the affectionate, intimate, sensual, erotic, and existential value of sensory intelligence of the insular position, students may turn into superefficient thinking machines, but tend to remain psychologically limited as far as human wisdom, intimacy and spontaneity are concerned. Goleman's book, *Emotional Intelligence* (1995), exemplifies this perspective with very impressive data.

Through its generalizing power, the might of the polarized position can produce omissions and disturbances of basic existential conditions, whose fixated symbols will be jettisoned to the shadow. The saying "the more ego in consciousness, the more ego in shadow" applies more to the polarized position of the patriarchal archetype than to any other.

The dialectic position follows the polarized position in symbolic elaboration and makes it all the more complex, since, apart from separating and forming the reality of the ego and the other, as the insular and polarized positions do, it adds dialectic interaction between them. In this sense, the dialectic position bears certain close and individualized aspects of the insular position, like intimacy, emotions, and empathy, yet differs from it because it operates by seeking conscious and coherent contact with totality, which includes the polarized position. The dialectic position maintains the polarized position's aspects of abstraction, coherence, and continuity of identity, yet differs from it in admitting in theory that the ego can present all the features of the other and vice versa, within the pursuit of totality. Its essence is the dialectical of dialectic encounter between the ego and the other so much enphasized by Jung.

## The Creationist-Evolutionist Polarity

Alterity is very important and includes the discussion of the creationist-evolutionist polarity that divides the field of education today. Some teach creationism as truth and others choose evolutionism. When we take into account the archetypal positions of consciousness, we see that both positions are right when used correctly and both are wrong if used incorrectly.

Creationism expresses a vision of creation through the magical-mythical mentality, which animates and endows creation with image and magical causality, corresponding to the insular matriarchal worldview. Evolutionism expresses a vision of creation through materialistic scientific mentality, which precludes animism and intentions in the objective world. Creationism expresses the fantastic imagination of myth, and evolutionism describes reality through the dialectical examination of the subject-object interaction restricted to objectivity. Each one is right in its archetypal dimension and wrong when it does not recognize the other's dimension as valid. The alterity archetype coordinates symbolic science, which includes creationism side by side with evolutionism.

The dialectic position opens consciousness to the mysterious, paradoxical, and synchronistic logic of opposites, where nothing is right or wrong a *priori*. What was good and desirable yesterday may be bad and harmful today. In this position, only the experience of deep symbolic elaboration reveals the positive and negative identifications to form the identity of the ego and the other in every new context. Its working principle, includes magical causality and reflexive causality, but also synchronicity, which transcends magical and reflexive causality. Synchronicity, as Jung (1952a) described it, is a principle of acausal relationship that explains reality as it is and not as we desire or plan it to be. Strictly speaking, synchronicity is not simply an acausal connecting principle. It does contain many causes but exactly because they are so many, the principle of causality becomes useless and the whole system can essentially be considered acausal. Causality, whether magical or rational, explains reality by the relation of cause and effect, whereas synchronicity conceives reality as a mystery made up of all the variables involved, whose interaction reveals meaning every time as something unique and extraordinary. Synchronicity depends on countless causes and all variables that systemically make up that moment, within a multiple feedback system, which includes unexpected and, therefore, even chaotic events.

Normally, as in the rest of his life, a man looks through the window and then leaves the house through the door. His leaving the house is regulated by the insular and polarized positions. Door is door and window is window. You go out through the door; you look out through the window when you wish it or need it. One day, he dreams he has left the house through the window. He does not understand the dream at all. Three days later, he wakes up in the middle of the night with the smell of smoke. There is a short circuit in the house and a fire has started in the living room. He runs down the stairs, but the smoke is so thick that he comes back choking. He ties a sheet and climbs out through the window. This happened at home, but it might have happened symbolically in married life, at the office, in the car, or in the stock market. In many of life's difficulties, logical, rational causality is useless. In these situations regular keys do not open the normal doors. The mystery reveals itself through keys that lie in the hands of synchronicity and the dialectic position. This calls for creativity! So there is no pre-established solution and we have to open ourselves to each and every circumstance that might help us discover the keys to transformation, survival and even salvation. The dialectic position, through synchronicity, expresses the pattern of the archetype of alterity, which includes the archetypes of anima and animus described by Jung.

The contemplative position is more differentiated than its four antecedents, for it structures the identities of the ego and of the other to form a gestalt that allows wholeness to be contemplated beyond polarities. The archetype that best expresses the contemplative position is the archetype of totality.

This position crowns the process of symbolic elaboration and is very well expressed in the emblem of Taoism, called *tai-chi,* ☯ the ultimate supreme reality of Tao (Lao Tse, sixth century B.C.). To accomplish the union of opposites within the whole with Oriental subtlety, in the middle of the black area there is a white dot, and vice versa. The ancient civilizations of India, China, Japan, and Tibet cultivate the contemplative position through the practice of meditation. Its wisdom lies in daily practices that ritualize total detachment and enter into direct contact with wholeness. This permits one to experience a state of consciousness that harmonizes, strengthens, and helps consciousness to proceed with the symbolic elaborations being carried out in other positions. Meditation practices vary from one school to another but generally give the most importance to detachment from symbols and direct contact with the center.

The five positions described express the symbolic elaboration in life and in symbolic teaching and therefore have to be thoroughly known in the theory and practice of Jungian symbolic education. Symbolic elaboration passes through the five positions in a relatively evolutionary way and considers the estimated time necessary for the ego-other relation to articulate each position. The ideal is for the ego to be always available to resume any position in the elaboration of existential situations. Even though these have already been elaborated, this availability is very enriching, for it enables us to maintain the ego-other positions as open channels of intelligence to reinvigorate our attitude toward learning within the totality of being.

This evolutionary characteristic of the developmental process deserves careful consideration not to repress but, on the contrary, to preserve the insular matriarchal pattern when the polarized patriarchal pattern is constellated. This can only be fully accomplished through the activation of the dialectical archetype of alterity. The radical implantation of the polarized patriarchal pattern with repression or "sublimation" of the insular matriarchal pattern has been a source of intense psychological deformation in many theories of education and of individual and collective development.

# Chapter 7

# THE INSULAR MATRIARCHAL POSITION IN TEACHING

The identification of the matriarchal archetype with the feminine and the patriarchal archetype with the masculine, caused by the identification of these archetypes with the historical circumstances of their cultural implantation, has been a great limitation. The matriarchal was identified with the feminine because the image of the mother, especially the aspects of pregnancy and breast-feeding, expressed significantly the exuberant sensuality and fertility of the matriarchal archetype. This imagery was historically so meaningful that the matriarchal archetype was named the great mother archetype.

Similarly, the physical strength of men, their heroic deeds in battle, and their commanding role in the family and in society established the image of the father as a fitting expression of the father archetype.

However, the phenomenology of the process of individuation and the description of the anima and animus archetypes by Jung clearly registered the presence of feminine characteristics in the personalities of men and masculine characteristics in the personalities of women. It was this fact that led Jungian symbolic psychology to realize that the phenomena that describe the great mother archetype correspond basically to sensuality and fertility present in the personalities of both men and women, while those that describe the father archetype correspond essentially to the capacity to abstract and organize polarities, which can also be seen in the personalities of both men and women. This fact allows us to conceive an archetypal typology as already mentioned with a dominance of the matriarchal or patriarchal archetypes in the individual and the cultural Self.

We may observe, for instance, that many women, in families and in society, are more capable of expressing the organizational capacity of the polarized patriarchal pattern than many men. Likewise, there are men who express, in a more refined way the sensuality of the matriarchal pattern within themselves, in their homes, with their children, and in society. From this perspective, identifying father and man with the patriarchal and mother and woman with the matriarchal is a great limitation, even though this has been historically the case in social roles, and recently in the studies of Erich Neumann (1949) following Bachofen (1967).

One of the main differences between analytical psychology and Jungian symbolic psychology is that analytical psychology interprets *participation mystique* as unconscious identity, instead of as the insular ego-other position of the matriarchal archetype. This reduction unduly exaggerated the extension of the collective unconscious to the detriment of the very existence and fundamental importance of the insular matriarchal position in consciousness.

When we consider the insular matriarchal ego-other position, which is predominant in many cultures and in childhood, expressing myth, emotion, magic, dream, or the pleasure principle, to be unconscious, we enormously reduce the scope of consciousness and become easy prey to the unilateral patriarchal historical dominance, which severely limited the matriarchal pattern. This dominance has not only disqualified the importance of the insular matriarchal position, conceiving it as unconscious and primitive, but it has also injured it through unbridled repression and violence, which has deformed many dimensions of the cultural Self during the implantation of civilization over the past ten thousand years.

Recognition that the insular matriarchal position operates consciously and unconsciously, together with the other four archetypal positions, allows us to extend the concept of the archetype to encompass the individual and collective unconscious together with individual and collective consciousness.

Due to the characteristic intimacy of the ego-other relationship in the insular matriarchal position, the symbiotic structuring function is prominent in symbolic elaboration in order to shape the identity of the ego and the other. This fact intensifies the literality of symbols and restricts their abstraction to such an extent that many authors have overlooked and even denied its symbolic property, as did, for instance, Piaget (1963) when he described it reductively as the sensory-motor stage of intelligence prior to the capacity of symbol formation. I emphatically insist that the abstract perception of symbols is one thing and their structuring symbolic force, which can be exercised even though literally and unconsciously in the insular matriarchal and in the sensory-motor stage of intelligence, is quite another. We should not, therefore, reduce symbolization exclusively to abstraction and consciousness. When we do so, we favor a false superiority of the patriarchal pattern to the detriment of the matriarchal. This has been one of the major drawbacks of traditional psychology, of constructivist teaching, and of classical anthropology. From the standpoint of producing abstraction, the patriarchal archetype and the polarized position are superior to the matriarchal archetype and its insular position. But from the standpoint of the symbolic productivity to form the identity of the ego and other, the opposite is true. The insular matriarchal archetype is by far superior to the patriarchal in identity formation because the symbiosis, intimacy, and imitative structuring functions are much more intense in the insular matriarchal position. What strongly corroborates this assertion is the fact that practically all primordial identity formation of the ego-other polarity, which lays the foundation of personality, occurs in the insular position expressing the symbolic elaboration coordinated by the matriarchal archetype. We do not identify with our parents and all our primary relationships through what they say (conceptual intelligence) but in how we experience and identify with who they are (sensory-motor intelligence).

Understanding this pejorative treatment of the matriarchal by the patriarchal pattern in its historical dominance over more than ten thousand years is an important step toward freeing the matriarchal archetype to be considered one of the four ruling archetypes around the central archetype. In the core of the soul, freedom is the sister of truth. The essence of full symbolic elaboration includes freedom, and there is no freedom without equal rights for truthful and compassionate expression by all archetypes including all their differences.

The sensory-motor literality of the symbol experienced in the matriarchal pattern greatly limits its abstraction and, consequently, the formation of logical chains that gather together the structuring functions and complexes into the structuring systems of logical abstract intelligence. It is one thing to say that a carrot is edible and to teach a recipe for making a delicious *soufflé* with it. It is quite another to locate it in its botanical family, relating it to other species, genera, and families. But the essential thing is that the lower degree of abstraction does not coincide with a lesser effect of the structuring symbol on the shaping of the identity of the ego and the other. Often the opposite can happen: we grow tired of knowing a subject abstractly, and then suddenly the impact of its literality on a given experience transforms and deepens our understanding of it. I have a friend who has many degrees in economy and theories about the need for total implementation of the market economy in Brazil. Then, on a hiking trip, he got lost and spent a few days in the forest without food or proper equipment. Sleeping very badly at night, bitten by mosquitoes and ants, and without any medical assistance, he returned to civilization exhausted, sick, and undernourished. Later, he told me that up until that day he had been familiar with the economy of affluent societies and the laws of the market, but that he had come face to face with the economy of survival and marginality. He felt that now he knew far better the socio-economic reality of a great part of the Brazilian people.

The literality of the symbol may contain a powerful structuring symbolic charge. The proximity of the ego with the other, including the teacher-student polarity, confers to the insular matriarchal pattern the supreme position in the pedagogy of imitation. This pedagogy is not the cynical "do as I say, but not as I do", but rather the more authentic and much more efficacious "do as I do" and also "do as I say, experiencing it as I do."

Imitative pedagogy has been neglected along with the matriarchal pattern and attributed to somewhat unintelligent people because its dominant component is sensory-perception and its degree of abstraction is small. The symbolic efficacy of the matriarchal pattern is not recognized and duly praised, and thus its structuring function of imitation has been bundled together with the simplest of the predominant patriarchal teaching methods, namely, rote learning, knowing by heart, repeating automatically to learn without living.

Imitative pedagogy is characteristic of childhood because of the difficulty of abstracting. The ego has an intimate symbiotic relation with parents and siblings, which creates an opening of the child to intensely apprehend the world and experiences. The Gospels refer to this capacity of children in Jesus' words:

> At the same time came the disciples unto Jesus, saying, Who is the greatest in the kingdom of heaven? And Jesus called a little child unto him and set him in the midst of them, And

said, verily I say unto you, Except ye be converted, and become
as little children, ye shall not enter into the kingdom of
heaven. (Matthew 18:1–3)

Any adult who tries to explain things not in the polarized position but instead entering an insular relation of imitative apprenticeship will see that learning speed will increase considerably. Many methods of teaching languages already incorporate these features of learning through intimacy, spontaneity, and imitation.

It is a great indiscrimination to place imitative pedagogy alongside non-experienced, patriarchal, stereotyped repetitiveness. A conscious initiation into the matriarchal, imitative pedagogic method is necessary to realize how it is at one and the same time imitative, spontaneous, and lively. This is its secret and its efficacy. The point is that the structuring function of imitation must not be subordinated here to some abstract, patriarchal finality that is pre-formulated, but rather to the overall performance of being. What surrounds and permeates this method of learning is the ego being intimately related to the other in the insular position, even more than the content of teaching.

A German family came to live in São Paulo. They were relatives of a Brazilian family. Each family had a twelve-year-old boy. The Brazilian boy had taken German lessons for four years but his progress was mediocre. They lived together for six months until the German family found a home. Both families were surprised at how quickly the German boy learned Portuguese, and even more so when the Brazilian boy began to speak German fluently.

I have a friend, a young engineer, who wanted to learn to dance, in particular, "those modern dances, to be able to court the women better." He joined a dance studio, in São Paulo, where the teacher was highly qualified, had a wide repertoire of dances, and could explain all the steps better than anyone else. The teacher had a master's and a Ph.D. in dancing. His method consisted of describing the steps without music and having his pupils repeat them until they were memorized. Then he would put on the music and tell them to dance. It is obvious that this teacher was using the patriarchal pattern for a rational, repetitive, abstract method of learning through conceptual intelligence, rather than a dance method having the spontaneous sensory-motor intelligence of the insular matriarchal position. Many pupils danced, others thought they were dancing but it was more like marching. And what became of my friend?

He did not lack intelligence. At once he understood the steps and began to repeat them, and soon he felt like an expert. When the music was put on, he realized to his embarrassment that he could not manage to adapt the steps to the rhythm of the music. He felt two forces in his body—the head giving orders and the body wanting to do something else. Two classes later, he began to feel back pains. He slept poorly. He visited an orthopedist and was told he had "twisted something" and that it would soon go away. He lost two weeks of classes. The pains went away. When he returned to his dancing classes, the pain came back, this time also affecting the ankle. He had to stop the course. The worst thing is that now, when he danced at parties, he felt he was dancing worse than before. He gave up trying to improve and went on courting the women as best he knew.

Years later, he started seeing a girl who attended a dance school. She thought the teacher was wonderful. What was the teacher like? She could not say. She only knew was that she was a *mulattress* who had come from Bahia. São Paulo, which is in the southeast of Brazil, has many people of European descent in its population, while Bahia is a northeastern Brazilian state with a very high Negro population and famous for its food, popular music, singing, dancing, and religiousness. My friend decided to try again. When he got there, he found a different method. "A real mess, a lot of noisy *Axé* music", he told me. *Axé* is the Yoruba word for energy; the Yoruba language came from Africa and has enriched Portuguese with many words. The first day was a cha-cha-cha class. He did not know the dance. The teacher turned on the music, told the couples to start dancing, and instructed him as follows: "You don't dance with anyone. Just loosen up and move among the others with the rhythm and keep your eyes on me." "But how many steps do I move there and back?" he wanted to know, remembering his old classes. "Don't you worry about that, just look at me and let your body swing to the rhythm as if the music were the sea and you were floating on top of the waves of sound. The rest will come later." And so it was that my friend began to love dancing again. To this day he does not really know if he is actually dancing the cha-cha-cha, but he loves it, and his girlfriend, too.

What happened is that he already had rhythm and dancing in his body through imitative, spontaneous, and natural learning. However, by submitting it to the rational, abstract, patriarchal method, he lost his natural coordination and with it the essence of rhythm and dancing with the entire body.

Such cases of fast learning through imitation and creative spontaneity are common, but educators did not have a theoretical archetypal framework and method to explain the difference between spontaneous, imitative teaching and the traditional abstract theoretical model. Jungian symbolic education applies the model of the natural development of the personality to learning. In this sense, the facilities and difficulties in shaping the identity of the ego and the other in developmental psychology constitute precious knowledge for teaching methods.

It is a current observation that children identify with their parents' characteristics, independent of gender, both in creative and defensive structures. Children learn to imitate the strategies parents use to elaborate their symbols, whether they are normal or pathological. To understand many of the child's normal or defensive procedures, it is not enough to know the child's history. It is important to understand how the child experienced the parents' reactions symbolically. Identification is often more influenced by the parents' reaction to events than by the events themselves, that is, identification takes place more through the attributes of symbols than through their obvious, literal meanings.

I have seen children of parents who lost everything be little affected by this because their parents were able to absorb the losses and get on with life. I have also seen children of parents who lost everything for whom this became the catastrophic mark of their lives; the parents were so distressed that they never emotionally overcame the event. An aggravating factor exists when one parent expresses his or her inability to elaborate the trauma by blaming and attacking the other. In other words, identification happens more with the reaction toward the symbolic meaning of the event than with its literal aspect. It is common for a pupil to like a subject not so much for its content but for the enthusiasm and affection that the teacher lends to it.

The influence of reactions of the personality on the shaping of identity, which is more powerful than that of the events themselves, is explained by the fact that one of the major, if not *the* major, structuring function of the central archetype is the function of elaborating structuring symbols. In fact, the human personality and human culture are great factories of symbolic elaboration. That is why what matters most for our development is not just the knowledge of things in and of themselves but what they mean to the life process and what we do with them in school and in life.

We may say, then, that the more independent parts of the personality which are not accommodated are always seeking a persona to elaborate symbols. When we meet people who give us this opportunity, we tend to imitate them. This characteristic has to be acknowledged in teaching methods and used far more than it is today. This includes how teachers dress and how they physically express themselves all the way to how they feel deep inside themselves toward the subject they teach and the kind of emotions they share with their students during classes.

## The Symbolic Body and the Insular Matriarchal Pattern

For didactic purposes, we may group together the symbolic characteristics of the psyche into several large dimensions, such as, the body, society, nature, idea, image, emotion, word, sound, silence, number, and behavior. The dimension of the body is the most archaic and primary dimension for expressing symbols. This archaism explains why the corporal dimension expresses symbols mainly through sensory-motor intelligence and the insular matriarchal archetype. Following psychoanalysis, medicine has wrongly labeled all corporal expressions of emotions as a conversion syndrome, hysterical conversion, buffers, or the like, as though the body should not naturally express psychic contents and the insular matriarchal position could only express them in dissociative syndromes formerly called hysteria.

This is not the position of Jungian symbolic psychology, for which the body is one of the basic expressive dimensions of symbols that make up the totality of the Self. The symbolic expression of the body is normal, natural, and necessary. Our body posture is in itself a complete language in normal daily life. The mere fact that we are bipedal and have the primary organs for four out of five senses in the head attributes many special characteristics to how we experience the polarities of above and below, front and back. The position of the eyes and nose on the front of the head also significantly marks the polarity of front and back, conscious and unconscious. The fact that most of us are right handed influences significantly the symbolism of right and left. Language symbolism and the overall functioning of consciousness, for instance, as regarding inside and outside and all bodily functions are also inseparably intertwined. We have headaches, we blush or turn pale, become nauseated, and even vomit to express emotions. We have diarrhea and urinate from fear; the back is sore when we are stressed with excessive emotional loads, and the language of our heart needs an encyclopedia to express all its meanings (Ramos 1990). This is all perfectly normal, and all of us have experienced this numerous times along with reactions of anxiety, since childhood, for instance, in that frightening first day at school. Defensive corporal expression is abnormal and occurs when symbolic creative expression is dissociated, fixated, and denied. Otherwise it is normal. This undue pathologization of the body comes from the historical subject-object dissociation described earlier. In the Western medical tradition, emotions have been reduced to the subjective and physical characteristics to the objective, creating the mind-body split. The defensively isolated body could no longer have emotions in normal circumstances, but only in a pathological context. This medical attitude that refuses to accept the expression of the symbolic body is unfortunately still very common nowadays, and it induces channeling of corporal symbolic expression into pathological syndromes and exaggerated medication. Any emotion expressed by the body is immediately labeled pathological. So many people rush to the doctor with their symbolic corporal expression already labeled as some clinical symptom. If the doctor is not prepared to "listen to" this as an expression on the normal, emotional, and symbolic level, corporal manifestations are medicated and thereby transformed into symptoms. In these cases, the language of the symbolic body is not understood; it is pathologized and treated as a disease. The pathological expressiveness of the symbolic body is erroneously labeled psychosomatic medicine because it situates the symbolic body out of the psychic dimension.

The expressiveness of the normal symbolic body should be taught in all schools, starting by medical schools. Knowing that the body's emotional manifestations are so important, rather than being left exclusively to doctors, their teaching should be part of basic education. The prejudice against associating body anatomy and functions, including the neurosciences, to normal symbolic reactions has prevented relating important contents of geography, science, the arts, physics, and chemistry to the normal functioning of the human body. Of course, the mind differs from the body in its capacity for abstract representation, which is the root of imagination and metaphor, but together they form the mind-body psychological polarity, one of the main symbolic expressions of being and of psiche as duality in unity (Byington 1965).

The body is host to symbolic reactions that range from the most archaic and undifferentiated to the most differentiated. Our feces and urine are part of the ecosystem, just like the oxygen we breathe in and the carbon dioxide we breathe out. Separation from the atmosphere for more than four minutes, without inhaling oxygen, can damage our brain. Without exhaling carbon dioxide, our respiratory center becomes paralyzed. Oxygen, carbon, nitrogen, and hydrogen keep us absolutely dependent on and inseparable from nature. Our separation from the milieu, on this level, spells death. At the same time, without the differentiation of the mind-body and mind-nature polarities (Whitehead 1929), we could never have discovered microbes and atoms, managed to contemplate the stars, or experience the ecstasy of a sunset. One of the great examples of the association of polarities of body and mind to propitiate psychological development is yoga, where positions and body functions are practiced together with meditation to enlarge the capacities of consciousness. Within the numerous branches of yoga where different aspects of the mind-body polarity are practiced, there exists *hatha*-yoga, where special body positions or asanas are associated with different mental states; *pranayama* yoga, coordinated by breathing, which is specially important in states of anxiety and stress; and *kundalini* yoga, which expresses countless meanings of bodily functions grouped around the seven chakras (energetic symbolic centers) along the spinal cord (Eliade 1954; Avalon 1918).

These extremes of nondifferentiation and differentiation that the body expresses can influence education in two quite different and fundamentally important ways. One has to do with the expressive techniques that activate the archetypal roots of symbols to build symbolic teaching. The symbolic corporal positions, such as the *asanas* of *hatha* yoga, the lotus position in meditation, dramatization, and dance, are examples of these techniques. The other way is the very rich source of examples of biological, physical-chemical, and symbolic expression of body phenomena that can illustrate learning with human corporal reality. A great deal of what physics, chemistry, and biology teach about the world and life can and should be experienced and exemplified corporally by students from primary school onward. The denial of subjectivity in rational teaching has contributed a great deal to the exclusion of the functioning of our bodies as an instrument for teaching. One teacher argued with me that someone who teaches languages or history would then have to study medicine. With that comment, she illustrated the problem well. Having a Ph.D. in geography, she feels that only medical doctors have to know how her body works. This is so because her teaching did not include her pupils' bodies or her own in the experiences and analogies with the content of teaching. She thinks the Gaia theory (Lovelock 1979) with its broad analogy between the human body and our planet does not include her students or herself. Compartmentalized teaching has reached extremes of alienation. In this case, the teacher had just given a test on the Andes and the Inca civilization, on the mountains of Asia, and on the habitat of the Eskimos in Alaska, and she believed this had nothing to do with the functioning of the body. Yet if she related altitude with the production of red cells by the bone marrow and the regulation of body temperature with resistance to cold, she would have made learning much more integrated and unforgettable. She could have shown the National Geographic Society video about the ambition to conquer the Everest, which would show the mountains of Asia along with features of the human body. Mountain climbers died in avalanches, others lost toes through frostbite. Beside them, we see members of the Sherpa tribe managing to haul heavy equipment because their bodies produce more red cells to compensate for the lack of oxygen at great heights. History, geography, medicine, psychology, anthropology, biology, physics, chemistry, and botany: integrated multidisciplinary teaching through body experience, which could be further improved by an exercise in pulmonary hyperventilation to experience the increase of apnea through the diminution of carbon dioxide in the blood, and so on.

If students stand up and do a few minutes of exercise in between classes, it is good for the blood circulation, for relaxation from mental concentration, and also to develop body consciousness during schoolwork. Whenever possible, teachers should relate teaching to the functions of the body because the development of body consciousness will then accompany the ethical construction of self-esteem. This lays the foundations for understanding the necessity of sleep, correct eating, with as little as possible salt, sugar, and fried food, and exercise, as well as encouraging students to avoid smoking and alcohol not as dogmatic prohibitions but simply to protect the body from intoxication. The best way to teach such ethical procedures is not with sermons on behavior, but rather with fundamental knowledge of body functions. In such a way, the symbolic body also becomes the guardian of ethics along with the mind.

Given the intense closeness of the ego-other relation that characterizes it, the insular matriarchal position is expressed a great deal through image and personal relationships with which we are familiar. In societies of great matriarchal exuberance like we have in Latin American countries, we know the importance of personal recommendations or requests made *viva voce* or "being physically present" to obtain something. So, too, teaching exemplified with our own bodies is very important to humanize the content of learning and make it a part of our sensations. Similarly, it is very important to illustrate teaching by means of animals and fruit trees at school. If there is only one fruit tree and a single cat, turtle, bird, or dog, that will suffice, especially if they are animated with names and personal histories, which accompany the whole course. Studying the history of the earth's crust and the ecosystem associated to the roots of the avocado tree and the functioning of the organism of Rex the dog, Princess the cat, or Speedy the turtle, with whom the pupils share their childhood, can have a learning effect for the rest of their lives precisely because of that personalized intimacy of sensory-motor intelligence and right brain hemisphere symbolism that makes human experiences unforgettable.

Because it can express symbolic meanings in a very archaic form, the body can operate with the ego and other polarities in stages of very little differentiation. When we are angry, we can unwittingly express our aggression by bumping our leg against a piece of furniture or slamming the door on our hand. Pain from chronic marriage suffering has been related to breast and womb cancer. The body is at one and the same time ego and other in this aggression. In extreme situations, some people can feel deep hatred and commit suicide to hurt another person.

We should not disdain this archaism of our body and reduce its expressiveness and that of the sensory-motor intelligence exclusively to primitivism, ignorance, and unconscious participation mystique because it is exactly due to this archaism that the body and sensory-motor intelligence are capable of grasping phenomena from afar and experiencing them deeply. I had an acquaintance that ate some seaweed in an Oriental restaurant and almost died of intoxication. Years later, having completely forgotten the episode, he wanted to go back to a similar restaurant but felt a strong nausea at the door and could not enter the place. His more rational ego had forgiven the seaweed, yet his bodily irrational ego had not. The memory of the threat he had undergone was still alive and decisive within his vegetative system. Many of the most important reactions that we show are rooted in and explained by this emotional bodily dimension.

Long before a volcano erupts, seismographers register its vibrations in the depths of the earth. Human volcanic eruptions express love, religious ecstasy, political revolution, intellectual creation, sickness, and death. Our seismographers are our dreams or the physical manifestations of anxiety, discomfort, depression, and malaise that reveal the functioning of these deep reactions. Profound sensitivity, intelligence, integrity, and creativity often emerge undifferentiated through the archaic dimension of the body. Instead of repressing or ignoring it, wisdom consists of listening to it, perceiving it, living with it, elaborating and teaching it symbolically. Traditional teaching tends to do the opposite. Due to the objective-subjective dissociation equated with rational-irrational, mind-body, and mind-nature dissociations, the teaching methods that come from our European tradition cultivated mostly the rational (conceptual intelligence) and banished the irrational and, along with it, sensory-motor intelligence and the body. In the nervous system, traditional education restricted the pedagogical method only to the cognitive centers of the brain and excluded from the classroom the rest of the brain and the nervous system.

To cope with the body in these zones and functions that express undifferentiated psychic life, one has to perceive it beyond its literal appearance. It is indispensable to know the symbolic body and its meanings. It is necessary to learn that for some people certain matters are a headache. Others cannot manage to digest certain sticky situations. Some mull over their problems until they develop ulcers or erode their teeth. Others stiffen with rheumatism. The symbolic body is a body whose anatomy and physiology have many metaphorical meanings, which can be worked out in many ways. One of the most repressive is to sit it down in a chair and not allow it to take part in teaching. I knew of a student who used to throw paper balls on the floor to have the excuse to leave his chair to pick them up and move around a little. Many pupils labeled as cases of attention-deficit hyperactivity disorder, depression, or inability to learn because of bad behavior or lack of interest are actually pupils with great corporal vitality who do not manage to fit into the teaching method that dissociates mind from body and imprisons the body in chairs during long periods in the classroom. To execute symbolic teaching, the chairs in the classroom must be movable, so that at any moment during the class or between classes they can be pushed aside to open up space for corporal expressiveness.

The body's symbolic dimension lends itself fantastically to the interaction of the conscious-unconscious, rational-irrational polarities in symbolic education because of the existence of the two parts conjugated in the nervous system: on one hand, the motivational cerebral-spinal nervous system that controls movements and senses, and can be subject to consciousness and will; on the other hand, the vegetative nervous system, which is affected little by will and operates dominantly, involuntarily, unconsciously, and even during sleep and coma.

It so happens that these two seemingly separate parts of the body are integrated by the nervous and glandular system into a common whole that is expressed and affected symbolically. When teaching is subordinated to sensory-motor intelligence rather than exclusively to conceptual intelligence, the vegetative nervous system will contribute to enhance emotional memory together with the motivational nervous system, which dominantly fosters rational memory.

We have registered this polarity even in the cerebral cortex. We now know that there is a tendency toward greater rationality on the left side of the brain, which is more verbal, logical, and analytical compared with the right side, which tends to be more imaginal, intuitive, gestalt-analogical, and musical. We must not forget, however, that in a minority of people these centers can be anatomically inverted. Teaching already makes use of these differences but it has to accompany the development of neuropsychological research to make use of its discoveries in school. As new discoveries are now being made very frequently, it is important for teachers to be continually informed about them. For Jungian symbolic education, music is indispensable in the classroom, as are materials for drawing, painting, and sculpture, so that pupils can experience learning equally by words and through sound and image. The performance of popular or classical music and the expressiveness of singing and dancing can make teaching any subject more pleasant and interesting.

My dear friend Cecília Conde is a well-known teacher in Rio de Janeiro who was entrusted to study the learning difficulties of children who live in Mangueira, a very poor area of Rio famous for its brilliant performances in Carnival Samba schools. The majority of children could not learn to read or write and had a great resistance to attending school.

There were many explanations for the children's learning difficulties, ranging from brain damage due to lack of protein in their diet to moral dysfunction acquired from the high criminality present in their family life.

Cecília began to talk to the few who came to school, trying to discover how they lived, what they ate, and what they liked to do. No doubt they lived among criminals, many of them drug addicts who seduced children to deliver drugs. Most of them had an insufficient and inadequate diet. Boys loved to play and watch soccer. Girls preferred TV serials, but what both of them loved the most was to dance in rehearsals preparing for the great carnival parade and competition with other carnival schools the following year.

Each carnival school creates a song every year which everyone learns at rehearsals, while the children also practice drumming, singing, and dancing.

Cecília had an intuition and asked the few who came to school to tell their classmates that from then on classes would teach writing and learning their "song of the year." The next day, the class was full. Chairs were moved to a corner and drumming, singing, and dancing began. Meanwhile, Cecília went to the blackboard and wrote down the sentences of the song. After half an hour she asked the children to bring back the chairs, sit down, and start learning to read and write. They all did it with much interest. After an hour, she asked them to move the chairs again and to dance and sing while watching the words on the blackboard. Homework was to write down whatever words they remembered and ask their parents to help them. When the semester ended, just about everyone in the class was well underway to learning how to read and write.

Let us now take the structuring function of breathing, which is the central function of *pranayama* yoga. On the one hand, it is subject to will, that is, to the motivational system. We breathe when we want to and can even hold our breath up to a point. On the other hand, it functions viscerally and automatically even during sleep or coma (vegetative nervous system). This duality opens up a channel, a language, or a technique to deal with and elaborate different experiences. Through breathing (*pranayama*, the breathing path, the way of *prana*), we can elaborate any structuring function, from affection, anger, envy, or anxiety. Breathing exercises in the classroom thus become a great pedagogical source to teach the functioning of the volitive nervous system, subject to the will, and the characteristics of the visceral dimension subject to the autonomic nervous system to control emotions.

The polarity which I just named—that is, the motivation rational nervous system and the visceral, automatic, or vegetative nervous system—is very broad and oversimplified. To the reader who wants to go deeper into this subject, I recommend Goleman, *Emotional Intelligence* (1995), and Solm and Turnbull, *The Brain and the Inner World* (2002).

How can India's geography and history be studied without experiencing the characteristics of breathing, meditation, and body positions in the science of yoga? A sleepy, bored class can always wake up by using the corporal expressive techniques of meditation, breathing, singing, and dancing. Using meditation and breathing along with the material taught can calm a very moved and anxious class, and at the same time help to focus attention and imagination on the subject being taught.

The educator able to open up to the experience of the symbolic body will see that pedagogic transference is a continuation of family transference, even of structuring functions and body symbols. Education is enriched when one knows that primary experiences with feeding, caring, and loving were in fact the first classes in life. What was learned in family transference, on the level of the symbolic body, will become part of pedagogic transference on the corporal, emotional, and ideation levels. A teacher's words are food to be digested and are archetypally linked to reactions that involve feeding, caring, and loving offered to the child and the adult during the life process. The insular position of the matriarchal pattern is present throughout life and the symbolic body is a permanent creative structuring function. This broad archetypal perspective is what enables Jungian symbolic education to unlock and use the teaching methods in all symbolic dimensions.

## The Importance of the Hands in Symbolic Learning

The increase of abstract polarized patriarchal conceptual intelligence after the second year of life is proportional to the development of the symbolic capacity of the ego and to the increase of representations employed by the brain. This process propitiates the differentiation of the mind-body, mind-nature and ego-other polarities progressively. As the mind grows with the maturing of the nervous system, the ego separates more and more from the other. As human nature develops, consciousness continues to separate from other animals and also from our instincts. This is the great virtue of our species and at the same time its major dilemma, because when the mind is distant from the instincts and consequently the ego from the other, the ego tends to look down on other people, the body, and nature, which is the way to inflation and omnipotence.

In this respect, culture seeks to compensate for this separation by cultivating the consideration of the ego for the other in various symbolic dimensions, such as religious animism, to maintain ego-other relationship with nature, and yoga, to maintain it with the body. The opposition of the thumb, present in the primates, equips the hands with an extraordinary complexity of movement. The interaction between cortex and hands is remarkably important in civilization. Manual work introduces the imagination to the world and the most abstract thinking possible through the body. The absence of the hands in learning, except for the teacher writing on the blackboard and the pupils taking notes, is one of the mutilations of traditional teaching. This lack of "the hand on the plough" is perhaps the most cogent illustration of the absence of experience in our traditional teaching methods. This deformity symbolically accompanies the dissociation between mind and body, the subjective and the objective, and teaching and work. That high school should exist separately from the forces of production is in itself a dissociation. That this should occur with university teaching is an aberration. Learning ought never to be exercised separately from doing, at the risk of becoming dissociated in the individual and cultural Self. Doing with the hands in learning has to be symbolically related to the application of teaching at home and at the sources of production, from the first day in school. Instead of children making drawings of little houses and people to hang on walls, why not work on mechanics, dressmaking, cooking, ceramics, and first aid from the very beginning?

In this sense, homework that repeats what was said in class does not take into account the fact that students at home have available to them other conditions of time, space, equipment, and social situations to express what they have learned. Should there be a need to do any work at home, the teacher has to reject the idea of boring, repetitive "homework" and imagine some intelligent and creative activity outside school to illustrate the meaning and utility of what is being taught, whenever possible through handwork. During any learning outside school, it is very important that students should feel creative doing something pleasant and interesting instead of feeling they have to take care of an obligation. If students have homework during which they apply productively what they have learned so as to impress their parents and neighbors, they will come back to school full of enthusiasm the next day. The permanence of learning through doing is a central theme of Jungian symbolic education and a positive conditioning reinforcement of great value not only in acquiring and retaining knowledge but also in building self-esteem.

The proximity and constant interaction between rational-irrational, differentiated-undifferentiated, sensory-motor-vegetative that goes on in the body is used abundantly by the matriarchal pattern in symbolic elaboration. Ever since the formation of consciousness, the orientation of space and time, the organization of data gathered by the senses, the alimentary experiences of hunger and satiation, company, loneliness, and care are all coordinated by the insular matriarchal pattern and expressed through the body. To disregard the insular matriarchal pattern in teaching is to enter the illusion that the base is formed and that we have no further need to work with undifferentiated parts to develop and teach the differentiated parts. A great deal of what this book sets out to show is that this notion is wrong. Just as any neuron needs water in order to function, so conceptual intelligence is nourished by and permanently interacts with the primary sensual concreteness of things. The sensory-motor intelligence is often more sound and existentially more accurate than abstract intelligence.

Imitative learning, which is characteristic of the insular matriarchal pattern, uses these body functions to a great degree, for they are rooted in the everyday life which the symbolic body permanently inhabits and in which it expresses itself. Speech, look, gesture, postures, and expressions are functions of the imitative pedagogic transference that the matriarchal pattern cannot do without.

## Teaching through Videogames:
## The Crowning of Symbolic Constructivism

The computerized videogames that fascinate children today are a good example of the hand-brain, mind-body, and mind-nature relationship, which is so useful for learning, because they associate the sensory-motor intelligence with abstract intelligence. It is a pity that the subjects of these games are, as yet, still mostly restricted to friend-enemy fighting and romantic adventures, like treasure hunting. If all subjects of teaching were expressed through videogames as an expressive technique, I have no doubt that learning would profit from this method incredibly. In this sense, all the objective world could be animated: alchemy would be resurrected, the subjective-objective split would be cured, the symbolic dimension would be crowned in education, and all this would be accomplished within the hand-brain polarity and the creative interaction of the insular matriarchal and sensory-motor intelligence associated with the polarized patriarchal and the conceptual intelligence.

## Feeling and Intuition in the Insular Matriarchal Pattern

The absence of conscious articulated polarities in the insular matriarchal position prevents the abstraction and formation of characteristic systems of patriarchal *a priori* planning. Matriarchal conscious organization is expressed as islands of experience that relate to one another mostly unconsciously by the necessities of life rather than by the abstract logic of their meanings. This type of archetypal coordination of symbolic elaboration provides great freedom for the preservation of diversity, liveliness, playing, and spontaneity. There is no assignment of the body functions, with their rights, duties, and hierarchical needs and performances to a specific plan. This does not prevent us from looking for food when we are hungry or rising from table at a certain moment to go to the toilet or feeling sleepy and turning off the television in the middle of a good film to go to bed. The point is that each one of these functions operates on a matriarchal island whose ensemble is coordinated by the necessities of the organism integrated into the ecosystem. If in mother's heart there is always room for another child, so in the psychic field of the matriarchal pattern there is always room for another structuring function, which expresses the senses. Among others, we may distinguish feeling, intuition, affection, coziness, the five senses, and also the sixth sense, the playful spirit, imagination, and pleasure, all especially important for symbolic education.

I have described the matriarchal/patriarchal typology in the individual and in culture and have drawn attention to the importance of the predominance of one or another pattern in the functioning of consciousness and in forming the shadow through fixation and defensive structures.

As I have formulated in an archetypal theory of history (Byington 1982a, 1983, 2008), the Christian myth was the great structuring function of the implantation of the alterity archetype in Western culture. It corresponds to the Buddha myth in the East, to Tao in China, Zen in Japan, Sufism in Islam, and the Exu myth in the Yoruba culture. Due to the predominance of the patriarchal model in Jewish and Roman cultures, the Christian myth suffered a defensive patriarchalization and deformation actively expressed for centuries by the repressive virulence of the Inquisition, which dissociated the good and evil polarity of the cultural Self as expressed by the Christ-Devil dichotomy.

When science took over teaching in the universities in the eighteenth century, it equated the experimental method and its search for truth with the objective dimension and dissociated it from the subjective dimension equated with faith, dogmatism, superstition, magic, and error.

This pathological split in Western culture, subordinated to the defensive patriarchal pattern, gave birth to positivism and materialism in the nineteenth century. The experimental method favored extraversion, thinking, and sensation, while the repressed subjective dimension included introversion, feeling, and intuition, together with an intense defensive restriction of the insular matriarchal archetype.

Unfortunately, when we refer to the extraversion of Western culture and compare it to the introversion of Eastern cultures, or when we praise the scientific development of industrialized societies and compare it to a supposed underdevelopment of tribal societies, we frequently forget to take into account that within the extraordinary creativity of the natural sciences occurred a fixation that formed a huge pathological subjective-objective split. This dissociation gave rise to and maintains the gigantic shadow of Western culture and its scientific humanism.

The structuring function of feeling regulates the affectionate relationship between the ego and the other. Abstraction distances the ego from the other in the patriarchal pattern, which fosters the exercise of the thinking function. The closeness of the ego and the other in the matriarchal pattern permits an intimacy that privileges the feeling function and permeates relationships with Eros. The absence of *a priori* codifications limits deductive reasoning and favors intuition, which leads us to experience things with affection and sensuality that are great sources of pleasure.

The patriarchal pattern abstracts conduct and rationally determines behavior "from the top down" in the form of orders and tasks that become challenges. Success will bring satisfaction and feasting, but when it is exaggerated, it establishes feats that must be performed with earnestness, perfectionism, and fear of error. There is little happiness, pleasure, or playfulness during its execution, and often we find the predominance of guilt linked to the principle of perfectionism, repressive, intolerant, and dogmatic power which tends to generate frustration and aggression. The task or challenge is then treated as an enemy, to be fought and conquered. Tasks become battles and life a great struggle. If the task lasts a week, all that time must be spent amid frustration and anxiety for fear of error, failure, or blame. Aggression and competition become closely related. The development of a high degree of technological precision in institutional life has increased human responsibility and promotes the inadmissibility of error. Joy comes only at the end, and only if the result is a satisfactory one. Otherwise we experience defeat, failure, guilt, and depression. One lives in an atmosphere of anxiety, aggression, competition, fear, and guilt, due to the intense cultivated responsibility and success accompanied by the dread of failure. This is a stern-faced, "preoccupied" pattern, which does not mean that the patriarchal pattern cannot also be experienced in a warm, understanding, and loving way when it is associated to the matriarchal pattern. Nevertheless, due to its intense component of demanding, competition, task, and challenge, it commonly tends toward overdemanding, guilt, repression, intolerance, and the rigidity of power. It is the heat of the sun that dries and transforms forests into deserts instead of nourishing them.

As for the matriarchal pattern, due to the lack of obligatory articulated polarities, it tends to form ego-other islands in consciousness, each with its own function. One island exercises anger, another affection, a third one struggles with persons, things, and tasks. Amid the islands flow unconscious psychic currents. Due to the dominance of unconscious characteristics, these islands can express the existential whole, but they cannot be joined by conscious abstraction and coordination. The ego and the other are very intimate and symbiotic, which precludes such abstraction. This separation is not dissociation. Through conscious-unconscious intuition we move constantly from one island to another, guided by desire and the necessities of life. This brings a "thrill", sensuality and spontaneity, even when one repeats what has always been done. These changes of the habitual are a constant source of sensual pleasure. Everything that is done leads us to move from one island to another, and wet our feet in the waters of the unknown and of emotion. There are people who love to wash dishes because they feel they are playing with water. Here the connection between frustration, execution, failure, and success is very quick, intimate and continuous, which prevents the long expectation that makes us tense and drives us to anxious and earnest rigidity within the patriarchal pattern.

Intimacy, affection, play, and pleasure were so identified with the matriarchal pattern and the subjective that patriarchal dominance, which cultivated objectivity, banished them from teaching and from psychology. Due to the intense relationship of the matriarchal to the pleasure principle, psychoanalysis has often gone to the extreme of identifying many expressions of matriarchal pattern with the pleasure principle, primary narcissism, irresponsible, immature, undifferentiated and unconscious childishness, setting these characteristics against the seriousness and responsibility of the patriarchal, pompously and prejudicially identified with the reality principle, as a synonym of adult, ethical life and maturity. Due to the same patriarchal dominance, traditional teaching banned pleasure, sensuality, and nondifferentiation along with the body and the insular matriarchal pattern. Speaking at a meeting for educators on redeeming pleasure, the playful, and affection in teaching, I was asked by one indignant teacher: "But how are the kids going to learn if all they think about is pleasure?" The result of this true massacre of the matriarchal pattern dissociated the school from the club and turned learning into something boring and erotically lifeless, a tedious task to be carried out in order to become someone in life, someone with a degree, a professional who goes into the work market at the cost of loss of pleasure, loss of the joyful spirit and love for learning. Basically oriented exclusively by competition and money, people easily become workaholics enslaved by the power drive. That alone already justifies a good deal of the resistance toward learning with pleasure and love.

However, we should also beware of idealizing the matriarchal pattern. Were its sensuality, joy, and emotion proportionate to its creativity, humanity would not have remained for ninety-nine percent of its history in the Paleolithic stage, when the matriarchal archetype was probably dominant. The proximity of the ego-other relationship presents so much intimacy, affectionateness, superstition, and magic in life that it also bears with it a sensual attachment to habit that can make it extraordinarily reactionary to progress. Absurd forms of conduct and belief learned through imitation are perpetuated and resist change, simply because "that is the way we've always done it". It is very difficult to change a superstition or a deep-rooted cultural custom, as for instance, food habits. Ingrained habits are as difficult to change as the symptoms of matriarchally dominated clinical syndromes, such as drug addiction, alcoholism, character and eating disorders, and neurotic emotional chronic defenses. It is one thing to use the insular matriarchal pattern to convey knowledge and quite another thing to try to change it once it is rooted in popular and individual habits. The same sensual attachment that permits imitative learning makes bad habits that are acquired very difficult to change. All analysts know that defenses of matriarchal dominance are immensely resistant, to the point of requiring ritualistic group support when treated, such as Alcoholics Anonymous, Weight Watchers, and drug addiction group therapies.

We still have to understand the structuring functions of intuition and imagination in their relationship with the matriarchal pattern and symbolic education. In as much as the matriarchal pattern tends to situate the ego-other relation intimately in islands of consciousness, it favors the feeling function and makes abstract thought difficult. The function of sensation is anchored in the senses and feeds attachment to the literality of symbols. And what about intuition? We know that it was banned from science and teaching along with subjectivity and the matriarchal pattern. But why?

Intuition is a structuring function that is especially feared and antagonized along with the matriarchal pattern because, due to its tendency toward omniscience and ubiquity in time and space, it is able to interlink unconsciously, irrationally, and inexplicably the islands of matriarchal consciousness in divination. Intuition can never be rationally deduced. It simply breaks out in consciousness like volcanic islands that appear in the middle of the ocean. Intuition is unpredictable and is therefore felt as irrational by the ego. We know that it expresses some part of the whole, but we do not know why that part was chosen in that way at that moment. Feeling and emotion that unite the ego and the other in intimacy by resisting and relinquishing abstraction stimulate intuition in the form of divination. That is why it became the main function of oracular divination that played and still plays such an important role in many cultures. Its unconscious components are very much stressed and enriched through rituals of possession. The main feature of intuition is to join one thing to another or to the whole, unbeknown to consciousness, as though it were an electric current: a button is pressed, and although nothing is seen, lamps are lit. The great difficulty in rationally dealing with the explanations of intuitives is that they generally explain things backward. They begin Napoleon's story with the description of his death on the Isle of Elba. A friend once remarked that intuitives should never be promoted to commanding generals because, in retreat, they would probably order bridges to be burned before their troops had crossed them. To be used in the patriarchal pattern, intuition is generally subordinated to thought and sensation. This subordination is seen in the use of intuition to choose how to carry out tasks that have been programmed and well-defined beforehand.

One has to remember that the islands of matriarchal consciousness take shape within the process of symbolic elaboration of the Self and so even without conscious memory they are coherently united by the memory of life within the process of being-in-the-world. Intuition is capable of following this path and detecting these mysterious connections. Due to the fact that abstract thought is little favored in the matriarchal pattern, intuition is made possible and even elected, along with feeling, as the function that connects parts to one another and to the whole. Its enormous acceptance and habitual exercise in the matriarchal pattern favor the development of foreknowledge, the sixth sense, which is the conscious and unconscious perception of the relationship of parts among one another and to the whole. This state of clairvoyance favors visions that spontaneously cross the mind. This is the sight of the "third eye" present in esoteric literature. When intuition is banned from consciousness, it appears in the shadow as an expression of menacing "occult forces", superstition, and witchcraft.

However, as already said, feeling, intuition, and the matriarchal pattern were not banned from teaching during the scientific dissociation just because they were associated with the subjective dimension. Their banishment had already been decreed through the centuries, largely by patriarchal dominance in the Judaic and Roman cultures, which greatly influenced institutional Christianity.

In proposing that the subjective and the matriarchal pattern be reclaimed in teaching, with all the wealth that they bring, we cannot fail to realize how they complicate the exercise of the scientific experimental method, precisely because they privilege the feeling and intuition functions, along with attachment to sensuality. The point is that, if, on the one hand, feeling brings us involvement with the pleasure of learning, it also brings resistance to facing the frustrations inherent in the daily routine. And if intuition makes us interested in fantasy and stimulates the minds of children and fascinates them with learning, it likewise makes recognition of the objective difficult by allowing it to be confused with the subjective in the imagination. That is why the patriarchal pattern also has its reasons for antagonizing, repudiating, and repressing the matriarchal, as we shall see further ahead. It is not an accident that one of the chief occupations of the archetype of alterity is to coordinate the symbolic elaboration performed by these two giants, which are so well represented in Murray Stein's book, *Solar Conscience, Lunar Conscience* (1993).

## Ritual and Play in the Insular Matriarchal Pattern

From time immemorial, ritual has been adopted as a structuring function to propitiate the symbolic elaboration of experiences. The expressive techniques that we propose for the purpose of animating objective teaching with subjectivity are actually individual and group rituals to invoke and provide for full participation of being in learning.

Due to the great amount of unconscious energy present in the symbolic elaboration of the insular matriarchal pattern, rituals function as channels to maintain ego-other identity during and after elaboration. Without rituals, the unconscious energy easily dominates the experience and the ego-other polarity may become undiscriminated, automatic, and consciously confused. Therefore rhythms, which accompany corporal movements like dancing and singing, operate ritualistically to keep and develop the symbolic elaboration in certain dimensions.

Rituals can fall flat and become stereotyped and automatic if discriminations already achieved through elaboration are automatically repeated without being able to mobilize the archetypal charge of the structuring symbols that gave rise to them. In the case of the patriarchal pattern, rituals are frequently weakened by the predominance of verbal expressiveness, which easily abstracts the experience of sensuality and leads spiritual and social practices to become automatic and lose their significance and transforming potential. This happens frequently in the ritual of prayer, as King Claudius says in Shakespeare's *Hamlet* (act 3, scene 3): "My words fly up to heaven, my thoughts remain below. Words without thoughts, never to heaven go." On the other hand, in the matriarchal pattern, with its abundance of corporal expressiveness through singing and dancing, the emotional level is maintained with greater ease in the rituals. A good illustration is the present popular revival of the Catholic Mass in Brazil, celebrated by singing priests.

The ritualistic function of play is often used to produce symbolic elaboration in the matriarchal pattern because play is capable of fostering a joyful, pleasurable, and unpredictable component. It is obvious that we can also use the structuring function of play dominantly in the patriarchal pattern, as for example in competitive games where the performance is reduced to dispute and win without significant spontaneous creativity. The importance of using play and joyful elements in teaching in the matriarchal pattern is to maintain a certain level of pleasure that makes learning lively and attractive.

Games have a high structuring power proportional to their capacity for emotional mobilization due to the structuring functions of luck, creativity, and mystery. They are especially useful for animating mathematics, which is one of the most abstract functions of the symbolic dimension. Games express the unforeseeable characteristic of the process of symbolic elaboration that is revealed while happening. Educators often fail to recognize the structuring capacity of play and do not value sports, such as soccer, which has immense collective repercussions in Europe and in Latin countries, with increasing popularity all over the planet, including in the United States. Through an understanding of the patriarchal, alterity, and totality patterns, conjugated with matriarchal pattern, we can comprehend the symbolic richness and cultural importance of games like soccer, which, under the dominance of the dialectic position of the alterity archetype, embrace the four ruling archetypes as structuring functions of the Self (Byington 1982a).

The decreasing amount of ritual in modern societies seduces the young to consume novelties. We already mentioned how this limits education in dealing with omnipotence, frustrations, and character formation. The introduction of expressive techniques such as imagination, music and dance, plastic arts, and acting is a creative way to ritualize regular teaching, but it also can ritualize the different phases that mark students' lives and identity. The beginning and end of each year, especially in high school and college but also in grade school, are very important times to be meaningfully ritualized. The inclusion of the life and death archetypes in these rituals marks what is to be left behind and what lays ahead (Byington 1996) and is thus an important component.

# Chapter 8

# THE POLARIZED PATRIARCHAL PATTERN IN TEACHING

Although we have underscored the importance of the matriarchal pattern in teaching and called attention to the fact that it is undervalued and underutilized largely due to the historical patriarchal predominance in our traditional teaching, we must not make the patriarchal archetype the villain of ruling archetypes. On the contrary, its dominance over the matriarchal pattern just goes to show its power and importance. When the matriarchal pattern was dominant, the earth was peopled initially with nomadic hunting and gathering groups and then with tribes; it was the dominance of the patriarchal archetype that propitiated settling.

The patriarchal pattern became dominant in many cultures as a consequence of the agricultural revolution, which occurred around ten thousand years ago, followed by the first cities, built around the fifth millennium B.C. (Hawkes 1963). It was unquestionably the invention of the wheel, the plough, and storage, soon followed by irrigation, that made it possible for the cultural Self to be expressed through villages and then cities, which allowed for extensive social organization through patriarchal dominance. Up until then, among the hunting-collecting groups, women could participate in harvesting in the fields close to their camps, which enabled them to work side by side with men in feeding the family. The plough and the domestication of horses propitiated agriculture in areas distant from home and village and allowed for the storage of food, which was the basic condition for the hunting-gathering groups to settle (Leakey 1977). The main event that marked this transformation archetypally was the institutionalization of private property at the center of individual families and the organization of society into classes, which evolved to form the state (Engels 1884).

Roaming hunting-gathering groups were detached from possessions, which probably favored the expression of the matriarchal archetype centered on feeding and reproduction. Settling and private property, on the contrary, brought attachment to possessions to the foreground, together with the power principle to organize, legislate, defend, and attack. Cities were formed and walls built around them; social organization and abstract law guaranteed security and inheritance of private property, ensured by patrilineal continuity. Thus began capitalism and the state coordinated dominantly by the polarized position of the patriarchal archetype (Engels 1884). During the last ten thousand years, the patriarchal pattern due to its extraordinary ability to abstract and capacity to organize gradually implanted its dominance. It developed the industrial-technological civilization on the planet and subjugated most other species and a great deal of nature, along with almost all the cultures of matriarchal dominance. The relation of the matriarchal and patriarchal patterns in each culture and in the individual personality is quite variable nowadays. There are cultures, especially in the developing countries, in which the matriarchal pattern is very lively and in many respects predominates.

Due to its capacity for organization, the patriarchal archetype is expressed in consciousness through the ego-other and other-other polarities which include all polarities besides the ego-other. These polarities are organized dominantly by the power principle in such a way that one pole is privileged above the other, as for instance nice over nasty, clean over dirty, beautiful over ugly, brave over cowardly, virtuous over sinful, and pride over shame. This psychological organization of consciousness structures a persona, which is very productive for organized reality, but which is also very unilateral. This pattern does not enhance the equal elaboration of polarities and thus favors fixations of the nonelaborated poles, forming defenses and shadow. This fact makes the patriarchal archetype the most powerful source of shadow formation during individual and collective development. Such fixations have been so destructive that they threaten the survival of our species, such as, for instance, arms for mass destruction, economic exploration, the depletion of reserves, the devastating imbalance of the ecosystem, and pollution. This is why, especially in the second half of the last century, since World War II, one sees distrust and discrediting of the patriarchal pattern throughout the planet. We have seen an increase in movements with matriarchal dominance, such as, the Woodstock Festival, in 1969. However, the great archetypal paradigm announced for the third millennium, which is developing in intensity, is the pattern of alterity, which conjugates dialectically and democratically the matriarchal and patriarchal patterns and proposes production sustentability.

The patriarchal pattern is expressed by the principles of power, duty, organization, codification of law and order, cultivating tradition, honor, responsibility, justice, stressing perfectionism, guilt, and punishment, that is, the organization of symbolic elaboration through abstraction and codified behavior established beforehand. Because of these characteristics of the archetype, its polarized pattern of ego-other relationship in consciousness presents itself in an asymmetrical, elitist, authoritarian, imposing, and dominating manner. Both the ego and the other, be they person or thing, are under subjection, obedience, and inferiority or in command, privilege, and superiority. To understand the activity of the patriarchal pattern in teaching, I shall begin with a brief analysis of Adam and Eve's departure from paradise in the Genesis of the Old Testament, which describes a myth of learning predominantly within the patriarchal pattern.

Myths generally explain reality through the imagination based on the insular matriarchal pattern. Everything is expressed fantastically through animation of facts and relationships, which include objective reality subordinated to subjective hypothesis guided by the imagination. Some myths are dominantly expressed in the polarized position of the patriarchal archetype, without losing the main matriarchal characteristics of fantastic imagination to animate reality. This is the case of the myth of Genesis.

The myth of Genesis relates the development of consciousness inseparably from the acquisition of learning through the creative structuring function of envy, which is here defensively stigmatized as destructive (Byington 2002a). The function of myths is to express, through fiction that includes supernatural forces, the symbolic elaboration of experiences with a great power to transform individual and collective consciousness. Myths are the dreams of cultures. Myths of creation like the Genesis story are true landmarks of civilization for the prospective structuring of collective consciousness.

The episode of the expulsion from paradise in the book of Genesis shows us a great differentiation of consciousness. The myth expresses an immense cultural transformation of collective consciousness in which human beings begin to elaborate, under the dominance of the polarized position of the patriarchal archetype, important psychic functions that until then had been lived under the sensuous elaboration of the insular dominance of the matriarchal archetype. The passage from one state of consciousness to another is clearly characterized by an experience of discovery and apprenticeship.

However, the story, which is largely repressive, that is, in the defensive patriarchal pattern, adds specific connotations of transgression, punishment, and guilt to envy and creativity, characteristics that certainly marked and influenced Judaism and the doctrine of original sin in Christian theology.

The tone of patriarchal repression and prohibition that pervades the event and considers envy so destructive is evident in that the transformation of consciousness is referred to as "the fall of man", an expression used to denote punishment for acquiring greater consciousness to operate the ethical condition in the polarized position. This immense change of consciousness through transgression was experienced as a crime and punished by expulsion from paradise. The patriarchal pattern cultivates tradition and the elitist power of one pole over another in all polarities in order to preserve the organization achieved in the past. That is why the acquisition of knowledge, which diminishes the God-human (central archetype–ego) asymmetry, is defensively forbidden and its achievement considered a crime to be severely punished. A matriarchal or alterity reading of this episode might call it "the great discovery of Eve and Adam through the creative structuring function of envy" or "the marvelous change of humanity".

So much for the title; now let us see to the text.

> Now the serpent was more astute than any beast that the Lord God had made. And he said unto the woman, Yea, hath God said, Ye shall not eat of any tree of the garden? And the woman said unto the serpent, Ye may eat of the fruit of the trees of the garden: But of the fruit of the tree which is in the midst of the garden, God hath said, Ye shall not eat of it, neither shall ye touch it lest ye die. And the serpent said unto the woman, Ye shall not surely die: For God doth know that in the day ye eat thereof, then your eyes shall be opened, and ye shall be as gods, knowing good and evil. (Genesis 3:1–5)

Temptation, covetousness, and envy are natural structuring functions in the development of personality and knowledge. Jungian symbolic education includes within its practice all these functions of great subjective mobilization to vitalize knowledge. If the educator can apply expressive techniques that make the day's material the target of temptation, covetousness, and envy, so much the better. So the serpent is not necessarily doing anything wrong. As a symbol of a vital and archaic archetypal part of the Self, its creativity expresses the psychological mobilization toward a transformation that includes an enormous acquisition of learning. It is not by chance that the serpent is the central structuring symbol of the development of consciousness in *kundalini* yoga (Eliade 1954; Avalon 1918) and as the *spiritus mercurius* in European alchemy (Jung 1911). When the serpent in each one of us fails to fulfill this function, we run the risk of moral stupor and psychic stagnation. What makes the serpent's temptation satanic is the patriarchal pattern, which, in order to maintain order and tradition, has to control and often limit knowledge of the new. It has to keep knowledge as a privilege of the elite, in this case, the divinity itself, and it has to consider the democracy of knowledge as a crime. Therefore, the acquisition of knowledge had to be prevented by the threat of repression and even by capital punishment ("so that you do not die"). By denying the threat of death and denouncing its patriarchal manipulation, the serpent undoes the mystification and unveils the true patriarchal polarizing essence ("I do not want you to have the same power as I have") that often hides behind the paternalistic, manipulating attitude ("I forbid you to eat to protect your life").

How many times do we see this defensive psychopathic manipulation in the teacher-pupil relationship in order to preserve dominion and asymmetry: "I stand and move, you remain seated and motionless"; "you listen, I talk"; "I know, you don't"; *but* "I teach (in this boring, uncreative way) doing you a great favor so that one day you will become someone." And what's more, "you amuse yourselves, you talk and don't acknowledge my work and my dedication to you (oh! how virtuous I am and how you are immature, irresponsible and ungrateful)."

So we see that the oppressed is one of the poles of the ego-other relation in the patriarchal pattern. Oppression is also an archetypal structuring function. It is a matter of ideological bias to follow the famous Brazilian educator Paulo Freire (1970) and reduce the "teaching of the oppressed" only to class struggle and socioeconomic factors. When we do so, we take the lamb from one wolf's mouth and leave it to the mercy of other wolves. When the patriarchal pattern is accused and reduced to a single cause, it only licks its chops, for its essence has not been unveiled and it goes on predominating and eating the lambs, because the old lambs have changed into wolves and the ex-wolves into lambs. So let us carry on and learn a little more about the relation between lambs and wolves.

> And when the woman saw that the tree was good for food, and
> that it was pleasant to the eyes, and a tree to be desired to
> make one wise, she took of the fruit thereof, and did eat, and
> also gave unto her husband with her; and he did eat. (Genesis
> 3:6)

The woman's voracity and envy inclines her to follow the serpent, while the man follows the woman. In the traditional patriarchal pattern man was granted the privilege of commanding, while woman had the function of obeying. The most contained, however, was the serpent: the most creative, archaic structuring function of the psyche, "more astute than any beast that the Lord God had made". When any great change takes place, that which is most revolutionary is considered the most subversive. Yet it must be noted that he who most commands, the man in this case, may be the most restricted and, in the long run, the most deformed, passive, and obedient. In short, all are dogmatically and repressively controlled: by law, by order, and "for their own good". Diabolical? Yes, because diabolical is the patriarchal shadow defensively projected onto the serpent when it revolts and transgresses, moved by creative envy (Byington 2002a).

> And the eyes of them both were opened, and they knew that
> they were naked: and they sewed fig leaves together, and
> made themselves aprons. (Genesis 3:7)

The structuring function of shame was constellated in order to continue the symbolic elaboration of the new discoveries (here the verb "to constellate" designates the activation of archetypes or structuring functions). Shame expressed in covering the genitals means situating sexuality in the intimacy of being and transforming the private-public dimension into a polarity. The responsible, optional activity of sex is here associated with dressing. This discrimination is of fundamental importance in structuring the persona of the patriarchally oriented family and society, which intensifies the incest taboo and regulates customs, inheritance, government, laws, and property. The patriarchal context considers this distinction transgression and uses shame defensively to make demands and punishment. Therefore, a great differentiation of individual and collective consciousness comes to be experienced in a highly persecutory atmosphere that is liable to punishment as though it were a crime.

> And they heard the voice of the Lord God walking in the
> garden in the cool of the day: and Adam and his wife hid
> themselves from the presence of the Lord God amongst the
> trees of the garden. And the Lord God called unto Adam and
> said unto him, Where art thou? And he said, I heard thy voice
> in the garden, and I was afraid, because I was naked, and I hid
> myself. And he said, Who told thee that thou wast naked?
> Hast thou eaten of the tree, whereof I commanded thee that
> thou shouldest not eat? And the man said, The woman whom
> thou givest to be with me, she gave me of the tree, and I did
> eat. And the Lord God said unto the woman, What is this that
> thou hast done? And the woman said, The serpent beguiled
> me, and I did eat. And the Lord God said unto the serpent,
> Because thou hast done this, thou art cursed above all cattle
> and above every beast of the field; upon thy belly shall thou
> go, and thus shalt thou eat all the days of thy life. And I will put
> enmity between thee and the woman, and between thy seed
> and her seed; she will bruise thy head and thou shalt bruise
> her heel. (Genesis 3:8–15)

In this atmosphere of repression, guilt, and fear, people tend to become cowards and lose their individuality. In failing to accept what we are, we tend to hold others responsible for it. The patriarchal pattern favors the preservation of organization and tradition at the cost of development of deep individuality and defensive projection of the shadow, forming the well-known scapegoat complex. It enables us to keep our projections and introjections defensively fixated at a halfway point, without integrating them as we could. Eve does not fully integrate the serpent's pedagogic curiosity and transgression, and Adam even less so.

Through time and the repressive tradition of generations (the curse and descent), the patriarchal pattern led us to live in conflict with our sensuous vegetative world, which expresses a great deal of the matriarchal archetype. The patriarchal pattern conditions us to disdain the sensory-motor intelligence within us that is archaic and creative precisely because it is not "bipedal", because it creeps and keeps permanent contact with the earth. The patriarchal pattern separates us from the serpent's power, from the permanent contact with the transcendent function of imagination of the Self that joins earth and heaven, sensuality and its spiritual meanings. In establishing the asymmetry between the ego and the other, and between all polarities, by the force of its power of perfectionist organization, the patriarchal pattern prevents dialectic and harmonic experience between the poles of the polarities of all symbols, between the foot and head of the Ouroboros (the alchemical dragon that swallows its own tail), symbol of the union of the beginning and end of all things (Avalon 1918).

Its organizing might is also its great limitation to integrating the polarities into a whole. In a group experience that I coordinated at the Second São Paulo Congress of Secondary Schools in 1992 (Byington 1992a) on the relationship between teaching in the West and the myth of Genesis, I asked the participants to approach the serpent using psychodramatic techniques in the experience of two different moments. The first was the episode of temptation. Participants were to imagine themselves as Eve being fully tempted by the serpent into envy. They should touch it and feel how its cold skin expresses the transcendence of life in another world, in the archaic, vegetative world where our entrails lie around the solar plexus, then to look deep into its eyes and feel the call to something revolutionary, adventurous, fascinating, dangerous, tempting, voluptuous, extraordinarily promising, and finally ecstatically irresistible.

The second moment was after the curse and the separation of the woman and the serpent. The participants were to imagine again Eve carrying a pitcher to fill at the fountain and, at home, waiting for her and hungry for lunch, Adam, Cain, and Abel, now grown up. The serpent crosses her path. Eve almost steps on it and it bares its fangs at her heel. There is a moment of great conflict, of antagonism, fear, aggression, and suddenly a flash of the memory of the other encounter in paradise. "Oh! For time not to have gone by! What longing! What absurd antagonism for that fascinating encounter with creative envy!"

In the patriarchal context of order and tradition, control over envy and creativity and the marvelous pain of childbirth were transformed into a suffering filled with fear (anxiety), curse, and tension. In this politically correct environment reigned the painless virtue of repetition. From then on the extraordinary discovery of good and evil lived amid creativity, persecutory fear, and defensive envy and pain. As women were capable of sheltering a new being and feeding it during its most vulnerable phase of life, they came to be the most exuberant expression of the matriarchal archetype, and consequently a great target for patriarchal control: in the beginning, creatively, to organize and protect, but eventually, defensively, to repress, accuse, persecute, abuse, and even torture, damaging sensuality and fertility through bullying and concupiscence.

Why is it that so many women from matriarchally oriented tribal cultures are capable of giving birth in a squatting position, cutting the cord, and then carrying the baby, while so many mothers in industrialized societies have to take classes to reduce the fear and anxiety with which they await childbirth?

> Unto the woman he said, I will greatly multiply thy sorrow and thy conception. In sorrow thou shalt bring forth children, and thy desire shall be to thy husband, and he shall rule over thee. (Genesis 3:16)

Freud was very creative in perceiving psychological development as sublimation, for it fits like a glove the process of symbolic elaboration coordinated by the patriarchal pattern. Sublimation is the direct transformation of a solid into a gas without there being an intermediate liquid state as is the case of water. The mathaphor is strongler and more meaningful than the process of liquefying. Sublimation as a psychic structuring function expresses well the growth of consciousness through the process of symbolic transformation of the matriarchal into the patriarchal pattern. The asymmetry in the ego-other relationship, maintained by the controlling power of the patriarchal pattern, is the condition for such intense delimiting of symbolic elaboration. Without an authoritarian asymmetry in the teacher-pupil relationship, young people cannot be told to wake up early and spend a beautiful sunny morning stuck to chairs "for your comfort", without spontaneity, play, joy, and pleasure.

What Freud did not realize was that there exist three other patterns (matriarchal, alterity, and totality) that rule symbolic elaboration without the exclusive delimiting and sublimating pressure that characterizes the patriarchal pattern. In fact, at the end of his work, when the great master complained of the unhappiness of mankind because of our tendency toward dominion and war, he bases his diagnosis on the need to repress Thanatos, the death instinct, rather than on the need to elaborate Eros and transcend patriarchal dominance of culture by functions other than sublimation (Freud 1929).

In this context, mankind's fantastic commitment to changing the world through work, one of the marvels of creation, becomes the expression of a crime to be punished. The patriarchal defensive pattern, through its power of expansion, transforms the very earth that is trodden and the air that is breathed into a great obligation and a great sin. This is the curse of toiling on earth and work in general, which subordinates all human activities to the reign of guilt.

The experiences in themselves are not necessarily imbued with the crime of transgression, for they are actually the great marvels of humanity. The way they are elaborated and exercised within patriarchal defensive pattern is what imbues them with illegal transgression, perfectionism, guilt, punishment, obligation, and their destructive consequences.

> And unto Adam he said, because thou hast harkened unto the voice of thy wife, and has eaten of the tree of which I commanded thee, saying Thou shalt not eat of it: cursed is the ground for thy sake; in sorrow thou shalt eat of it all the days of thy life. Thorns also and thistles shall it bring forth to thee, and thou shalt eat of the herb of the field. In the sweat of thy face shalt thou eat bread, till thou return to the ground, for out of it wast thou taken: for dust thou art, and unto dust shalt thou return. (Genesis 3:17–19)

Finally the myth tackles death and finiteness and situates the problem within the same punitive context as all the rest. "From dust we came and unto dust we must return" was a discovery that science needed the atomic theory to prove. The myth precedes it with disconcerting creativity. Each step of the discovery of the composition of matter led us to the knowledge of atomic composition common to human beings, nature, and the cosmos. Only in the twentieth century, after so many scientific steps, could Teilhard de Chardin (1950) conceive the prospective differentiation of cosmic matter toward the formation of the human brain and consciousness.

The elaboration of symbols and structuring functions of death and finitude are frightening, which explains their control during elaboration. But the myth also assures us that "nothing is lost, all is transformed" ("because thou are dust and to dust shall return") and thus introduces scientifically the theme of eternity. For humankind to be and return to dust means that our atoms, protons, and electrons will always remain. Despite the discomfiting restriction with which patriarchal pattern colors it, the myth wisely affirms that death is not the end; it reiterates the material impossibility of our leaving matter, the cosmos, or God.

Concluding its description of human life, Genesis formulates another prohibition, not of the tree of good and evil this time, but of the tree of life. The prohibition to eat from the tree of good and evil showed the creativity and transgression of the ethical function on the cultural Self expressed by the serpent and the punishment for them. The new prohibition shows a new temptation in the Judaic cultural Self, which is extraordinary and messianic and will be continued in the New Testament.

> And the Lord God said, Behold, the man is become as one of us, to know good and evil: and now, lest he put forth his hand, and take also of the tree of life, and eat, and live for ever: Therefore the Lord God sent him forth from the garden of Eden, to till the ground from whence he was taken. So he drove out the man, and he placed at the east of the Garden of Eden cherubim, and a flaming sword which turned every way, to keep the way of the tree of life. (Genesis 3:22–24).

In fact, the myth that followed it—the myth of incarnation in the New Testament—is the symbolic consequence of the ingestion of the fruit of the tree of good and evil together with the fruit of the tree of life. It is the confrontation of the shadow and of sin through death and resurrection. It is the myth of the democratic dialectic relationship between the ego and the other, which includes the dialectic confrontation between good and evil in each human heart, in each day's work, a process described by Jung as the individuation process (1935), which expresses the integration of another polarized archetypal position in consciousness. It transcends the productive capacity of the position of the patriarchal archetype in symbolic elaboration and introduces us to the dialectical position of the alterity archetype.

The transcendent function of imagination of the Self, represented by the serpent as the spirit of knowledge in Genesis, reappears millennia later to Mary, this time to enter her body as the Holy Ghost. With the same force that made Eve and Adam eat of the tree of good and evil, the product of her gestation will surpass the spade of the cherubim to reach the tree of life and assume eternity as a dimension of human condition: "I am the resurrection and the life. He that believeth in me, though he were dead, yet shall he live" (John 11:25).

The creative strength of the psyche allows the transformation of consciousness through the confrontation and integration of the dark side of the soul, sin, or shadow through the polarity of the archetype of life and death, which is equivalent to the permanent elaboration of what has to die and be reborn transformed (Byington 1996). This other myth, however, although it continues the themes of Genesis, elaborates envy, transformation, creativity, and shame within another archetypal pattern, the dialectical pattern of the archetype of alterity, which we shall describe in greater detail in the next chapter.

## The Civilizing Efficiency of the Patriarchal Pattern

It is important for the educator to realize to what extent patriarchal predominance tends to discard the characteristics of the matriarchal pattern of teaching and rids it of the playful, imaginative, affective, intuitive, spontaneous, savory, and pleasurable elements. It is likewise important for the educator to realize that the dissociation of subject and object in our traditional teaching must not be seen as synonymous with patriarchal pattern, nor be attributed to it. This dissociation is rooted in the pathology of the cultural Self of the West and occurred along with the preexisting historical patriarchal dominance which continued after it. The unmotivating, inartistic, and unattractive picture of our pedagogic tradition is due to the imposition of the subject-object dissociation that took place in the late eighteenth century within the patriarchal predominance that had existed for many centuries and which was exacerbated in positivism and in materialism.

The fact that we avoid the dominance of the patriarchal pattern in teaching by no means implies that we wish to exclude it. Due to its extraordinary archetypal importance in symbolic elaboration, this would obviously be impossible and unthinkable. What we need is to keep it in its proper place, complementing the matriarchal pattern, and subordinated to the pattern of alterity in constructivism, science, love, creativity, and democracy. Freedom can only prosper if a sharp distinction between the boundaries of the ego and the other is patriarchally delimited and respected as formulated by Descartes (1637). Without the sharp, patriarchal delimitation of responsibility, the fire of freedom will burn down its oven, as happened in the French Revolution.

The patriarchal pattern is extremely useful when there is a need to abstract, organize, and plan. Its massive utilization in computer technology is the only efficient way to work out countless needs of modern society, without which life in the big cities and on the planet would long ago have become impractical. Services concerned with production, marketing, transportation, supply, health, safety, banking, housing, hygiene, and the whole of institutional life in industrialized societies would not survive half an hour without abstract patriarchal organization. Even the democratic model of alterity of sustainable economy cannot be exercised without balancing the sensual components of survival of the insular matriarchal pattern and the components of abstract coherence, organization, planning, and responsibility of the polarized patriarchal pattern.

# Chapter 9

# THE DIALECTIC POSITION
# AND THE ALTERITY PATTERN
# IN TEACHING

The alterity archetype allows for maximum productivity in the process of symbolic elaboration of personality and cultural development and therefore also in education. As the archetypal foundation of constructivism, including symbolic constructivism, this archetype coordinates the quaternary dialectic interaction of the ego and the other, an interaction which forms systems within the total process. The quaternary relation of the ego with the other and the other with all others is only possible when both admit their opposition and equality, for example, right-wrong, in which case the ego opens up to perceive itself as right or wrong, just as the other does. This is the archetype of dialectics, mutuality, compassion, conjunction, and encounter. It coordinates the differentiation of consciousness to integrate right and wrong, good and evil, sickness and health, sin and salvation, life and death, and all the other polarities in the existential process, including mind and body and mind and nature.

Archetypes are always a function of the whole, through the coordination of the central archetype. Still, on coordinating the quaternary dialectic interaction between the ego and the other related to wholeness, the alterity archetype can achieve an incomparable degree of productivity in elaborating symbols, greater in extension and depth than any other archetype. It includes the anima and animus archetypes, described by Jung as psychopomps, that is, archetypes that lead the process of individuation in the second half of life.

When we consider imagination to be the structuring function that best expresses the reach of psychic totality, this superior capacity to produce symbolic meanings makes the pattern of alterity the chief archetype for coordinating the objective and subjective through imagination in Jungian symbolic education.

All archetypes coordinate symbolic elaboration through relationships that affect the ego-other polarity. Coordinating the quaternary dialectic interaction of polarities, the alterity archetype allows for maximum differentiation of the ego and the other, and, consequently, it is constellated in all the existential situations that seek this total differentiation. I call the relationship quaternary when a person can relate to another, for example, a teacher with a pupil, admitting his or her shadow in the expectation that the other may do likewise. The same happens in the ego-other relationship in the individual Self and among institutions in the cultural Self. So we have the encounter of the ego with the other and also with the shadow of the ego and the shadow of the other. It is difficult to describe and even more difficult to experience, but when it happens in a productive way, it is very life enriching. This is the path of the scientific method, of artistic creativity, of love, of democracy, and of symbolic education.

Among religions we see the alterity archetype especially activated in Hinduism, Sufism, Buddhism (Zen Buddhism), Taoism, Christianity, Hassidism, the Jewish Cabal, and in the Yoruba pantheon, among others. In the sociopolitical sphere, it is the archetype of democracy (Byington 1992b). The pattern of alterity is also the chief archetypal pattern that grants to consciousness the conception of the scientific vision of the right-wrong relationship, especially when this also includes the subject-object interaction, as is the case in the paradigm of symbolic science (Byington 1990c). In medicine, it allows us to understand the antigen-antibody interactions at the core of immunology, and the symptom-normal interaction in general medicine and in dynamic psychotherapy. In ecology, it coordinates the complex multiple feedback relation in nature. In education, it is the archetype of constructivism. Like the other archetypes, the immense power of differentiation of consciousness by the pattern of alterity must not be idealized. Its dysfunctions, brought on by defensive structures and by the intrusion of other archetypes in its symbolic elaboration, can turn its expressions into a caricature of its potential. The demagogy and corruption that exist in today's world in the name of democracy, the depletion of natural resources for the sake of progress, and the ecological destruction in the name of free enterprise suffice to give us an idea of how the archetypal expressiveness of the alterity pattern can become diluted and contaminated during symbolic elaboration, remaining deformed and fixated in the shadow and falling far short of its extraordinary structuring potential.

## Alterity is not Synonymous with Equality

The dialectic relationship among polarities in the pattern of alterity does not mean that the poles, including the ego and the other, are considered equal. What this pattern permits is for the poles to interact with equal opportunity to express their similarities and differences, that is, for the ego and the other and all other polarities to interrelate in freedom and to experience their full reality.

This differentiating force of alterity even goes so far as to enable the two poles to change position in order to reveal themselves fully. Here lies the origin of the biblical proposal, in the face of adversity, to offer the other cheek or put yourself in the place of the other to know the question better. This most important fact changes the notion of identity in Aristotelian logic, which is firmly established in patriarchal pattern, according to which A equals A and is different from B. When consciousness is ruled by the pattern of alterity, A may be equal to A and in very special cases of paradox also equal to B. This, for instance, is the case of a microbe that causes an infectious disease. If A is the disease and B the remedy, A = A and B = B and A is opposite B. Nevertheless, when this same microbe that causes the disease also functions as vaccine and remedy, A becomes equal to B. So, A = A and is different from B in one situation and A = B in another. This logic, typical of the pattern of alterity, gives rise to paradox, which includes, for instance, the famous esoteric paradox of the equality of opposites that permeated occultism and alchemy within the symbol of the emerald tablet and had so much influence on the whole of Jung's work (Hermes Trismegistus, II to IV Cent.).

It is crucial for us to differentiate the logic of alterity (in which, in very special and objective cases, A is different from B and equal to B) from the logic of matriarchal predominance (in which A becomes different from A and equal to B due to changes in the conditions of sensuality, fertility, and desire rather than also by objective reality). In the matriarchal pattern, subjective and objective identities are too labile because the attachment to sensuality is extraordinarily strong. The saying "in a house without bread, people may argue endlessly and no one is ever right" fits very well here, for it shows reason as subordinate to desire and frustration. Hunger, covetousness, envy, passion, jealousy, hatred, spite, and magic can color objective reality with all the possible hues by involving and even inverting yes and no, right and wrong, beautiful and ugly. Here A = A and A = B because of the subjective rather than because of its objective function. This almost complete lack of objectivity is well expressed in another saying: "whoever loves the ugly sees it as beautiful", or: "the grass is always greener on the other side of the fence". This emotional exaggeration of the matriarchal pattern in describing reality according to the subject's desire creates and cultivates most beliefs and superstitions, one of the main causes that led to the subjective being expelled from the experimental method developed by nineteenth-century scientific mentality. The subject-object dissociation that occurred at that time defensively entrenched truth and the objective along with patriarchal pattern and also defensively jettisoned obscurantism along with the subjective and the matriarchal pattern.

The pattern of alterity, given its archetypal dialectic nature, has been experienced one way or another by all those who delved deep into the existential mystery of human life in the cosmos, long before it was exercised in the scientific method. Since time immemorial, its great paradox for humanity has always been the fact that we are so fleeting and insignificant, while at the same time able to perceive the immensity of cosmic space-time. In the religious and esoteric dimensions, where realities are affirmed chiefly by imagination and without concern for demonstrative explanation, the pattern of alterity is often intuited and mentioned as the secret of secrets and mystery of mysteries.

## The Revealed Identity of Opposites in the Paradox of Alterity

In the esoteric tradition we have the famous example of the Emerald Tablet (*Tabula Smaragdina*), mentioned in the book of initiation, *Corpus Hermeticum* by Hermes Trismegistus (n.d.) where we read: "What is below is the same as what is above and what is above is the same as what is below". This dictate permeates the whole of alchemical thinking that preceded the modern sciences as a fundamental truth. This expresses esoterically (experienced and affirmed without demonstration) the pattern of alterity within alchemy, which was most important in forming and differentiating the scientific mind, illustrated by the postulation of the equality of the upper and the lower as the essence of the equality of opposites. For centuries this initially intuitive affirmation stimulated scientific research to transcend the polarized patriarchal experience of reality and find universal laws or truths common to different and even opposite manifestations in all dimensions of humanism, including ethics and science.

Albert Sabin experienced this paradox, expressed in the *Tabula Smaragdina,* of the equality of opposites in modern science when he discovered the vaccine for polio. The polio virus expresses the disease and opposite to health. On transforming the virus into a vaccine, Sabin also equated it to health and discovered the mysterious identity of opposites in this disease, to his own joy and that of all humankind. Freud experienced the same when he discovered the cure for neurosis within itself. This was also Einstein's dream in the broad theory of relativity, through which he sought a common denominator for the macrocosm and microcosm. Today we are still trying to confirm the similarity of forces inside the atom to those of the macrocosm and so discover in physics where the smaller is the same as the greater. Part of what today is science was experienced by very differentiated persons and for a long time was expressed esoterically. The pattern of alterity, like any other archetypal pattern, may be experienced emotionally, mythologically, and affirmed esoterically long before it is understood rationally and applied objectively. One of its great illustrations in religion is found in the core of Christianity where sin is the opposite of salvation but at the same time its essential condition.

The dialectical pattern of alterity surpasses the insular matriarchal pattern (sensuality) and the polarized patriarchal pattern (organization and power) in efficiency when it comes to creating meaning in symbolic elaboration in proportion to its capacity for detachment from sensuality and power. We must realize this to understand that the pattern of alterity is the essence of scientific creativity. If anything is fundamental to science, it is detachment from subjective and objective appearances in order to find the great universal laws and truths. Can there be anything more instrumental in causing detachment from appearances than formulating the equality of opposites that was repeated so often by the alchemists? It is hard to imagine a greater incentive to research the reality that lies beyond the appearances of opposition than the paradox that opposites are mysteriously the same in many different and very specific situations. "Where and how are they the same?", was asked endless times by neophytes. "Pray, read, read, read again, research, and you'll find out" (*ora, lege, lege, relege, labora et invenies*) has been endlessly taught by the masters (for example, the work of [Jacobus Sulat?] Altus [1677], in de Rola 1988, p. 481). It is the logic of alterity that explains for us the wisdom of the paradox. Wasn't this the path that led to the discovery of the atomic theory and to the knowledge of the combination of the elements to demonstrate the common atomic denominator of matter, under the most different appearances possible? The mysterious phrase "the equality of opposites" is a leitmotiv of Taoism, expressed in the *Tào Tè Ching*. It is also a Zen Buddhist koan, used to break the attachment of the ego to the appearance of reality registered by the senses and by patriarchal logic, under which the same are equal and the opposites are different and that's the end of it!

The equality of opposites is also perceived in psychopathology when we study it in the pattern of alterity. In this manner we penetrate the mystery of symptoms as defensive structuring symbols and functions to discover their normal characteristics and decode the neurosis. Freud and Josef Breuer were still working together when they made the ingenious discovery that the key to health lay within neurosis. Is this not the same paradox that mysteriously equates virtue and sin in salvation? In order to discover how to produce a vaccine from a microbe, one has to penetrate deep inside the immunological dialectic relationship of antigen-antibody. That is what we do when we perceive the symptoms of psychopathology as structuring symbols and study how they function in the Self. Only then can we remove them from the defensive structures (shadow and symptoms, both circumstantial and chronic) and elaborate them through creative structures (normal growth of the personality). The constructivist method does the same in education, since it considers creativity to be as important for the teacher as for the pupil, perceiving them as opposites that, in very special conditions, are also mysteriously equal in apprenticeship.

Psychodrama, founded by Jacob Moreno, includes role playing, which allows the ego to dramatically interact with the other, in its wealth of symbolic elaboration. Active imagination, an expressive technique described by Jung, and inner psychodrama enable the ego-other relationship to be imaginatively dramatized to the same end (Bustos 1979).

Being the essence of the mystery of paradox, "the sameness of opposites" is not to be generalized and taken literally. On the contrary, when understood or exercised literally, "the sameness of opposites" is absurd, silly, and monstrous. Imagine the epidemiological catastrophe that its literal use would provoke, for instance, if a population were inoculated with a pathological virus simply for the purpose of "vaccinating" it!

"The equality of opposites" is a mystery in religions and in esotericism and it is very difficult to employ in scientific, political, psychotherapeutic, humanistic thinking and education due to the countless variations of the relationship of opposites. The equivalence of opposites is mysterious because it is concealed from appearances in some extraordinary condition, which must be revealed or discovered. It is initiatory, for only those who have lived and suffered deep passion and tragedy beyond conventions can understand that right and wrong, ugly and beautiful, good and evil, health and disease, virtue and sin are polarities whose interchangeable identities carve the way of the soul toward self-fulfillment.

The pattern of alterity seeks to differentiate all the manifestations of symbols, complexes, and functions in order to fulfill the very special and unique condition of its here and now. The result is that it operates simultaneously within the magical causality of the insular matriarchal pattern, the objective causality of the polarized patriarchal position, and synchronicity, which makes the alterity pattern always creative and absolutely unique. In this pattern, each case really is a unique situation. Only by bearing this in mind can we attempt to discover the mystery of the sameness of opposites in any given situation. It is this mysterious situation in learning that characterizes symbolic constructivism resulting in Jungian symbolic education. A great degree of existential intelligence, honesty, and sensibility is needed by the teacher to detect emphatically these most creative situations, where the student is also a teacher and the teacher also a student, that is, when student and teacher, although opposites, become the same.

The pattern of alterity is as deep and marvelous as its shadow can be improper, terrible, and grotesque. Standing before the marvel of a city lit up by atomic energy or seeing the miracle of the eradication of polio, on the one hand, and the horrors of Chernobyl or the disaster that is AIDS, on the other, we realize the extent of the constructive and destructive power of this archetype. Its scope and complexity are what make it so difficult for consciousness to exercise it. This means that the conscious ego often lacks the ability to undertake the proposed symbolic elaboration and allows the shadow to be formed. The great shadow formed by the archetype of alterity, be it in politics, science, education, or love, is treason and imposture in which the encounter of opposites for the elaboration of life is falsified and becomes a caricature of what it could be.

## Matriarchal-Patriarchal Coordination by Alterity

One of the most important functions of the pattern of alterity in the psychodynamics of the humanities, including teaching coordinated by the ruling archetypal quaternio, is to undertake the creative interaction between the matriarchal and patriarchal patterns. It is one thing to construct rationally the dialectic encounter between the ego and the other in a given situation in consciousness and shadow; it is another thing to construct symbolically the relation between the innumerable existential situations coordinated by the matriarchal and patriarchal archetypes that is between sensory-motor intelligence and conceptual intelligence. From the differences we have seen between these two patterns in the two preceding chapters, we can imagine how extraordinarily difficult is the search for their permanent dialectic interaction, be it in democracy, in science, in art, in love, or in education. In fact, many of the major items on the list of evils of individual life and civilization are caused by the wounds and deformities that result from the conflicts between the matriarchal and patriarchal patterns in symbolic elaboration.

In order to function, the pattern of alterity requires great power of transcendence to allow for relative detachment both on the matriarchal level (partial detachment from sensuality) and on the patriarchal (partial detachment from power to control) so as to perceive their common denominator and the relative importance of each in the development of the whole (see *Instinct,* a 1999 film directed by Jon Turteltaub). At the same time, it is necessary to understand the essence of these two patterns to be able to coordinate them. It is difficult to exercise alterity if we lack a deep experience of the nature of the matriarchal and patriarchal patterns in our own existential and cultural processes.

## Archetypal Evolution—A New Concept of Cultural Education

The concept of evolution applied to culture, which identified progress with the collective implantation of the patriarchal archetype, was a disaster for humanism. It not only sanctioned, morally and scientifically, and celebrated with medals and parades the atrocities committed to nature and society coordinated by the patriarchal archetype, but it created an immense scientific and cultural prejudice against the sensuality, fertility, and pleasure of the matriarchal archetype, generating the epithets of primitive, savage, barbaric, immature, undeveloped, childish, ignorant, irrational, hysterical, lazy, immoral, perverse, and even unconscious.

This unilateral and prejudiced labeling became so exaggerated that it created a defensive compensatory reaction, a defensive *enantiodromia* (flowing toward the opposite), which disqualified and negated any evolutionist concept in culture whatsoever. This negation was positive, on the one hand, because it at least protected the matriarchal archetype from intellectual prejudice, but on the other hand, it was negative in that it left countless atrocities coordinated by the patriarchal archetype praised as great feats of humanity and identified with progress and the goal of cultural development.

However, when we consider the symbolic elaboration of individual and collective archetypal development, evolution can be seen clearly not in patriarchal dominance, but in the progressive dialectic coordination of the matriarchal and patriarchal by the alterity archetype.

Therefore, the theory of cultural evolution must be reconsidered and taught in psychology, sociology, and history to identify, cultivate, and pursue the highest values of humanism through the progressive implantation of the dialectical archetype of alterity.

## Matriarchal-Patriarchal Interaction in Learning

The coordination of the dialectics of the matriarchal-patriarchal patterns in school is one of the most important activities of symbolic constructivism in teaching.

Patriarchally, the school has to teach a program by means of classes in a determined place and within a predetermined time period. This program, however variable it may be, must comply with the legal norms of the country and insert its content in the institutional cultural life that coordinates the future with the past. The school, therefore, has to select, contract, train, pay, and improve teachers and workers to maintain the conditions of teaching, organization, security, and hygiene. The school must have a budget and an efficient accounting system for income and outlay. It needs to plan prevention of accidents and first aid. It has to organize a method of evaluating and improving pupils' and teachers' results, cope with problem pupils, and take care of the interaction between the school and parents. It is necessary to formulate an inspiring ideal and goal for the school, as well as humanistic guidelines that express the essence of short- and long-term daily activities and set significant dates for institutional festivities. All this has to be planned, organized, executed, controlled, evaluated, and periodically recycled.

Matriarchally, the school requires a campus linked to nature, preferably close to the pupils' homes, a safe and comfortable building, with a reasonable number of pupils in each class, and a sizeable recreational area. The teaching should be rooted in the experience of the body, emotions, and expressive techniques that make it as pleasurable, playful, and dramatic as possible. Intimacy with the subject taught should be encouraged to the maximum through direct experience: fruit trees, animals, kitchen, laboratory, singing, dancing and music, games, a joyful atmosphere that is intimate and affectionate, and plastically expressive materials; a direct intimate experience of the microcosm and macrocosm through the microscope and telescope; rituals that foster these features, above all in the expressive techniques of symbolic elaboration. The teacher-pupil transference relationship is the great nest where archetypal patterns can be sheltered. The commemorative rituals of the school at the beginning and end of the school year and on national dates and feast days, as well as the elaboration of individual benchmarks such as birthdays, weddings, deaths, and tragic accidents involving teachers and pupils emotionally, are all particularly significant for the expression of the insular matriarchal pattern because of the degree of human warmth and intimacy they convey.

The association of the matriarchal and patriarchal patterns enriches the content that is learned, along with the method of learning. The material that is learned is associated to the totality of being through experience, which makes it richer and more difficult to forget. For example, it is one thing for the pupil to have learned patriarchally that the first French republic ended in political terror which favored Napoleon's expansionist, belligerent dictatorship; it is another, completely different, thing to experience a dramatic representation of these events by the entire class, representing the monarchy, clergy, people, and parliament, with Georges Danton, Maximilien Robespierre, and Jean-Paul Marat defending laws for the people and at the same time scheming to send one another to the guillotine. These dramatic classes combine the tragic and the comic and are never forgotten. Students will never know whether they remember Danton's heroic tragedy for his sake or because of the expression on the face of a classmate on hearing his death sentence! The presence of the pattern of alterity lies in the fact that the symbolic meanings of the French Revolution are extracted from objective facts of patriarchal logic and associated with the matriarchal immediacy of emotion imagined by the students in expressing what they felt in this historical search for democracy between civil war and terror and the pursuit of freedom and hope.

A class that is constantly taught using acting may achieve a dramatic expressiveness that is significant in itself. "But do you want to teach history or theater?", one teacher asked me. As a matter of fact, Jungian symbolic education seeks to teach both, for it aims to form people and not just scholars who can recite the dates and facts of the French Revolution without being able to have a human feeling for its symbols due to the lack of emotional and existential experience. One cannot learn science existentially without art. Human imagination and the nervous system always include content and form, meaning and style. What happens in exclusively rational learning is that memory tends to remain merely in the cognitive level of the ego. It generally lasts until the test and what has been learned is very likely to be forgotten at once, because, even when constructed, it was not experienced. The memory of the Self is much fuller, deeper, and more lasting than that of the ego. The memory of the Self is the memory of experience and existence, brought about by words and images, thoughts and emotions, science and art, rational and irrational, conscious and unconscious participation.

Because we have expanded the notion of archetype to include consciousness and thus managed to describe the archetypal patterns of the ego-other relationship, we may use the pattern of alterity to conjugate the matriarchal and patriarchal patterns, within expressive techniques of symbolic elaboration. The purely rational perspective is quite limited, due to the essentially different and often conflicting nature of the two archetypes. How to maintain emotion, joy, and discipline in a class at the same time without resorting to expressive techniques? How to make learning attractive and tasty when faced with insipid subjects, generally taught only with explanations? How to maintain intimacy in a big class with only abstract themes? How to cultivate the playful and the spontaneous alongside the organized and directive? How to conjugate such diverging polarities and all the others that would take forever to list? The exclusively rational method is too limited to undertake the task. Only the initiatory, experiential method is capable of making it operational.

The experiential (simultaneously rational and irrational) path of symbolic elaboration involving the totality of the Self and consequently also the functions of feeling, intuition, and introversion, side by side with thinking, sensation, and extraversion, is the path of opposites, ideal for symbolic constructivism. Jungian symbolic education, in spite of being the fruit of a philosophy of education and humanism, is not necessarily erudite, sophisticated, or intellectualized. By the experiential nature of its conceptual bases, it is dominantly creative and natural, because it is essentially affectionate and ontological, that is, existential. If we want to formulate its philosophical and scientific basis, as we are doing, we have to undertake a long and strenuous journey. In order to exercise Jungian symbolic education, intellectual sophistication is often more of a drawback than an aid. In developing countries, at least, the classes centered around popular culture are generally more able to intuit it, because popular culture has preserved the matriarchal archetype, the subjective-objective relationship, affection, intuition, and bodily expression to an incomparably greater degree than the more traditional academic classes.

Popular culture in Brazil, for instance, is very diversified, open to the new, and frequently expressed by body language through music and dance (Conde 1978). One promising fact is that the opening of private schools to symbolic teaching is on the rise, at least as far as I have been able to observe in many secondary schools in São Paulo. It is a pity, though, that the public school system, at least in Brazil, is still very much centered around the classical European model of patriarchal dominance or Piaget's rational constructivism and is very resistant to the symbolic approach.

The teacher-student polarity, as in all symbolic elaboration, begins with the unilateral dominance of the passive position, lived by students, and tends to be reversed during learning. During the process of apprenticeship, students become more active and teachers become more passive, repeating the model of the parent-child relationship. It so happens, however, that not all students develop to the same degree and many become much more active before others. To attend to these differences in the classroom, teachers should delegate the active position in teaching to the more advanced students, having them help those who have remained in a more passive position. In symbolic education this is important for character formation of students, who learn that those with more can give to those who have less. It is also productive to provide the brighter ones with a creative stimulus to prevent them from feeling bored. The class can thus function as a dynamic learning system in which opposite poles of apprenticeship operate dialectically.

When used directly in symbolic elaboration, the pattern of alterity naturally includes coordination of the balance between matriarchal and patriarchal patterns, and extends even to the pattern of totality. This occurs because the scope of symbolic elaboration in the pattern of alterity is such that it requires the full exercise of the whole ruling archetypal quaternio.

To exercise the pattern of alterity in symbolic constructivism, it is especially necessary to surrender to the imagination. The development of the teachers' symbolic capacity and the experience of how to apply it in teaching are fundamental. To give flight to the imagination in order to teach actually means to allow the imagination to use the wings that it already has. The imagination is the creative essence of the psyche; it joins all the polarities, including conscious-unconscious and normal-pathological, in symbolic elaboration. Its scope knows no frontiers for its reach intuits eternity and infinity. Artistic creativity is its exercise on the predominantly subjective level, and scientific creativity on the predominantly objective level, but both are needed to express the subjective and the objective on the symbolic level. It is a matter of training educators who have the vocation to teach with their whole personality and not just with their cognitive ability. Such educators already exist in countless numbers but a considerable part of their teaching potential is neglected and restrained within exclusively rational constructivism.

Fantasy is the imagination of vigil, as corporal sensations are the imagination of the body. The creative structures tend to express fully the imagination, while the defensive structures tend to limit it because of fixation. Delirium is the pathological imagination of the insane, myths are the imagination of cultures, and dreams are the imagination of sleep.

The disposition to express the full symbolic elaboration of alterity for the exercise of symbolic teaching is proportional to the educator's being open to the imagination. It calls for the gift of creativity and the disposition to practice art and science within the whole. It is art allied to science that fosters subjective and objective union in symbolic science as a result of the expansion of the symbols through the imagination.

## The Symbolic Method

The teaching of Jungian symbolic education is performed through expansion of the symbolic meanings of the content being studied in order for it to be grasped experientially on the level of the Self rather than the ego. The pattern of alterity is distinguished from the other patterns of the ruling archetypal quaternio by its capacity to seek the greatest possible number of meanings of symbols. This is why alterity is the privileged pattern for the method of symbolic constructivism in Jungian symbolic education.

We have already seen the wealth inherent in the master-apprentice archetype (chapter 5), which allows us the creative exercise of fantasy and transference in teaching. Within the pattern of alterity, the interaction of the teacher-pupil polarity may reach the extreme of inversion, in which the teaching capacity of the pupil and the learning capacity of the teacher are being fully exercised. This means that teachers should be open to identifying those students in the class who can make the best use of the experience of symbolic education and encourage them to actively participate in the function of teaching.

Knowing the archetypal patterns of consciousness is useful for understanding and exercising the symbolic method through the alterity archetype, without diminishing the patriarchal organization and responsibility of the roles of teachers and pupils. The patriarchal pattern preserves the identity, the roles and responsibilities, of pupils and teachers in the class and school. Many schools that have tried to shed traditional patriarchal predominance by turning to alternative teaching methods have failed due to wholesale adoption of the matriarchal with no concern for preserving the patriarchal pattern, which maintains limits in the roles of teachers and pupils. This fact underscores the notion that all the archetypes are necessary; none is more important than the other in an absolute sense, for they are all more important in the specific functions that best express their nature within the context of their elaboration.

The increased number of meanings brought about by the subjective-objective interaction in learning leaves the pupils more exposed. Their intimate lives can open up before the teacher and the class, as, for instance, when students start to tell their dreams and personal problems. In such cases, the teacher must treat the meanings of such intimate symbols with the greatest care. This opening can arouse in the teacher the temptation to use what is revealed for patriarchal control of behavior and learning, which would be an abuse of power on the part of the educator (Guggenbühl-Craig 1971). This must be avoided at all costs in exercising symbolic teaching. Such abuse of power is frequently expressed by the omnipotent defensive interpretation, by which I mean one person interpreting another without permission, to manipulate and control, which is the shadow of power in the social dimension. Unfortunately, defensive interpretation is becoming widespread in culture through the popularization of psychological theories and their usage in education. It is not just a matter of preventing the educator from posing as therapist. The problem is far greater and also involves therapists. For both therapists and educators, interpretation should arise from symbolic elaboration rather than from the defensive projection of stereotypes. In the symbolic method, the difference between educator and therapist, in relation to interpretation, lies in the content of their theoretical approach. Education is centered on elaboration of growth, whereas therapy is centered on the elaboration of the shadow with fixations and defenses. Of course, there exists a gray area between education and therapy, in which the educator, and especially the psychological coordinator, uses symbolic constructivism to elaborate existential problems that are directly linked to learning or even to the relationship with classmates and family members. Nevertheless, the utmost care should be taken lest interpretation be used defensively. What I recommend is that teachers use the intimate material of students that appears in class only where it refers to the subject taught or to the pedagogic transference, without revealing the intimacy of the students, which must be protected at all costs.

On applying the symbolic method through the pattern of alterity, we manage the feat of bringing together art and science in education. This is the great door that opens to computerized education in the third millennium. Imagine what the world would be like if the creativity of the Disney and Nintendo studios were dedicated to education: videogames the world over dedicated to studying anthropology, medicine, history, and geography with Scrooge, Goofy, Mickey Mouse, and all other popular figures; a thousand creators following in the footsteps of Monteiro Lobato, a Brazilian author of superb educational children's books; role-playing games with the more advanced technologies. Then imagine a great many of the animated drawings of the world dedicated to education on discs and on the Internet; artists and scientists joined together to convey learning through experience. Imagine children rushing home to play videogames and, with joy and satisfaction, participating in the games, dancing, singing, acting, crying and laughing, full of animation, and all this for the sake of studying, knowing life . . . living! And taking all this back to school the following day for interactive study! Instead of videogames whose characters are disconnected from science, why don't we have games, for instance, between characters that represent the chemical elements, which fight, join together and separate, love and hate one another, marry and have children by virtue of their strictly objective physical-chemical properties? Imagine detective stories in videogames with plots centered on the great discoveries of science! This is the dialectics of right and wrong, good and evil taking root symbolically within scientific, existential learning.

By bringing together art and science in everyday teaching within the pattern of alterity, we come face to face with the great phantom that massacred culture in the West: the subject-object dissociation. To attempt such a feat of confrontation, we need to resort to fantasy and to our creative imaginations. If the previous epoch was that of the educator who transmitted erudition, the Jungian symbolic education of the future will belong to the creative educator who teaches life. For us to have access to this degree of imagination in our institutions for the teaching of science and art within experience, it is useful to understand what has happened historically to the imagination since the cultural dissociation of subject and object. I feel that this is a way to reclaim imagination from its imprisonment and deformation in Western tradition. (I shall take this up again in chapter 12, exploring the meaning of the Christian myth and the alchemical imagination at the birth of modern science, based on the archetypal theory of history.)

## Alterity, Detachment, Initiatory Method, and Constructivism

Based on the archetypal symbolic perspective, I reached the conclusion that the initiatory method in symbolic teaching is predominantly founded on the archetype of alterity. To generate learning in the pupil through constructivism, within the pattern of alterity, the teacher and pupil first have to undergo frustration. The teacher has to be frustrated through detachment from the dominant position of owner of knowledge and the pupil from the passive position identified with ignorance and swallowing without chewing. Teacher and student have to resist the laziness of mere opposition and search for encounters in which opposites become equal, that is, when both teachers and students teach and learn. When perceived archetypally, initiatory and constructivist teaching is an illustrative example of the relative detachment of the matriarchal and patriarchal patterns necessary for alterity to be exercised. In this sense, I would like to present an analogy between constructivist initiatory teaching and the symbolic elaboration of dynamic psychotherapy, since both require frustration to be expressed within the dialectical position.

Psychotherapy that analyses conscious and unconscious symbolic contents takes place within a context of relative frustration such that symbolic elaboration can achieve great depth. The goal of this frustration is to produce a relative detachment of the matriarchal and patriarchal patterns, which will allow the full productivity of the pattern of alterity. This differentiation of symbolic meanings is so important and necessary because often only one of the countless meanings is the path that leads to transformation and cure.

Frustration forces detachment of the ego-other polarity from its usual functioning and makes room for the transcendence in which the archetypal matrices of the psyche become active, with the possible appearance of new conscious and unconscious components. Frustration favors detachment from established points of view, which propitiates the activation of archetypal psychic creativity, a process Erich Neumann called centroversion. Piaget's school refers to this necessary detachment from the old as the need to unbalance (*deséquilibrer*) consciousness in order to construct the new. When elaboration is not restricted to either the matriarchal or the patriarchal pattern, frustration activates the pattern of alterity, which can lead to the deep elaboration of symbols with the perception of their countless meanings.

Any analyst (psychodynamic psychotherapist) knows that the analytical process must take place within a relationship in which the patient's experiences are worked through, without the analyst actively intervening to resolve them in the patient's life. The analyst can neither actively satisfy the patient's needs (matriarchal attachment) nor direct the patient to satisfy them (patriarchal attachment). Insight, existential solutions, and the resulting conduct must emerge from the therapeutic Self, that is, from symbolic elaboration within the transference of the therapist-patient relationship. This means that insight is constructed in the therapeutic Self within the pattern of alterity and the principle of synchronicity. Insight is thus not produced by the analyst and handed over to the analysand. Analysis goes on within the frustration and lacunae that derive from detachment from the matriarchal and patriarchal patterns. This is also the pedagogy of *wu wei* (not doing) of Taoism and Zen Buddhism. It also recalls Teresa of Ávila's "doing without doing", an inherent part of the state of grace of Christian practice.

The primary importance of the analyst's intervention can be deeply understood only through the interrelation of the ruling archetypal patterns. Mere counseling makes it difficult for latent archetypal components to be experienced. If an unmarried thirty-year-old man tells his therapist that he is always fighting with his mother at home, and the therapist tells him that it is time he lived on his own, it is obvious that such directive intervention limits the elaboration of archetypal feelings of defensive attachment (conscious and unconscious), which prevent him from maturing and separating psychologically from his mother. If he follows this advice, he will receive a fish but will not learn how to fish. In other words, he will leave home and not fight so much with his mother, but instead of depending on her, he will depend on his therapist, or he will seek a girlfriend he can depend on. In short, he will not integrate the maternal function that generates dependence and will not mature, as he needs to.

Likewise, if a man says repeatedly that he hates his father and yearns for a good father, and the therapist points out that now he is going to feel better because he has found a good father in his new boss, the therapist is making it difficult for him to remain in a state of frustration until possible amorous archetypal components (conscious and unconscious) can be elaborated in the father-son polarity of the Self.

Many cultures have used frustration to force the matriarchal to submit to the patriarchal pattern, such as for example, the so-called Spartan education, which refers to any rigorously frustrating patriarchal method of education. This is the type of education developed by Moritz Schreber (1808–1861) in the German tradition, which had wide repercussions in Brazilian education at the beginning of the twentieth century. In this case, frustration can force detachment from matriarchal pattern at the cost of an exaggerated attachment to the organizing power of patriarchal pattern, with the subsequent limitations to exercising the pattern of alterity. This often happens in imposed practices of abstinence, whether from sex, drugs, food, comfort, sleep, or any other habit or function.

There also exists the counterpart of complete detachment from the patriarchal pattern because of matriarchal predominance, which also makes it difficult and even impossible to exercise alterity. This is the case, for instance, with orgies of a ritualistic cultural nature, such as Carnival through the ages and around the world, of extensive parties with drink, sex, and drugs, and of the lifestyle practiced by many families nowadays of eating, drinking, and living around the television.

The detachment of sensuality and power seems to be what we seek both in psychotherapy with an analytical base and in symbolic constructivism to express the archetype of alterity. When we do this, we acquire an increased capacity for symbolic expansion, the elaboration of which permits us to integrate many aspects that cannot be reached by matriarchally or patriarchally dominated elaboration. The initiatory transmission of knowledge as a method of teaching is archetypal and exercised through the dominant coordination of the pattern of alterity. Detachment from matriarchal or patriarchal dominance does not eliminate the functions of these archetypes but, on the contrary, is the way to allow these archetypes to function dialectically, side by side.

There is a Hindu legend in which a master was traveling along a road, talking to a disciple about detachment from sensuality. As they were about to cross a creek, they saw a beautiful girl hesitating to cross for fear of getting her dress wet. The master did not think twice. He lifted her in his arms and carried her over the creek. Master and disciple continued to walk along silently, when suddenly the disciple showed great indignation and asked the master why he had broken the rule of detachment so shamelessly. The master answered that he had done so to continue his journey freely and not to remain paralyzed and a slave of desire by fighting it repressively as the disciple had done.

The disciple was practicing matriarchal detachment based on patriarchal dominance. According to this perspective, the master should have repressed completely matriarchal sensuality and not even looked at the girl, much less carried her over the creek. However, by not doing so, the master had detached from matriarchal involvement by not avoiding desire completely and had also detached from patriarchal dominance by not having remained attached to power through repression. This was a great lesson to the disciple about detachment in the dialectical pattern of alterity. The main teaching was that the patriarchal pattern can express detachment of matriarchal sensuality by repression but that this is not sufficient to elaborate completely the function of detachment because repression tends to fixate elaboration together with attachment to power.

## The Scope of the Pattern of Alterity

The initiatory method is at one and the same time experiential and comprehensive, and therefore so profound that many religions and esoteric practices (symbolic experiences without any rational explanation) kept it hermetic (restricted to the initiated). Its difficulty is rooted in its complexity and in the difficulty of understanding what is experienced, chiefly with regard to the interrelation of the parts to one another and simultaneously to the whole. Here lies the unbound capacity of the archetype of alterity to elaborate symbolic meanings in the development of being. Thus, in order to exercise the initiatory method, the educator is called to a true creative initiation in the nature of learning. Many scholars employ the words *hermetic* and *initiatory* as synonyms of *secretly*. In this context, initiatory means profoundly experienced.

The ritual can become a secret teaching limited to the initiated because of its depth, which resists verbal transmission, and because of the psychological value it contains, which must be protected from superficial mundane usage. In this sense, symbolic education is initiatory but not hermetic.

The scope of symbolic elaboration of the archetype of alterity is based on its capacity for quaternary elaboration. Jung described the quaternio as one of the main symbols of psychic totality. It is not by chance that we generally dwell in houses and rooms with doors and windows, sleep in beds, and play in fields that are all quadrangular in shape. We divide time into four seasons and space according to the four cardinal points. In the pattern of alterity, the structuring function of the quaternio exercises its full capacity for symbolic elaboration and psychic productivity. The teacher's ego is capable of opening to archetypal transcendence just as it can create the space for the students to do so. The teacher admits to recognizing his or her own shadow in the same way that he or she points out the students' shadows. However, like all archetypal patterns, this refers to a potential pattern, a goal to be sought.

The importance of the pattern of alterity is shown by the large number of its cultural manifestations, which feature among civilization's greatest achievements. Its depth in the functioning of consciousness has been praised in many cultures as the highest possible state of human differentiation aspired to by those who dedicate themselves to the paths of wisdom. The Tao of Taoism, the middle path and Nirvana of Buddhism, the Zen of Zen Buddhism, the wisdom of Sufism, Samadhi or Moksha of Hinduism, the Metron of the Greeks, the secret of the Kabbalah of Judaism, and the state of grace of Christianity all refer specifically to this state of illumination that perceives the conflict and the equality of opposites to express meanings.

In numerous cultures since ancient times, attempts have been made to cultivate the spirit by relinquishing the sensuality of the flesh and the regalia of power. In this psychological language, this ever-sought "spirit" refers to the full amplitude of symbolic meanings to experience wholeness. To relinquish the sensuality of the flesh is equivalent to detachment from matriarchal dominance; to give up the regalia of power means detaching oneself from the organizing and controlling domination of the patriarchal pattern. It may be concluded that a significant part of mankind's spiritual development has consisted of the search for existence within the predominance of alterity.

The *yin yang* symbol of Taoism, ☯ , which unites black and white inside a circle, is an especially strong expression of duality within unity; it is so complete that it includes a white dot in the black space and a black dot in the white space. Through the essence of Tao and alterity, the *Tao Te Ching*—the sacred book of Taoism—expresses detachment from polarities in order to experience their common essence (Lao Tzu, sixth century B.C.).

## Unity in Diversity (*Dao de Jing*, verse one)

> The Tao that can be expressed
> Is not the eternal Tao.
> The name that can be named
> Is not the eternal name.
> Non-existence I call the beginning of Heaven and Earth
> Existence I call the mother of individual beings
> Therefore does the direction towards non–existence
> Lead to the sight of the miraculous essence,
> The direction towards existence
> To the sight of spatial limitations
> Both are one in origin
> And different only in name
> In its unity is called the secret.
> The secret's still deeper secret
> Is the gateway through
> which all miracles emerge. (Wilhelm 1923)

The *Tao Te Ching* is a book of wisdom conceived within the patterns of alterity and totality. This can be better understood when we consider the Commandments of Christianity, in which patriarchal dominance is evident because detachment from sensuality and moral rules of conduct are dogmatically imposed.

> I am the Lord your God.
> You shall have no other gods before me.
> You shall not make for yourself an idol.
> You shall not make wrongful use of the name of your God.
> Remember the Sabbath and keep it holy.
> Honor your mother and father.
> You shall not murder.
> You shall not commit adultery.
> You shall not steal.
> You shall not bear false witness against your neighbor.
> You shall not covet your neighbor's wife.
> You shall not covet anything that belongs to your neighbor.

In these well-named "commandments" we find a clear illustration of the dogmatic organizing characteristics of the patriarchal pattern codifying the relationship with God, family, and society. In the *Tao Te Ching*, however, we identify the coordination of the alterity archetype searching for a conscious attitude with a common denominator between polarities through detachment of any dogmatic attitude. Verse one of the *Tao Te Ching* above describes the experience of transcendence, of unity in diversity. The first two lines of verse two describe the detachment of one polarity in favor of its counterpole, saying that the one generates the other, and then goes on to express once more duality in unity.

## Synthesis of Antithesis

If all on earth acknowledge the beautiful as beautiful
Then thereby the ugly is already posited
If all on earth acknowledge the good as good
Then thereby is the non-good already posited
For existence and non-existence generate each other
Heavy and light complete each other.
Long and short shape each other.
High and deep convert each other.
Thus also is the Man of calling
He dwells in effectiveness without action.
He practices teaching without talking.
All beings emerge
And does not refuse himself to them
He generates and yet possesses nothing.
He is effective and keeps nothing.
When the work is done
He does not dwell with it.
And just because he does not dwell
He remains undeserted. (Wilhelm 1923)

This is no doubt initiatory or symbolic constructivist teaching because it is trans-rational and the ego detaches itself from polarities to express totality through the dialectical relationship of duality within unity (Byington 1965). It is a *wu wei* teaching of non-action that happens in *kairos,* in the symbolic timing of the master-apprentice relationship. This is the true initiation in learning, the profound teaching of things and of life, which become wisdom. Especially meaningful to this philosophy of teaching is a legend according to which Lao Tzu left this life confessing that his greatest sin had been the writing of the *Tao Tè Ching*. Possibly, the master meant that the description of the mysterious *Tao* in a written text was a mistake, because it could lead many people into the illusion that *Tao* can be taught cognitively and not exclusively through initiatory, that is, symbolic experience.

Another outstanding text that exemplifies most significantly the archetype of alterity and totality in Chinese culture is the *I Ching*. Starting with the fundamental polarity *yang* (the creative) and *yin* (the receptive), it builds eight trigrams that give rise to sixty-four hexagrams, which form a complex dialectical frame to elaborate symbolically and constructively all life situations. Consulting the *I Ching*, one is again and again amazed by the inexhaustible richness of meaning created by the combination of polarities within a coherent system, due to the fact that these polarities vary all the way from opposition to equality.

In the introduction of Richard Wilhelm's 1923 translation of the *I Ching* into German, he gives a brief survey of the eight trigrams (see table 1).

Table 1. Eight Trigrams of the *I Ching*

| Name | Attribute | Image | Family |
|---|---|---|---|
| Chi'ien (the creative) | strong | heaven | father |
| K'un (the receptive) | yielding | earth | mother |
| Ch'en (the arousing) | inciting | thunder | first son |
| K'an (the abysmal) | dangerous | water | second son |
| Kên (Keeping) | resting | mountain | third son |
| Sun (the gentle) | penetrating | wind, wood | first daughter |
| Li (the Clinging) | light-giving | fire | second daughter |
| Tui (joyous) | joyful | lake | third daughter |

Professor Corrêa Pinto (now a monk who goes by Shogyo), who translated Wilhelm's German version of the *I Ching* into Portuguese together with Alayde Mutzenbecher (1982), has called my attention to the son and daughter principles representing dialectical modes of action and reaction between the father-mother, *yang-yin* principles. According to him, we can imagine the first daughter representing the modification brought about in the father's anima by his first contact with the mother. Through the birth of his first daughter, the father becomes gentle as the wind. In the same manner, the mother's animus is modified in the *coniunctio* with the father and becomes aroused and inciting, like thunder, through the birth of the first son.

The marriage *coniunctio* and changes in the father and mother principles, in the anima-animus syzygy, continue through the birth of the second son and daughter. The dominantly narcissistic creativity of pure yang becomes clinging and light, like fire, through the second daughter. Correspondingly, the total passivity of the mother principle becomes threateningly dangerous, like the abyss of deep waters, as expressed by the second son.

As combination and change between *yang* and *yin* continue, through the birth of the third daughter, father yang becomes joyous and calm as the lake, whereas mother *yin*, through the arrival of the third son, now rests thoroughly settled and appeased, as a mountain.

Such poetic abundance of meanings created through the centuries around the *I Ching* express quite well how the principle of synchronicity is the principle through which the archetype of alterity coordinates the elaboration of countless meanings of symbols. From this standpoint, it is easier to see how much more limited are the matriarchal archetype (principle of magical causality) and the patriarchal archetype (principle of reflective causality) in their individual capacities to produce meaning through symbolic elaboration.

The archetype of alterity coordinates the experience of totality through the creative interaction of polarities in the process of transformation. Therefore, the *I Ching* is appropriately considered *The Book of Changes*. The archetype of alterity experiences totality mainly through the dialectical position whereas the archetype of totality experiences totality directly through the contemplative position of the ego-other and other-other polarities, as we shall see in the next chapter.

# Chapter 10

# THE CONTEMPLATIVE POSITION AND THE TOTALITY PATTERN IN TEACHING

The archetype of totality operates within the ruling archetypal quaternio and around the central archetype by directly coordinating experiences of totality.

Imagine that the four regent archetypes that make up the ruling archetypal quaternio are psychic forces—intelligences or fields—that typically elaborate symbols based on the coordinating function of the central archetype. This means that each experience becomes a symbol of being inasmuch as it is centralized and coordinated with experiences of the past, the present, and those prospectively foreseen for the future. When postulated in this manner, the central archetype covers the potential totality of the Self. This elaborating, integrating, and coordinating function is exercised through the four ruling archetypal patterns. These four patterns are the main strategies by which the central archetype coordinates the process of symbolic life: in the matriarchal pattern, basically through instinctive sensuality; in the patriarchal pattern, through abstract organization; in alterity, essentially through the dialectics of opposites; and in totality, through the direct experience of wholeness. Each pattern expresses the central archetype and thus operates from and toward wholeness, through its own characteristics.

Symbols that express the potential of full realization of the central archetype in the Self, such as the cross, the tree, pearl, child, egg, mandalas, and the *anthropos*, may be more or less dominantly elaborated by one of the four ruling archetypal patterns.

The advantage of underscoring the strategy of each of the ruling archetypes is, on the one hand, to frame the four great archetypal intelligences of symbolic elaboration and, on the other, to draw attention to the complexity of the centralizing function of the central archetype, which includes the competition among the four patterns for symbolic elaboration. At first this competition may be incomprehensible, when the characteristics of omnipresence and omniscience inherent in the central archetype are idealized. However, if we admit that this competition does exist—and that it is as dramatic as a contest between giants in the psyche—but nevertheless accept the coordinating function of the central archetype, then we achieve some notion of its complexity. It is partial and at the same time global.

This complexity increases extraordinarily when we consider the interrelation of the defensive and creative patterns in the centralizing function of the central archetype, that is, the polarity of good and evil. How can this archetype privilege a neurotic, psychopathic, borderline, or even psychotic defensive structure to the detriment of its creative counterpart? If the shadow is evil, how can the central archetype allow its expression to the detriment of the light and good of consciousness? Although paradoxical, this is nonetheless a psychic reality according to the perspective of Jungian symbolic psychology, on which Jungian symbolic pedagogy is based. This de-idealized notion of the central archetype comes from the theoretical concept and from the existential and clinical experience of the major psychic function being symbolic expressiveness. This being so, the central archetype can express its function even by including the strategy of the psychotic pattern. It is being that drags itself along in naked flesh, bleeding and suffering in the depth of abysses to proceed on its path (Byington 1992c). Amidst the relative existential inadequacy of neurosis or the extreme inadequacy of psychosis, there persists the expressiveness of symbols and the effort of the Self to exist by coordinating the meanings of experience in whatever possible fashion, through health and disease, virtue and sin, good and evil, consciousness and shadow (Silveira 1981). It is necessary to understand that the expressive capacity of the vital functions far surpasses the borders of normality. The nervous system, blood circulation, and cellular metabolism go on working in a gangrene-infected limb. Moonlight and dawn continue to occur and influence the imagination to write poetry inspired on Hiroshima and Nagasaki.

This complexity of the central archetype—including polarities such as right and wrong, health and disease, good and evil, sin and virtue—is difficult to understand, especially from the ethical and religious points of view. For a Christian, for instance, it is difficult to accept the road to salvation through the symbolic elaboration of sin, as Christ preached when he called the sinners to him. To admit sin within the nature of God, however, is far more difficult. In psychological terms this means that it is one thing for us to admit neurosis, psychopathy, and psychosis as archetypal dysfunctions or ego defense mechanisms and quite another to agree that these dysfunctions are used as existential archetypal strategies by the central archetype. The fact that we now know the genetic basis of many mental pathological symptoms does not mitigate the complexity of the central archetype but rather increases it, for the coordination of the development of the personality—and of culture and the overall functioning of the brain, which include and express these pathological dysfunctions.

The proposed reunion of the subjective and objective in symbolic elaboration includes the reunion of mind and body through the creative or defensive experience of the symbolic body. The educator often comes across the phenomenon of a child who has difficulties with relationship and communication and whose school performance is poor. In these cases, the possibility of organic autism, brain paralysis, and other neurological disorders has to be discussed, along with psychodynamic autistic defense and isolation of normally timid and introverted children. Due to the mind-body dissociation, neurologists, psychologists, and educators often fail to reach a common approach for coping with the child and to orient the school and the family. In a case like this, we have to differentiate the autistic neurological disorder from the autistic psychodynamic defense that is developed to express symbols outside consciousness and becomes defensively fixated in symbolic elaboration.

Due to the enormous complexity of the functioning of the central archetype, which embraces so many different things, I have chosen the archetype of totality as the fourth archetypal pattern of the ruling archetypal quaternio to emphasize exclusively the totalizing psychic experience by consciousness. Through it, we can emphasize this totalizing strategy of the central archetype that elaborates structuring symbols and brings to consciousness the overall notion of the psychic moment, an actual accounting whose gestalt is a balance sheet.

During the lengthy and complex process of circumstantial development of the individual and of the collective Self—a lifelong symbolic process—

there are innumerable situations that foster the experience of totality. On the individual level, we have circumstances of realization of the whole with its positive and negative aspects, interaction, direction, balance and unbalance, losses and creative possibilities, all forming a global gestalt. This synthesis allows us to experience common reactions to the present general state of our process of being: "How good it is to be alive!", "I don't know what is the use of living!", "How difficult life is!" as momentary daily experiences that express the archetype of totality. On the collective level, these totalizing experiences are often expressed by representative leaders who bring to consciousness the notion of the state of the community, of culture, of the planet, and—more and more—of our being in the cosmos (Worldwatch 2010). In school and in class, this experience of totality is very important, for this is what enables us each and every day to evaluate the general learning disposition of a class or the general functioning of the institution. It is also fundamental in coping with the general state of teaching in our city and country, and even in thinking of teaching as a whole worldwide, as a manifestation of self-reflection of the humanized cosmic Self.

The difference between the archetype of totality and the central archetype may be hard to understand because many authors use the latter to express all psychic experiences of totality. To Jungian symbolic psychology, the concept of the central archetype expresses totality through all symbols and archetypes, whereas the archetype of totality is conceived to elaborate exclusively the direct experience of totality by the central archetype. The inclusion of the archetype of totality among the psyche's four main patterns of symbolic elaboration is meant to address specifically the direct relationship of consciousness with the phenomenon of totality of the central archetype in symbolic elaboration.

During day-to-day activities, we often appraise situations. This is a matter for the structuring function of evaluation, which always occupies a key position in symbolic elaboration. This function was described by Freud as the superego and attributed to the introjection of cultural values (Freud 1913). Without disclaiming this cultural component, like all the other structuring functions, the evaluation function is here considered archetypal, that is, innate and normally operative in symbolic elaboration. It may be in harmony with the values of the traditional cultural Self, which form the superego, or it may contradict them due to special dynamics of the individual Self. When this function is operating defensively, we become neurotic perfectionists, which makes reflection obsessive, inadequate, nonproductive, and exhaustive (Freud 1909). Normally, however, the evaluation function is one of the most important activities of the process of reflection within symbolic elaboration. It is what makes us constantly reflect on the results of the elaboration that are gathered from behavior.

Like all symbols and structuring functions, the evaluation function (both creative and defensive) may be dominantly coordinated by one of the four ruling patterns. In matriarchal pattern, the main polarities elaborated are I like–I don't like, I want–I don't want, useful–useless, pleasure–frustration, I need–I don't need, intimacy–distancing, and so forth. In the patriarchal pattern, elaboration is generally undertaken through the polarities of right–wrong, I must–I mustn't, important–insignificant, rational–irrational, and so on. In the pattern of alterity, there is a predominance of the dialectic confrontation of all the poles of polarities that belong to the experience of the situation in question. Finally, in the pattern of totality, elaboration with the evaluation function is carried out by grasping the situation as a whole in itself and, at the same time, within the whole existential process. It is extremely important that we realize this archetypal variation of the evaluation function: it makes us aware that the evaluation of learning by examinations and grades only is quite limited in that it is exercised exclusively in the patriarchal pattern of the polarity of right–wrong. It is also crucial to appraise, for instance, whether a pupil studies because of the pleasure to learn or due to competition and anxiety of being left behind or just to accomplish tasks. It is also important to know the interaction between grades and behavior, such as self-esteem, jealousy, envy, sexuality, and all the other structuring functions. There are pupils who get poor grades to compete with a sibling who is an excellent student (defensive competition). Others do not know why they study and the learning function operates exclusively on an island of the personality. There are still others who foster an inferiority complex and so await the first opportunity to quit studying for good. Evaluation on the level of totality enables us to situate the moment of learning systemically in the general panorama of the student's life. Exclusively objective teaching tends to convert the pupils into motivated robots, in which case individuality appears as a dysfunction of learning. It is nevertheless obvious that each person experiences learning with particular meanings, that is, whether consciously or not, students experience learning symbolically. Taking this into account, the teacher and the school can become much more efficient.

Let us take as an example the extensive and well-illustrated clinical case presented by Gerhard Adler in his book *The Living Symbol* (1960). Prose and poetry, paintings, corporal expression, active imagination, and elaboration of dreams demonstrate the importance of the use of expressive techniques for symbolic elaboration, forming a true apprenticeship of the overall expressive capacity of being in Jungian analysis. The clinical case concerns a middle-aged woman prone to panic attacks. Inspired by one of these attacks, which lasted several days, she wrote the following poem:

> The Eye and the Wilderness
> The lightning strikes the granite peaks;
> They cannot writhe, they cannot scream.
> Their wounds bleed stones, their helpless rocks
> Roll grinding in the glacier stream.
>
> All night, a mad malignant wind
> Buffets the ridge with blow on blow
> And from the high tormented crest
> Draws out a shrieking plume of snow.
>
> The bridge of logs is swept away,
> The path stops short on the moraine
> At the black gulf where nothing lives
> Except the night's inhuman pain.
>
> No voice, no face, no living soul
> Only the two of us are there:
> The Eye looks at the wilderness,
> The wilderness returns its stare. (Adler, 1960, p. 52)

In the ruling archetypal quaternio, we see several important aspects of the symbols that make up the poem and contribute to an understanding of the general state of the personality. The title draws our attention to confrontation and the possibility of exercising the dialectic of encounter that is peculiar to the pattern of alterity. Indeed, the fact that the patient has written a poem about such an overwhelming emotional crisis is already an indication that the pattern of alterity is activated. It is the attitude of alterity that inspires someone to creatively seek a more profound meaning of a psychic state such as a panic attack. Its terribly painful, threatening, undesirable, and sickly sense permeates the matriarchal and patriarchal patterns and prevents the perception of anything necessary, productive, healthy, or beneficial. In fact a panic attack creates such a threatening psychic state that many psychiatrists limit themselves to attempting to eliminate it thoroughly by drugs, a patriarchal approach. They do not dare to enter the terrain of alterity and seek out the more complex meanings in the suffering, which only the alterity pattern can reveal. Although the poem, by its creation, its title, and in the last two stanzas, shows the intense elaborating presence of the alterity pattern, all the other patterns are also present in an important sense. The poem illustrates very well the interaction that takes place in the regent quaternio for the elaboration of these structuring functions and symbols.

Matriarchal dynamics elaborate an intense suffering expressed by solitude, freezing of Eros and all nature, mountains being struck by lightning, and the fall of the bridge, a symbol of dissociation and the threat of total isolation and the interruption of life itself. The intense suffering alerts us to the danger of suicide, especially if the psychodynamics of the case lead to defensive depression, that is, if the suffering in question cannot be faced openly and creatively and the patient starts to recriminate herself for what is not her fault. The terrifying suffering of the panic attack makes it extremely difficult to elaborate in the pattern of alterity and is the main cause of the defensive attachment of therapists and patients to the literal experience of crises in matriarchal and patriarchal patterns. This dreadful suffering induces them to reduce everything to the body and nervous system in a cause-effect relation, a reduction that makes therapists incapable of a broader symbolic understanding and leads them to use medication and cognitive behavior psychology defensively without any deeper symbolic elaboration. It is one thing to prescribe a drug to alleviate a symptom and to help in understanding its symbolic significance; it is quite another to get rid of the symptom by repressing with it the patient's existential drama. In the same way that there are teachers who are not the least interested in their pupils' lives, there are psychiatrists and neurologists who are not interested in understanding their patients' life processes.

The presence of the patriarchal pattern in the poem is not as easy to detect as the other patterns of the quaternio, since here it acts in a defensive and consequently somewhat deformed way. If the patriarchal pattern were to function here creatively, as an organizing and conquering mission, we might find it expressed as a heroic rescue mission to repair the destroyed bridge. Instead, it appears defensively as the aggressive lightning and wild wind that attacks the glacier, tears at the mountains, and closes the path. In fact, many situations in which the matriarchal pattern is wounded also present serious defensive patriarchal dysfunctions, which contribute to and aggravate the wounds. In such cases, the wound is treated with a whip, which favors the inculcation of a depressive, suicidal, or sadomasochistic pattern. We often see the dynamics of personality presenting the patriarchal disorder as exaggerated perfectionism expressed by the critical and intolerant judgment of an evil superego, an implacable punisher of suffering. The panic attack is symbolically expressed in this poem by the movement of the glacier representing the wounded matriarchal pattern, along with the attack of the evil wind as the limiting, merciless criticism of a defensive patriarchal pattern. This does not invalidate the presence of specific neurological and genetic components in the patient that might have enhanced the expression of the existential problem specifically through the defensive strategy of the panic syndrome.

The pattern of alterity is clearly presented throughout the poem by the confrontation of polarities that begin to inspire the personality and will eventually lead it to the analytical process. Identified and dominated for decades by neurotic defenses, the Self—by virtue of age, disillusioned with the exaggerated pride and omnipotence that derive from patriarchal defenses, and the very suffering and gravity of panic attacks—presents a transformation in which the archetype of alterity is activated to coordinate the position of dialectic confrontation of the problem by the ego. The eye that confronts the wilderness in the poem dramatically expresses the dialectic interaction of the ego and the other as the chronic shadow in the pattern of alterity (*Auseinandersetzung*). Hermeneutics are important here for understanding symbolically the sentences of the poem either in the study of literature or psychopathology.

All this leads to the archetype of totality and illustrates the function of its pattern in the symbolic elaboration of the poem. This presence stands out in the gestalt, in what it conveys explicitly and implicitly. It is very important to realize to what extent perception of the implicit action of the pattern of totality is produced by the pattern of alterity. Due to the confrontation of polarities in harmony and in conflict within the literary creativity of alterity, especially those polarities related to the matriarchal and patriarchal giants, at each and every moment, we experience detachment and transcendence. In the pattern of alterity, the ego is oriented by a psychological pattern in which none of the poles is exclusively right, because the two opposites make up life. This leads to detachment either from one pole or the other and reminds the ego that this can only occur because a greater force rules them. This constant experience of detachment and transcendence in the pattern of alterity allows the structuring symbols and functions to be elaborated in the pattern of totality.

Within the gestalt of totality in this case, we experience a Self that embraces all its parts meaningfully. We have seen these parts in the matriarchal, patriarchal, and alterity patterns embedded in the poem. Much suffering, critical repression and disposition, opening and courage to seek understanding creatively within the suffering of this enormous psychic conflict explodes in panic attacks! We feel a *kairos*, the mysterious time of the existential process in the fourth decade of a woman's life where all this is happening. Based on the reunion of all these partial experiences, a gestalt is formed that the pattern of totality brings to consciousness. Something transcendent, mysterious, and global floods the Self and thus we experience synchronistically in an absolute and factual way a whole that is unique in that life situation.

The experience of the pattern of totality is fundamental for the orientation of being: where to follow, what to do, what positions to take—all this is influenced by it. Of course, the matriarchal pattern guides us by sensual desire, patriarchal by the rules of order and duty, alterity by creativity of confrontation, but in a subliminal way, with omnipresent and omniscient characteristics, the pattern of totality affects our lives through the necessity of wholeness, genuineness and coherency, joining together everything that has to do with the process of being (Byington 1965). It is very important for the educator to reserve some room in daily tasks for this experience, which underscores the values and priorities in the learning process. When the educator is closed to this archetype, there is the risk of being buried by innumerable daily chores, which limit reflection and prevent the correction of the daily itinerary through values that lend a larger meaning to professional engagement.

Based on the symbols elaborated in the poem, which so deeply express the archetypal forces of the complexity of her being, what overall orientation will predominate in this woman's life? Is her being heading for depression and suicide? Will she resort to some lifelong anti-anxiety medication, and if so, how will she cope with the side effects and the risk of drug dependence? Will she begin a process of analysis to elaborate old and strongly structured defenses? Will her defenses join together in the panic attacks and change to a physical clinical syndrome? Will she find courage in her being to face other crises and go on using her creative literary abilities to elaborate them? All these paths are possible. But there is a whole, a totality that can appear mysteriously and uniquely during elaboration and more or less express her ontological identity and influence the existential process. This experience of totality, as we have seen, is fleeting, yet its range is spread all over the space-time, present-past-future dimensions with the tendency to grasp the consequences, possibilities, direction, and sense of the whole existential process.

Consciousness of the existence of the pattern of totality and its exercise through proper positioning of the ego can greatly increase the integrity of the personality and the wisdom of living. This is one of the inestimable functions of meditation, the practice of which has brought so much depth and growth to the psychological development of individuals and cultures. The art of meditating teaches us, through the medium of time, to open the ego to detachment from parts, to experience transcendence and the whole, and this facilitates the constellation of the pattern of totality in symbolic elaboration. The patient chose the path of self-knowledge to rediscover the sense of her existential process, and Adler's book describes in detail and depth the path of Jungian psychotherapy she pursued.

## The Pattern of Totality in Teaching in General

In schools where the teachers are poorly paid, schools with precarious classrooms, unstable atmosphere, and needy pupils with serious economic and social problems, such as for instance, criminality and drug addiction, the experience of the totality pattern is so swamped by the want and pathology experienced in matriarchal and patriarchal patterns that the dynamics of teaching are rarely realized in all their depth. The defensive predominance of these patterns activated by the pupils' precarious health, the teachers' low wages, and the disorganization of the educational network creates an immense frustration that appears to be the central problem of education, making it difficult to experience alterity and totality. It is an illusion to think that massive investments in education, with a significant raise in teachers' wages, funds for research, reform, and construction of new schools, acquisition of school materials, and improvement of health and meals in schools, will also solve these other problems of teaching. This is what has happened many times with the focus on the socioeconomic dimension of the problem of teaching, especially in developing countries. All these measures are necessary, yet they may obscure and fail to elaborate the problem of teaching as regards its content, the method of exercising it, and its function in the pupil's lives, the job market, society at large, and culture generally.

The struggle for better-equipped schools, better-paid teachers, and pupils in reasonable socioeconomic conditions should not hide the deep dissatisfaction that emerges from the limitations of teaching in itself, its method, aims and results. Realization of limitations of teaching proper and the measures to correct this may then be applied to all teaching institutions along with an attempt to attend basic needs. Clear identification of these limitations on different levels is of the utmost importance for a country like Brazil, which is going through a phase of basic teaching limitations never before known in its history.

The pattern of totality allows for the exercise of existential philosophy, the ontology of human dimensions. The perception of existential situations as a whole that are not necessarily desired, repudiated, or idealized but rather simply confronted as a real, human whole directs being to the philosophy of life, metaphysics, the essential questioning of the primordial why and what for. Exercising the totality pattern in education is highly important to enable us to separate the productive, necessary, and authentic from the useless, superfluous, and alienating. It is quite shocking when we become aware of the immense investment made in useless education whose inevitable result is to be forgotten.

## Basic Wants, Content, Method, and Aim

Thinking education within the pattern of totality becomes a philosophical reflection on teaching in general to be practiced at each bend on the road. This reflection needs first to identify the matriarchal needs of schools, pupils, and teachers and the patriarchal limitations of the organization of individual teaching and the school network. Next to be identified are the content, method, and aims of teaching, within the four ruling archetypal patterns. Satisfying the matriarchal and patriarchal wants requires resources and administration, which depend on the political and socioeconomic situation of the community. As for the content, purpose and method, these require being open to the reformulation of exclusively objective and rational traditional teaching, at the same time reflecting on the humanism in which the system of teaching is inserted.

The pattern of totality elaborates teaching in its overall why and wherefore and directs us to the humanism that formulates the sense of learning in the ontological identity of being. When we practice this elaboration, at whatever level of schooling, be it kindergarten or postgraduate, at each and every moment we can change the direction of teaching and redirect it toward the integrity of being in relation with work, social functioning of society, the meaning the individual lives of teachers and students, the culture we live in, and the planet on which our species experiences the cosmos. Exercising Jungian symbolic education is not just a matter of knowing and carrying out a program and a method, but rather of experiencing an ideal and reflecting on a day-to-day basis the course of its search. It is a matter of preserving and continuing the search of the great educators who always subordinated the paths of education to the values of humanism.

## The Totality Pattern and the Content of Teaching

The holistic perception of the content of teaching enables us to elaborate whether the parts form a coherent and creative whole. Unfortunately, what we perceive in a general sense, regardless of the socioeconomic level of the school and even the developmental level of the country where it is located, is a progressive fragmentation with defensive specialization and a plethora of pedagogic contents on all levels.

This state of teaching—fragmented and overburdened by the plethora of content—is so traditional that we consider it an objective fact and do not even question it. Frequently we teach history, geography, mathematics, science, languages, art, and education as separate sectors of existence that are only related in their application but have no interrelation in origin and development. Thus the very exercise of horizontal or interdisciplinary teaching is limited to sewing patches on a big patchwork quilt. This fragmentation extends to professional compartmentalization and defensive specializations. Students graduate with notable erudition in their fields but often have not the least notion how to articulate their knowledge at the existential and cultural level. It is no use trying to correct this distortion only by including humanism courses within specializations, since the fragmentation of learning comes before specializations and affects even the teaching of the humanities.

The main factor of fragmentation in teaching, which now occurs even in lower school, is due to the dissociation of subject and object, which is followed by the loss of concern for integrity of being and consequently also of learning. Exclusively objective and dominantly cognitive teaching stresses the differences between subjects and precludes the possibility of their interrelation and integrated exposition in the whole. Within this illusion, learning remains fragmented, subjects being learned and exercised in isolation. This limitation of teaching and its application lead to the learned contents not interacting within the Self and tending to remain isolated functions of consciousness. This feature fosters alienation of learning, makes it difficult to use what is learned in daily life, and favors its being forgotten. Perhaps the worst of all is that this method separates learning from love and aesthetics. It contaminates knowledge with the viruses of anti-Eros and disharmony. Love invokes the whole and repudiates partial relationships, while aesthetics calls for harmony through the coherent interrelationship of the truth of parts within a lifestyle related to wholeness.

The dissociation of subject and object prevents the critical subordination of the values of education to humanism. It is common for pupils to feel that they struggle to learn many different things without understanding what good they serve, except to take tests, pass on to the next year, and eventually get a diploma and a job. The worst part is that most of the time the teacher is in the same situation of fragmentation and alienation as the pupil.

From high school on, education suffers an increased tendency toward the cultural Babel of fragmentation and specialization of learning. Each subject, tends to become an independent discourse, and its distance from the others and the whole increases with its complexity. The transition from a single teacher for a whole grade to one teacher for each subject at the end of lower school is an important mark in discussing the problem of fragmentation of the pedagogic Self.

In Brazil, we have the same teacher for all subjects up to the fifth grade, and this makes the transference teaching relationship more personal and intimate, favoring the matriarchal pattern and preserving it somewhat, despite the fact that the dissociation of subject and object already jeopardizes its fully creative experience. The fact that the classes stay with the same teacher, usually a woman, encourages the continuity of parental transference through the teaching transference and articulates the intimate interaction of the family and the school Self. On the teacher's side, the long-term and daily exposure activates maternal or paternal characteristics in their personalities, which complement the pupil's transference. The fact that the subjects are not particularly complex, along with this activated transference intimacy, favors subjective-objective proximity, despite the methodological tendency that already appears at this point of teaching to separate them. This subject-object closeness, which survives in the lower-school period, affects imitative matriarchal education and often structures aptitudes in the pupils that remain throughout the rest of their lives. This does not disappear in the high-school period, for the pupil's emotional relation with the subject will continue to be very influenced by the pupil's emotional relation with the teacher, but the emotional relation with the school and with learning in general is quite different in high school, due to the change in the transference relation between teacher and pupil, among other variables, because of having a different teacher for each subject.

The transition from the fifth to the sixth grade subdivides the transference relationship in the pedagogic Self of the pupils, the teacher, and the class on both the subjective and objective levels. Accompanied by the subject-object dissociation, this subdivision of teaching aggravates the fragmentation of learning. It is not that the teacher's specialization should not exist, but its existence is another strong reason to seek overall, practical integration of contents of subjects and of the entire program, that is, the opposite of the tendency now observed in most schools.

The diversification of teachers and the resulting increased fragmentation of teaching from the sixth grade onward coincide with the emotional surcharge of puberty. Yet, because subjective factors are not taken into consideration, we have no rite of passage to offer our students, such as what happens in puberty in tribal cultures. Because of the materialistic rationalism that predominates in our culture, and the massive exclusion of subjectivity in teaching, all rituals have been greatly weakened and practically abandoned. The weakening of family collective rituals that could serve as a reference for the development of the personality of the young, which could intensely foster the humanist intimacy of the teacher-pupil relation, creates an enormous demand in modern society.

A good example of this lack of integration between subjective and objective is the sex education courses that begin in the fifth grade. Generally, an appropriate description of sexual anatomy and physiology is taught, which is considerable progress. Nevertheless sexuality remains an island, and a subjectively incomplete one at that, within the predominantly objective program of teaching. It is important that sexual education be carried out together with teaching the emotional development of the personality and the acquisition of the capacity to love. Indeed, the capacity to love, which includes the compassionate consideration of the other, encompassing the body, society, and nature, must be conveyed as the greatest acquisition of learning, with sexuality as one of its components. Tribal rites of initiation were not created artificially; they exist by virtue of the need for the personality to develop as a whole. When the educator opens up to the pupils' subjective needs, elaboration of the experiences exercised by means of rituals is immediately resumed. It is very alienating to teach sexuality outside the context of emotional identity formation of individuals and the loving relationship of humankind. This is so alienating because the main emotional interest of most students during high school is the construction of affectionate relationships.

Because this predominantly rational and objective teaching is not integrated with humanism, many fundamental manifestations of the Self cannot be elaborated consciously through the persona and will be acted out through the shadow. In most cases these symbols are expressed in the circumstantial shadow (the one that possesses circumstantial defenses which the ego can confront and elaborate), though this does not prevent symbols from being expressed improperly in the shadow of the group Self. The problems of drugs, sexual promiscuity, bullying, delinquency, and lack of interest in studies are among these expressions. Social pathology often shocks us without due perception of its psychodynamic roots in the defensive structuring functions that form the values of collective consciousness. The growing problem of adolescence in industrialized society, for example, cannot be understood if we do not take into account the fact that the liberation of customs afforded was not accompanied by the engagement of youth to construct responsible participation in labor and social welfare. This can be done through education focused on the immediate usage of what is learned in school within a social cooperative humanism.

A group of girls from a sixth-grade class began to ostracize a classmate, attacking her and accusing her of being a "hen" for having "necked" with three boys at the same party. This was clearly a case of competition and envy expressed with the defensive election of a scapegoat for projecting the group shadow. The rite of initiation of puberty was being experienced outside teaching and in the shadow, despite the fact that it was accompanied by the group's feeling that it knew everything about sex. The group's emotional problem was affecting the class Self and limiting learning.

When called upon to intervene, the psychological coordinator learned that one of the ways the group of girls had of attacking the scapegoat was to ridicule her still small breasts. The coordinator began to meet with the group and work through the structuring symbols of the insecurity of physical identity defensively projected onto the classmate. From the very beginning, it was obvious that these structuring symbols and functions of sexual identity involved opposite categories of superiority and inferiority: superiority because she had "won" three boys at a party at which many classmates had spent most of the time unaccompanied; inferiority because one characteristic mark of puberty in girls and of feminine physical identity—her breasts—had not yet fully developed.

In elaborating the symbols and functions of physical development, including the growth of the breasts and the capacity to find a boyfriend, the counselor asked each member of the group to tell how she felt about these in her own life and with respect to her own body. The appearance of anxiety and insecurity in the group was very intense. Weekly meetings were set up, and the many structuring symbols elaborated were gradually grouped around the symbolic body (the various meanings of each part of the body) and the formation of sexual identity. Due to the embarrassment expressed by the group, the coordinator resorted to her creativity and devised a form of expression. Each girl gave herself a grade (from zero to ten) for the self-esteem she felt for each part of her body, from feet to ears. The grades were placed in a jar and then selected at random for discussion without identifying the author. As the group revealed its intimacy and elaborated symbolically the feelings of insecurity about the various parts of the body, the coordinator debated the formation of woman's identity in our culture and offered objective and subjective instruction on how to cope with development, insecurity, and limitations. This is the symbolic teaching that conjugates the subjective and objective in learning and is so different from the rational, objective, and inexperienced teaching of sexuality which the group had already had and which proved to be useless in dealing with the crisis of puberty. After two meetings, the group's scapegoat could be invited to join and share in the problems which had been projected onto her, and which were then elaborated as problems of each one in the group.

The experience of adolescent crisis outside the curriculum is a glaring example of the alienated and alienating result of the subject-object dissociation and dehumanization of teaching. I do not know of any tribal culture that teaches objective data and deals with adolescence as if nothing were happening subjectively. It is no wonder that many adolescents in our culture do not have the least motivation to study, as the focus of their interest has no relation to the content of teaching, which, besides excluding emotion, has no practical usage and no immediate economic gain. It is not a surprise then that many youngsters are much more attracted to sexual promiscuity, drugs, purely entertaining videogames, computer addiction, and delinquency, finding these much more interesting than school. To be humanized, teaching has to be centered on what is going on within the students. It is the individual existential process inserted into the social dimension that must be the backbone of teaching, rather than specialized and partial learning separated from existence. The crisis of adolescence is centered in social assertion of structuring functions of self-esteem, emotion, sexuality, love, adventure, jealousy, envy, ambition, competition, insecurity, body symbolism, existential intelligence, and a thousand other subjective factors. The prevalence of mostly objective content in the teaching of adolescents is absurd because it bores them and does not prepare them for life. That is why symbolic teaching, which joins together the subjective and objective, must necessarily include fundamental changes in teacher training and program organization.

The totality pattern shows us that predominantly rational and objective teaching is not anthropocentric and therefore cannot claim to be humanistic. For it to be so, the program has to be centered on what the pupils do and how they live, rather than what they have to learn to correspond to the abstract erudition of specialists. If a program of teaching were set up that was anthropocentric, pragmatic and experience-based, rather than objective and centered on erudition like most of today's programs, perhaps we could greatly reduce its present content. Anyone with the archetype of totality even minimally activated realizes, on leafing through a high-school curriculum, that most of what is being taught is prone to being forgotten because it has no utility in the pupils' existential process. The specialists' awareness of the need for anthropocentric teaching should precede any movement toward interdisciplinary programming. This is the most important step toward joining with colleagues from other subjects to program and execute an existentially useful curriculum guided by daily practice. The teacher has to opt between creating existential bridges that insert knowledge in life and passing on alienated knowledge condemned to oblivion.

In the way that a good deal of today's teaching is programmed, the integrating activity of the central archetype is obstructed by this alienation, and the ego is unduly weighed down by the fragmentation of learning. The archetype of totality enables us to become aware, in an impressively reiterated manner, of the fragmentation of the pedagogic Self. However, because this fragmentation is in harmony with the very cultural pathology of subject-object dissociation that accompanied the universal institutionalization of modern scientific learning, nothing happens. The result is a loss of harmonious interaction of the forces of the ruling archetypal quaternio and a progressive increase of patriarchal dominance in learning. Teachers concentrate on delivering the program. Pupils strive to learn the program and take examinations to show their parents and teachers through their grades that they have learned it. One does not know who is more deluded, because compartmentalization precludes articulating teaching within the Self and the perception of its existential pertinence. This patriarchal exacerbation in the fragmentation of the pedagogic Self severs the emotional-affectionate relation with learning and diminishes the interest of the students. Under these limitations, when the examinations are over, pupils, parents, and teachers are exhausted without knowing quite why, yet the fact is that they have all contributed in their own way to making teaching persecutory, a boring obligation that many want to fulfill and then flee. Holidays take on a defensive connotation, since learning is subliminally or openly identified by pupils, teachers, and parents as a duty bereft of pleasure. Its practice is devitalized. In the short run, this type of learning builds up a prejudice against studying and learning in the pupil and in the collective consciousness.

An example: a twelve-year-old boy who loves to study was in the sixth grade learning grammatical agreement in Portuguese, Greek mythology in history, climate and winds in geography, breathing in science, and equations in mathematics. One Sunday, after doing his homework, he complained to his mother that he did not understand why he was studying these things. He argued that when he had sailing classes, he knew exactly what each part of the boat and each maneuver were for and how to use them, but at school it was just the opposite. He had not the slightest idea of what the things he studied were good for. No adult ever mentioned those things, and whenever he wanted them to explain his lessons, he realized that they had forgotten most of what they had learned. He concluded by asking his mother if he could go sailing all day and quit going to school.

His mother, a physician, told him that it was not quite like that, that what he was studying did make a lot of sense. Following her maternal intuition, she asked him the name of the watch he used in sailing competitions. "Chronometer". he replied at once. "*Chronos* is that great god of time you are studying in mythology, isn't he? He did not let his sons grow and swallowed them so that time would never pass, and he would always be the only one to rule. *Metro* means measurement, so you measure your regatta with a chronometer. See what the words you study in your Portuguese class are like? They were born and joined together over time, while people sailed over the seas and discovered the planet. Myths tell these stories. Numbers were also invented and used to name time and distances and many other relations between things, like words were invented and used to give a name to things, so that we could talk about the relationship between them and between us and things. That is why you are called Michael, and we have just celebrated your twelfth birthday. Mathematics, Portuguese, and English are brothers. Portuguese and English talk to one another in words and mathematics speaks through numbers. Together they express the communication of life. When you were in my belly, we only knew the number one. When you were born, we became two, and three counting Daddy. Then Helen was born and now we are four. The wind blows with our breathing. Winds are the breath of the lungs of the earth. When people smoke, they dirty their lungs, and when factories pollute the air, the winds pollute the earth and hurt its breath." In her motherly anxiety at seeing her son's idealism in jeopardy, she had plunged into a meandering lecture. All that she wanted to say was: "Go on studying, son, because studying is worth it. Though you might feel quite the opposite right now, learning is something marvelous that broadens consciousness and enriches life immeasurably. I love learning, because it gathers everything together in just one thing: the life of the universe and the affectionate relationship of all things and creatures."

The boy picked up on his mother's anxiety without understanding half of what she was saying. Suddenly he exclaimed: "Mother, if the wind is the breath of the earth and the number is the word's brother, then everything is connected. Wow! That's brilliant!" His mother began to cry, and they hugged each other. Little did they know that even Pythagoras found it wonderful that the boy, at least in that brief instant, understood through his mother's anxiety the Greek ideal of *paideia*: to teach human beings that all is one (*en to pan*).

## The Teaching Program

The school has to have a curriculum. The teachers have to cover the curriculum. The pupils have to study the curriculum. Evaluations are necessary to elaborate the efficacy of the teaching. Otherwise, the students will not pass their college boards. How were the university entrance exams devised? By the same system that made the curriculum. If we see that the pupils are studying an enormous amount of superfluous content that is bound for oblivion because it will never be used, what to do? One wonders whether the authors of the curricula would come up with the same programs if they made them to interact with the other subjects within life as a whole. But how can they do that if they consider their programs exclusively within their specializations and fail to interact with colleagues from other subjects? Just how to define the problem is very difficult, because it requires more than simply changing the programs; it also calls for a radical change in mentality toward learning.

The program springs from the same fragmented, alienated learning culture and is made by the same teachers who exercise and intensify this fragmentation daily. Insofar as the teachers fail to realize that this fragmentation of the pedagogic Self leads to the alienation of teaching and being, one cannot build a holistic program that contains what is really necessary for life, including cultural values that lend material and emotional dignity to the human being to fulfill its creative potential.

The use of the archetype of totality to analyze why teaching begins to become superfluous as early as the lower school level points to the subjective-objective dissociation as one of the major factors. To heal this pathological split the object should not occupy the center of the program. It has to be occupied by the pupil's experience in culture with regard to the stage of personality development, that is, by the symbolic perspective. The simultaneous experience of the subjective and the objective helps to delimit the field studied and situate the program within the interest and utility of the life of the pupil. Thus, re-associating the objective to the subjective within the symbolic dimension affects not only the teaching method but also its content and the organization of the program, because it makes learning symbolic and always related to the whole. This whole covers everything, from the pupils' daily life (the individual Self) to their family's social life (family and cultural Self), all the way to the planetary Self and the cosmic Self.

The subjective-objective dissociation created the false notion that the humanities and sciences should be taught separately, the former ruled by words and the latter by numbers. Then, the artificial separation constructed between mathematics and humanism began to be used as proof of the need for dichotomy between the humanities and sciences. This division radically dehumanized the teaching of science and cast it far from the daily life expressed by the body, home, food, clothes, means of locomotion, and domestic utilities. Once alienated in their islands of specialization, each sector of teaching followed its own path. More and more innovations were added based on the content of the subject itself, without due commitment to other subjects, the whole of teaching, or its applicability in the pupil's present or future daily existence. This is the prescription of the program, based on the pedagogic Babel, which was built in order to gain status and diplomas. The only evidence necessary to verify this supposition can be had by testing adults on how much they still know of what they learned in school. In this sense, the permanent encounter of the objective and subjective within the symbolic in itself can become the great regulating factor of the existential applicability of teaching in the daily life of the student. The reclaiming of the subjectivity of numbers becomes an important task for the teacher inasmuch as this constitutes a strategic bridge to join the humanities and sciences and re-humanize teaching.

Comparative anthropology is an inexhaustible source of information for symbolic education because it allows us to amplify, using the experiences of other cultures, learning situations and their symbolic relationships with the cultural Self. Tribal cultures know much less in objective knowledge but often much more in wisdom. In the absence of the subjective-objective dissociation, tribal societies practice education inseparably from myths, the development of individual and social life, the body, and the immediate needs of each and every day. With this method, in which content and finality are integrated in life, teaching is much more interesting and far less likely to be forgotten. This is a holistic, ontological teaching because at each moment it relates being with life, myth, and the cosmos. In this perspective, no learned meaning remains abstractly fragmented and consequently alienating and condemned to oblivion.

Learning in tribal societies is shaped by the stages of life and the formation of identity through development of the body. Each stage—birth, childhood, puberty, marriage, old age, and death, with their concomitant acceptance of responsibility, participation in social organization, professional obligations, and seasonal festivities—is lived in rituals that integrate the development of individual identity and body changes with the functioning of the family and society. Because the myths are the symbolic history and the foundation of these rituals, individual development itself embraces a vast amount of learning, the symbolic experience of which is filled with subjective and objective meanings that are difficult to forget. Tribal cultures cannot conceive of learning something that is isolated from the individual existential and social whole. In a system like this, there is no possibility of learning and the teacher being separated from life as a whole. Here learning is always subordinated to its existential applicability and is never situated outside what is useful.

In a seminar on the family crisis of adolescence, when I was discussing the symbolism of young people who do not want to attend school, an adolescent said that she found herself in that situation because she saw no relation between the subjects taught in school and the interests of her life at the moment. Every day she went to school feeling more and more alienated, and so she had decided to quit.

We saw above that at the start of his adolescence young Michael had complained of the compartmentalization of learning, and that his mother's reassurance that learning integrated things within the whole rather than isolating them reminded us of *paideia,* the Greek ideal of education. For the Greeks, to fail to subordinate anything to the one was equivalent to disrespecting the gods and committing *hybris* (hubris), the omnipotence that jeopardizes *metron*, the just measure, the very balance of life, for which one was liable to punishment. By repudiating alienated learning, don't our adolescents want to avoid *hybris?*

There is an enormous difference between Indian tribal societies and ours! When I did medical research among the Carajá Indians on the Araguaia River in central Brazil, I was surprised one day to see three adolescents painted black with *genipapo* ink. One was not supposed to address them because they were dead and waiting for the festival to be born into adult life. What a rich and unforgettable lesson that was, relating sexual development, individual and sexual identity, adult responsibility, and the archetype of life and death in the individuation and the humanization process.

In every tribal culture, we observe at each and every moment the integration of learning and life. In his book on the Caiapó-Xicrin Indians of Brazil, anthropologist Lux Vidal describes innumerable customs in which we see the interrelation between learning, utilization and integration in the socio-cultural-mythical-cosmic whole (Vidal 1977). The most precious teachings are all inserted within a system of rules or taboos inherent to life from birth to death. It is inconceivable for anything to be learned or exercised existentially and socially dissociated from the individual and cultural Self.

When a Caiapó-Xicrin child learns to walk, its mother throws its dried umbilical chord, which has been kept aside, into the river in order to receive its strength and health. The objective learning to walk is symbolized together with the subjective by expressing important meanings of the symbolic body that integrate walking into the existential process amidst nature. In this ritual, the merely physiological walking that depends on the progressive myelin development of the nervous system is symbolized as a second stage of maturing of the Self, the first being birth and separation from the placenta. However, to prevent this second separation from becoming fragmented and subliminally expressing the idea "I can walk now and no longer need anyone", the dried umbilical chord is not thrown away but rather returned to the river, and this will lend strength and health. Objectively speaking, this is a bunch of nonsense, as it has never been shown scientifically that throwing dried umbilical chords into rivers has ever brought anyone strength and health. Symbolically and existentially speaking, however, this is very wise, for it makes the umbilical chord part of the symbolic body and inserts its detachment at birth in the emotional, cultural, and even ecological process. The blood that flows between mother and child becomes analogous to the water of the river, which flows between us and Mother Earth or nature. This is the metaphoric meaning, which relates symbolically the individual, family, cultural, and planetary Self in the existential process.

When the child walks, it separates for the second time physically from its maternal dependence. Further separations will go on occurring throughout life to form and develop the identity of the ego based on symbiotic dependencies. Nevertheless, it is of the utmost importance for each step of the development of the ego to preserve an opening to the transcendent function of the imagination, which maintains the relationship of the ego with the archetypes that coordinate the formation of past, present, and future steps. By so doing, the ego exercises *yoga*, the link with centroversion, the symbolic dimension that shapes and transforms it. The ritual of throwing the dried umbilical chord into the river could be expressed as: "You can now walk away from your mother because your bond with her has been transferred to Mother Nature within the life process."

When the ego fills with pride and believes that it is independent and no longer needs anything, a state of psychic disharmony sets in, which Freud called omnipotence and Jung called inflation. This fact is so important that cultures recognize and attempt to avoid it. The Greeks called it *hybris*, for

Christians it is arrogance, and to Hindus it is Maya (illusion). These are not exactly equivalent expressions, but they all point to this psychological state in which the ego becomes attached to the literality of experience and loses the notion of transcendence and totality. Abandoning this attachment to literality and fragmentation is what saves us from illusion and enables us to remain in the *metron*, the just measure of the Greeks, or the middle path of Buddhism, the *wu wei* of Taoism, the *zen* of Zen Buddhism, or the "doing by not doing" of Saint Teresa of Ávila.

The mother returning the dried umbilical chord to the river to ensure the strength and health of her child who is learning to walk is a detachment from the literality of the umbilical chord, an homage to the symbol of the river and a veneration of all nature. It is admitting that the ability to learn to walk signifies a strong acquisition of physical and emotional independence by the child, but that the great force of life is not therefore subject to the ego and will always transcend its power, for it is part of the ecosystem and the cosmos.

The act of delivering the umbilical chord to the river becomes sacrificial in this context: *sacrifice* from the Latin *sacer* (sacred) and *facere* (to make). In the psychological dimension we can understand the phenomenon of sacrifice, which is common to all cultures and religions, as a ritual of the ego–central archetype relationship as well as that of the ego to all other archetypes. This allows one the perception of the umbilical chord not as something only objective but as a structuring symbol within the transcendent function of imagination of the Self. In this sense, the umbilical chord becomes sacred because it is perceived as a transforming agent within the totality of the Self. In psychological sacrifice the ego detaches itself from the meanings already lived to attain new meanings through which it is renewed and maintains its link to totality. The umbilical chord has been made sacred because it has linked the personal mother with Mother Nature, as an ecological blood vessel, which feeds the individual, society, and planetary life.

In the perspective of Jungian symbolic psychology and education, things are also always structuring symbols. Everything is symbolic and everything can become sacred, because everything is also always archetypal. The ego, however, despite being permanently formed and transformed through the symbols that transcend it, repeatedly forgets it, when guided unilaterally by the matriarchal or patriarchal archetypes. Because it ignores this and identifies with the transcendental root of transformation, it always relapses into inflation, omnipotence, *hybris,* and Maya. The ritual of sacrifice, guided by the archetypes of alterity and of totality, diminishes the arrogance of the ego and allows it to follow the path of relativity and humility, between right and wrong, good and evil, life and death, the middle path, the path between polarities that embraces and transcends them in the creative symbolic process.

As so well expressed in the myth of Prometheus, if the acquisition of learning is not accompanied by sacrifice, it becomes an act of usurpation. It is the sacrificial offering of learning that makes it sacred, surrounded by the wisdom of the cosmos that transforms and transcends it. To offer the dried umbilical chord to the river at the moment the child learns to walk is to perceive the umbilical chord and the river as structuring symbols, to give them significance, to make them sacred, and to recognize that life and death are transcended by a greater force that articulates them during the permanent archetypal transformation of consciousness and the ego.

The sacrificial attitude toward learning precludes the vain, arrogant, and compartmentalized mentality of specialization. To sacrifice and to make learning sacred is to acknowledge its inseparability from the whole before, during, and after it is acquired. This is done by connecting theory with the banal moments of daily activity and by relating these moments to totality. Making learning sacred transforms the voracity of learning and the pride of possessing what has been learned into the humility of those who give thanks for a gift received from a source that knows and can provide infinitely more.

To understand better the nature of symbolic learning integrated by the archetype of totality, I shall sketch some ideas of the curriculum in general, and mathematics in particular, in symbolic constructivism teaching and evaluation.

## Symbolic Systemic Constructivist Evaluation

The symbolic systemic constructivist evaluation is a process inseparable from teaching that elaborates learning through the interaction of teacher, student, school, family, society, planet, and cosmos. This perspective positions teaching and evaluation in the existential process of symbolic elaboration, which forms and transforms ego and other identity throughout the individual's life.

### The Theoretical Frame for Constructing Systemic Symbolic Evaluation

Evaluation is constructive when it is carried out through a quaternary dialectical relationship of the alterity archetype between teacher and student wherein both are evaluated together with their relationship. Each of them has consciousness and shadow, which are seen to interact in the process of learning when examined in the dialectic of alterity. Both admit in advance that they can be right or wrong. Thus teachers are not the owners of knowledge and students are not exclusively responsible for the limitations of the learning process.

Jungian symbolic education disagrees with the notion that the most efficient teaching occurs predominantly through reason and postulates that the most productive education is both rational and irrational because it is rooted in symbolic experience. Jungian symbolic education introduces being into the classroom through natural learning with experience. The evaluation of this philosophy and method of teaching follows the same path. This model of learning is based on the identity constructed as a result of primary relationships in childhood through imitation or reactive formation, not through reasoning. This evaluation is symbolic and systemic because it is positioned in the interacting field of student-teacher-family-school-society-planet-cosmos.

Plato wrote that "to know is to remember", possibly because to know the world is to know the wisdom that has always been within us. In this sense, the evaluation of teaching includes perception of the degree to which students and teachers are aware of their relationship to wholeness, together with their knowledge of parts.

The complexity of our nervous system endows consciousness with the capacity to relate the same theme learned with the individual, family, cultural, planetary, and cosmic Selves. Each one of these is a dimension of totality and one encompasses the other. In this manner the evaluation of teaching at any moment, coordinated by the totality archetype, can show an alienating distortion in anyone of these dimensions and correct it.

Cognitive difficulties in learning are rarely solved without going beyond cognition into the emotional existential context. Reducing learning difficulties to the cognitive realm frequently creates defensive rationalization.

The immense amount of knowledge taught only rationally, without students really knowing how to use it, is not experienced existentially and is liable to be soon forgotten. The worst aspect is that students associate this useless knowledge with culture and learning and stay away from them for the rest of their lives. In such cases an aversive defense is formed, which is the last thing we want to have in education.

Exclusively rational teaching must be clearly identified by evaluation and denounced as a poison that will distance students from knowledge and from culture. The construction of systemic symbolic evaluation challenges teachers to open themselves to considering the learning difficulties of students in their emotional, family, and cultural realities and not simply as an individual and rational problem.

During this evaluation, it is important to look for possible learning gaps that prevent the student from understanding the present due to lack of knowledge that should have been acquired in the past. In such cases, evaluation must carefully consider how far back a student needs to go to recuperate the knowledge needed. It is fundamental that the student acquire matriarchal intimacy with the essence of the subject taught and be protected from falling into robotic thinking to cover up the gap defensively. To differentiate this experience in learning, teachers must be accustomed to transmitting the essence of the subjects taught together with their content. A great limitation in identifying the characteristics of problem students lies with teachers who do not practice evaluation in direct contact with the student and leave it instead to testing.

As referred to in chapter 4, Jungian typology is very useful for evaluating many problems in education. Latin American collective typology, which privileges intuition and feeling, was very much influenced by Iberian, Indian, and African cultures with their exuberant matriarchal archetype. The European method of teaching, mainly French, was traditionally adapted to the thinking-sensation typology. Thus students with this typology obtain better results in examinations than those who have the intuition-feeling typology, which came to be considered less intelligent. Frequently, those with intuition-feeling typology, not being correctly understood and taught, are delayed in the learning process, tend to lose interest in studying, form learning gaps, and become prone to suffering aversion to studying. Their learning evaluation needs the identification of their typology to ransom their lowered self-esteem and correctly elaborate their learning difficulties.

One aspect that complicates the due evaluation of the intuitive-feeling polarity versus the thinking-sensation type in teaching is the matriarchal-patriarchal polarity and the polarity of right hemisphere versus left hemisphere. Frequently, but not always, thinking-sensation becomes associated with the patriarchal and left hemisphere dominance in the personality. On the other hand, feeling-intuitive typology frequently becomes associated with matriarchal and right hemisphere dominance. When this association occurs, as seems to be predominantly the case in Latin American countries, we find it even more difficult to teach according to the European tradition, which presents a predominantly thinking-sensation typology with patriarchal and possibly left hemisphere dominance. Another important point is that in the thinking-sensation typology, the patriarchal and frequently the left hemisphere dominance correspond to the traditional masculine identity, while in the feeling-intuitive typology, the matriarchal and commonly the right hemisphere dominance correspond to the traditional feminine identity.

Therefore, learning evaluation needs to consider Jungian typology and such correlations in order not to fall into traditional cultural stereotypes and also to consider every institutional case individually. It is important to realize that Jungian symbolic education, being centered on the dialectic position of the alterity archetype, needs all four functions as well as introversion and extraversion and the matriarchal-patriarchal polarity for symbolic teaching. Consequently, any psychological type needs its complementary polarity to participate fully in teaching and learning.

## The Practical Construction of Systemic Symbolic Evaluation

Jungian symbolic education is centered on the elaboration of symbols and therefore understands that any event in education already contains its own evaluation within itself. The evaluating structuring function is archetypal as we see in figure 10.1 (p. 238). The evaluator, therefore, has to become conscious of something that is already present and revealed during teaching. Teaching and evaluation must be practiced as two faces of the same coin.

In this perspective, teachers can identify students with learning difficulties by their relationship to the teacher and to classmates, by their physical posture, by their capacity to concentrate and the attention or lack thereof shown in their eyes, by their capacity to participate in symbolic constructivism and finally, by homework, exams, and grades.

Lower school and high school teachers who cannot assess the learning difficulties of students without tests should reconsider their choice of profession. In the same way that a competent mother realizes that her baby is not feeling well, without necessarily consulting a pediatrician, every good teacher is able to become aware that a student is having difficulties following the class before being submitted to tests. After this basic perception, careful examination should be made to determine if the limitation is in the eyesight or hearing capacity of the student or in the neurological, emotional, cognitive, circumstantial, or chronic shadow.

Once the limitation is perceived, the teacher begins to act immediately to understand its nature, seeing the student after classes. If need be, the teacher must be open in this evaluation to understanding the student's problem symbolically, within the teaching transference and the interrelationship of student, teacher, school, family, and society. Only when the problem cannot be elaborated within the transference relationship should the student be sent to the teaching coordinator. This, of course, is an ideal situation; teachers may not be able to carry through on this for lack of time, and in such a case the student has to be sent to the teaching coordinator from the very beginning for evaluation.

Recognizing virtues is as important as identifying limitations in teaching. Therefore, during evaluation, the perception of normal creative structuring functions is as valuable as identifying defensive functions, which form the shadow. In evaluating a learning difficulty, the teacher needs to discriminate normal functions that are not producing sufficiently due to lack of dedication by the student from defensive functions that are fixed and subject to repetition compulsion in the shadow. Every teacher must train to differentiate these two functions because this is crucial for handling any difficulty in learning. Where a normal function lacks dedication, the teacher can help the student with encouragement and work out with, him/her whether tutoring is needed. If the difficulty shows itself to be resistant to conscious efforts and is accompanied by other emotional or physical symptoms indicating a defense, then the teacher must try to locate it in one dimension of the Self—such as in the class, in the teaching transference, in the family, or elsewhere. After doing this, the teacher will be able to assess whether it is a fixation in the circumstantial shadow that can be elaborated in class or something more serious that points to a chronic shadow and needs special attention in psychotherapy. Whatever the case may be, there is no excuse for waiting for low grades to detect a student's difficulties in learning.

In lower school and high school, the positive characteristics and the shadow observed by the teacher should be communicated to the class coordinator throughout the school year. With this information, the class coordinator has a fair idea of the development process of the personality of each student and the students' relationships with each other. This is very useful for orienting teachers and parents on how to help students in the most productive way.

## The Role of Students in Symbolic Evaluation

Students can contribute significantly to the evaluation of teaching by listing their reactions. What follows are the reactions of a student in his last year in high school, preparing for his college-board exams. His typology is feeling-intuitive introversion with matriarchal and right hemisphere dominance with a strong aversion to the thinking-sensation extraverted typology present in the avalanche of subjects of Brazilian college boards. He had begun to present anxiety, stress, and aversive reactions, which limited his learning capacity. To evaluate better the stress and the aversive reactions, I asked him to make a list of his classes, pointing out any difficultly experienced and attributing to each class a grade from 1 to 10.

Table 2. Student Self-evaluation

|  | Monday | Tuesday | Wednesday | Thursday | Friday |
|---|---|---|---|---|---|
| 7:15 | Composition 8 | World History 3 sleep | Literature I 5 distraction conversation | Math I 7 | Geometry 9 |
| 8:05 | Composition 7 | Math III 4 cognitive block | General Geography 8 | Chemistry I 6 distraction drawing | Math II 6 cognitive difficulty |
| 8:55 | Break | Break | Break | Break | Break |
| 09:05 | Chemistry II 6 distraction, conversation | Brazilian History 6 distraction | Literature II 7 | Physics II 6 distraction, conversation | Geometry 8 |
| 09:55 | Physics I 5 cognitive difficulty | Biology I 8 | General Geography 7 | Math II 6 drawing | Brazilian Geography 7 |
| 0:45 | Break | Break | Break | Break | Break |
| 1:05 | World History 4 block | Brazilian History 7 | Physics II 6 distraction, drawing | Biology III 9 | Chemistry I 4 block |
| 1:55 | Physics III 5 distraction | Math II 6 desinterest | Physics I 7 | Biology IV 9 | Brazilian Geography 8 |

Using the evaluations he brought to me weekly, we could assess where his difficulties lay and elaborate them with each subject and each teacher. Helped by reinforcements in the afternoon period, he could cope with the stress and aversive reactions and successfully overcome the exhausting pressure of his college boards.

## Systemic Symbolic Evaluation and Expressive Techniques

Expressive technique is any teaching procedure used to work through the content of teaching within the symbolic dimension. Expressive techniques favor evaluation beyond verbal communication because they confront difficult themes in teaching through a number of strategies that propitiate comprehending the psychodynamics of the learning experience consciously and unconsciously. Expressive techniques produce not only symbolic elaboration for better understanding the meaning of the subjects taught but also the emotional relationship to the teacher and the subject, which amplifies greatly the scope of evaluation.

The main expressive techniques I use for evaluation are also used for symbolic elaboration in general: *psychoplastic* (drawing, painting, and sculpture), *written* (composition, story telling, poetry, letter writing, and descriptive essays), *dramatic* (playing, singing, dancing, playing musical instruments), and *imaginal* (active imagination and directive imagination {Désoille 1961}, spontaneous and directive meditation, imagination with figures, such as sand play and marionettes) (Byington 1993a).

## Integration of Symbolic Constructivism in the Curriculum

When we wish to teach for the totality of being, we face the immediate challenge of joining subject and object in the method of learning and then reformulating the curriculum so that it also expresses this integration. It is necessary to recognize that subject-object dissociation has caused not only the elimination of the subjective in the teacher-pupil rapport and in learning, but has also affected learning in its fragmentation, existential alienation and the very selection of content. The following considerations do not claim to cover the immense and complex theme of the composition of the curriculum, but only to touch on some essential points in an attempt to diminish the fragmentation of learning and stimulate multidisciplinary coordination of the teaching function.

To reclaim the systemic integration of the subjects taught, one has to imagine them as structuring functions of education, operating in complementary dimensions to one another within the individual, cultural, planetary, and cosmic whole (diagram 1, p. 240). This perspective directly affects each teacher and each subject and calls for building a symbolic mentality so that the subjects are perceived as different expressions of the whole. To this end, regular meetings of teachers of the same and different subjects should be a fundamental part of education. It is necessary for teachers of different subjects to interact and regularly present their ways of teaching in order to bring together the objective and the subjective and apply teaching to the daily lives of the pupils. In their weekly meetings, teachers can show their colleagues how they incorporate their subjects into the pupils' lives and their interaction with the pedagogic whole. In the course of the school year, each teacher will endeavor to convince the others of the utility of the subject he or she teaches for the student's lives, as well as showing how to make the material taught playful, attractive, and even fascinating. Demonstrating how to build symbolic teaching by integrating the objective and subjective dimensions in each discipline in the daily lives of students, each teacher will teach and learn along with the others. In this manner, the competitive and creative structuring functions are exercised in the construction of an existentially integrated and useful curriculum. The systemic experience of multiple feedback reactions in the teaching team will make each teacher aware of the creativity and limitations of his or her symbolic capacity. If these meetings are videotaped, a library of symbolic education techniques can be organized by subject, to be consulted by teachers in the following years. This material will then become a source of inspiration for symbolic teaching.

The schema shown in diagram 1 represents the symbolic integration of the program in modern lower school and high school education.

*Diagram 1.* Pedagogic Self

| |
|---|
| **PEDAGOGIC SELF** |
| **Symbolic Pedagogic Elaboration** |
| **Structuring Functions and Systems of the Curriculum** |
| **The Ontologization of the Curriculum** |

| Dimension of Artistic Creativity | | Dimension of Communication |
|---|---|---|
| Native Language & Arts | | Foreign Languages & Numbers |
| | Dimension of Totality | |
| | General Coordination of Teaching | |
| | Content Coordination & Psychological Coordination | |
| Dimension of | Dimension of Structure | Dimension of |
| Space and | & Functioning | the Physical Vitality |
| of Time | of Nature | & of the Unpredictable |
| History & Geography | Physics-Chemistry-Biology | Sports & Games |

The relationship among subjects is one of the highest aims of Jungian symbolic education. The endeavor to integrate each dimension of each subject in the curriculum with the whole is exercised in the mentality each teacher gradually shapes as he or she demonstrates the utility of the subject in the practical lives of students, as well as the symbolic form in which it will be taught. Teacher training integrated by the symbolic mentality is indispensable in the practice of Jungian symbolic education (Furlanetto 1997). Once there is an understanding of the function of each subject and its relation to the others in the lives of the pupils, the predominantly compartmentalized mentality gives way to a holistic, dialectic, and pragmatic mentality (Furlanetto 1986). Largely theoretical and alienated abstract teaching is gradually replaced by an integrated, practical, and symbolic teaching that is reinforced by the subjective-objective reunion used in each subject via the experiences made possible by expressive techniques. The following roles are suggested for the practice of Jungian symbolic education in lower school and high school.

General pedagogic coordinator (GPeC)—this role oversees the content of teaching and the creativity of teachers within the symbolic perspective.

General psychological coordinator (GPsyC)—this role oversees the capacity of teachers to relate to students, observing their characteristics and responding to them with empathy, coaching, and affection.

Together, these two coordinators select, organize, and supervise the orchestra of symbolic teaching.

Class coordinator (CC)—this role is chosen among the teachers of a class and elected annually by them.

Department representative (DR)—this role is chosen among the teachers of each subject and elected annually.

The school must hold regular meetings to propitiate the interaction of teachers to cultivate a symbolic teaching mentality. The following schedule is suggested, to be organized by the two general coordinators.

Weekly meeting of class coordinators (CC)—these meetings should include class coordinators of each grade.

Weekly meetings of department representatives (DR)—these meetings should include department representatives of each subject, including grades. Selected teachers can present expressive techniques they have created. This presentation and discussion should be videotaped and catalogued in the school library to be consulted by other teachers during the following years. Prizes should be given to the best presentations each year in each subject.

Monthly meeting of all school teachers—in these meetings, teachers will see and discuss presentations selected in the meetings of the department representatives. Each month they will discuss one or more presentations selected from the different subjects to express symbolic education.

Weekly classes in existential-pedagogic orientation—for all classes of each grade organized by the two general coordinators and the class coordinators.

Monthly meeting of class coordinators and department representatives—with the two general teaching coordinators.

Weekly classes in existential-pedagogic orientation explicitly coordinate the rapport between learning and the lives of the pupils. The meetings should include themes such as friendship, love, sexuality (gynecological assistance, nature and prevention of infectious diseases, pregnancy, birth control, and abortion), drug addiction, smoking, alcoholism, bullying, community activities, civil rights activities, and others. These discussions should be oriented by the psychological coordinator with reference to the individual and collective development of consciousness as described by Jungian symbolic psychology, which must include the difference between normal and pathological development. These lectures will also include teachings on the development of the individual and social psyche, which are considered especially pertinent to the existential and cultural phase that the pupils pass through. The teaching of these topics may be enriched with the participation of special guests, animated by the discussion of films, plays, expositions, and a wide range of existential and cultural issues of students with these guests and among themselves.

## Parents' Association

The monthly meetings of class coordinators and departament representations with the students' families of each grade will point necessarily to certain general themes that acquire central importance. The formation of parents' associations at every school can be oriented by the two general coordinators in the organization of monthly meetings to discuss general themes related to education. The intention is to discuss these themes with parents in relation to their sons' and daughters' existential necessities and at the same time enhance their own cultural and psychological development. These meetings can be coordinated by the two general coordinators, assisted by class coordinators and department representatives, in such a way as to elaborate school life with family, social, and cultural life, a true education of society within the student-teacher-school-family quaternary relationship.

## The Structuring Function of Ethics and Jungian Symbolic Education

The extension of the concept of symbol and archetype to include conscious and unconscious characteristics of all things formulated by Jungian symbolic psychology is the basis of Jungian symbolic education. This extension of the concept of the archetype to encompass structuring symbols, complexes, functions, and systems is the condition to describe scientifically the structuring function of ethics as inherent to any symbolic elaboration of the personality and of culture. This conceptual frame allows us to teach ethics together with all psychological development and to see consciousness and shadow formation as the permanent fight between good and evil in daily life.

The great difficulty in understanding this theoretical perspective is that students, teachers, and parents see in the world around them evil frequently practiced consciously within the increasing corruption of values of modern society.

To explain this crucial conceptual difficulty, it is important to know the difference between the neurotic defense and the psychopathic defense. The neurotic defense, which everyone has in varying degrees, is mostly unconscious, and when it becomes conscious it is accompanied by guilt because it is something not desired by the personality. Psychopathic or character defense, on the contrary, dominates the voluntary function of the ego and therefore is not accompanied by guilt. In this defense, a person acts out the shadow unconsciously but also consciously because the structuring function of intention has become fixated and defensive. In such cases, consciousness is dominated by the shadow and acts evilly. When this defensive acting out occurs in the social dimension, the psychopathic defense is also called sociopathic defense.

The penal code distinguishes between voluntary and involuntary crime. In Jungian symbolic psychology, we also distinguish between evil practiced involuntarily in the shadow of neurosis and psychosis from evil practiced voluntarily through the psychopathic defense. This voluntary evil, which we see practiced daily around us in demagoguery, corruption, and outright dishonesty is the expression of evil through the psychopathic defense in the cultural shadow. The defensive persona, which covers up this criminal behavior by disguising it as normal, is called the normopathic defense and is complementary to the psychopathic defense (Byington 2006a).

The psychopathic defense can express the circumstantial or the chronic shadow. In the circumstantial shadow it is found in many existential circumstances, for instance, in the lying of adolescents. In the chronic shadow the psychopathic defense becomes a serious ethical dysfunction of the personality and is very limiting for psychological development to the point of forming the psychopathic personality (Byington 2008).

The nonrecognition of the psychopathic defense within dynamic psychopathology as a fixation of the normal structuring function of ethics has prevented the recognition and prevention of this ethical dysfunction during symbolic elaboration in adolescence that is essential for the understanding and teaching of ethics.

In addition to the law, religion also expresses in various ways the difference between good and evil, including the dimension of life after death. Christianity, for instance, situates good and evil in heaven, purgatory, and hell. Symbolically, we can see these places as psychological states, corresponding to well-elaborated symbols (heaven) and fixed defenses in the shadow (hell), whose torments Freud so well described in the repetition-compulsion of chronic defenses. In an intermediary state, we have the elaboration of symbols between normality and fixation that we experience daily (purgatory).

In ancient Greece, good and evil were also partly elaborated with the symbol of Hades, the underworld, where some of those considered evil during life suffered punishment through fixation and repetitive compulsion after death, like Sisyphus, Tantalus, and the Danaids.

All these, however, are representations of the good-evil polarity in the form of projection, and the fixation of the will, which characterizes the psychopathic defense, is not clearly differentiated. One event in the Passion of Christ, however, is very meaningful in this context. It occurs when Jesus is being tortured by Roman soldiers and cries out: "Father, forgive them for they know not what they do" (Luke 23:34). It is evident that the soldiers were torturing Jesus intentionally. However, Jesus affirms that they are not conscious of what they are doing, which can be explained through the psychopathic defense: the intention has become defensive, expressing the shadow, and therefore the ego acts but is not fully conscious of its actions. The psychopathic defense is frequently expressed by military men who commit crimes and afterward justify themselves by saying they received orders from their commanders, many instances of which came up in the Nuremberg trials.

Historically, the applications of the ethical function were bound first to religious contexts and later to legal formulations, and thus have codified traditions. Neither tradition, however, teaches ethics from within, as a psychological archetypal function.

Education generally also teaches ethics from without, from a traditional viewpoint, either religious or legal, and little has been added to this teaching from a scientific perspective, except for the concept of the superego in psychoanalysis. In this sense, the teaching of ethics is generally based on a traditional moral code or collective superego, which is taught as a set of rules to be obeyed to avoid transgression. This leaves ethics under the coordination of the polarized patriarchal archetype, which is difficult to convey to youngsters, who require transgression as a normal function in order to separate from their parents and to develop.

What Jungian symbolic education proposes, instead of the traditional superego model of sermon and punishment for transgression, is the formation of character through the structuring function of ethics elaborating transgression and frustration within the transference relationship of students and teachers. This is the concept of ethics of individuation as described by Erich Neumann in his book *Depth Psychology and a New Ethic* (1948).

Three students from the eighth grade (fourteen years old), decided one afternoon to "baptize" a classmate through bullying, throwing eggs at him as they were leaving school. The boy ran into a supermarket but was dragged out by his three classmates and smeared with eggs. The families became involved, and their classmates were also shocked by the event, which was taken by the class coordinator to a meeting with the two general coordinators. There was no doubt in their evaluation that the action involved the structuring functions of bullying, defensive aggression, and ethics in the formation of character. Both sides were heard separately. The victim was a very timid and introverted student. The offenders admitted their aggression and justified themselves by saying that it had been a mere joke. Their report showed their conduct to be the acting out of bullying through a psychopathic circumstantial defense expressed intentionally in a cowardly manner.

The class coordinator divided the class into two groups and sat them facing each other. After describing what had happened, which everyone had known about and had been commenting on for the last two days, he directed the class to use a dramatic expressive technique. Half the class would represent the aggressors and half the class the victim. One side would describe episodes of bullying in which they had participated as offenders, and the other side would speak about experiences as victims. The two sides then switched positions, a role-playing technique used in psychodrama.

After forty minutes of interaction, the class counselor remarked how aggressors and victims had humiliated and had been humiliated by thoughts or actions during the course of their lives, and how much suffering such an experience can cause. He told them about creative transgression, which calls for dignity and courage and the expression of which is important to avoid having it become fixated and form defenses. Next, he pointed out to them how bullying the classmate had been a usage of transgression deformed by cowardice. It was an excellent opportunity for the class to experience the function of ethics from within and to realize how much education is learning consideration for others in the formation of character.

Adolescence is a fertile field for the appearance of the circumstantial psychopathic defense, as in this case, because the normal differentiation of adolescents from their families occurs through polarization and transgression within the social dimension. Adolescents are the following generation, which will transcend the present generation commanded by their parents. One of the main characteristics of adolescence is to discover the new and endorse its conflict with traditions represented by the attitudes, authority, and ideology of the preceding generation. This conflict often leaves adolescents indiscriminate, really dizzy and divided, for they stand and fight for a cause still greatly unknown to them against another which had been theirs since birth. In this manner they are easy prey for the latest novelties, many of which clearly transgress traditions and expose them to all kinds of risk. Whether in the dimension of sexuality, political ideologies, drugs, or dangerous behavior, the crisis of adolescence expresses itself in an archetypal field highly charged by the hero archetype and by the archetype of alterity, which includes the anima and animus archetypes, described by Jung to explain the immense fascination we experience toward the other sex and serving as the psychopomps of the individuation process.

The confrontation or polarization with tradition through the activation of the hero archetype makes the adolescent, on one side, inflated and arrogant, but on the other confused and insecure, needing reinforcement from a group or gang. The fidelity code of the adolescent group reinforces the defensive persona of self-sufficiency, which covers up weakness and insecurity and makes frequent use of the structuring function of lying to cover up transgression and guilt. Knowing this, the teacher can greatly contribute to the formation of character in adolescence, perhaps the most precious contribution of education during that phase of life.

In spite of hiding inside the group, the adolescent generally experiences the emergence of individuality amidst much anxiety, because the polarizing mission to defy grown-ups requires competition and performances, which are very stressful and often accompanied by suffering, especially humiliation. The experiences of inferiority and failure frequently suffer fixations and form defenses. Initially this shadow may be circumstantial, in which case the school and the family have a golden opportunity to intervene. The emotional holding and understanding afforded by parents and teachers, accompanied by a firm attitude, preferably without prescribed solutions, can revert fixations and propitiate very creative elaborations. Instead of offering ready-made solutions, the capacity of adults to elaborate difficult life situations holding conflict and anxiety may teach the adolescent to contain and elaborate frustrations and thus avoid precipitating precocious action, which is one of the tendencies of shadow behavior.

The individual Self in childhood is very much impregnated by magic, *participation mystique,* and omnipotence due to the exuberance of the insular matriarchal position and is mostly contained by symbiosis within the family Self. Adolescents become very powerful, this being the age at which they acquire the physical capacity to reproduce and to kill. Through this energy, the progressive integration of the matriarchal (sensuality) and patriarchal (order) archetypes and the nascent integration of the alterity archetype (encounter) due to the hormonal activation of the anima/animus archetypes, lead the adolescent to polarize with the family Self while plunging into the cultural Self. The central problem of the ethical function in adolescence is that this polarization with the family Self includes antagonizing and transgressing the ethical universe structured by the symbolic elaboration of past generations. Until they construct the ethical view of their new adult generation, adolescents roughly between 10 and 20 years of age undergo a great ethical indiscrimination during which they take a polarized position vis-à-vis conventional ethics without having yet constructed their own.

When parents do not understand that adolescents need to transgress and approach the young mainly with their own ethical stereotypes and repressive sermons, the young sincerely believe that adults really do not know how to deal with good and evil. This is the ethical loneliness of adolescence. The young know what they disagree with because they do not accept tradition based on stereotypes, but they do not yet know what they propose instead. Teachers and parents should refrain from presenting a ready-made recipe, because what the adolescent really needs is to learn to elaborate ethical problems from within, together with their individual differentiation, and not from an outside superego.

Like all other structuring functions, ethics can be constructed. When an adult brings to the young a ready-made answer, this demonstrates ignorance; when we live with the ethical function archetypally, its elaboration and construction come from within the heart and not from some rational rule (Stein 1993). The ethical function thus is inseparable from the feeling function, because it coordinates the affectionate consideration of the ego for the other and vice versa. To teach ethics, the educator must not train the students to repeat good sermons, for what needs to be taught is not what good and evil are but their dialectical elaboration. In the case discussed above of bullying elaborated through dramatic exercise, the psychological coordinator from the start made it quite clear that he was not judging or accusing anyone but only elaborating the meaning of bullying and teaching the students how each one had already suffered by being persecuted and humiliated.

> And the scribes and Pharisees brought unto him a woman taken in adultery; and when they had set her in the midst, They said unto him, Master, this woman was taken in adultery, in the very act. Now Moses in the law commanded us, that such should be stoned: but what sayest thou? This they said, tempting him, that they might have to accuse him. But Jesus stooped down, and with his finger wrote on the ground, as though he heard them not.
> So when they continued asking him, he lifted up himself, and said unto them, He that is without sin among you, let him first cast a stone at her. And again he stooped down, and wrote on the ground. And they which heard it, being convicted by their own conscience, went out one by one, beginning at the eldest, even unto the last: and Jesus was left alone, and the woman standing in the midst. When Jesus had lifted up himself, and saw none but the woman, he said unto her, Woman, where are thine accusers? Hath no man condemned thee? She said,

No man, Lord. And Jesus said unto her, Neither do I condemn
thee: go, and sin no more. John 8:3–11)

The formation of character in adolescence continues that which was
begun in childhood, mainly through the primary identifications of ego with
parents, siblings, the family atmosphere, the relationship between parents,
and the child's reactions. It is well known that the way parents relate will affect
the ego-other polarity in the identity of the child and in the way boys and girls
begin to relate in adolescence. Amidst these acquired characteristics, it has
special importance for the way a child learns to deal with frustration, anger,
and transgression. This capacity, acquired in childhood, will be highly useful
for avoiding the formation of fixations and defenses during the intense
frustrations of adolescence. In this sense, it is fundamentally important to
educate parents not to punish children but to let the children experience the
frustrations that life normally brings. Instead of imposing a rule to turn the
television off at 10 p.m., it is better to repeatedly stress the importance of sleep
for their brains, so that they will be able to function intelligently the next day.

In today's unstable society, educators occupy a key position in dealing
with the crisis of adolescence, because they are, at the same time, a
representative of the past generation and a witness and a bridge to elaborate
new propositions for the future. The educator teaches in the crossroad of
history. Constructing knowledge symbolically within the student-teacher-
school–family quaternio, teachers work in the melting pot of character
formation where the ethical function of the new generation is molded.

The understanding of the crisis of adolescence allows parents and
educators to become aware of why these youngsters are so resistant to sermons,
advices, orders, and moral orientation imposed patriarchally from the outside
and not symbolically and dialectically constructed from within. If the function
of the crisis of adolescence is to question traditional values, how can anyone
imagine that adolescents will passively accept their imposition? Precisely
because adolescents confront their parents and society patriarchally, expressing
an antithesis to every thesis through the polarized position, parents and
educators need to know how to exercise the dialectical position of the archetype
of alterity to elaborate conflicts and, in so doing, teach youngsters to construct
syntheses.

With the maturation of the sexual glands and the acquisition of physical
strength, the insular matriarchal archetype of sensuality is also strongly
activated in adolescence, predominantly in the active position through the

functions of sexuality, competition, creativity, aggression, curiosity, and vanity. The patriarchal archetype is also constellated in the active position, which explains why adolescents are so eager for power and have such an extraordinary capacity of polarization.

Traditionally, the crisis of adolescence was greatly restrained and the patriarchal archetype directed with strong disciplinary measures to "educate" the ego, conditioning it to submission in the passive position. Children were taught to repeat their parents' thoughts and beliefs. Today, however, the crisis of adolescence, fully acknowledged in Western societies, propitiates a war of archetypes to differentiate the individual Self of youth from the family Self, which harbors the traditional Self. In this sense, ethical symbolic education of the individuation process is the opposite of traditional superego education, which taught how to repeat tradition. According to the apocryphal Gospel of Thomas, Jesus said:

> Whoever does not hate his father and his mother in My way will not be able to be (one disciple) to me. And whoever does (not) love his father and his mother in My way will not be able to be a (disciple) to me. (Thom. 101)

In the construction of the ethical function, the archetype of totality will be the guardian that will propitiate the systemic inclusion of the crisis of adolescence in the individual, family, cultural, planetary, and cosmic Self, because the good and evil polarity will only be properly constructed when its elaboration is related to wholeness.

## Integrating Mathematics Within Wholeness

Mathematics is the subject most difficult to insert into the dimension of symbolic teaching, both in relation to the other subjects and to the pedagogical-existential whole because number is a symbol with one of the highest degrees of abstraction. This is why math teachers should be given special attention when they meet to coordinate symbolic teaching.

The abstract characteristic of mathematics in itself facilitates objectivity and specialization, but the fact that it has been used defensively to express rational-materialistic scientific development, utterly dissociated from subjective reality, is what has determined its reification, compartmentalization, and an enormous contribution to shadow formation in materialism. The abstract expression of this dissociation was so extreme that it became enormously difficult to teach math within the symbolic reality articulated with the whole. Based on this perspective, math teachers usually face the greatest difficulties in symbolizing and re-humanizing teaching. This leads math teachers to fall victim to arrogance, a defensive pride that transforms abstraction, isolation, and alienation into compensatory defensive feelings of nobility and self-sufficiency.

In order to situate the teaching of mathematics in the symbolic dimension, it is not merely a matter of teaching it with subjective characteristics that help in understanding its operations and applying them in practice. It is indispensable for mathematics to be taught inseparably from its utility and application in daily life. But that is not all. Something further has to be done to redeem mathematics from dissociation and to apply it within the subjective-objective relation: teachers and students need to learn to experience mathematics as a structuring function of relationship, as a language of communication in the relation of the ego with things and things with one another. The difference between the decimal system of ancient Egypt and the system based on the number six, which appeared in ancient Babylonia and is still used today by us to measure time, is one place to start to exemplify two languages within mathematics. The division of mathematics into arithmetic, algebra, and geometry can also exemplify its linguistic, polyglot nature. The fact that our hands have ten fingers, that we begin to learn arithmetic by finger counting, and that the decimal system prevailed worldwide should be used to relate math to subjectivity. We relate to life through abstract representations expressed in numbers, images, and words in the same way that we manipulate the world, first with our hands and then with tools.

However, it is crucial to begin by demystifying the notion that mathematics can only exist in things, independently from being. All things are symbols of the Self, and numbers too must be perceived as such to promote the articulation of things with one another and with the whole (von Franz 1980). Things are symbols of the Self because they articulate functionally with the whole through their meanings. Through the symbolic dimension, the part is inseparable from the whole, the *en to pan,* the all in one of the Greeks. Self is the whole, the great one, the universe. All other things and all other numbers are part of the one. Things symbolically perceived form the languages of relationship and communication. So do numbers. Within this perspective, all mathematics encompasses a great system of relationship of the parts with the whole. To gain this understanding, teachers of math have to study the philosophy of mathematics as discussed by the great masters who speculated about the nature of numbers, which shows their transcendent and symbolic reality through which they are linked to all other symbols, to express knowledge.

The whole process of symbolic working through consists in the differentiation of the psychic dimension of cosmos to form the ego-other and the other-other identities in consciousness through the experience of symbols in the dimensions of body, nature, society, idea, image, emotion, word, number, sound, silence, and behavior. This differentiation from the whole creates the identity of things and at the same time the words, images, and numbers to express interrelationship and communication.

The symbol is the part and the whole into which the part is archetypally inserted. In "Om", India perceives the mystic syllable that expresses the origin of words, life itself and the Universe. That is why it should be pronounced by breathing "ooommm" in order to realize the *pneuma* expressing the Atman, the universal Self. The one in mathematics is the "Om" in Hinduism, it is Atman, it is totality, the cosmic Self. All numbers are parts of the great one, that is, the Self. All the integer numbers, before becoming multiples of one, are fractions of one. The number two is formed by two ones (a multiple) but at the same time it expresses two parts, within the whole. When I speak of three matches, I refer to three parts of the whole and attribute to them a category that relates to the great one. When we refer to pure mathematics, we are not limiting ourselves to the numbers in themselves but rather experiencing the parts of the Self and their abstract relation to one another and with the whole.

Mathematics, then, is one of the main structuring functions of relationship and, therefore, is not alien to love. It was our pathological traditional culture that reduced it exclusively to objectivity and separated it from subjectivity and the whole. Affection joins the parts harmonically and, born of frustration, aggression shows their discrepancy. Love is an erotic link between parts and, as already mentioned, encompasses affection and aggression. As in life, so too in mathematics: it is love that exercises the evaluation function of the mathematical operation. The exact calculation is accompanied by satisfaction and pleasure, and error brings frustration, anxiety, and irritation, just like words in communication, images in aesthetics, and sound in music. Numbers and equations are the family of the one, as symbols of other dimensions are the family of the Self from the atom all the way to the great family of the galaxies. Many mystics, chose an esoteric language, to express the sacred. By analogy, we may say that pure mathematics is the abstract language of parts with one another in communicating with the whole. Mathematics and music are two dear languages of God. A marvelous example of this is the golden mean, which is present in music, in the human body, in works of art, and also abundantly in nature. Another example is the equation $E = mc^2$, which expresses the *coniunctio* of energy and matter through the speed of light. This approach to mathematics makes numbers both symbolic and sacred in the Pythagorean sense. The understanding of this symbolic and archetypal reading of number in general as part of the number one, which is the very Self, is fundamental for enabling teachers to remove mathematics from defensive specialization and to teach it within the symbolic process to re-humanize education. Exactly because math is one of the most abstract of all symbolic dimensions, it is capable of representing objectivity isolated from subjectivity, which contributed very much to the chronic condition of the subject-object dissociation in modern sciences. For this very same reason, however, math teachers are the ones who can most significantly contribute to overcoming this dissociation and practicing symbolic humanism.

## Mnemosyne's Revenge

In a lecture given at the opening of the I Group Congress (São Paulo High Schools), in 1991, I attempted to represent symbolically the failure of compartmentalized knowledge, exclusively objective, exclusively taught through rational teaching in the West (Byington 1991c). I imagined a fable.

A secondary school in São Paulo had courageously undertaken to conduct a survey to determine statistically what had remained of schooling in adults. A very important meeting was called of parents of high school pupils. They believed it was to discuss some problem with the graduation diplomas at the end of the course, and they turned out en masse. Upon arriving at the meeting, they were surprised to be given a test, not for their children, but for themselves. The school had decided to test them with the same program given to their children. Some of the parents took the test for junior high, the rest for senior high. The parents nearly panicked. A lawyer almost passed out, and an engineer tried to slip out the window. Calm was restored after the school reassured them that the purpose of the examination was exclusively statistical and that it would be impersonal and destroyed as soon as the results were obtained. Even so, there was a lot of sighing, cheating, and requests to go to the toilet during the exam.

The school did not complete the evaluation of the test. When the results reached the point where 90 percent of the questions answered were wrong or left blank, the examination was brought to an end and the tests were destroyed. The parents swore solemnly not to tell their friends or even comment any further on the matter among themselves, so ashamed they were.

During the exam, a fax was received from the Ministry of Foreign Affairs and the Superior War School, requesting the director of the school to go to Brasilia on a matter of national security. The presidential jet was waiting at the São Paulo airport. From Brasilia, our director was dispatched to an emergency meeting of UNESCO in Paris. Her husband was very jealous about it all, but seeing the importance of the mission, agreed to the trip.

On landing, as the official representative of the developing countries she was called before a joint European, American, and Japanese council. To her astonishment, she was informed that NATO had learned of her experiment with the parents and invited her to a debate. Similar examinations had been carried out in major universities with the same results. This was perceived to be an international epidemic, a public calamity, and kept as a state secret. Were it to be disclosed, the epidemic would spread even wider: children would not want to go to school any more, parents would not pay, and governments would cut funding for education. It would be the end of modern teaching. The situation called for immediate correction. But, how to discover its cause?

Having exhausted all the resources known to objective, rational teaching so far, the members of the council went off to bed depressed and desperate. That night, they all had the same dream in which they went to Greece to consult the Delphic oracle. When they gathered together the next morning, the Brazilian school director told her dream and was surprised when the council members' decided that she should leave for Delphi at once. No one said that they had had the same dream. The criterion suggested was that Brazil had already all races and forms of the esoteric on the planet, and so the oracle would surely give her a good welcome.

Arriving there, our director came to a pile of ruins, but the guard explained to her exactly where the Pythian priestess spoke Apollo's pronouncements. She waited and, since there were no tourists in sight, hid among the stones of the shrine to spend the night. She fell asleep and had the following dream:

Apollo appeared all-radiant and showed her the way to Olympus. Boarding Helio's carriage, our director reached the mountain and was ushered to a goddess who asked her what she wanted. As she explained her mission, the goddess called in nine younger goddesses. Sadly, they gathered around their mother. Day broke on Mount Parnassus. The morning mist slowly disappeared. After hearing what she had known for a long time already, the goddess spoke:

_ "I am Mnemosyne, the Goddess of Memory. These are my daughters by the great Zeus, he who stands for the intelligence of the world. They are the muses that inspire art and knowledge. You limited their creative imagination and separated them from one another. You became arrogant with the little knowledge you gained and offended Zeus with indifference, vanity, and pride. You fell victim to *hybris* and in your madness decided to rationally and objectively control knowledge. You cast out imagination from the temple of education and transformed it into a cultural Babel. You disrespected my daughters by manipulating them without inspiration or love. On your altar, you adored reason, and in its name you used science to build the genocidal mushroom. Our grief is infinite. At the request of Zeus, as punishment, I have sent against your alienated learning the mantle of oblivion. That's what you discovered in your survey."

Our director woke up warmed by the sun. Her back was stiff and her chest was soaked. She thought it must have rained during the night, but then realized she was wet from her own tears, which kept on falling. She had not understood rationally the extent of the goddess's pronouncement, but being a woman and a mother, she was deeply moved by her suffering and vengeance.

The council members awaited her, anxiously pressured by their ministers of state. She could not explain much. Her tears confounded them. Weeping at such an objective, urgent problem only made things worse. "Just like a woman, and a Latin to boot," they thought to themselves.

The meeting was videotaped and then examined by experts, who reached no conclusion. The only words they caught were *culture, oblivion, knowledge, love, meaning, imagination, creativity, arrogance, existence, wisdom,* and *wholeness.*

These eleven words were examined by the world's latest technology. The conclusion of this project was set for the distant future. In the meantime, the results of the unbelievable examination remain a state secret, kept under lock and key.

## Direct Contact with the Center

The archetype of totality coordinates one of the pearls of the teaching of wisdom, which is the direct contact with the central archetype. Religions like Hinduism, Buddhism, and Taoism have taught this relationship through meditation. Western culture has had a certain difficulty with meditation as practiced in the East, because prayer in Judaism, Islamism, and Christianity do not include regular mental concentration exercises to cultivate detachment and to experience totality through emptiness.

Richard Wilhelm was a German protestant minister who lived in China in the beginning of the twentieth century. He translated the *I Ching, the Book of Changes*, and brought it to Europe. This book is an oracle of wisdom, which propitiates a very intensive experience of the dialectics of opposites within totality.

It was a synchronistic event that, in 1928, he sent the book *The Secret of the Golden Flower* to Jung (1961), who was studying mandalas and conceiving the Self as the central archetype of the psyche. It is important to differentiate archetypally the teaching of Jung's active imagination from the Taoist meditation, taught in the *Golden Flower,* to experience the center and live Tao.

Active imagination is an extraordinary expressive technique to propitiate the dramatic dialectic of opposites (*Auseinandersetzung*), which is characteristic of the alterity archetype (anima and animus) within totality. It requires only partial detachment of the polarities from both matriarchal and patriarchal patterns to be able to relate polarities within totality without taking sides, but it needs attachment to identify emotionally with each side.

The totality archetype, on the contrary, needs complete detachment from polarities in order to live totality. *The Secret of the Golden Flower* is a treatise to teach meditation and direct contact with the center in order to live totality fully and experience Tao through the mental experience of emptiness.

Within the countless forms of meditation, direct meditation on the center requires total detachment from symbols to experience emptiness. This is the direct experience of totality, which transcends the opposites. This is the living of God without a name, completely uncontrolled, unfathomable, perceived in infinity and eternity because it is mediated by the practice of experiencing emptiness. When we call on God, at first we praise him, but soon the ego begins to appropriate totality to personalize it and manipulate it politically. The phenomenon is common to all religions, and this is why the commandment that prohibits using the name of the Lord in vain is a way to prevent egoic manipulation of the transcendent dimension. Prayer and mantras are also directed to concentrate the mind, to go beyond duality and experience unity through transcendence of daily matters by their very repetition.

It seems to me that the main distinction between Confucianism and Taoism, the two great philosophical systems of ancient Chinese culture, can be better understood through the difference of the archetypes of alterity and of totality. Confucianism, which today has been rescued from oblivion and intensely influences education in China, has the great ideal of cultivating totality in changing society through the dialectical interrelationship of opposites; it therefore chose the *I Ching, the Book of Changes*, as its main guide. This book is an extraordinary expression of the alterity archetype. Taoism, on the other hand, cultivated wisdom and totality by detaching from opposites and establishing their mysterious equality through the contemplative conscious position of the totality archetype and chose the *Tao Tê Ching* as its main reference. Both works, the *I Ching* and the *Tao Tê Ching*, exemplify respectively in a very extraordinary way the archetype of alterity and the archetype of totality.

This direct experience of the intelligent essence of the universe is the core of the religiosity of Hinduism, Buddhism, and Taoism and also of the modern sciences, when we are able to get beyond its subject-object dissociation. As Einstein expressed so well:

> Religions always fought science and persecuted scientists ... However, I affirm that the cosmic religious feeling is the most intense and the noblest motivation of scientific research. Only those who become aware of the immense effort, and above all of the devotion required by pioneer work in theoretical science can understand the emotion of this effort which is experienced far away from the daily realities of life ... It is the cosmic religious feeling which gives a human being the strength to pursue this task. A contemporary has affirmed that in the

materialistic times we live, the serious scientific researchers
are the only persons profoundly religious. (1930, p. 28)

It is the concept of the central archetype, as the center of the creation
and transformation of consciousness of being-in-the-world (Heidegger 1927),
that allows us to live this religiosity scientifically within the study of the reality
of nature and of personality development as an unitarian experience. It links
the gnôthi s'autón, "know thyself" of ancient Greece, with the knowledge of all
things around us in the *paideia*, the knowledge of being, including its subjective
and objective reality.

The recognition of the method of direct meditation on the center
through the contemplative position of the archetype of totality is fundamental
to teaching meditation in school. This allows teaching the ancient wisdom of
the East within the Western cultural Self. The psychological skill of
detachment, which is fundamental to the exercise of transcendence, reaches
its highest degree in the contemplative position of consciousness of the totality
archetype, so important for the elaboration process in symbolic teaching.

## The Symbolic Teaching of Meditation and the Experience of Totality

The scientific method developed over five centuries the knowledge of
Western culture, and has its equivalent in meditation, which built its wisdom
during thousands of years in the construction of Eastern traditional cultures.

The resistance of Western culture to teaching meditation regularly is a
sign of its limited introspective capacity, which is rooted in its subjective-
objective dissociation. Our predominantly extraverted teaching is capable of
achieving a Ph.D. in the exact sciences or in the humanities without ever
having studied the nature of love, the meaning of self-realization, or the
experience of infinity, eternity, and enlightenment. Today bookshops are
saturated with best-sellers that teach magical recipes for making money,
achieving success, or being happy. Cognitive behavior therapies are gaining
more ground on psychiatry every day, directing thoughts toward sane attitudes.
This is the beginning of introspection, although still in a very limited patriarchal
way.

Meditation is an introspective activity, which teaches us to introvert
the ego and develop the ability to concentrate and direct attention to any
chosen theme. This greatly enhances the subjective dimension in symbolic
elaboration. Through meditation one practices to deconstruct learning (Piaget
1967) and opens the mind to fresh and new creativity. This is why meditation

revitalizes the self and encourages learning with more existential intelligence. Through this subjective development, the masters of the East acquired much wisdom and attained mental states of great differentiation and extraordinary depth, which they try to transmit to their followers in schools and theories of spiritual development. In Taoism, Hinduism, and Buddhism, meditation is as natural as brushing the teeth, doing morning calisthenics, or having breakfast in the West. Learning to meditate for them is like learning to read and write for us. Western culture is so ignorant of the subjective dimension that most people do not even understand what this subject is about.

To meditate is an initiatory practice; like swimming, it is necessary to do it to know what it is. I will describe a meditation exercise to illustrate symbolic elaboration of the ego-central archetype relationship through the contemplative position of the totality archetype.

### Meditation Exercise
### Part I

### The Tree of Life and the Structuring Function of Breathing
### Learning to Pass from the Executive Rhythm
### to the Vegetative Rhythm

Choose a quiet place, sit in a comfortable position (lotus position if you can), and close your eyes. Imagine entering and walking in an enchanted forest with huge and beautiful trees where you will meditate. It is a sunny day. A gnome guides you to find your tree of life in the forest. It is a lovely and gigantic tree.

You sit underneath it. The trunk is very thick; it would take four people to embrace it. The tree is very tall and has many branches. Among the leaves there are countless small red apples. They represent all your ego activities. When you awake and open your eyes every morning, the brushing of one little apple corresponds to this action. When you get out of bed, another. When you take a shower, a third one, and so on.

Your brain, with its one hundred billion ($10^{11}$) neurons (Kandel et al. 2000), has countless activities in consciousness. Your ego is responsible for the execution of the conscious activity. In this meditation exercise, your ego is represented by a little monkey, which jumps from branch to branch in your life tree, brushing with a small cloth the little apples that correspond to your desired actions. Its rhythm is frenetic. He knows and obeys your commands. Now you tell him to stop all activity, come down and lie on the first branch of the tree, about twelve feet above your head. He obeys and comes down and lies beside his cousin, the sloth, who began climbing the tree when you were born and has only now reached the first branch. The little monkey stretches comfortably and closes one eye, half asleep, lazily watching your meditation.

Focus your attention on the rhythm of your breathing: inhale, exhale, inhale, exhale. If any other activity comes to mind, it is because the little monkey has disobeyed and is polishing some little apple. Don't scold him. Just withdraw your attention from what he has done, and he will know that he has to come back and lie down again on the first branch. Continue to contemplate your breathing. Inhale, exhale. This is the *pranayama*, the yoga path of breathing toward spiritual knowledge. Your nervous system has abandoned the executive rhythm, which obeys rational commands, and is progressively adopting the contemplation of vegetative functions, which are mostly subcortical and unconscious. This is the rhythm of breathing when you sleep and also the rhythm of all sensorial functions such as digestion, blood circulation, cell metabolism, and basic life activity. Inhale, exhale. The little monkey has now ceased all his executive activities, you have detached from the very stressful performance rhythm, and you are increasingly tuning into the vegetative rhythm, the basic life rhythm of your body and of nature. Inhale, exhale. Relax and open yourself to life.

Focus your attention now on the miraculous aspect of breathing, which celebrates life in every movement. During inspiration you receive oxygen produced by plants to maintain all animals alive. In expiration you eliminate carbon dioxide ($CO_2$), the final product of vital activity, and return it to plants. Focus your attention on the life miracle. Oxygen represents life, and carbon dioxide represents that which has died. Life and death interact in every breath. Inhale, exhale.

Become aware of the intelligence of the universe, which has created life and the relationship between plants and animals. Inhale, exhale. Inhale, exhale. Contemplate the oxygen entering your lungs and think about the three hundred million alveoli that receive oxygen and allow it to pass into the blood. The oxygen enters the blood capillaries and is absorbed by the blood cells to combine with hemoglobin, a very large protein molecule, to form oxyhemoglobin, which gives blood its red color. The blood cells are now full of life. Watch them sail through your whole body, pumped by your heart. Think of the tissues receiving oxygen in your feet, legs, thighs, sexual glands, belly, lungs, heart, arms, hands, neck, face, ears, and finally your brain. Accompany the cell metabolism going on and rejoice for being alive. Register the reunion of subjective and objective dimensions. Don't leave your breathing rhythm. Inhale, exhale.

Imagine the oxygen that has been used up in the tissues returning as carbon dioxide within the blood cells. They are not red anymore. Hemoglobin has combined with $CO_2$ and turned into carboxylhemoglobin, which makes the blood blue, returning through the veins toward the lungs. Carbon dioxide passes through the alveoli in the lungs and out into nature. Inhale, exhale. Relax and open yourself to life.

Contemplate now the miraculous transformation of carbon dioxide back into oxygen. This occurs in plants fueled by nitrates produced by bacteria from the soil and solar energy in photosynthesis. See how plants give back oxygen to maintain all animal life. This is the fundamental symbiosis of life on our planet. Rejoice for the privilege of living in it. Inhale, exhale. Relax and open yourself to life.

Consider that around 4.5 billion years ago the earth was formed. Millions of years afterward, life began and there was no free oxygen in the atmosphere. Minuscule unicellular life forms were slowly transformed into multicellular organisms, which became plants. Some of them acquired the capacity to produce free oxygen and release it into the atmosphere.

Concentrate your attention on solar energy, which travels 92 million miles to get to the earth and participate in the miracle of life. Offer reverence to the sun, a small star among 100 billion stars present in our galaxy, which is called the Milky Way because it looks like drops of milk spilled in the sky. The stars are the origin of all the hydrogen, oxygen, carbon, nitrogen, and iron atoms, and all other atoms, that formed the earth and created life and your body. Inhale, exhale. Relax and open yourself to the miracle of life.

Continue in the vegetative rhythm, which you began to follow when the little monkey (the executive rhythm) stopped. Be aware of the state of relaxation and the absence of anxiety and stress that you have enjoyed in the *pranayama*, which has established this vegetative harmony between you, the plants, and planetary life. Notice the difference between what you are feeling now and the running around of your daily life with the little monkey polishing countless little apples. You are now detached from all daily worries. Through the vegetative rhythm you followed the roots of your life tree and realized the importance of all plants in your life. Remember this state of mind. You can return to the magic forest through your imagination whenever you wish. The gnome and the sloth will be there to welcome you and help you rest and contemplate the life miracle, through which you can be revitalized and become aware through compassion and intelligence of the profound nature of the universe .

This meditation illustrates the theory and practice of Jungian symbolic education, where all things and functions are experienced subjectively and objectively and become structuring symbols, complexes, functions, and systems of consciousness. In this example, meditation is taught through the function of imagination, including the functions of breathing, blood circulation, the function of oxygen and carbon dioxide in the metabolism of animals and in the photosynthesis of plants in the animal-plant symbiosis. At the same time, this meditation experiences the subjective functions of magic, attachment-detachment, admiration, praise, transcendence, religiosity, reverence, and gratitude for the life phenomenon. The exercise continues as follows to go more deeply into the transcendent dimension of the cosmic Self. The ideal proposition is that students begin practicing this first meditation in junior high and the second meditation in high school.

## Meditation Exercise
## Part II

### The Cosmic Voyage of the Spirit and the Preparation of Consciousness for Life after Death

Accommodate yourself under your life tree. Concentrate on the breathing rhythm and then on the light of photosynthesis; follow it to outer space. Leave your body and the earth and enter space, which contains the matter of the universe. Imagine seeing your body, your life tree, and the gnome way down on earth. Inhale, exhale. Relax and open yourself to the universe. Continue your trip.

Look around you now and see countless galaxies with their countless stars. Become aware that you are in infinite space, which contains all the matter of the universe and all the forms of being that were and will be. Become aware that infinite space is the temple of the creative spirit. Call the creative spirit God if you like but you do not have to. Feel welcomed. It has always been and it shall always be your home. Enjoy your stay. Know peace and gratitude to partake this dwelling.

You have discovered totality through emptiness, where you will always be free from attachment and breathe enlightenment. You can return as often as you feel like.

Now you return to earth, to your body. The little monkey polishes one apple, you open your eyes and go back to your daily activities, but now you know the way to infinite space. You can undertake this experience as often as you like and prepare your final voyage when you leave your body for the last time to live in your eternal home forever.

# Chapter 11

# SYMBOLIC SYSTEMIC CONSTRUCTIVISM

César Coll Salvador writes in his book *School Learning and the Construction of Knowledge* (1994):

> To speak of significant learning means above all else setting in relief the process of constructing meanings as the central element in the teaching-learning process ... the pupil may also learn ... in a purely memorizing sense ... and repeat mechanically without understanding.(p. 148)
>
> In Piaget's terms, we might say that we construct meanings by integrating or assimilating the new learning material to the schemes we already possess with respect to a comprehension of reality. (p. 149)
>
> A radically constructivist interpretation of the concept of learning forces us to go beyond simply considering the pupil's cognitive processes as the mediating element of teaching. Constructing meanings involves the pupil in his/her totality, not just in his/her previous knowledge and ability to establish substantive relations between these and the new material to be learned. (p. 153)

These observations allow a few further considerations on the method of Jungian symbolic education and constructivism perceived existentially and systemically through the symbolic perspective. The question is complex, for it involves a whole epistemological focus that embraces the very concept of symbol and in final analysis also the concept of existential intelligence at the service of the Self in the symbolic process of development of individual and collective consciousness. Existential intelligence obviously includes the intellect side by side with emotional intelligence.

Despite being a highly promising and creative challenge, it is not easy to integrate the concept of archetypal and symbolic dimension with the constructivist concept, as the Piaget school formulates it, within Jungian symbolic education. Piaget's approach has a typological perspective, which tends to consider cognition essentially expressed by the functions of thinking and sensation and the attitude of extraversion, to the detriment of the functions of feeling and intuition and the introverted attitude. There are students who find it hard to explain their thoughts and actions, yet intuit the ways of life, or follow the truth of the heart, or find their behavior guided by some intimate mediumistic perception. Are they necessarily less intelligent than those who explain their motivations through the logic of objective facts? What I most miss in the notion of conceptual intelligence and cognition in Piaget's constructivism is precisely the fact that feeling, intuition, and introversion are not considered as important as thinking, sensation, and extraversion. From the perspective of Jungian symbolic education, learning is not separated into subjective and objective dimensions, and therefore all four psychological functions and both attitudes of consciousness described by Jung are equally important.

Piaget wrote that:

> Jung is an extraordinary constructor, but a certain despising for logic and rational activity which he picked up in the daily contact with mythological and symbolic thought made him perhaps not too demanding with regard to verifications. To sympathize more with the realities he speaks about, he adopts an anti-rationalist attitude and the surprising suggestions that he possesses the secret at times actually discomfit the critical reader. (1964, p. 252)

## Jung and Piaget and the Historical Opposition Between Intuition and Sensation

Here we have two problems, one is typological and the other has to do with scientific tradition. With respect to the former, I believe that Jung and Piaget are situated at the typological extremities of the intuition-sensation polarity. Jung is the intuitive type who flies to past and future along with the possible meanings of symbols, and Piaget is the sensation type who latches on to the immediate characteristics of symbols in order to study them. This may be one reason why Piaget complains in the above quotation of Jung's cultivation of mythological and symbolic thought and not being sufficiently demanding as to verifications, which are so vital to the sensation type. On the one hand, the dreamer intuiting the nature of the image on the horizon; on the other, the person fascinated with understanding the here-and-now. There is no doubt that both are complementary and for that very reason necessary in human reality, scientific research, and teaching. This opposite typology makes Jung's and Piaget's thoughts and works difficult to compare, especially when one considers that this typological opposition is also historical.

As mentioned before, Jungian symbolic psychology has amplified Jung's concept of the individual Self and also described the cultural Self, which can present the same archetypes, symbols, complexes, and functions to structure collective consciousness. This theoretical approach allows us to realize that the two opposite typological perspectives of Jung and Piaget—regarding intuition-sensation, introversion-extraversion and subjective-objective—are not only personal. They also represent a polarity which we find in the scientific tradition and which was expressed in psychology by two prevailing trends in the twentieth century: the psychology of unconscious processes, depth psychology, or dynamic psychology on one extreme and behavioral and cognitive psychology on the other. It is important to observe, however, that within the psychodynamic current, Freud dwelt far longer on the cause, infancy, and genesis of development and is therefore expressing sensation typology, which makes him, in this sense, closer to Piaget than to Jung. Based on the prospective poles of archetypes and symbols, Jung dealt intuitively with depth psychology, searching more for the prospective or teleological where-to, which led him to formulate the individuation process.

## The Typology and Scientific Traditions of Jung, Piaget, and Freud

Jung's and Piaget's typologies are highly meaningful when related to European scientific tradition regarding the extraversion-introversion, intuition-sensation, and thinking-feeling polarities. From opposite types on the intuition-sensation and introverted-extraverted polarities, Jung and Piaget have in common the fact that the thinking function is more privileged than the feeling function in both of them. Jung situates his scientific perspective in the introverted attitude, thereby privileging the subjective aspects (internal adaptation of the ego). Piaget's work shows a dominant attitude of extraversion and so focuses mainly on objective aspects (external adaptation of the ego). This resulted in Jung adopting the concept of archetype from Plato, another great intuitive introvert, as the internal matrix of images, whereas Piaget chose Aristotle's extraverted way, the method of direct, pragmatic observation of the development of the child's intelligence, beginning with his own children. In so doing, Piaget coincided with the positivist, causal, materialistic, rationalist, and objective tradition of the nineteenth century. On the other hand, Jung's intuition-thinking-introversion typology is more closely linked to the typology of the monastic life of the Middle Ages that preceded the lay university, as mentioned in chapter 2.

Monastic life was dominantly influenced by Neoplatonic philosophy, essentially intuitive and introverted, whereas the universities, which followed the monasteries, were guided by the ideas of Aristotle, essentially rational and extraverted (Jung 1921). This helps to explain in part the widespread labeling of Jung as an occultist, begun by Freud (1921), and Piaget's criticism of Jung's methodology (Piaget 1964). It is important to note that in the second half of the twentieth century, mainly after World War II, a new cultural wave arose redeeming the value of sensuality of the insular matriarchal pattern (see chapter 7), feeling, intuition, and introversion, within the democratic pattern of alterity, continuing the creative trend of the Western cultural Self to heal the rationalistic, materialistic, positivist dissociation of the nineteenth century.

Jungian analyst Edward C. Whitmont agrees with this analysis and illustrates it with the following extract from Piaget's book, *The Language and Thought of the Child:*

> Psychoanalysts were made to distinguish two fundamentally different ways of thinking: directed or intelligent thought, and non-directed or, as Bleuler suggested putting it, autistic thought. Direct thinking is conscious, that is, it pursues an objective that is present in the mind of the person who is thinking; it is intelligent, which means it is adapted to reality (external reality) and tries to influence it; it admits the possibility of being true or false (empirical or logically true), and may be communicated through language. Autistic thinking is subconscious, which means that the objectives it pursues

and the problems it tries to solve are not conscious; it is not adapted to reality, but creates for itself an oneiric world of the imagination; rather than to establish truths, it tends to satisfy desires and remains strictly individual and incommunicable by means of language. On the contrary, it acts mainly through images, and in order to express itself, it resorts to indirect methods that evoke by myth and symbol the sentiment that it directs. (1959, p. 43)

Whitmont's comments are as follows:

Autistic thinking (non-conceptual, imagistic thought, more associative than causally logical) is implicitly devalued here by Piaget ... his value judgment seems to be that reality is only to be found in the world of exterior objects, so the only adaptation to reality is based on that type of mental attitude, described as directed thought, that is grounded on concepts, directed by will and orientated by causality, and is thus appropriate for making the exterior world usable. The experience of each one's internal world, which happens through thought by images, does not appear to be reality and is viewed only as something primitive, inferior, and pathological. This is the prejudice of extraverted positivism (Whitmont 1969, p. 25).

Freud had also the sensation function and extraverted typology in his scientific formulations. It is striking how the same positivist ideology that overestimates and equates the objective with the conscious, the normal, the mature, and the real and scorns the subjective by likening it to the unconscious, desire, the childish, and the pathological also permeates his work. In *The Formulation of Two Principles of Mental Functioning*, Freud wrote:

We have observed for a long time that all neuroses result in, and are therefore probably also the purpose of, drawing the patient from real life, alienating him from reality ... And now we are faced with the task of investigating the development of the relation between neurotics and humanity in general, and thereby to find the psychological significance of the external, real world for the structure of our theories ... we have grown used to taking as a starting point the unconscious mental processes ... we feel that they are the oldest, primary processes, remnants of a phase of development when they were the only type of mental process ... This is described as the principle of pleasure-pain ... Our dreams ... are vestiges

> of the predominance of this principle .... The psychic apparatus
> had to form a concept of the real circumstances in the external
> world ... A new principle of mental functioning was thus
> introduced ... this setting down the principle of reality proved
> to be an auspicious step. (1911, p. 277)

Jungian symbolic education seeks to integrate these two types of thought—first, the magic, mythical thought directed by sensuality and desire as an expression of the sensory-motor insular matriarchal archetypal intelligence, and, second, the rational, logical, organized, and executive thought as an expression of the conceptual polarized position of the patriarchal archetypal intelligence. The concepts of structuring symbols, complexes, functions, and symptoms as psychic structural and functional dimensions of the Self embrace all polarities, which allows Jungian symbolic education to formulate the concept of symbolic constructivism, associating these two types of intelligence within the dialect position of intelligence of the alterity archetype.

## Systemic Symbolic Constructivism

My intention in proposing symbolic constructivism is to continue Piaget's constructivism along with Jung's notion of the process of individuation and Freud's concepts of the ego and the repressed unconscious with its defenses, basing these three perspectives on the concepts of structuring symbols, complexes, functions, and systems. Symbolic constructivism is cognitive, emotional, developmental, and systemic. It is exercised based on the symbolic elaboration of the material to be learned together with the emotional reactions of students and teachers, within a multiple feedback system, which makes it also dialectical, systemic, and symbolic. This is the concept of *systemic symbolic constructivism*.

Systemic symbolic constructivism is deployed through the student-teacher-school-family transference relationship on two fronts. On the objective front of the symbolic material, the student-teacher-school-family quaternio opens up to study the world and the life processes through the archetypal nature of the imagination, that is, through the transcendent existential meanings of the material to be taught, rather than just the literal ones. In order to do this, expressive techniques are employed, which may include dramatic, corporal, playful, and plastic (drawing, painting, and modeling) techniques, games (including videogames), music, dancing, popular and classical singing, as well as the emotions, dreams, and experiences of the teacher and the pupils, especially those connected with the material taught. The class taps into mythical, historical, and legendary stories, fairy tales, literary and theatrical arts, oracles, and the pupils' own creativity so that the wings of the imagination can develop the objective contents of symbols and pollinate psychic life. The objective physical, chemical, biological, and mathematical features of the symbols are thus thoroughly scrutinized, reviewed, and regrouped in a dynamic, holistic manner and always reformulated and animated within the symbolic-existential perspective. This is the praxis of systemic symbolic constructivism, which continuously reviews the curriculum so as to adapt it to the existential reality of the pupils.

On the subjective front of symbols, the student-teacher-school-family quaternio assumes an attitude of amorous transcendence of the ego within the totality of the learning and existential process. This means that conscious systemic and symbolic teaching is not confined to the teacher-pupil interaction, since it is practiced within a commitment to the process of individuation of teachers and pupils and to the process of symbolic development of the humanization of the Self of the school and of the planet. This commitment has to occur in all symbolic dimensions of the Self: body, nature, society, idea, image, emotion, word, number, sound, silence, and behavior. Because of all this, systemic symbolic constructivism is ontological: it eschews the erudition that is limited to the cult of rational knowledge and pursues wisdom by significantly activating the dialectics of the subjective-objective relation of being-in-the-world. In this sense it is experiential and pragmatic, but always holistic, through the transcendent experience of the part and its link to the whole.

## Systemic Symbolic Constructivism and the Process of Individuation

One of the central characteristics of symbolic constructivism carried out at the systemic level is that it is perceived within the process of the person's individuation and the symbolic development of the group and cultural Self. One of the perils of conceptualizing constructivism in education is that it can remain imprisoned in the rationalism that is deeply rooted in subject-object dissociation and be unable to reach the desired range; that is, "constructing meanings involves the pupils in their totality" (Salvador 1994, p. 153). Often the constructivist and systemic perspectives (holism) are desired, but in excluding the subjective and archetypal from this approach, the irrational elements necessary for achieving this totality are relinquished, and they escape from us. In such cases, despite the full intention to situate systemic constructivism in totality, this is not attained and one continues limited and alienated in rationalism. The rationalist prison only releases us when we situate rational-irrational, conscious-unconscious, subject-object, and teacher-pupil symbolically side by side, all interacting amorously, cognitively, and dialectically as a function of the whole in the process of teaching. To achieve this totality, we must situate constructivism and the systemic perspective within the process of symbolic development of the teacher and of the pupil, that is, within the process of individuation and the process of archetypal humanization of the group, be it a class, a school, a nation, a continent, or global society. The difference between ontic and ontological identity can help us expand the symbolic experience in question.

## Ontological Identity and Systemic Symbolic Constructivism

During a symbolic supervision of class coordinators, one of them presented me with the following problematic situation: the opening of a senior high cycle in the school brought in new teachers to make up the teaching staff along with teachers who had accompanied the pupils since the fifth grade. Some of the new teachers received high praise from many of the pupils, who explained that they were performing better because they were more affectionate and participative.

One class counselor suggested an interpretation, saying that the new teachers treated the pupils more like children, while the old ones treated them more like grown-ups. Quoting Piaget, she argued that it was as if the old teachers in the school believed that the pupils had already fully acquired formal thinking, whereas the new teachers did not make this assumption. Based on this diagnosis, she suggested that the old teachers should go back to treating the ninth-graders more like children, feeling that in this way they would obtain the same performance as the new teachers.

I tried to draw their attention to the cognitive bias in the counselor's reasoning. She was reducing the emotional and affectionate experience in learning to a childish and less developed stage of intelligence. Given that the new teachers were more affectionate and participative, she reckoned that the pupils were performing better because "they were cognitively more childish". In this context, I suggested that, since they were less formal in their conduct, the new teachers had intuited far better the insular matriarchal aspects of adolescents. It seemed to me that the better constructivist performance the new teachers had achieved was due to a better pedagogical transference with affection and empathy, without necessarily having to be explained in terms of the stages of development of intelligence. In reality there exist various forms of intelligence that differ according to the structuring functions chosen for learning and teaching, and these should not be labeled as better or worse, superior or inferior, more advanced or more primitive. As Gardner (1983) has described, these forms of intelligence, each in its own manner, tackle different aspects of life's vicissitudes. Likewise Jung's psychological types are different strategies to express the intelligence of the Self. The feeling function, for instance, is a form of intelligence, "the intelligence of the heart", according to Pascal. The fact that Jungian symbolic psychology considers the four regent archetypes to be the four main types of intelligence of the Self situates the symbolic elaboration in education within the ontological dimension.

Following Martin Heidegger (1927), I described the ontic and ontological identities to differentiate two important characteristics of personality and of teaching. Ontic identity—or ego, persona, and shadow—includes isolated data regarding color, profession, residence, age, parents, and all the endless characteristics of each person, including passport and identity cards. In teaching, the ontic identity of the object refers to the thing in itself (Kant's *das Ding an sich*) to be studied. Ontological identity—or identity of the Self—includes all symbols and their archetypal roots forming what Jung called the personal myth, which is the sense of each person's individuation process, or the collective myth of a group, society, or even a set of societies (Byington 2000). Heidegger's ontic-ontological polarity (*Seiende-Sein*) can perhaps be better understood when associated with Alfred North Whitehead's polarity (1929) of entity and process in his theory of knowledge.

The attachment inherent in the matriarchal and patriarchal patterns favors the perception of ontic identity, while the detachment patterns characteristic of alterity and totality enable us to experience ontological identity, that is, the process of significant systemic linking of each person's symbols.

A middle-age woman who is a psychologist, a painter, and a writer had the following dream:

> I'm going to travel abroad with my husband and children. On reaching the airport, I realize I've forgotten my passport. My husband gets angry. A great calm comes over me. Quite cool and collected, I tell him I'll have time to go back and get my passport. He claims I won't be able to do it. I return to fetch my passport, but surprisingly I don't go to my house but to Rita's, a childhood friend who always cultivated Hindu mysticism. Along with the passport, she gives me a carousel, which, when you spin it, displays lovely figures, and a glass seal.

Using Freud's method of free association, she associated the symbols of Rita and India with dedication to the introverted values of meditation and creativity, which she herself practiced when she wrote her stories, essays, and poems. The carousel was associated with the precise articulation of moving parts with the whole, and the figure of seal with the capacity of meditation and creativity to dive down below the surface. Employing Jung's method of amplification, we may also see the carousel within the circus as the playful and creative dimension of a mandala producing transcendent experiences, which are integrated into totality. Amplifying the seal symbol, we also saw the seal as the great hunter of the Artic, a creature that separates from the group and dives alone for food in unknown depths, in the same way as the ego is guided by creativity in all forms to grow and renew itself during centroversion.

This analysand had two well-delineated worlds that were in conflict: one with her husband, children, home, and social commitments and the other with her introverted and creative experiences. The dream privileged the latter in order to harbor her forgotten identity (her passport was at her friend's house) on her existential journey. In this case, consciousness had to be called by her ontological identity through certain ontic characteristics that she was leaving on a secondary level. The fact that her husband did not believe she would be able to fetch her passport and return in time for her flight points out to the conflict that her family role played in her ontological process of individuation. On the objective level, her husband is a man of the sensation type, extraverted and materialistic, and therefore, on her subjective level, he represents the patriarchal tradition, which prevents the integration of the dialectic relation of alterity and totality in all activities and tasks during the ontological journey. The patriarchal polarized position represented by the husband separates rigidly extraversion from introversion and hampers the creative dialectical association of ontic and ontological identities.

Educators need to bear in mind the difference between ontic and ontological identity in order to differentiate authentic teaching that corresponds to the true needs of the pupil's life from the alienated teaching that piles together a great deal of ontic notions that, once learned, will provide the student with a diploma but will fail to correspond to the pupil's ontological process.

The conceptual difference between ontological teaching and teaching that is alienated because it is exclusively ontic, fragmented, and basically subordinated to formal programs is not restricted to the individual Self and also applies to the group and cultural Self. This means that the collective Self also has an ontic and an ontological identity. Negro students in the northeastern part of Brazil (Bahia), for instance, experienced an enormous upgrade in learning when their curriculum was taught including references to traditional Afro-Brazilian cultures.

Among the alienating aspects present in teaching programs, we can specifically identify those that stem from the rationalist dissociation that separates knowing from practical usage. Teaching according to constructivism may include any procedure as long as it is experienced and useful. Lino de Macedo, in a lecture on constructivism and pedagogic practice (1993), taught that to be a constructivist would entail treating education as an investigation, as an experiment. In this way he showed that even a copy can be constructivist, as long as it bears the characteristic of research.

I explain symbolic constructivism as something essentially characterized by the emotional experience of symbolic elaboration. The more adequate emotion there is in teaching, the more psychic energy the Self will invest in symbolic elaboration, and the more holistic it will be. Of course, for this to happen it is necessary to vivify, that is, to matriarchally animate the objective content of teaching, the participation of teacher and pupil, and their transference relationship in the subjective and objective dimension.

To construct teaching symbolically is to transform it into useful experience and to elaborate it as far as possible. To do so, education has to use imagination in science and art, with as many expressive techniques as it can. It is not enough for teachers to understand theoretically the intention of the symbolic constructivist method. They have to be trained in the use of expressive techniques at the service of the imagination experienced and related to the process of individuation. The learning and usage of expressive techniques in symbolic constructivism require of educators some degree of self-knowledge, such that they can also recognize the nature of their circumstantial and chronic shadows and employ this knowledge with their students. Through their capacity to mobilize the pupil's personality, potentially existing defenses may trigger clinical symptoms or aggravate others already present, and the teacher must be able to recognize this and deal with it adequately.

Symbolic constructivist education is also systemic. It is practiced within the totality of the teaching Self, in the teacher-pupil relationship, class, school, family, and culture. This holistic feature of the dynamic relation between parts and the whole is analogous to the multiple feedback system studied in the concepts of homeostasis in cybernetics and biological ecosystems (von Bertalanffy 1968). The interaction between parts and the whole occurs within the process of symbolic elaboration coordinated by the ruling archetypal quaternio around the central archetype to form consciousness. The interaction of the parts within the Self may therefore occur under one of the four basic archetypal patterns and under the domination of the creative and defensive structuring functions, and this will influence symbolic constructivism in typical ways. For Jungian symbolic education, what characterizes the symbolic constructivist method and the systemic perspective is the symbolic elaboration of learning with all the attributes described in the preceding chapters. So, when we practice the systemic constructivist method, it is necessary to choose the adequate archetypal pattern to elaborate any given situation and to pay attention to the possible presence of defenses. The desire to be interactive and holistic is not enough. It is necessary to be interactive and holistic archetypally and ontologically, rather than just rationally and ontically. I have observed that many theories that praise holism end up frustrated because they do not recognize irrational elements, which are not explicit in the system but which are nonetheless present and active. I refer to these elements as irrational not because they are so in themselves but because they do not appear within the logical explicit context. If they are disregarded, these elements will remain in the shadow of the system constructed and will limit the holistic approach.

The archetypal elements that embrace the subject-object relation act in a transcendent, prospective manner. They may not be visible in the objective form, either because they conceal themselves from the network of conscious meanings or because they are dissociated in the shadow or because they reveal themselves in the form of images whose archetypal roots are often very distant from consciousness. When they remain unperceived or unsought, all talk of a systemic and constructivist approach will lack holism and will repeat the old rationalist ego-centered perspective with all its omnipotence and limitation. There will be an illusion about wholeness and the dialectic freedom between parts that are never achieved. In these cases, the theory will be radically different from reality. When the holistic perspective is not symbol-centered and does not include the subjective-objective and the ontic-ontological aspects of events, it will be a lopsided discourse because certain experiences will be privileged to the detriment of others. The symbolic perspective is a method that permanently transcends the ego perspective and so prevents the rationalist sidetracking that frustrates authentic research within holism. The symbolic holistic perspective requires of educators humility, maturity, and detachment in order to transmit knowledge, while being receptive to evaluate the discrepancy between their goal and the limitations of their achievements.

## Systemic Symbolic Constructivism and Dominance in the Ruling Archetypal Quaternio

The constructivist and systemic symbolic methods in teaching tend to privilege the pattern of alterity. Both were historically created to improve teaching (constructivism) and communication (the systemic approach) beyond the traditional patriarchal pattern.

Piaget's school expressed a radical change in the traditional method of teaching in Western culture, which tended to be based on learning through rational understanding and repetition of what teachers said. The premise was that teachers knew things and pupils did not, which expresses the polarized position of the patriarchal pattern. The poles are separated as radically different entities and one pole acts causally on the other. In this context, the teacher is identified with knowledge and transmits it to passive pupils.

Likewise, before cybernetics and von Bertalanffy's description of open systems in living organisms, the interaction of energetic forces tended to be perceived as acting causally in a mechanical, linear way. The explanation for tuberculosis, for example, was reduced to the penetration of Koch's bacillus into the organism. In the same manner, neurology explained that the hand reaching for a fork as a vision that showed the brain the fork's location. The concept of the multiple feedback system introduced a new view of interaction that transcended the causal, unilateral, and mechanical explanations. Understanding of reality became far more satisfactory. It is not just Koch's bacillus entering the organism that causes tuberculosis but rather the feedback relationship between the bacteria and the organism, within the individual, family, and cultural Self. Disease is a whole and its parts (bacillus, genetic predisposition, age, incidence of disease, conditions of the organism, food, rest, housing) are all structuring symbols, complexes and functions full of different meanings that interact with each other and within the whole. In the same way, it is not only the vision of the fork that guides the brain and the hand to hold it, but rather the dynamic interrelationship between hand and fork image, brain and progressive reduction of space that explains the final grasping of the fork. It is a set or system of actions and reactions. In constructivism and in systems, the principle of synchronicity plays a primary role and the principle of causality becomes secondary because of the fact that there is never only a single cause for the phenomenon. There are always so many causes interacting in the field where the phenomenon takes place that in one way we can consider it acausal. The fact that one cause is singled out for study should by no means exclude others. The interaction of parts seen within the principle of synchronicity, which includes programmed and spontaneous unpredictable events in systemic symbolic constructivism, substitutes an attitude of expectation, revelation, and mystery for the rational causal certainty.

Thus alchemists used the expression "if God wishes it" (*Deo concedente*), for they transcended the materialistic rational causality of the polarized patriarchal pattern to include faith and the unforeseeable within the alterity pattern of synchronicity.

The constructivism of Piaget's school and the systemic theory share the common denominator of interaction by multiple returns within a whole. The teacher activates in the pupil the archetypal opening to learning, just as the pupil stimulates in the teacher the desire to teach. Teaching is symbolically constructed within this interaction. The function of the teacher, as we saw in chapter 5 on the archetype of the master-apprentice, is to generate learning in the pupil's psyche. The German word for "convincing" is meaningful in this context: *überzeugen* is made up of *über* (over) and *zeugen* (to generate). To teach is to convince the student of something, that is, to activate its generation in the Self of the student. Education, from the Latin *educare*, is made up of *e* (out) and *ducere* (to lead, to draw, to bring), drawing out someone's capacity.

Although he did not fully conceive of the psyche as functioning like a multiple feedback system, Jung came very close to a constructivist psychotherapy because he always considered the dialectic conscious and unconscious interrelationship between patient and therapist expressed in the face-to-face dialogue. He conceived the creative interaction of opposites through the action of the transcendent function in the dialectics of neurosis and normality, in the polarity of typological functions, in the pursuit of homeostasis via compensation, and also in his formulation of the principle of synchronicity as an acausal relation between subject and object.

As I have already mentioned, constructivism and the systemic perspective express the multidisciplinary emergence of the implantation of the archetype of alterity in the collective consciousness of the cultural Self. This implantation can also be seen in mathematical functions, in cybernetics, in the antigen-antibody interaction of immunology, in the concept of gravity in astronomy, in all artistic and creative processes, in the functioning of the neuroendocrine system, in the dynamic understanding of the ecosystem, in the democratic interaction of family and government, and in intimate interpersonal relationships. In all these life dimensions, we witness the relation of parts through a multiple feedback mechanism within a systemic whole.

The recognition of the importance of the archetype of alterity should not be used to disqualify the other three regent archetypes, because to exercise alterity, it is necessary to have the capacity to elaborate symbols also coordinated by the matriarchal and patriarchal patterns. Detachment from them does not mean eliminating them from symbolic elaboration. On the contrary, they must be integrated so that they can be adequately submitted to alterity. It is crucial to realize that the principle of synchronicity and the multiple feedback mechanism that characterizes the systemic perspective are the core of the pattern of alterity, utilized democratically to integrate dialectic and the different forms of intelligence, including those of the matriarchal, patriarchal, and totality archetypes.

## Imitation and Copy in Teaching

Automatic imitation should be distinguished from copying carried out as a planned task, or even as a duty. Automatic imitation is one of the main characteristics in identity formation coordinated by the matriarchal pattern, whereas required copying is mostly a feature of the patriarchal pattern. Systemic symbolic constructivism should not exclude either automatic imitation or required copy, for both can be productively used in learning.

As we saw in chapter 7, the matriarchal pattern coordinates symbolic elaboration in a close, symbiotic relationship in which the ego and the other are so intimate that they may easily experience identification. Children may feel great intimacy with teachers and spontaneously imitate them, just as they imitate mother, father, siblings, and whoever lives with them (Levy-Brühl's *participation mystique* adopted by Jung). This facility for imitation is due to the insular position of consciousness characteristic of the matriarchal pattern, described in chapter 7.

Automatic imitation is very intense in early childhood and in personalities with strong affinity for the matriarchal archetype and, like any other structuring function, it may act creatively or defensively. It may lead to positive identification and enhance learning or to negative identification with the shadow, limiting learning unconsciously. Defensive or negative identification may also lead to identification with the opposite characteristics of the other person, which is called reactive formation, in which case the student feels aversion to the subject taught. The importance of automatic imitation in early life is such that we may consider it the most profound and influential social factor in identity formation. Even when not recognized, it is always present and active in teaching due to the learning transference, which is unavoidable even at the most advanced post-graduate level. However brilliant and original the pupils may be, they always bear identifications with their teachers. The greatest danger of negative identification or reactive formation in teaching is the aversive reaction of students, the worst enemy of education. Many students become "allergic" to mathematics, history, or languages due to a defensive identification with their first teachers.

As we saw in chapter 8, the patriarchal pattern coordinates symbolic elaboration in an abstract, organizing, planning, dogmatic and task-conditioned relationship in which the ego-other polarity of consciousness comes face to face with symbols and transforms identity through idealism, imposition, demands, and guilt (Freud's sublimation), which gives rise to superego identification with the ideal of learning. Personally, I do not recommend copying as a method in teaching, but I think that we must admit that when it is chosen by a student, voluntary copying may act as a structuring function that enhances memory and learning through the patriarchal pattern.

This being so, the archetypal structuring functions that propitiate automatic imitation and voluntary copying cannot be excluded from learning, since they always occur, whether they are accepted or not. What can and should be done with them in systemic symbolic constructivism is first to make sure that they operate creatively rather than defensively, and second, that they are subordinated to the pattern of alterity.

Automatic imitation may also become defensive. These are the cases where positive or negative identifications between teachers and pupils, instead of enhancing the productivity of learning, lead to blocks and resistance. We should not forget that many defenses stem from the automatic imitation of parents' defensive behavior. This is the case, for instance, of the pupil who loses enthusiasm for studying a certain subject because of defensive automatic imitation of a teacher who is undergoing a crisis of depression, who is bored, or who is resistant to the call of teaching.

Likewise, voluntary imitation may become defensive when its meaning is not perceived and taken into account in the overall dialectic context of alterity. These are cases where voluntary copying can give students the false impression that this is the best that learning can render, in which case it can generate tedium, resistance, and automatic learning that prevent intensifying the elaboration of the symbol in question.

To subordinate the structuring functions of automatic imitation and required copying to the pattern of alterity means to perceive and place them in the context of the whole, so that they may operate creatively and their symbolic attributes be incorporated in wider and deeper elaborations in the teaching project.

For constructivism to become symbolic, it is necessary to be open to elaborating symbols in teaching through every and any structuring function, through the four structuring functions of consciousness that, as we know, are complementary to one another and together form a whole. If I claim that the planet was subdivided into meridians and parallels in order to identify the four directions—north, south, east and west—despite understanding this theme rationally, on experiencing it symbolically I still have another three functions and two attitudes to elaborate. Intuition may ask how these were used in the past and what use they will be in the future. Sensation may want to know how they can be determined in the air, at sea, and on land. Feeling may express the affects of its reactions on what lies in each direction. Extraversion may take care to perceive the world through them, and introversion may try to point out how our ego reacts to them, all within the individual and collective levels. The north-south polarity in the United States, for instance, formed a complex, symbolically charged with intense emotional characteristics, as a symbolic reaction to the civil war. Most nations have a symbolic experience with cardinal points due to their history and traditions. Symbolic learning is achieved through intelligence and existential cognition. It is important to note that, just as each person has a specific typological dominance, each one's intelligence and cognition operate characteristically through this particular typology.

As pointed out in chapter 4, teachers should know Jungian typology to improve their professional performance. With this knowledge, they avoid reducing their teaching performance to their main typological function and become able to associate the difficulties of many students to the fact that their typologies are opposite.

By so doing, we shall be exercising a systemic symbolic constructivism rid of the surveillance of the traditional IQ measure, in which intelligence and cognitive ability are exclusively subordinated to the functions of thinking and sensation and to extraverted attitude. Elaborating the content of teaching by the creative and defensive structuring functions in the archetypal patterns and by all the typological functions and attitudes within the whole is the method that directs the practical exercise of systemic symbolic constructivism.

When systemic symbolic constructivism uses the typological tool, it can take into account the particular difficulties that students with the feeling-intuitive typology experience in traditional teaching, especially male students who present the neurological dominance of the right brain hemisphere accompanied by a strong presence of the matriarchal archetype. Jungian symbolic education emphasizes the value of the matriarchal archetype and the functions of feeling and intuition because of their facility to experience emotion and imagination.

Systemic symbolic constructivist evaluation is carried out through the student-teacher-school-family quaternio within the Self. This is the frame that enables us to evaluate the symbols of the education process related to each other and to the whole. This frame is important to avoid reducing difficulties of the education process to only one of its components. These four components interact dynamically, and so the symbolic focus of any dysfunction requires its elaboration in light of this quaternio. A certain pupil may have learning difficulties that unquestionably express a schoolwide problem that has to be examined. Difficulties of another pupil may expose his or her teacher's limitations. Pupils have problems that undeniably express their families' crises or chronic problems and can only be worked through with the families' participation. And of course, there also exist learning disorders whose primary dimension is the actual personality of the student.

### The Self in Education
#### General Teaching Coordination

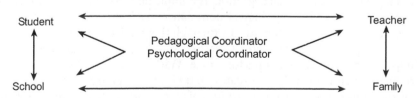

Evaluation carried out within systemic symbolic constructivism has two great advantages. First, it helps avoid reductionism, whereby the problems of teaching are unilaterally focused. Second, because this evaluation reverts to all the dimensions of the system, it does not end once the problem itself has been worked through, but rather reflects on all the dynamics of the Self, which allows for the continuous reassessment of the whole system of education.

This method of evaluating permits the elaboration of teaching guidelines for the class and the school throughout the entire school year. To undertake it, it is necessary to map out the creative and defensive dynamic forces operating in each class and in the school as a whole, on the cognitive and emotional levels, by the class coordinator from the start of the year. The interaction of teachers with one another and with coordinators has special value in this connection. This mapping out of class psychodynamics should include the pupils' normal characteristics, such as typology, learning process, capacity for emotional expression, and group rapport, as well as the difficulties, including those of a physical, emotional, rational, social (with the class), family, and academic results. This mapping of the characteristics of the pupils allows for the composition of the psychodynamic forces that act in the class as a whole. This perspective enables the class coordinator and teachers to adopt creative strategies to enhance the teaching and help solve the circumstantial problems that crop up during the school year. It is also especially useful for evaluating changes in the makeup of the classes passing on to the year ahead.

## The Consequences of Systemic Symbolic Constructivism for the Personality of Students

The fact that the teacher participates with mind and heart in the construction of teaching creates a teaching transference relationship that will influence the development of the student's personality, including character formation, which is unthinkable in purely cognitive constructivism. It is in this emotional and cognitive learning vessel that we can create the psychological and ethical standards of what is constructive and destructive in character formation and in life. Including the physiological and biochemical functions of the body to illustrate teaching whenever possible significantly favors the understanding of the constructive-destructive polarity by helping to assess the danger of behaviors involving risk activities, violence, drugs, alcohol, and smoking in the life of the young.

The function of ethics centered on the constructive-destructive polarity of systemic symbolic constructivism must occupy a crucial position in the curriculum. It is subordinated to the general coordination of teaching, and it must be a general concern for all teachers and the whole school. Without any preestablished dogmatic morality, the constructive-destructive polarity of good and evil must underlie every symbolic elaboration of the shadow in teaching. The preoccupation with the symbolic construction of ethics and character by joining knowledge and love with the development of the individual, family, and society in teaching and the perception of the formation of the shadow through fixations and defenses is the way in which Jungian symbolic education contributes toward the ethical construction of humanism. Dignifying responsible and productive work is one of the great challenges of education for helping modern society cultivate meaning for individual and social life as an antidote to drugs, cynicism, corruption, and delinquency. A healthier culture that cultivates sustainable economy and respect for human beings and nature in search for self-fulfillment and preservation of dignity of life on earth is the central aim of Jungian symbolic education.

## Systemic Symbolic Constructivism and the Ideal of Teaching

Symbolic education is dedicated to building symbolic humanism. The dialectic experience of parts related to wholeness in the existential process creates a direction and a sense in being. When it is auspicious, there arises the symbol of the north, the guiding star. When desperate, there emerges the symbol of the abyss, which in the case of teaching is the absence of perspective on the individual and cultural transmission of human values. The north of the teacher's function is to reveal this ideal of individual Self, being aware that, in doing it, the teacher will never be alone because he or she will be followed by the students. The teacher must be open to feel this ideal and to work for it in the school Self and the cultural Self, as part of the striving for symbolic education within the cultural Self and the cosmic Self.

School and society need to have an ideal for teaching, and it is this ideal that guides the teacher's training and daily work. That which is achieved always falls far short of what is desired. The ideal is the compass that points the way and at the same time permits elaboration and awareness of mistakes and limitations. It is during the permanent elaboration of this goal that all the ideal of the student-teacher-school-family quaternio should be undertaken. It is from this interaction that a society's guidelines for teaching should emerge. This process necessarily includes the search for light side by side with the permanent confrontation of shadow, keeping in mind that, as in any apprenticeship, a well-elaborated error may teach more than the right answer.

When teaching is guided by a humanistic ideal, which in the case of Jungian symbolic education is the ideal of symbolic humanism, it includes cognitive instruction along with the shaping of character and the whole personality, which enables students to acquire the ethical capacity to differentiate good from evil. This means that teaching is guided by the developmental processes of human beings, whose conquests of freedom, human rights, and fraternity stand for that which is most valued in civilization. Yet this is not a matter of including sermons in the curriculum, but rather of training teachers to teach a program with important objective contents to pupils whose personality is being shaped both objectively and subjectively. The construction of symbolic teaching is not limited to using the subjective to increase the quality of objective teaching but also aims at developing character and shaping the entire personality during the acquisition of objective knowledge. It is a question of shaping the professional personality, and at the same time the personality of the national and international citizen through knowledge.

The path of symbolic constructivism uses in its daily work the reunion of the subjective and objective in the construction of knowledge, and therefore, the very method of teaching transcends the teacher-student cognitive relation and opens the teaching transference relation to intellectual and emotional intimacy. Within this context, the sermon is redundant and superfluous because the teaching experience already covers the emotional elaboration of satisfaction and frustration, right and wrong, good and evil in everyday human reality. It is never a matter of knowing only where Egypt lies or the Nile flows and on what date the pyramids were built, but also always of trying to understand how the ancient Egyptians who built the pyramids lived and conceived of life after death, inseparably from what the pupil and the class feel about creativity and life and death. In the intimacy of symbolic constructivism, it is practically impossible to avoid the permanent elaboration of existential problems such as virtue and evil and life and death along with learning. Nevertheless, attention must also be paid to avoiding exaggerated subjectivity, as when teachers become counselors and involve themselves inadequately with the intimate lives of pupils and families. This would be the omnipotence (*hybris*) of subjectivism, as bad as the omnipotence of objectivism that excluded the subjective from teaching altogether. The intention is not to teach good and evil patriarchally in a polarized position, because this any lower school student already knows. The aim is not to codify what is good and what is evil but to construct the ethical capacity to elaborate the difference between good and evil through the understanding of what is destructive and constructive in the development of the individual, of the family, of culture, and of society.

# Chapter 12

# JUNGIAN SYMBOLIC EDUCATION AND THE IMAGINATION

One of modern psychology's greatest discoveries is the archetypal nature of the imagination on the conscious and unconscious levels of the Self. The discovery of the repressed unconscious, which inaugurated psychoanalysis, overshadowed the major discovery of the creative power of conscious and unconscious imagination. When we examine the facts, the immense importance of archetypal imagination found in myths, works of art and in emotional, scientific, pedagogical, and political creativity, and even in psychological symptoms, is undeniable. The path to psychic self-fulfillment is guided by the imagination. The conscious-unconscious polarity is one of its by-products. The Self imagines conscious and unconscious reality by means of symbols.

The development of modern psychology can be highlighted by eight main ideas. First, Pierre Janet recognizes the neuroses but reduces them to mental degeneration. This was the beginning of psychodynamics and, at the same time, a reduction to organicism. Second, together with Anna O., Breuer discovers and cures the first neurotic symptom psychodynamically. Anna had not drunk any water for weeks without knowing why (hysterical water phobia). Hypnosis revealed that she had seen the dog of her hateful governess drinking water from a glass on a table. On emerging from hypnosis, her symptom vanished (Breuer 1893). The third is a group of ideas: Freud's psychoanalysis, including free association, resistance, repression, infantile sexuality, the

Oedipus complex, normal and abnormal formation of the ego through psychological relationships of early childhood and transference.

The fourth idea was behaviorism, initiated by Pavlov, developed by Watson and Skinner, and culminating in Piaget's cognitive psychology. The fifth was Jung's analytical psychology, including the concepts of libido as psychic energy, the complexes, symbol, the archetypes and their prospective characteristics, the individuation process, the transcendent function, psychological typology, persona, shadow, psyche, and synchronicity. The sixth idea is the relationship of the psychological dimension with existential philosophy. The seventh is the contribution made by transpersonal psychology to different states of consciousness.

The eighth idea is the archetypal perspective that includes subject and object in the formation and transformation of individual and collective consciousness through the elaboration of structuring symbols, complexes, functions, and systems coordinated by the four ruling archetypes, which function around a central archetype. Resulting from the association of the work of Freud, Jung, and the behavioral, existential, and transpersonal schools of thought, this idea is based on the perception that the central archetype consciously and unconsciously coordinates, by means of the structuring symbols and functions of normal and defensive imagination, the identity formation of the ego and the other, in consciousness and in the shadow, a process we refer to as creative and defensive symbolic elaboration. This eighth idea identifies the psyche with representation of the cosmos. It is the basis of symbolic humanism and amplifies the conception of development of personality described by Jung in the individuation process with that of culture as an expression of the process of cosmic humanization (Teilhard de Chardin 1950). Furthermore, this dimension can be taught through symbolic elaboration in education in the same way that the identities of the ego and the shadow are formed in early childhood.

The fact that we can perceive everything in life as a structuring symbol, complex, function, or system gathering the subjective and the objective dimensions together in the Self enables us to seek this symbolic scope in what used to be seen only from the rational and objective point of view in traditional teaching. One of the main structuring functions of the ego in this framework is the imagination, since it consciously and unconsciously expresses the creative essence of the central archetype in the development of the Self. Anna O. was perfectly aware of the negative feelings she had for her governess and the disgust she felt for the little dog drinking water from the glass. What she was not aware of was that this was used unconsciously by her imagination to construct a phobic reaction to water. What neither she nor any one else knew was that the central archetype of the Self has the capacity to transform these facts into a symptom associating their symbolic meanings through the structuring function of the imagination.

When Breuer and Anna O. linked the episode of the dog drinking from the glass with the symptom of hysterical phobia of water and the symptom vanished, they discovered something more essential and wide sweeping than the dynamic unconscious. They discovered that the psyche expresses itself and develops through the attributes of things chosen by the imagination on the conscious and the unconscious levels, in normality as well as in pathology. They discovered that neurotic symptoms are products of the imagination (conscious and unconscious), and this opened the door for us to see that symbols are elaborated consciously and unconsciously, creatively and defensively, by the central archetype, through the structuring function of the imagination. This allows us to claim the imagination as one of the main archetypal structuring functions of the Self, which includes the transcendent function and all symbolic elaboration on the conscious and unconscious level. This fact is of great importance for Jungian symbolic education, for it makes it clear that when objective facts are perceived and taught as structuring symbols, which include their subjective aspects, we are using the structuring function of the imagination, that is, the same function that has always been used by the central archetype to coordinate the symbolic development of the whole personality. This enables the educator to conceive and engage the imagination on the level of the Self, rather than on the exclusively rational level of the ego. The use of the imagination in the perspective of the Self protects knowledge from simple erudition and subordinates it to wisdom.

The structuring function of imagination embraces what Jung called the transcendent function, and thus it can be conceived as the transcendent function of the imagination. Jung, like Freud, was also fascinated by the discovery of the unconscious. Freud formulated the theory of repression and then that of the life and death instincts of the id. Jung conceived the theory of the collective unconscious, to which he reduced the archetypes. This reduction to "the unconscious" lent primal *status* to it and transformed it into a place overshadowing the discovery that all symbols have personal and archetypal as well as conscious and unconscious characteristics. The link between the little dog drinking water and Anna O.'s phobia of water was repressed by an unconscious defense, but in forming the symbol of phobia of water, conscious and unconscious components were articulated by the imagination of the Self.

Jung went beyond Freud's reductionism to sexuality and equated libido to psychic energy, in the expression of all symbols. Nonetheless, on reducing the concept of the archetype exclusively to unconscious factors, he prevented his concept of the libido from being used also to cover the archetypal functions of consciousness and of education. A significant part of this book is devoted to showing educators that they can consciously choose one or another ruling archetype to elaborate symbols during teaching. If the archetypes were only unconscious, they could not be included in teaching, and Jungian symbolic education would not exist. The important concept, which we draw from this extension of the concept of archetype to encompass individual and collective consciousness, is that the process of individuation and of humanization can be symbolically taught through symbolic constructivism.

By dynamic psychology I mean the psychology that deals with the interaction of psychic structures significantly in the development of personality based primarily on the conscious-unconscious polarity. The marked reductionism of dynamic psychology to the unconscious aspects of the psyche— which is why led it to be called depth psychology—separated dynamic psychology from behavioral psychology. It also distanced dynamic psychology from the exact sciences, philosophy, anthropology, sociology, and education. By viewing the unconscious as the primary source of the conscious, a good deal of the findings and concepts of these disciplines were considered by-products of unconscious activities. This precluded understanding of the psychic scope of the imagination, in science and in all human creativity, and its historical mutilation in the West, along with the disappearance of alchemy. The transformation of imagination into a mere projection of the unconscious, whether personal or collective, largely confounded the understanding of its conscious and unconscious creativity on the individual, historical, and cultural levels. The eighteenth and nineteenth centuries overvalued the rational and the conscious, to the detriment of the imagination. After the discovery of the dynamic unconscious, dynamic psychology subordinated the imagination to it. In both cases, that is, in positivism and beyond, the dimension of the bipolar conscious and unconscious scope of the imagination was severely limited.

Overvaluation of the unconscious to the detriment of the dynamic importance of the conscious inundated dynamic psychology with intense unilaterality. All psychic phenomena were colored by this asymmetry. Take dreams for example. For Freud, the dream remembered at dawn was the conscious manifest content that conceals the true latent meaning, which remained unconscious (Freud 1900). For Jung, dreams generally stand for the archetypal creativity of the unconscious that compensates the unilateral positions of consciousness (Jung 1934). In reducing the archetypes to the collective unconscious, Jung overvalued unconscious characteristics to such an extent that he began his *Memories* with the phrase: "My life is the story of an unconscious that fulfilled itself" (Jung 1961). It is quite clear that Jung is expressing his lifelong dedication to the development of the archetypal potential of his personality. But why equate it to the unconscious? Were the conscious components of his fantasies, dreams, and creativity so secondary that they should be considered a mere by-product of the unconscious components? Why equate the structuring function of compensation to unconscious activity and not to the function of the imagination coordinated by the central archetype which encompasses unconscious and conscious creativity?

When we accept archetypes as the coordinating factors of symbolic elaboration on both conscious and unconscious levels of the Self equally, we realize that the archetypal structuring function of imagination can express symbols both in normality and pathology, which means both in education and in mental disease. This is the basis of Jungian symbolic psychology and of symbolic psychopathology that significantly gathers together the cultural dimensions of education and mental health. The importance of this focus lies in the opportunity to understand mental disease symbolically, as well as the whole development of the personality from the beginning to the end of life, including the archetype of life and death (Byington 1996).

## The Importance of the Imagination

If the psyche were a bird, its wings would be the imagination. In fact, if we wanted to choose the most important and essential structuring function of symbolic elaboration, the transcendent function of the imagination would certainly win first place. Jung grasped fully the importance of imagination, naming it fantasy:

The psyche creates reality every day. The only expression I can use for this activity is fantasy. Fantasy is just as much feeling as thinking, as much intuition as sensation. There is no psychic function that through fantasy is not inextricably bound up with the other psychic functions. Sometimes it appears in primordial form, sometimes it is the ultimate and boldest product of all our faculties combined. Fantasy, therefore, seems to me the clearest expression of the specific activity of the psyche. It is, pre-eminently, the creative activity from which the answers to all answerable questions come; it is the mother of all possibilities, where, like all psychological opposites, the inner and the outer worlds are joined together in living union. Fantasy it was and ever is which fashions the bridge between the irreconcilable claims of subject and object, introversion and extraversion. In fantasy, alone both mechanisms are united. (Jung 1921, par. 78; see also Grinberg 2003)

Whereas behavior belongs to the here-and-now, elaborating symbols in greater or lesser depth by pragmatic commitment, imagination opens the wings of the psyche to elaborate symbols and produce meanings ranging from their immediate and literal appearance to their most remote and mysterious reality. Thus, the imagination can follow the archetypal roots and branches of symbols to the borders of eternity and infinity. It is imagination that enables us to visit the immensity of the cosmos and, in so doing, to experience the breathing of psyche within the intelligence of the universe. Modern physics teaches that the speed limit in the universe is the speed of light. Anyone can experience the fact that the speed of imagination greatly transcends the speed of light. In a fraction of a second we can imagine a galaxy millions of light-years distant from the earth. This is enough to remind us of how much the nature of psychic reality and the capacity of its imagination transcend our present knowledge. Imagine now Proxima Centauri, the star nearest to the sun, situated forty-one thousand billion kilometers or 4.2 light-years away, and it comes instantaneously to your mind.

## A Historical Perspective of Imagination in the West

Understanding the phenomenon of the imagination and its use is fundamental to the theory and technique of Jungian symbolic education. The prejudice that places imagination outside objective reality reduces its systemic application and symbolic understanding. This prejudice has historical roots that need to be archetypally understood so as to be avoided. It consists of the defensive literalization of the psychic dimension, which is a symptom of subject-object dissociation that originated and flourished in the materialistic world of the nineteenth century. Here I shall continue the reasoning developed in chapter 2, now taking into account the interrelated patterns of the four ruling archetypes.

I shall make use of some symbols from the Christian myth to exemplify the creativity of the imagination in the cultural Self. My aim is to show the creativity of imagination on both the subjective and objective levels, as well as in the individual and the collective dimensions. The Christian myth lends itself extraordinarily well to this demonstration because, to a large extent, the cultural archetypal imagination used its symbols on the subjective level and, at the same time, on the objective level to transform culture. On the subjective level it prepared the social mentality for democracy and Western humanism. On the objective level it laid the groundwork for the scientific knowledge of nature. This example is a rich expression of the central role of imagination and symbols in the development of culture, as Jungian symbolic psychology describes in its archetypal theory of history.

Very briefly, we may say that the conflict between Israel and Rome (two civilizations of marked patriarchal dominance) at the start of our era intensively activated through the imagination the alterity pattern in the messianic tradition of the Judaic cultural Self, giving rise to the Christian myth of the incarnation and the preaching of love, compassion, sacrifice, death, and resurrection (Byington 1983).

The imminence of another genocide within the patriarchal pattern put into question the philosophical, religious, political, and moral capability of the patriarchal archetype to elaborate the agreement-conflict polarity in the individual and collective civilizing function of the Self. The patriarchal pattern sponsored the monotheism of "the chosen people" and the wars to conquer the Promised Land, as well as the growth and expansion of Rome and other empires. The cultural atmosphere of the beginning of our era showed clearly the long tension and incompatibility between two cultures of great patriarchal organization heading for genocidal confrontation. Compare the armed struggle against the Assyrian invaders that culminated in the first destruction of the Temple against the decades-long historical tension between Israel and

Rome, oscillating between the diplomacy of submission, indignation at religious profanation, armed struggle, and the clear possibility of genocide. From the core of the Judaic cultural Self, and as a continuation of its patriarchal messianic tradition, the cultural imagination was extraordinarily mobilized on the eve of the holocaust and gave birth to the emergence of the Christian myth. This historical, archetypal mobilization led to a colossal activation of the archetype of alterity and its democratic pattern to cope with the agreement-conflict polarity. It was as if the cultural Self of Judaism had constellated, along with the threat of genocide, a new archetypal pattern to propitiate symbolically the very survival of the species.

After reaching Rome and converting the empire, this myth became the most popular religion in the West and the chief civilizing structuring function and system that for two millennia has been shaping the identity and development of many nations in the direction of science, art, and democracy (Byington 1992b). As I mentioned in chapter 2, the elaboration of the Christian myth within the church and its messianic proposal, coordinated by the pattern of alterity, required liberty, spontaneity, love, and creativity to exercise so much imagination. However, after the conversion of Constantine and the Roman Empire in 325 A.D., the creative imagination necessary to elaborate the myth clashed head-on with the gigantic task of organizing and institutionalizing an empire with a strongly dominating patriarchal tradition. The outcome, with the passing of the centuries, was the growing defensive patriarchalization of the myth, the limitation of the imagination in the alterity pattern, and the consequent reduction of many of its symbols to mere literal meanings. Such dogmatization confined the wings of imagination, especially when accompanied by the iron arm of the Holy Office and the Inquisition, which not only rigidly codified interpretation and practice but also brutally repressed the variants of the elaborating imagination of the myth, after pejoratively labeling them heresies. The Greek word *hairesis* derives from *hairein*, "to take, to choose" and the Latin *haeresis,* which means "a school of thought", whether religious or philosophical, "a doctrine, opinion, or set of opinions or principles at variance with established or generally received views or doctrines, as in politics, morality, philosophy" (*Webster's Unabridged Dictionary*).

Christianity is a religion of mystery and revelation that expresses the importance of the alterity archetype in individual and cultural life. The patriarchal archetype's lesser capacity for symbolic breadth failed to elaborate the Christian myth in its psychological depth and, therefore, literalized and reduced many of its components in order to organize it politically during its institutionalization. The heresies, which were important imaginal variants for the symbolic elaboration of the myth and their incorporation into the dynamics of individual and collective consciousness, were mostly extinguished. Among them, we distinguish Gnosticism, whose great power of elaborating imagination became apparent only after the discovery of the Nag Hammadi Library in Egypt in 1945. These papyri were written in the Coptic language (the Egyptian language written in the Greek alphabet), perhaps in the fourth century A.D., and then buried in the early fifth century. Their content presents a wealth of imagination in the reports and commentaries of the apostles attributed to the Gnostics, including variants of the canonical Gospels, which are important for a better elaboration of many meanings of the myth.

The Church's patriarchal repression of the heresies and the predominantly patriarchal pedagogy adopted to transmit the myth literalized its teachings and turned the Christian community into a homogenous flock, ill prepared to experience the transforming power of the myth in each one's life. The mystery of the Passion projected exclusively onto Christ nailed to the cross and experienced weekly at mass was patriarchally taught to submit the community to the authority of the Church and manipulate the myth defensively. Initiation, characteristic to all mystery religions, was abolished in the practice of Christianity by the patriarchalization of the myth during institutionalization. Officiated exclusively by male priests, under oaths of celibacy, poverty, and obedience within a rigid hierarchical organization, Christians—kneeling and praying to the crucified Messiah—were left with little to do but repeat stereotyped prayers and obey without being able to experience, imagine, or integrate the myth into the dialectics of their own individuation processes. At the core of the ritual, where imagination was most restricted by this rigid patriarchal codification, stands the defensive practice of confession, in which the faithful reveal their shadow to Christ, a central symbol of alterity, for elaboration, integration, and redemption.

The list of sins and their prescribed absolution in exchange for codified prayers—and later for payment—impoverished the imagination necessary for the dialectic ego-shadow elaboration in the enormously constructive transforming power of consciousness in confession. Originally Christian confession probably practiced the symbolic constructivism of the systemic relationship of the shadow with the psychic whole. Its progressively defensive codification removed its constructivist and systemic features through repression of the archetype of alterity by the patriarchal archetype. The impoverishment of the imagination, and thus psychic life, by the patriarchalization of confession is analogous nowadays to the impoverishment of psychotherapy and teaching, when the consulting room and the school are transformed (by drugs in the case of the consulting room and by rationalism in the school) into places of reductive, repetitive, and directive practices. The liberation of the imagination in the West had to wait until the twentieth century and the arrival of psychotherapy, social democratic ideology, constructivism in teaching, and the liberation of creativity in arts, human rights, and culture in general.

Patriarchalization of the Christian myth intensely repressed imagination in the cultural Self and produced four great schisms within the Church. The first, between the West and the East, gave rise to the Orthodox churches in 1040 A.D. The second, in the sixteenth century, was the division between Protestantism and Catholicism. The third, between science and religion, and the fourth, between religion and the state, which took place in the eighteenth century. Between the first schism and the second, in the Middle Ages, as imagination became progressively limited through the organization and institutionalization of the myth, the monasteries were spared to some degree. They became the institutions where the creative elaboration of the myth was at least partly exercised through religious meditation, study, and discussion, and through the examination of consciousness in the search to relate sin to salvation in the sacrifice of the Messiah. Among the cultural activities of monasteries, it is important to distinguish dialectics, the art and science of thought and argument, the practice of which, over the course of more than a millennium, prepared the European cultural Self for the elaboration of truth and error within the scientific mentality. Translating everything they could find, from Greek, Aramaic, and Arabic to Latin, the monasteries began to operate as universal generators and distributors of culture. They became the forerunners of Europe's universities, and they began to elaborate the Christian myth alongside the classical culture of the Mediterranean.

The imagination's creative work of elaborating the difference between sin and virtue, undertaken in the introverted dimension of the monasteries, strengthened the practice of the dialectics of the ego-other relation so that the ego was able to reach a state of great authenticity separated from the inauthentic, represented by sin and perdition before God (Byington 1965).

During the Middle Ages, the experience of the creative imagination in the monasteries produced a profound elaboration of the myth with regard to the Passion and death of the Messiah, anticipating the fantastic imagination of the glory of the resurrection which exploded in the Renaissance. Along with the ability to think, developed in the study and practice of dialectics, the creative imagination, in the first millennium of Christianity, was directed through introversion and depression toward the ego-other relationship on the dominant level of subjectivity and progressively extraverted to the world at the end of the Middle Ages. It was this ability to elaborate sin and virtue symbolically in introversion that trained the imagination of the cultural Self to elaborate error and truth in extraversion through the scientific method of experiment, which gave birth to the modern natural sciences.

## Imagination in the Middle Ages and Demonology

The might of the Christian myth managed to overcome the repression promoted by the Holy Office and exercise the creative imagination to begin integrating important aspects of the pattern of alterity, for instance, in the art of dialectics and the pursuit of understanding of the function of sin (shadow) in the psychological development of the soul. Nevertheless, many aspects of the structuring symbols and functions of the Messiah's life and Passion were left aside by the Church's increasing puritanical patriarchal codification, and formed the immense shadow of Christianity, expressed defensively in the terrible psychopathic sadism of the Inquisition. These characteristics were expressed by the creative imagination in the shadow of the cultural Self increasingly through the symbol of the Devil, as differentiated from Satan in the Old Testament, who was recognized as a son and even messenger of God: "On the day when God's sons came to present themselves before the Lord, Satan also came among them" (Job 1:6).

In the history of Christianity, we see the figure of the Devil dissociating more and more from the figure of Satan, son of God, and, through defensive imagination, growing progressively stronger to become the Antichrist, to the same extent that the figure of Christ and the myth of transformation through salvation lost their potency in the growth of repression sponsored by the Inquisition (Byington 1991a).

It is not by chance that school and teaching in Western culture often associate education with suffering, Puritanism, seriousness, and rationality, setting aside joy, sensuality, pleasure, drama, and play for recreation time, to be experienced at home, in the street, in entertainment events, everywhere except in the classroom. It was the patriarchalization of teaching that led to this because the Holy Office controlled all knowledge for most of fifteen centuries. More than three centuries after Gutenberg invented moveable type and mechanized printing (1440), every book printed in Catholic countries still had to have the Holy Office's authorization stamps (*nihil obstat* and *imprimatur*).

It is perhaps difficult to realize that the patriarchalization of scientific learning and teaching in the West has its roots in the dissociated patriarchalization of the Christian myth, dissociated because it was undertaken at the cost of repression of the matriarchal and alterity patterns and created an immense pathological shadow in the cultural Self (Byington 1986). On describing the repression of sexuality in the Victorian era, Freud revealed the tip of the iceberg of the sensual insular matriarchal archetype repressed in the cultural Self.

Like interconnected vessels, the defensive imagination of the symbol of the Devil increased qualitatively and quantitatively to the extent that the creative elaboration of the Messiah became defensively patriarchalized and restricted. Qualitatively, because the characteristics that the imagination expressed through the Devil in the shadow became increasingly varied: sensuality, omnipotence, magic, aggression, humor, omniscience, intelligence, falsity, treachery, seduction, simulation, theatricality, cruelty, envy, covetousness, jealousy, and many others. Quantitatively, because the imagination of the Church and of the people concerned themselves more and more with the symbol of the Devil instead of the symbol of Christ.

This situation proffers abundant illustrations of the dialectic relationship of the ego of consciousness with the ego of the shadow in the individual and collective Self. If the central archetype is not successful in elaborating a symbol necessary to life through a conscious creative attitude, it will probably express it through defenses in the shadow. The central archetype, through the imagination, seeks to express life, either in good or in evil.

In Christianity, because the Devil stands for the fixated and defensive symbol of Christ as the Antichrist in the chronic shadow, the imagination of the Self was expressed through the Devil in a way that was immense, albeit distorted, inadequate, and destructive. Only the creativity of the imagination would be capable of engendering such a drama. When we grasp the imagination's capacity to form the shadow, we can relate meaningfully to any person or group that fails to elaborate certain symbols and is expressing them in the shadow.

For example, suppose a geography teacher is giving a lesson on the structure and movement of the Earth's crust. Half the class is almost asleep and the other half is becoming more and more undisciplined, a clear case of circumstantial shadow formation. By resorting to symbolic imagination, the teacher can act creatively and shift the psychic energy, which is being experienced more and more through the shadow, and redirect it toward the objective subject being taught. He or she might, for instance, make use of the expressive technique of dramatization. The class is divided into four groups and assigned to represent the continents, the volcanic and nonvolcanic islands, the oceans, and the fire at the core of the planet. The class becomes "re-animated". They dramatize the elements involved in volcanic explosions, destruction of cities and creation of islands, the vitality of the earth's crust when its layers shift, and the ecological complaints of civilization. The half-asleep students wake up and influence the others to exercise their creativity and aggression in consciousness and learning, rather than in shadow and defensive transgression.

The history of Christianity shows us the dramatic expression of imagination through normal elaboration and fixation. The defensive patriarchalization of the Christian myth within the Church reached the end of the Middle Ages with an intense repression of the symbol of the Messiah and his priests. Repressed by patriarchal tradition and in contradiction to the essence of the Christian message, women did not administer the sacraments. Men did so under obligatory vows of chastity, poverty, and obedience, that is, through detachment from matriarchal sensuality reinforced by attachment to the patriarchal pattern. This prevented them from elaborating the myth within alterity. There is an enormous difference between choosing detachment through poverty, silence, chastity, or fasting in the search for spiritual development (alterity pattern) and adopting abstinence dogmatically and repressively as a general rule (patriarchal pattern). It is no surprise that such defensively repressed sexuality formed an intense shadow which is now being expressed in countless cases of pedophilia. Indeed, for the wings of imagination to fly fully in the pattern of alterity, more than anything else they need freedom and love. As far back as the fifth century, Saint Augustine expressed his profound experience of mystic grandeur of the myth that illuminated his life through the ethical saying, "Love and do as you will".

Christianity is a myth of love and compassion, and the archetypal imagination could not do without conjugal romanticism as a variant of its elaboration. The archetype of love involves the imagination with the archetype of the *coniunctio* (the psychic function that separates and joins the polarities) and fertilizes its creativity in conjugality through the anima and animus archetypes. While the troubadours began to sing of romantic love and the art of chivalry against the brutality of the Middle Ages, the figure of Mary Magdalene was gradually detached from the Messiah and replaced by the cult of the Virgin Mary. The anima archetype, an inseparable companion to the hero archetype of alterity, was demonically labeled a prostitute, on one side, and on the other, reduced to the idealized mother figure, weakening the alterity archetype proportionately. What a difference between Mary Magdalene as an ostracized prostitute possessed by the Devil in the liturgy of the Church and the Messiah's companion and favorite disciple, as described in the Nag Hammadi gospels! Her affectionate relationship with Jesus and the confirmation of her extraordinary spiritual development are clearly stated here:

> The Lord's companion is Mary Magdalene. Christ loved her more than all His disciples . . . . They asked Him: Why do you love her more than us? The Savior answered them: Why do I not love you like her? When a blind man and a person who can see are in the dark, there is no difference between them. When the light appears, the one who can see will see, but the blind man will remain in the dark. (Gospel of Philip 63:5–64:10)

The repression of the imagination in the myth included the repression of romantic love. If romantic love between Mary Magdalene and Jesus were admitted in the myth, with all its matriarchal and sensual attachment, creative imagination would have had to develop much more to elaborate the Messiah's sacrificial detachment and the spiritual initiation of a Devil-possessed prostitute. To search for detachment within the alterity pattern is much more difficult than in either the matriarchal or patriarchal patterns, where it is practiced in a very particular and selective way and very differently in every case. In this manner, erotic mysticism, which is a profound religious expression of the archetype of alterity, was repressed in the Christian myth. To get an idea of how far it might have gone without repression, we can study the god Krishna and his relationship with Radha in Hindu mysticism (Guerra, 2001).

The symbols of Jesus and Mary Magdalene as the messianic mystical *coniunctio*, the sacred bond of the archetypal syzygy of alterity, of anima and animus, were patriarchally repressed together with the men and women priests. Jesus came to be adored unilaterally as a miraculous child in his mother's lap or dead and imprisoned in martyrdom on the cross. Instead of denouncing the cross as the terrible repression of alterity by the patriarchal pattern, Christianity began to worship it as the representation of "He who died for us". All this evaded the recognition of the ferocious collision of the patriarchal and the alterity archetypes within the myth.

By no means do I wish to underestimate the symbols of the child or the cross; the archetypal might of both is enormous. I do want to draw attention to the fact that great emphasis was laid defensively on the symbols of the child and the dead Messiah to the detriment of the splendor of His resurrection. This reduction weakened the heroic, revolutionary, and culturally leading messianic figure of alterity. Above all, it overshadowed the civilizing function of the myth as a great prospective force that leads the patriarchal archetype to alterity.

The encounter with Christ was postponed to the Last Judgment. Christians were deprived of the daily companionship of the hero and guide to symbolic life. Parallel to this, the image of Mary Magdalene was weakened, deformed, and reduced to being exclusively represented as sinner and repentant prostitute, to the detriment of her role as the Messiah's companion and disciple. Mary Magdalene's psychological development as a medium was more differentiated than that of any other apostle, and as such it brought her the acknowledgment of the resurrected Jesus before the others and despite their disbelief, even in John's canonical Gospel. In failing to recognize Mary Magdalene's initiation by Jesus and the depth of her imaginative power, the institutionalization of the myth dug a veritable black hole in the imagination of Christian erotic mysticism.

> But Mary stood outside the sepulcher weeping: and as she wept, she stooped down and looked into the sepulcher. And seeth two angels in white sitting, the one at the head, and the other at the feet, where the body of Jesus had lain. And they said unto her: Woman, why weepest thou? She saith unto

them, Because they have taken away my Lord, and I know
not where they have laid him. And when she had thus said,
she turned herself back, and saw Jesus standing, and knew not
that it was Jesus. Jesus saith unto her, Woman, why weepest
thou? She, supposing him to be the gardener, saith unto him,
Sir, if thou have borne Him hence, tell me where thou hast
laid Him, and I will take Him away. Jesus saith unto her, Mary.
She turned herself, and saith unto Him, Rabboni; which is to
say, Master. Jesus saith unto her, Touch me not; for I am not
yet ascended to my Father: but go to my brethren, and say
unto them, I ascend unto my Father, and your Father; and to
my God, and your God. (John 20:11–17)

To complement the repression of imagination along with the erotic
feminine initiated in the mystery of alterity, we shall see at the end of the
Middle Ages the massive, exclusive deposition of this feminine on the image
of the Virgin Mary. She was cultivated as a virgin because she was believed not
to have conceived the Messiah through Joseph. In this manner she was not
recognized symbolically as the initiated virgin, who conceived through Joseph
as a manifestation of the Holy Spirit and gave birth to the incarnated child
who came to save mankind (Byington 1993c). The virginity of Mary is not to
be taken literally but has to be imagined as the beginning of her initiation,
which will continue after the crucifixion. The blocking of the imagination
brought about by the Inquisition literalized the symbol of the Virgin Mary,
reducing it to the concrete simplicity of physical virginity, which invalidated
the symbolic understanding of the miracle. On withdrawing the physical
sexuality of Mary, theology dehumanized her and deprived her of her major
greatness, which was the simplicity of having been the human mother of God.
The desexualization of the Virgin Mary accompanied the disqualification of
Mary Magdalene as the Messiah's companion. In this way the hero of alterity
was castrated and human sexuality was profaned and condemned to be lived
without love in the cultural shadow, where it waited for C. G. Jung to redeem
it archetypally.

In the Nag Hammadi Gospels, we see that the creative imagination of
the Gnostics was able to elaborate the archetypal symbolic meaning of father
and mother. They associated the symbol of the Virgin Mother with initiatory
experience, that is, the birth of the adult enlightened with the consciousness of
alterity. It is a matter of understanding the difference between the biological
mother and father and the initiatory mother and father, which is only possible
when the imagination operates in the alterity pattern of consciousness.

> Jesus said: He who does not hate his father and mother as I do
> will not be my disciple. And he who does not love his father
> and mother as I do will not be my disciple. My mother gave
> me falsity, but my true mother gave me life. (Gospel of Saint
> Thomas, v. 101)

The imagination allows us to realize that the biological mother is mythologically left behind in the psychological development of alterity and transformed by initiation into the sacred mother, in this case the Virgin Mary, experienced by Jesus. On imagining himself the Messiah incarnated to live out the Passion, Jesus is initiated and his biological mother becomes the Immaculate Virgin. On imagining that she had given birth to the one who was to incarnate the myth, Mary was initiated and saw herself as the Virgin Mother, for she realized that she was mother of Jesus, the man, by Joseph, and of Christ, the God, by the Holy Spirit, to incarnate the mystery of the Passion. This imagination of initiatory life, as the symbolic life that is characteristic of those who open themselves to the elaboration of the imaginary meanings of the process of individuation, is also to be found in Jesus' dialogue with Nicodemus:

> Nicodemus saith unto him, how can a man be born when he is
> old? Can he enter a second time into his mother's womb, and
> be born? Jesus answered, Verily, verily, I say unto thee, Except
> a man be born of water and of the Spirit, he cannot enter into
> the kingdom of God. That which is born of the flesh is flesh;
> and that which is born of the Spirit is spirit. Marvel not that I
> say unto thee, Ye must be born again. (John 3:4–7)

One might ask if that which is imagined is the truth. The question indicates ignorance, for imagination is a structuring function and not a mere attribute to be catalogued as truth or lie. Truth and lie are attributes of things in determined contexts of their symbolic elaboration. Imagination is a central structuring function in symbolic elaboration through which the psyche flies about the world to gather and separate right from wrong, subjective from objective, true from false, authentic from inauthentic. This being so, everything that is imagined has its reality in some existential dimension. The true-false, right-wrong, concrete-abstract polarities belong to the process of elaboration of the imagination to search truth, which corresponds to the elaboration of any symbol in the development of the Self. We see again and again during psychotherapy how the imagination can lead to the fixation of a symbol, turning it into a neurotic symptom.

One has to recognize the historic roots of our cultural repression and the dark fantasies that accompany it in order to understand the resistance that even nowadays we show in liberating the imagination in teaching. The repercussions of this repression still echo among us, as for instance in what, according to Jung, was Freud's preoccupation with avoiding "the black slime of the occult" in establishing the dogma of sexuality.

> I still have alive in my memory Freud saying: My dear Jung, promise me never to give up the sexual theory. That is what matters, essentially. Look, we have to make it a dogma, an unshakable bulwark . . . A bit in awe, I asked him: A bulwark against what? He answered me: Against the wave of the black slime (here he hesitated a moment before adding) of the occult. (Jung 1961, p. 150)

To understand the power of the imagination within the individual and cultural Self of our historic Christian tradition, the Self has to be seen as a multiple feedback system where the symbol of the Devil attained the height of its intensity at the expense of Christ's messianic might. In the same manner, parallel with the ostracizing of Mary Magdalene, we see an increase of the cult of Mary the Mother and the immeasurable growth of the magical, destructive power of the witch, priestess and companion to the Devil, expressed in countless cases of hysteria. Gifted with all the sensuality, aggression, and creativity of the feminine that were puritanically repressed in Mary the Mother, the witch was patriarchally reduced, along with the romanticism and mediumistic qualities of Mary Magdalene, to the sewers of sin, psychotic hysteria, and prostitution. The distortion of the expression of imagination in the pathological shadow reached that point where the repressed Christ was cultivated as the *fiancé* of the Church, while the ritual of the Black Mass, the Satanic Sabbath, arose in the margins to celebrate the union of the "prince of the night" with his concubines, a fantastic *coniunctio* experiencing the syzygy in sin and shadow (Kramer and Sprenger 1484).

It is in this crucial dilemma between the immensely creative power of the Christ symbol on one side and its repression and distortion defensively expressed by the symbol of the Devil on the other, that the cultural expression of the myth made its way toward the Renaissance. Symbolically seen, the depressive darkness of the Middle Ages corresponded to the crucifixion and death of the Messiah while the Renaissance expressed His resurrection and the immense cultural transformation to come. The imagination of the cultural Self repressed the heroic couple of alterity in the institution, and the immense power of the Devil and the witch, persecuted, tortured, hanged, and burned to death, demoralized the compassion preached in the myth and proclaimed the victory of the shadow and of ethical dissociation. The creative energy of the myth greatly intensified the imagination to elaborate the symbol of the resurrection in the dimensions of ideas, emotions, society, body, and nature. Due to the fact that the social and the bodily dimensions were repressed by the Inquisition, the imagination channeled this immense amount of energy through the Renaissance into nature to elaborate the greatest and most creative of all heresies: the modern sciences.

For many rationalists and materialists who still act out our historical subjective-objective dissociation, and who are blind to the scope of the prospective creative power of the cultural imagination within the structuring function of the myth, the natural sciences were born out of the blue. One fine day, Europe simply threw away "all that faith nonsense" and began to think properly, based on the scientific method. To these thinkers, the miracle of scientific learning that changed the world, created industrialization, and characterized the modern planet arose by chance in Europe like a meteor fallen from heaven. For them, the Middle Ages are a time of darkness during which nothing happened, an era of cultural stagnation with much ignorance, plague, and little creativity. It is as though the marvelous development of the modern sciences could have occurred in any place, in any culture, and with any myth. This materialist rationalism dissociated from the subjective is incapable of accompanying the gigantic step taken by the imagination in continuing the sociocultural implantation of the myth, except that this time it was compelled by the Church to live it on the outside. Only through empathy with the creative, archetypal capacity of imagination guided by the force of the Christian myth in the European cultural Self, can we realize that the scientific method was the continuation, on the extraverted and objective level, of the examination of consciousness undertaken in the monasteries as initiation on the introverted subjective level. The research that science undertook on nature, within the dialectic relation of trial and error, had been experienced by religion on emotions within the dialectic relation of virtue and sin. Symbolic recognition of the power of the imagination in history shows us that error became the shadow of truth in the scientific method in the same way that sin was considered the shadow of virtue in Christianity. The scientific method and examination of conscience are the dialectic expression of the ego-other relation in the archetype of alterity expressed through the messianic message of the Christian myth. Creative imagination, increasingly repressed by the reactionary forces of the Inquisition within the Church, began to be exercised full steam ahead outside the Church in the natural sciences.

There exists an important symbol, a name the Inquisition gave the Devil—Lucifer—a true historical *lapsus linguae* that foretold that the civilizing path of the myth, chosen by the imagination, would basically lie outside the Church.

As mentioned above, in the history of the cultural implantation of the myth, its mystery was experienced, among other ways, through the path of monastic reclusion dedicated to understanding the martyrdom of the Messiah within the life-death polarity. The experience of the resurrection came with the light of art, science, sociopolitics, with the intelligence dedicated to reclaiming the world from darkness, from the theology of original sin, from innocence and ignorance, and it unveiled the profundity of the mysterious and miraculous, eternal and infinite work that is the universe.

When the Inquisition began to call the Devil Lucifer (he who produces light), this cultural *lapsus linguae*, by which the Inquisition admitted its separation from Christ, revealed the extent to which it projected onto his great enemy the capacity to create light, to broaden consciousness, undoubtedly the greatest of all the treasures sponsored by the Messiah. It should be noted that the name Lucifer does not occur in the Gospels; it reemerges halfway through the Middle Ages, from ancient Judaic legends of the fallen angel. In projecting the ability to create light onto the Antichrist, it became clear that the Church's reactionary attitude toward the myth had condemned it to stagnation and alienation in regard to the three great treasures that would arise from the cultural implantation of the Resurrection: the arts, the modern sciences, and the sociopolitical transformation of the monarchic state into the republic and thence to industrialization and democracy. The persecution of scientific and sociopolitical modern humanism, labeling them heresy at the service of Lucifer, was a natural consequence, the expression by the cultural imagination of a reactionary attitude that diminished greatly the creative power of the myth of alterity within the Church.

## Alchemy and Creative Imagination

Psychic changes take place through structuring symbols that act as energy transformers. The archetypes of the Self are expressed by means of structuring symbols, complexes, functions, and systems whose elaboration leads to consciousness formation and transformation. To conscious perception, initially, things are literalized symbols. When the educator broadens the symbolic dimension of things by setting them on the wings of the imagination, he or she allows them to be elaborated in the field of the creative imagination of the whole Self rather than just the conscious ego. This extension of the meaning of things through the imagination allows students to experience symbolic constructive learning. In the same manner, in scientific research the imagination looks for creative ways to broaden the merely rational and objective approach (Byington 1995). This is what happened to alchemy and science. Understanding the role of alchemy in the development of science is a creative way to widen our grasp of the role of the imagination in this development and its distortion in our tradition.

When we consider an object in the context of fantasy and activate the imagination, there are two possible consequences. One is productive and enriches learning, the other is nonproductive and stagnating. Productivity comes from increasing the perspective of study and our understanding of the object. In this case, our initial inability to discriminate and our confusion in symbolic elaboration are followed by a greater scope that enriches understanding. A case in point: in the middle of a class, a sixth-grade pupil told his science teacher that studying botany was awful, boring and dull, and that he could not stand memorizing all those classifications without even knowing what they were for. Consulted on how to respond, I advised the teacher to symbolize the subject by adding subjective components using imagination and to tell the pupils a story, for instance, Buddha's sermon of the flower:

> One day, the disciples asked the master what the search for truth and love meant. He picked a flower from the garden, placed it in his hand, and looked at it for a long while in silence. That was his explanation. The disciples understood nothing. Only Ananda, the much-loved disciple, grasped the message.

When they heard the story the pupils were very impressed. The teacher promised a surprise for the next class based on Buddha's teaching and asked them to recall the lesson on chlorophyll and plant reproduction, keeping in mind the sermon of the flower.

At the next class, the teacher told the pupils to arrange their chairs in a circle. In the center he placed a flowerpot with one red rose in the middle of some lush foliage. He then asked the pupils to talk about the function of chlorophyll in the life of the planet, observing the plant in front of them. When the function of chlorophyll in transforming carbon dioxide into oxygen using the light of the sun and the role of the flowering parts in plant reproduction had been once again made clear, the teacher asked them to remember Ananda, who had understood the master, and to intuit what had passed through his mind.

The resulting discussion was very exciting, connecting life, sex, beauty, and love to the ecosystem. The teacher then asked why florists in the United States advertise sales with the phrase "say it with flowers". Between the sermon of the flower, the function of chlorophyll in the ecosystem, preservation of life on the planet, affection, plant development, and human consciousness, spiced with emotions and even tears, the botany class gradually reanimated the pupils' imaginations and their interest in the subject. The student who had confessed disinterest thanked the teacher, who replied in front of the class that the student was the one to be thanked.

The immense power of the imagination, which has yet to be tapped in institutional education, is widely used in commercial advertising. It is unfortunate that the use of this teaching treasure is predominantly subordinated to increasing sales, often by presenting an illusory basis, which is ethically questionable.

The nonproductive and stagnant blocking of the imagination is due to its becoming fixated and defensive. This is the case with superstition, which fixes the subjective and the objective and prevents the progress of symbolic elaboration and of knowledge. Imagination once populated the unknown seas with such terrible monsters that, by the end of the Middle Ages, shipping captains found it very hard to contract sailors, so scared were they of what they believed to live under the waves. The imagination becomes unproductive when the lack of discrimination in fantasy is not sufficiently elaborated and ends up attributing subjective characteristics to the object, which distorts learning. Superstitions, popular beliefs, and errors of judgment generated by such distortions are the slime of the occult that Jung claimed was so feared by Freud, and they are part of the shadow of the structuring function of the imagination. Alchemy encompassed both aspects, the normal and the shadow. In the shadow, fixed imagination, which becomes defensive, is affirmed as objective knowledge although it is mostly subjective. A good part of the stagnation and underdevelopment of humanity is due to fixations of imagination in superstition and false knowledge.

In chapter 3 we saw that symbolic elaboration is done by introjection and projection to differentiate respectively the identity of the ego and the other. When the process of elaboration is interrupted by fixation, the ego may mistakenly conclude that the other possesses characteristics of the ego or vice versa. The creative structure of the imagination in this case suffers a fixation and begins to operate defensively and improperly in either a circumstantial shadow or the chronic shadow. In the circumstantial shadow, when the defensive structures are confronted by the ego, they may change into normal structures, thereby returning to the process of normal symbolic elaboration. In the chronic shadow, the defensive structures generally become permanent and compulsively resist any attempt of the ego of consciousness to face the fixated structuring symbols expressed by the defense and the ego of the shadow (repetition compulsion in psychoanalysis). Absurd ideas, beliefs, and superstitions are mostly fixations of the structuring function of the imagination in the elaboration of knowledge.

The belief in monsters of the unknown seas during the Middle Ages is a good example of the formation of superstition by incomplete symbolic elaboration. The imagined monsters represented the projection of little known animals such as giant squids, whales, and white sharks, coupled with lack of knowledge that the earth is round and that it rotates and moves around the sun. These monsters also represented the introjected fear of the unknown, including diseases such as scurvy and the suffering experienced during long sea voyages. Superstitions in culture hold on due to the interruption of the symbolic elaboration of the situations in question. Continuity of symbolic elaboration allows introjection and projection to interact, refining the identity formation of the ego and the other, subjective and objective, in order to know them better. In this sense it may be said that the process of symbolic elaboration is the source that produces human truth, always very relative because in the last analysis symbolic elaboration is the revelation of the permanent and infinite mystery of creation.

To the extent that the creative symbolic elaboration of the Christian myth gradually advanced in the monasteries on the introverted level, creative imagination began to express the path of its extraversion in the cultural Self. The symbols of the Passion, concerning the imprisonment, torture, crucifixion, and death linked by the mystics to the confrontation of sin in the dark night of the soul, were literally lived by the Messiah, which explains the immense necessity for introjection and introversion in the monasteries for Christians to find the meanings of this sacrifice in the Messiah's and in their own souls. The main pursuit in the monasteries was possibly the desire to feel deeply into the sacrifice of the Messiah and understand how the ego of the adept could position itself in the mystery. Considering the example of Christ, how was the believer to experience sin and virtue? What is it to feel deep down in the soul the absence or presence of God? If it suffices to behave obediently, why is it that many Christians, who follow all the rules of good conduct, still feel that life is empty, meaningless, and without God? If sin is inevitable, how does one deal with it under Christ's guidance and what is the meaning of salvation? These questions were elaborated predominantly on the introverted level. But the same could not be done with the Resurrection, especially if it was seen in its symbolic meaning as transformer of the Self on the individual and cultural levels, as a true awakening in alterity to individual, scientific, socioeconomic, and political life. Indeed, symbolically elaborated, the resurrection meant experiencing Christ as the *anima mundi*, which led Europe to rediscover the heavens from the Renaissance on.

The patriarchal interpretation of the Incarnation and the Resurrection as literal events gradually emphasized the conception of the second coming of the Messiah, putting it off to the first millennium and then to the end of time, the day of the last judgment. But those who experienced the myth within alterity felt the Resurrection as a symbolic phenomenon and wanted to live with Christ resurrected in the world. They would not accept the idea of a representative of Christ on earth, whom they had to obey, as the intermediary in their experience of sin and God. Intimacy with the resurrected Christ is defended, for instance, in three treatises in the Nag Hammadi Library: the Treatise of the Resurrection, Exegesis of the Soul, and the Gospel According to Philip. The idea that Christ is daily with us means that he is alive and permanently guiding Christians into creative transgression, forgiveness, compassion, love, and eternal life through the permanent disposition to rescue the symbols of the soul from sin, that is, from the shadow. This attitude calls for a direct initiatory relationship of the believer with Christ through the imagination. In other words, the orientation of Christian initiation has to be constructed symbolically within the pattern of alterity and cannot be imposed dogmatically. The patriarchal a priori reductive codification of sin literalizes it and prevents the profound symbolic elaboration thus transforming the power of the imagination in Christianity into a poor metaphor of its real meaning.

The imagination of the cultural Self prospectively sponsored extraversion to elaborate the myth experientially in the world. The institutionalization of the myth in the Church had been precociously based on the Roman, monarchist, patriarchal model, which made it very difficult for the sociocultural incarnation of the alterity pattern present in the myth to take place over the centuries. The mythical resurrection was expressed brilliantly in the Renaissance. We can see its preparation in the Church in Saint Thomas Aquinas's monumental *Summa Theologica* (1225–1274), which is the fruit of all the monastic philosophical progress of the Middle Ages and prepares the ground for the Aristotelian-Thomist synthesis that accompanied the extraversion of the Renaissance.

The imagination necessary for the extraverted elaboration of the myth had to be essentially different from the one experienced in introversion. Creative imagination lacked a symbolic source to approach the world and nature on the objective level. The central archetype constellated three sources: Greco-Roman mythology, astrology, and alchemy. Greco-Roman mythology lent animist representation to the forces of nature. Astrology functioned as a bridge to astronomy in cosmic physics and as a reunion of cosmic forces with terrestrial matter in physics and chemistry. Alchemy joined together the imagination on the nature of substances and their chemical relationship with the messianic experience of salvation proposed by the myth. These three dimensions propitiated the archetype of alterity expressed in the Christian myth to coordinate knowledge of the universe through the scientific mentality.

The eleventh, twelfth, and thirteenth centuries were times of prodigious translation of Arabic and Greek texts into Latin by the cultural elite: Christian, whether monastic or not, Arabian, and Judaic. This translating activity was responsible for the massive transference of Greek and Arabian culture to medieval Europe. Greco-Roman mythology flooded the European imagination with a cornucopia of mythical symbols expressing relations with nature, the body, family, and society. Along with mythology and astrology came alchemy, in a very special way. As Milton Vargas puts it:

> In the same way as Arabic alchemy, European alchemy was born ready. That is to say, in Europe there was none of that evolution from a magical-mythical technique to its final stage of learned interpretation of the transmutation of metals, as a parallel to a process of individual salvation ... However, as the wisdom that permeated the Arabic *opus* was the result of a Greek-Egyptian-Judaic-Chaldean syncretism, Christian re-interpretation found no obstacles to oblige it to make radical changes of meaning. (1987, p. 27)

The meeting of the extraverting movement of the implantation of the Christian myth and alchemy was a synchronicity that abundantly equipped the imagination for its activity as transformer of the cultural Self. The depth and sweep of this impact was important because it was there that the birth of a great deal of modern physics and chemistry and the scientific mentality took root prior to the subject-object dissociation that occurred in the late eighteenth century.

The magical-mythical activity of mining characterized alchemy in all the cultures in which it was practiced. There is always a psychological-ethical-spiritual procedure that culminates in obtaining a miraculous substance. The process involves the transformation of the practitioner along with the substance, and the result, whether an elixir or a stone, is the symbolic product of the relationship between human being and matter. We may say that alchemical practices are the true source of research and symbolic education, which shape the personality of the adept during apprenticeship and the undertaking of the task. Alchemy, in Chinese, Egyptian, Greek, Judaic, and Chaldean cultures, is an archetypal ritual meant to obtain knowledge by uniting objective and subjective within the whole to teach, learn, and work. Through the animated meanings of substances, the personality develops alongside research and labor, inseparably from the whole within the *labor + oratorium* (work and prayer, objective and subjective).

From the matriarchal perspective, in alchemy we have the immense world of nature with its infinite properties—color, weight, texture, taste, smell, physical states and dimensions—that arouse our sensuality, pleasure, displeasure, fear, ambition, vanity, and fertility, all coordinated by imagination. From the patriarchal perspective, we have organization, classification, and the technical procedures gradually developed to protect the substances and the very life of the alchemists and their assistants, along with discipline, dedication, cultivation of truth, and ethical precepts. In the pattern of alterity, we experience the numerous polarities of the characteristics of matter and their creative relationship in initiation into the mystery of salvation. Finally, in the pattern of totality we realize that nothing remains outside the whole and everything is composed and integrated in the work, the *opus,* as the alchemists called it.

Nevertheless, alchemy in non-Western cultures, despite its contribution to symbolic learning on the subjective and objective levels, failed to produce the creative impact on the imagination that resulted in the modern sciences, as occurred in the Renaissance. In the West, the central archetype coordinated the structuring function of the imagination to seize the countless meanings of the transformation of matter to continue the implantation of the archetype of alterity through the myth. The encounter of the alchemical process and the Christian myth transformed knowledge and salvation into the one and only thing. On equating Christ with the Son of the Philosophers, that is, with the philosophical stone itself, European alchemy made the process of discovering and knowing the world equivalent to the experience of salvation through the revelation of the mystery of the Resurrection. Everything that many Christians were unable to do with the soul because of the repression imposed by the Inquisition, they could now undertake through matter perceived symbolically. The terrible persecution of the Inquisition continued, but the objective terrain of research functioned, at least relatively, as a protective shield. The humanization of learning, made sacred through the archetype of alterity, brought the soul so close to nature that the two became inseparably related within the cosmos. The original sin used as a repressive tool by the inquisitor began to be experienced far more creatively as ignorance of God on the emotional level, as well as in cosmic matter by scientists. Nature was reanimated, but this time beyond magical-mythical matriarchal animism. The matriarchal paradigm of tribal cultures was transcended by the paradigm of alterity in the animism of the scientific method. It was the *magia naturalis* of Marcilio Ficino. This reanimation was inspired by and in turn inspired scientific research as the pursuit of knowledge as a sacred theme. It was this scientific magical-mythical reanimation of nature that brought us, through geniuses like Saint Francis of Assisi, to the theory of the ecosystem in the twentieth century, which will save us or not, depending on how we put it into practice. The dialectic of the ego with sin, as a function of the monastery-learned approximation of the soul to God, began to embrace the dialectic of the ego with error on the path of the scientific truth of the soul of the individual and of the world. Introversion and extraversion complemented one another in symbolic elaboration. The scientific geniuses of the Renaissance experienced the scientific method of trial and error as the spiritualization of the soul toward the light. Christ's Resurrection became experienced as the *anima mundi* that calls forth humanity to awaken from the sin of darkness to experience God as the intelligence of the universe.

Jung rescued European alchemy as far as the wealth of psychological meanings in the alchemic imagination is concerned. With regard to his interpretation of the relationship of alchemy to Christianity, however, he tended to consider Christianity exclusively as a masculine, patriarchal, and spiritual religion that was compensated by alchemy with its earthly, matriarchal, and feminine symbology. However, it was not the myth but the Roman-Judaic tradition and the Holy Office that reduced institutional Christianity to a masculine, patriarchal, and spiritual religion stripped of sensuality, earth, and the feminine. The Christian myth is a myth of the incarnation of the whole being, integrating man and woman, matriarchal and patriarchal archetypes, eros and logos, and flesh and spirit; from Jung's perspective, it becomes difficult to understand alchemy symbolically as the expression of alterity in the elaboration of nature. Alchemy ransoms the repressed earthly, matriarchal, and feminine symbology that had been repressed in the Christian myth and relates it dialectically to the spiritual, abstract, patriarchal pattern through the pattern of alterity that characterizes the myth. When Jung interprets alchemy as a compensatory undercurrent to Christianity, it seems to me that he is referring to institutionalized Christianity, which patriarchally deformed the myth, and not to the myth itself, with its inherent pattern of alterity, which was expressed exuberantly in alchemy. The evidence that alchemy expressed the myth fully is that the philosophical stone is not a chthonic counterpart of the "divine spiritual and heavenly son" but Christ himself, as the *Rosarium Philosophorum* represents in the final figure of the *opus*.

Jung writes:

> The point is that alchemy is rather like an undercurrent to
> the Christianity that ruled on the surface. It is to this surface
> as the dream is to consciousness, and just as the dream
> compensates the conflicts of the conscious mind, so alchemy
> endeavors to fill in the gaps left by the Christian tension of

opposites. Perhaps the most pregnant expression of this is the axiom of Maria Prophetissa quoted above, which runs like a leitmotif throughout almost the whole of the lifetime of alchemy, extending over more than seventeen centuries. In this aphorism the uneven numbers of Christian dogma are interpolated between the even numbers, which signify the female principle, earth, the regions under the earth, and evil itself. These are personified by the *serpens mercurii*, the dragon that creates and destroys itself and also represents the *prima materia*. This fundamental idea of alchemy goes back to the Tehom, the Tiamat with its dragon attribute, and thus to the primordial matriarchal world which, in the theomachy of the Marduk myth, was overcome by the masculine world of the father. The historical shift in the world's consciousness towards the masculine is compensated by the chthonic femininity of the unconscious. In certain pre-Christian religions the male principle had already been differentiated in the father-son specification, a change, which was to be of the utmost importance for Christianity. Were the unconscious merely complementary, this change of consciousness would have been accompanied by the production of a mother and daughter, for which the necessary material lay ready to hand in the myth of Demeter and Persephone. But as alchemy shows, the unconscious chose rather the Cybele-Attis type in the form of the *prima materia* and the *filius macrocosmi*, thus providing that it is not complementary but compensatory. This goes to show that the unconscious does not simply act contrary to the conscious mind but modifies it more in the manner of an opponent or partner. The son type does not call up a daughter as a complementary image from the depths of the "chthonic" unconscious—it calls up another son. This remarkable fact would seem to be connected with the incarnation in our earthly human nature of a purely spiritual God, brought about by the Holy Ghost impregnating the womb of the Blessed Virgin. Thus, the higher, the spiritual, the masculine inclines to the lower, the earthly, the feminine; and accordingly, the mother who was anterior to the world of the father, accommodates herself to the male principle and, with the aid of the human spirit (alchemy or "the philosophy"), produces a son—not the antithesis of Christ but rather his chthonic counterpart, not a divine man but a fabulous being conforming to the nature of the primordial mother. And just as the redemption of man the microcosm is the task of the "upper" son, so the "lower" son has the function of a *salvatori macrocosmi*. (1944, par. 26)

Jung seems to consider Christianity as finished and alchemy as a new stage in culture that would add to the Christian myth through compensation. This might have been the case were we not to take into account the intense distortion caused by the institutional patriarchalization imposed by the Holy Office and the unlimited structuring power of such a myth. Perhaps because they descended from families very much identified with institutional Christianity, Jung and Nietzsche did not clearly separate the myth from the deformation brought about by the institution. Nietzsche projected onto Dionysus the matriarchal characteristics of Christ repressed during institutionalization, which prevented him from seeing the Dionysian aspect of Christ. Jung also projected the matriarchal outside the Christian myth, but onto alchemy instead of Dionysus. Otherwise his attitude regarding Christianity was not the same as Nietzsche's, but as he did not clearly separate the myth from institutional Christianity, references to Christianity in his work are at times contradictory.

When we consider the deformation present in the cultural implantation of the myth, we can conceive alchemy as the creative, normal, prospective continuation of the genuine implantation of the myth outside the Church, in the heretical dimension of the natural sciences. This is important not just for understanding the role of alchemy in the formation of the scientific worldview, but also to understand the huge creative force of the archetypal imagination expressed by myth in the cultural Self. Having been compressed inside the Church, the creative prospective imaginary potential of the myth flowed outward toward nature and society, creating modern art, science, and the sociopolitical development that eventually fostered social democracy.

The Christian myth is above all else a myth of incarnation. Therefore, the sensory-motor aspect of the matriarchal archetype should be the last aspect removed from it, for incarnation comes from *incarnare* (to make flesh). We are dealing with a myth whose prospective end is to structure a worldview through the senses. All myths do this to some degree, but the Christian myth embraces human existence from conception to after death in such a manner that each existential aspect is emphasized. Jesus' preaching starts with a miracle, typically Dionysian, transforming water into wine at the wedding feast, the symbol of the erotic *coniunctio* at Canaan. There follows the miracle of the bread and fishes, also typical of matriarchal fertility. The Messiah's companion, before initiation, is a devil-possessed prostitute. The Passion of Christ is made real in flesh through the crucifixion. The resurrection is carried out through the real body after three days spent among the dead. (John 20:11-17)

When we start from the dissociated perspective of psyche-matter and psyche-body, which expressed the cultural subjective-objective dissociation, we tend to see alchemy as rescuing the psyche from the embrace of physics. However, when we adopt the holistic, symbolic, and ontological perspective of psyche as being, integrating the mind-matter, mind-body, and subjective-objective polarities, the worldview and Christian alchemy have a different meaning. In this case, alchemy is a redeeming process to reveal the psyche through knowledge of the composition of matter, that is, to continue the revelation of the spirit though matter, through the Incarnation and the Resurrection, exactly what Teilhard de Chardin (1950) described in the humanization process, which explains the formation of consciousness from the differentiation of cosmic matter.

European alchemy sought psychic redemption as the recognition of the intelligence of the universe incarnated in the matter of the cosmos, in the metals of the earth, symbols of the flesh of the Messiah from which his spirit rose up symbolically. According to the model of the myth, alchemy will seek the philosophical stone after the discovery of the characteristics of the metals found in the bowels of the earth. Jung himself acknowledges the innumerable parallels drawn by the alchemists between the philosophical stone and Christ. In the alchemical text *Rosarium Philosophorum*, which Jung used to symbolize transference in the therapeutic process (Jung 1946), the last figure depicted in the process, which Jung failed to include in his book, is Christ resurrected, emerging from the tomb as an expression of the philosophical stone, the finality of the *opus*. European alchemy, therefore, expresses symbolically Christ's Resurrection through the imagination of alterity in the modern sciences.

European alchemy resumes the Christian myth, repressed and dissociated by the Church, and reintegrates the ego-other, ego-sin (shadow) relation via the dialectics of the polarities of poison and health, destructive and constructive substances in the process of development. Alchemy brought a new impulse to the social implantation of the alterity of the myth, which was being asphyxiated by the dogmatic patriarchal dissociation of good and evil in the symbols of the Messiah and Lucifer. Reintegration of the opposites became a current theme represented by the dialectic relation of the constructive-destructive polarity, sulphur and mercury, the proper duality of the Mercurial Spirit itself, the winged and wingless dragon as prime matter, the sun and moon, the hermaphrodite, all preparatory to the final synthesis of the *coniunctio*, the philosophical stone, Christ. European alchemy was engulfed by the asphyxiated Christian myth to restore and continue the implantation of its messianic and redeeming message through the confused mass of *prima materia*, experienced as the ignorance of the original sin in the search for the philosophical stone. Christian alchemy consecrated material research, teaching the transmission of wisdom, and creative work which had been defensively prohibited within institutional Christianity.

It is important to distinguish between the functions of projection and introjection in elaborating the symbols of the Resurrection and the philosophical stone, which appear in the last figure of the *Rosarium*. If we see the function of projection-introjection only structuring the identity of the ego, we will interpret alchemy merely as projection of mind on matter, which was recollected to structure analytical psychology. When we do so, we reduce alchemy to a projection and do not recognize the presence of the psyche also in chemistry. When, however, we recognize the function of projection-introjection in the formation of the identity of the ego and of the other, we realize that the alchemist projected and introjected the archetype of alterity, which greatly influenced the development of analytical psychology and of chemistry. It is important to conclude then that alchemy contributed to form the ego-other or subjective-objective identities with concepts of the individuation process on the subjective level and simultaneously of modern chemistry on the objective level.

As a structuring function of immense vitality in the cultural Self, Western alchemy united two great psychic polarities: myth and matter, or Christ and the philosophical stone as duality in the unity of being. We have seen how Christ expressed the implantation of the alterity archetype through the incarnation of the God image in the myth. In the alchemy of many cultures, the philosophical stone represented the miraculous stone of wisdom, which can be constructed through metallurgy. The reunion of Hephaestus and Prometheus working on the matter of the universe discovered the presence of the God image in the organization of matter, as did Teilhard de Chardin. Western alchemy, through the symbol of the *anima mundi*, continued the myth of the incarnation of the Holy Ghost with the revelation of its presence in matter through the philosophical stone.

Jungian symbolic psychology includes in the psychic dimension the creative relationship of the polarities ego-other, consciousness-shadow, good-evil, and many more within the concept of normal and defensive structuring functions, which carry on the elaboration of all symbols, complexes, and functions in the formation of consciousness and shadow. Jungian symbolic psychology also integrates the dialectical relationship of polarities within the whole, which occupies a central position in alchemy through the conception of the archetypes of alterity and of totality within the regent archetypal quaternio, which leads to the formation of consciousness through the theory and practice of Jungian symbolic education.

This is not just a matter of redeeming the repressed matriarchal pattern with a simple return to a magical-mythical or animistic attitude toward nature, but rather, as Jung pointed out in the quotation above, a matter of searching for the archetype of the child on the cosmic level, that is, of the minute human in the infinite universe. The prospective symbolic content of alchemy was the full release of the creative imagination in the pattern of alterity in order to express the dialectics between all opposites, including the matriarchal-patriarchal polarity, and to conceive the scientific paradigm that has come to rule the planet. The philosophical stone is not simply a daughter of the earth, but rather a hermaphrodite joining opposites—matter and wisdom, heaven and earth, king and queen, sun and moon, myth and matter, micro and macro physics—and, like Christ, it is the symbol of alterity in totality.

When holistic, systemic and constructivist thought is emphasized in culture and education, it is essential to include alchemy as the mythical root of modern science so that we do not end up once again locked into rationalism, separated from the archetypal imagination, precisely that rationalism we want to flee from in order to operate truly within totality. We cannot go beyond rationalism without basing the development of consciousness on the symbols and archetypes that form and transform it through conscious and unconscious imagination in the subjective and objective dimensions as Jung expressed in the *Red Book* (Jung 2009).

## Alchemy, Christianity, and Creativity

European alchemy not only stressed the dialectics of opposites but also gave it emphasis within the process of creative pursuit of the *opus*, two of the essential characteristics of the Christian message and the expression of the archetype of alterity.

Alchemy, because it was engaged in relating opposites dialectically through the initiatory knowledge of nature, was able to resume the experience of the creative imagination as the best road for the encounter with the philosophical stone and Christ. The consequence of European alchemy was the reinstallation of the creativity of imagination in the essence of the myth, that is, the reclaiming of full alterity in the field of research, through the scientific method, which is indispensable for a scientific worldview encompassing subjective and objective reality.

The imagination of the cultural Self through alchemy amplified the virtue-sin polarity from the introverted dimension to apply it through the truth-error polarity in the extraverted dimension, which became the cornerstone of the scientific method.

When we consider the Christian myth as an expression of the archetype of alterity, we recognize without doubt that the dialectic proposal of the ego's relationship with sin involves confronting normal development with the shadow. In other words, in its essence, mythical Christianity not only proposes awareness of sin as a psychic dysfunction, but also the transformation and integration of its content in the same way that science deals with error. At the same time, it includes the search for totality through the creative development of all psychic potential. The call to salvation refers to the practice of alterity both in confrontation with the shadow and in pursuit of self-fulfillment of the creative potential of each person (individuation) and of each culture (humanization) in relationship with the cosmos. In this sense, sin is what we fixate defensively and express in symbolic elaboration and also what we fail to elaborate out of laziness, ignorance, cowardice, accommodation, or lack of opportunity. Thus, the sin that separates the Christian person from God can be both an act against the integration of totality and an omission of the fulfillment of the existential potential of being. In this respect, Paul Tillich's *The Courage to Be* (1952) and Rollo May's *The Courage to Create* (1975) are brought together.

The patriarchal deformation of the myth tended to diminish its expression by the archetype of alterity and to reduce sin simply to a transgression of morals patriarchally codified in a series of conventional precepts. This deformation distanced Christians from the symbolic notion of sin as the fixation of symbols indispensable for the soul's journey through creative imagination. How to elaborate sin symbolically and discover its meaning requires the work of the imagination through the dialectical ethics of alterity, buried during the centuries of repressed Christianity.

## The New Mutilation of the Imagination and the Death of Alchemy

Within the patriarchal repression of institutionalized Christianity, alchemists had to conceal their activity lest they be persecuted for heresy along with the rest of the scientific community. Moreover, they disguised their writings so that they could not be understood by the uninitiated, who sought only material profit from the transmutation of metals. The symbolic expression of the *opus* gathered the objective and the subjective predominantly under the imaginal in the insular matriarchal position to express the creativity of art, science, and religiosity. With the cultural implantation of the natural sciences, the passage from the dominant insular matriarchal archetype to the dominance of the polarized patriarchal archetype further effected the abandonment of alchemy. This passage was accompanied by a great abstraction and the rise of the importance of mathematics in the scientific worldview. Although this was not incompatible with alchemy, it had an important effect on its abandonment. All these factors greatly contributed to the separation of chemistry from subjectivity, but the final deathblow to alchemy was the objective-subjective dissociation that inaugurated rationalism, materialism, and positivism when the scientific mentality took over the command of learning in the university at the end of the eighteenth century. This argument is difficult for the scientific community to accept, for it rocks the narcissistic edifice of truth and freedom of thought centered exclusively in objectivity enthroned in the Enlightenment. However, it is difficult to deny that the subjective-objective dissociation reinstalled defensively, in the scientific thought of the European cultural Self, the Manichaeanism of the imagination which had been firmly established in Christian religious thought with the good-evil, Christ-Devil ethical dissociation.

The development of scientific thought, its abstraction in mathematics, and its mechanism are important elements (Capra 1982), but these aspects would not in themselves impose the subjective-objective dissociation. Proof of this is that the scientific geniuses of the Renaissance who constituted the pillars of modern science, such as Copernicus, Kepler, Galileo, Descartes, Leibniz, and Newton, even by making full use of mathematical abstraction within a mechanical world, continued to have a religious vision of the universe during and after their discoveries. Their subjective emotional mystical reality went hand in hand with objective knowledge of the world because the science they developed was in total agreement with the Christian myth as both expressed the alterity archetype. Science collided with the Inquisition, not with the Christian myth. Neither mechanization nor the mathematical abstraction of science would, by themselves, make science incompatible with the myth. Quite the contrary! The immensity and complexity of the universe that the new sciences announced corresponded on the subjective level to the ecstatic experience of the grandiosity of God, imagined in the Old and New Testaments. The message of love, tolerance, and compassion expressed in the myth, and so fully experienced with nature by Saint Francis of Assisi (1182–1226), was totally compatible with science. Further proof of this is found today in that it is being entirely reclaimed by modern ecology in the concept of the ecosystem. The mechanistic and mathematical view of the world did not introduce the repression of the subject or the limitation of totality, especially since number and machine are symbols and are therefore rooted in archetypal transcendence, which includes subjectivity and totality (von Franz 1980).

The subject-object dissociation in the European scientific imagination seems to have sprung mainly from an emotional reaction of aversion experienced by the scientific community, a paranoid and reactionary defensive formation in response to the centuries of prepotency, intolerance, repression, persecution, torture, and homicide patronized by the Church against free and creative learning (Byington 1991a). Due to the fact that, from then on, the scientific mentality considered only the objective and rational to be valid, this highly subjective emotional reaction of repulsion against subjectivity has remained hidden and has been frequently expressed in the shadow of research and teaching by intolerance of and prejudice against taking into account the subjective dimension. It was defensively rationalized by the exclusive objectification of truth, which makes it difficult for the history of science to detect and elaborate it and, consequently, to rescue completely the function of the subjective in the scientific paradigm.

The consequence of this new repression within the European cultural Self in the eighteenth century was that the fecundity of the imagination of alterity was again intensely limited, this time, however, in the name of objectivity, science, and truth; no longer under the command of the Holy Office but rather under the materialistic, ideological surveillance that began to direct the universities and dogmatically control dissociated learning. For seventeen centuries, alchemy had maintained creatively the subjective-objective interaction that was extinguished in the late eighteenth century. The channel of faith, based on subjectivity, had expressed the good-evil (Christ-Devil) dissociation during the Middle Ages. After alchemy, the dissociation of the cultural Self continued to be expressed through the dissociation of the subject-object polarity sponsored by the materialistic philosophy of science. Though situated on fundamentally opposite sides in the cultural Self, predominantly religious in the subjective dimension and scientific in the objective, in terms of cultural pathology these two dissociations were equally responsible for limiting the full creativity of the imagination. Since the eighteenth and the beginning of the nineteenth centuries, through literature, painting, sculpture, architecture, music, psychology, sociology, and the civil rights movement, the Western cultural Self expressed the creativity of the imagination in order to circumvent this restriction and continue to seek its full liberation.

## The Mutilated Twins of Alchemy: Chemistry and Psychology

Alchemy split into two mutilated fields: modern psychology and modern chemistry. Both denied their hermaphroditic heritage and were carried on in isolation. Chemistry fell prey to materialism and lost its soul, while psychology was injured by the dissociation of mind-body and mind-nature and lost both the body and the world. Jung dedicated much of his creativity to overcoming this split by strenuous theoretical efforts, conceiving the *unus mundus*, the psychoid, the principle of synchronicity, and the objective psyche. During his work he returned many times to the search to reunite the subjective and the objective affirming:

> All that is outside, also is inside, we could say with Goethe. But this "inside", which modern rationalism is so eager to derive from "outside", has an *a priori* structure of its own that antedates all conscious experience. (Jung 1954b, par. 181)

> A wrong functioning of the psyche can do much to injure the body, just as conversely a bodily illness can affect the psyche; for psyche and body are not separate entities, but one and the same life. (Jung 1943, par. 194)

> There is no difference in principle between organic and psychic formation. As a plant produces its flowers, so the psyche creates the symbols. (Jung 1964, p. 64)

> Since psyche and matter are conditioned in one and the same world, and moreover are in continuous contact with one another and ultimately rest on irrepresentable, transcendental

> factors, it is not only possible, but fairly probable, even, that psyche and matter are two different aspects of one and the same thing. (Jung 1954a, par. 418)
>
> Every science is a fountain of the psyche and all knowledge is rooted in it. The psyche is the greatest of all cosmic wonders. Ibid., par. 357)
>
> Far from being a material world, this is a psychic world, which allows us to make only indirect and hypothetical inferences about the real nature of matter ... we are steeped in a world that was created by our own psyche. Not only in the psyche of man is there something unknown but also in the physical. We should be able to include this unknown quantity in the total picture of man but we cannot. (Jung 1933, par. 765).

It seems to me that Jung's great difficulty in accomplishing this task was that, from the very beginning, he conceived psychological reality as subjective together with the concept of symbol and archetype. From then on, although he tried very hard to join the opposites, his initial presupposition of psyche as a counterpart of matter prevented him from formulating systematically the polar relationship of mind and body and of mind and matter within psyche.

The reunion of opposites of mind and matter and mind and body within psyche, in my view, only becomes possible with the extension of the concepts of archetype and symbol to encompass the subjective and the objective dimensions together with the concept of the psyche as the representation of being-in-the-world as Heidegger (1927) postulates.

## The Dysfunction of the Subjective and Objective Imagination in the Nineteenth and Twentieth Centuries: The Esoteric Avalanche and Freud's Slime of the Occult

One of the reactive formations to the materialist cult of objectivity in nineteenth-century Europe was the appearance of mystic subjectivism in various forms, with the tendency to label itself as objective in order to gain the *status* of materialistic science without due elaboration within the scientific method. I have already identified the subjective channel of esoteric ("interior") learning (derived from the Greek *eso*, meaning "internal"), in contrast to the exoteric course of the exact sciences (derived from the Greek *exo*, "external"). To elaborate and differentiate these two paths is of the utmost importance for the theory and practice of Jungian symbolic education, in view of the goal of elaborating symbols in both the subjective and objective dimensions.

In his book *Psychological Types* (1921), Jung described the introverted and extraverted attitudes. In the introverted attitude, the personality privileges the ego and the subjective reactions, leaving the other and the objective reality to a secondary plane. The extraverted attitude favors the other and the objective dimension in experiences, relegating the ego and subjective reality to a secondary position. One of the advantages of Jung's typology, as discussed in chapter 4, is that introversion, extraversion, and all the other typological polarities are recognized as complementary and are present in all individuals and cultures. The predominance of one function in a person or culture does not mean that they do not have the counter pole, but that this other pole exists in less-developed conditions in the personality or in the culture and requires supplementary dedication for development.

As in the individual Self, the cultural Self also needs all the functions and the two attitudes to elaborate a symbol and integrate its energetic contents in collective consciousness. That is why, when preponderance of the objective dimension succeeded that of the subjective at the close of the eighteenth century, it was to be expected that it would be followed by a new activation of subjectivity in the nineteenth. Symbolic elaboration is not performed by all the structuring functions at the same time. Structuring functions are bipolar and their poles do not participate simultaneously but rather alternate from the passive to the active position in symbolic elaboration. In this manner, introjection and projection alternate through objectivity and subjectivity to deepen and improve any symbolic elaboration. In the history of the individual Self, this alternating happens in years or over decades, but in the cultural Self, it occurs over decades, centuries, and even millennia. Objective and subjective poles, even when not fixed and dissociated, also alternate. Nevertheless, due to the subjective-objective dissociation fixed at the end of the eighteenth century, subjectivity was largely banned from the scientific mentality in the nineteenth century and could not be used creatively at the service of learning to the extent needed by the imagination of the cultural Self. What happens in these situations is that, due to the fact that the Self is a system, blocking one pole in consciousness leads its counter pole to be expressed in the shadow. It so happened that a flood of esoteric theories and practices were introduced in Europe in the nineteenth century to express—mostly incompletely, superstitiously, and improperly—the subjective elaboration of phenomena such as the psychic reality of death, the altered states of consciousness, and the so-called extrasensory perception, that is, the deep nature of the imagination.

The terms *esotericism* and *occultism* refer in this context to experiences of the imagination that are predominantly subjective. The continuity of life after death and the nature of mediumism are extremely difficult to explain and therefore need considerable symbolic elaboration in order to differentiate their objectivity from their subjectivity. In this sense, not only mysticism but also a large part of art in general is dominantly esoteric. The subject-object dissociation that occurred in European humanism made this elaboration difficult and allowed for the practice of a poorly elaborated esotericism that expressed its defensive and inadequate objectification, as happened with psychography in the work of Alice Bailey, with the work of Helen Blawatski in anthroposophy, with possession in Allan Kardec's spiritualism, with the psychology of past lives, and with the dynamics of dilution in homeopathic and orthomolecular medicine, to mention just a few. In this manner, many phenomena empirically observed were explained defensively and esoterically in a reductive rational and objective way, as though they were exoteric, which jeopardized continuation of the elaboration of these phenomena to reach a better understanding of their nature.

Speaking on the objective reality of the soul, for example, Allan Kardec writes:

> It is true that this is no more than a theory, even though it may be more rational than the other (on the existence of the soul). But it is already something that this theory does not even contradict reason or science. Besides this, if it is corroborated by the facts, it will have in its favor the sanction of reasoning and experience. We find the facts in the phenomenon of spiritualistic manifestations, which thus constitute the patent proof of the existence and survival of the soul. (1861, p 15).

Kardec applied the theory of the existence of the soul after death to explain the phenomena of possession and mediumistic capacity, while these same phenomena were used to prove the theory. This error of reasoning has been known in dialectics since time immemorial and consists of introducing as an argument of proof the conclusion to prove it. Kardec wants to prove that the psyche has a life after death. Possession and mediumistic phenomena are used to contact the dead through the imagination. Then possession and mediumistic capacity are used as proof of life after death. In this way, the elaboration of the nature of possession and the psychic dimension of death was interrupted by spiritualism and this made it difficult to study these phenomena in anthropology and psychology. It was no longer necessary to study possession, because spiritualism considered it an objective fact to demonstrate the functioning of the psyche after death. Such early and undue objectification of the imagination made it difficult to elaborate the observed empirical phenomenon and the complexity of the psyche.

This precocious objectification of the structuring symbols and functions of the imagination by the esotericism of the nineteenth century justified and exacerbated the dissociated scientific and academic reactionary attitudes centered in the objective. In a chain reaction (the biofeedback mechanism operating defensively), the materialistic exacerbation in turn promoted a new growth of this fixed and poorly elaborated esotericism, which posed an enormous cultural drawback since it stimulated a high degree of superstition and obscurantism. Here we see Freud's dread of the "slime of the occult" acting on two fronts, one creative and the other defensive. Its creative aspect objectively affirmed that this esoteric occultism fixated and limited symbolic elaboration and was thus a methodological error, which had to be condemned by scientific thought. On the defensive aspect, repressive academic reaction against the esoteric continued to limit its elaboration and favored reactionary subject-object dissociation, defensive materialism, and scientific intolerance.

The phenomenon of defensive objectification of symbols in esotericism leads to the fixation and non-elaborated transmission of phenomena, beliefs, and superstitions, which is undoubtedly one of the factors of the cultural stagnation of all times. We may even say that the undue elaboration of symbols is the pedagogic way to multiply ignorance. By no means does this imply, however, that we should give up elaborating the esoteric path and the beliefs and superstitions, myths and religions themselves and live in atheistic, exclusively rationalist and objective materialism. We saw how the positivism of European Enlightenment threw out the baby of subjectivity along with the bathwater of the obscurantist Inquisition.

In this way, in the twentieth century, Western culture inherited two complementary groups of subject-object dissociations structured in the nineteenth century. First, the materialistic current, inspired by the exoteric objective mentality, which identified itself with truth at the expense of excluding subjectivity. This tendency is especially active in many universities and in traditional science. The second group, inspired by the esoteric current but also reductive and dissociated, labels as truth its predominantly subjective imagination, which it defensively reduces to objectivity to achieve the *status* of traditional positivistic science. This group is mainly present and active in the so-called alternative sciences, in many of the doctrines and techniques imported from the East, and in endless beliefs, superstitions, and practices culled from all the cultures of all time. The creative esoteric vacuum left in culture by the dissociation of the Christian myth and the abandonment of alchemy by materialistic science largely explains this fertile, disorderly growth. Bitter enemies, these two dissociated groups defensively project their shadow complementarily between themselves. They both have in common the need for more symbolic elaboration of the imagination to emerge from the unilaterality in which they are methodologically imprisoned. One of the ways to fail to understand the symbolic constructivist proposal of Jungian symbolic education is to consider it only as an "alternative" school of education.

It is necessary to take into account all these cultural esoteric manifestations of the imagination, including fantasies and dreams, and instead of using or discarding them along with their undue objectification, proceed with their symbolic elaboration until the subjective components are more and better separated from the objective components that are ever present in symbols. The paths of esoteric dominance that privilege subjectivity and those of materialistic dominance that privilege objectivity are both valid and creative for religion, science, humanism, and education, provided that each continues the symbolic elaboration of reality through imagination, which suffices to construct their identity better and significantly differentiate themselves from their complementary pole. To this end, we need the comprehension and disposition to ransom both the dissociated materialists from wanting to rid themselves of beliefs, symbols, and myths, as well as the dissociated spiritualists who want to go on using incompletely elaborated phenomena as objective and "scientific". The educational intolerance going on between exclusive preferences for creationism or for evolutionism is a good example of what I mean and what we want to avoid by implementing the symbolic approach.

In order to understand better the phenomenon of undue objectification in esotericism, it must be remembered that it comes from the natural process of symbolic elaboration in the individual and cultural Self. When we come across it, we should not think only in terms of a regression to magical-mythical animism or sensorial intelligence to explain it. It is enough to remember that, in the process of elaborating any phenomenon, we pass through several positions in which the structuring function of projection is at odds with the structuring function of introjection in symbolic elaboration. Introjection leads symbolic meanings to the ego (to the subject), while projection leads them to the other (to the object). The dispute between the two functions, introjection and projection, is supervised by the structuring function of evaluation, which regulates the need to continue elaboration. Superstitions, beliefs, and the magical-mythical perspective err only when they usurp the objective nature of reality.

The two great wars of the twentieth century, including the genocide in the second, followed by the collapse of communism exposed the illusion of materialistic rationalism in claiming to understand and develop humanity without interaction with the subjective dimension—emotional, esoteric, religious, and magical-mythical—which forms humanism. The disintegration of the rationalist-materialist ideology and the weakening of the patriarchal pattern that supported it swept away the traditional family and institutional values of collective consciousness, in both communist and capitalist societies. (After all, were they not first cousins, children of the subject-object dissociation of the eighteenth century?) Postwar changes since the 1960s point to a new era of imagination in the symbolic elaboration of life and the world. The opening to the subjective after the 1960s was paramount in counterculture. Through it, our cultural Self was flooded by an avalanche of poorly elaborated esotericism from Oriental, African, and Indian cultures and from the European past, joined—as is always the case in such times—by opportunistic charlatans who infiltrate like rats hungry for fame and profit in this fertile ground of not yet discriminated structuring symbols, complexes, and functions. In the midst of this confused worldview, modern propaganda, marketing, and self-help literature flourished.

Among the beliefs that spring from incompletely elaborated phenomena, we have seen the emergence of a cornucopia of practices in medicine, psychology, and education that are being exercised as alternative novelties. An example is the therapy of past lives. This consists of producing an altered state of consciousness through relaxation and pulmonary hyperventilation (breathing quickly for a few minutes eliminates more carbon dioxide than usual and produces an alteration in the metabolism—gaseous alkalosis—that causes dizziness). In this altered state of consciousness, one imagines a past life, which is then considered to be the cause of and explanation for some present difficulty. The imagination of a hypothetical past life, which in principle can be very creative, is interrupted, fixated, and objectivated when one reduces the imagination to an objective past-life event. From then on, the literality of the imagination is defensively fixated and projected, and it evades the continuation of symbolic elaboration of the present difficulty. The alternative "treatment" consists of creating a new defense, which is the defensive displacement of the projection to a past-life event.

In spite of the cultural backwardness that this and other defensive alternative practices encourage, together with growing mystification and charlatanism, it is not adequate to simply repudiate them. Rather they call for continued symbolic elaboration to further discriminate the objective and subjective components within the imagination and thus to produce more adequate meanings. To carry out this task, it is important to be aware of two limitations that derive from the conceptions and practices of materialistic and rationalist science. The first is elimination of the subjective dimension from the construction of scientific knowledge. The second is the notion that objective truth can be completely attained and exclusively known in objectivity. Both of these conceptions jeopardize the use and full elaboration of imagination in Jungian symbolic education.

## Reducing the Subjective to the Objective by Materialistic Science

As mentioned above, the subject-object dissociation that took place in the Enlightenment dominated the eighteenth, nineteenth, and twentieth centuries and is still intensely active today. It refused the incorporation of subjectivity in scientific method and reduced the truth of the imagination to objectivity. This repudiation of the subjective was a major component in the eruption of unduly objectivated esotericism in the nineteenth century, which in turn opened the doors to the undue objectification in the "alternative" epidemic that flooded Western culture in the second half of the twentieth century, officially inaugurated at Woodstock in 1968.

However, to understand this symbolic dysfunction of the imagination it is not enough to deal with subjectivity alone. We also need to change our attitude toward objectivity and its usurpation of the subjective practiced by materialistic science. One unfortunate example of this is the organicism present in all allopathic medicine and especially in psychiatry, which has lately been increasing with the progress of the neurosciences and the refining of psychopharmacological drugs. It is not a matter of underestimating the advance of knowledge in the neurosciences, a laudable and significant scientific achievement, but rather of acknowledging its dissociated and defensive use by many practitioners of psychiatry, neurology, and clinical medicine. This resurgence of organicism—that is, reduction of the mind exclusively to the body in psychiatry—reminds us of the worst moments of the defensive organicism of the nineteenth century before the discovery of psychodynamic psychology.

The industrial-commercial-medical complex of powerful multinational companies, which have millions in funding available to mold public opinion by marketing, allied with scant medical knowledge of psychology and culture, has made an enormous contribution to this reduction of the subjective to the corporal objective and presents great resistance to the symbolic reintegration of the subjective. The situation is aggravated by the extraordinary growth of the international drug trade, which also has a root in the defensive use of the imagination through altered states of consciousness in present day consumer hedonism. The growing drug trade can be seen as a branch of the same tree that sponsors the production and commercialization of psychopharmacological products in order to repress indiscriminately the subjective components of anxiety and depression in the imagination, exclusively reduced to their neurophysiologic components. Both the drug trade and the psychopharmacological industry profit enormously from the repression of the subjective dimension of the imagination. We fight drug addiction and drug trafficking, but at the same time, dependence on medically prescribed drugs is not sufficiently evaluated and, on the contrary, it is frequently stimulated.

Jungian symbolic education, in its attempt to use imagination fully to practice research and teach the spread of culture and the pursuit of truth, needs to identify the distortion of objectification that comes from defensive esotericism, just as it has to identify the distortion of objectification that comes from denying the subjective and the symbolic dimension in traditional academic science. These two methodological biases are not autonomous aberrations but rather spring from a fixation, a defense that accompanies the historical subjective-objective dissociation which fixated the normal dispute of the structuring functions of projection and introjection in the process of symbolic elaboration. And there exists yet another important factor in scientific tradition that produces harmful objectification of the subjective and makes it difficult to fully elaborate the imagination—an attitude toward the truth.

## Undue Objectification of Truth in Scientific Tradition

We have seen extensively in the light of the subject-object dissociation that dominated the nineteenth century through rationalist materialism, that the experience of the subjective was repudiated and situated exclusively among the errors of elaboration. This prejudice lost the experience of full totality, which embraces the polarities, above all the subjective-objective. Nevertheless, the experience of totality did not disappear, nor could it, for it is an archetypal expression of the central archetype and of the archetype of totality. Any psychic function rejected in consciousness starts to act unconsciously in the shadow. In this way, the experience of totality began to take place in the shadow through dissociation and defensive projection of error in subjectivity. As the decades passed in the nineteenth century, academic science witnessed the sedimentation of the notion that creative imagination which leads the mind to truth should be exclusively objective. Thus, a scientific defensive Puritanism was constructed in which truth was equated with pure objectivity. In order to reach the truth, it would suffice for us to deal with the body and with nature detached from all subjectivity. The basic dimensions of body and nature, such as space, time, light, gravity, and electromagnetism, were considered exclusively objective and should be pursued as such. This attitude confounded the elaboration of imagination and led the philosophy of science into the materialist alienation.

The position of symbolic science, which inspires Jungian symbolic education and symbolic humanism, is quite different. For symbolic humanism, science is the symbolic representation of truth. The pursuit of truth is the path of the imagination of the cosmic being that unveils itself during its own existence and forms human consciousness with its subjective and objective components expressed in the ego-other identity. Human beings are made of stellar substances, same as the planet they inhabit. The era of travel to outer space celebrates the beginning of the visit of human beings to their ancestors, who maintain them alive through their radiations. The path of the imagination is archetypal, and its essence covers the conscious-unconscious and subjective-objective polarities to encompass the archetypal dimension of the eternal and of the infinite. In this sense, fundamental magnitudes such as space, time, light, energy, matter, electromagnetism, and gravity are imaginary subjective and objective expressions of the archetypes, which operate in the psyche as structuring functions, enriching consciousness through the process of symbolic elaboration to know them a little more every time. To affirm that these dimensions are exclusively objective is to remain in *Maya*, the dimension of appearance and literality that limits the flight of imagination toward wholeness.

## The Role of Fairy Tales, Dreams, Popular Beliefs, and Myths in Symbolic Education

Fairy tales, stories, dreams, popular beliefs, and myths occupy a key position in the education of all cultures expressing the imagination of the cultural Self. They gather symbols together in a creative context, which elaborates them up to a certain point on the collective, impersonal, or transpersonal level which leads to continued elaboration on the individual level. "Once upon a time" is one of the ways through which the imagination activates, guides, and frames the symbolic elaboration of the archetypes with countless symbols. In their context, all sorts of structuring functions are experienced and elaborated: fear, curiosity, covetousness, jealousy, envy, hope, longing, cowardice, hate, sickness, affection, guilt, ambition, repulsion, creativity, sex, scorn, death, fascination, transgression, power, shame, ridicule, humiliation, pride, heroism, ethics, daring, courage, honor, treachery, magic, despair, and countless others that exist in the psyche. Above, around, and amid them all, we perceive the structuring function of the imagination.

Traditional beliefs are to a great extent the wealth of a culture. These are the popular universities that pass on the cultural experience of the symbolic elaboration of many generations. As wisely put by the Brazilian Bororó indian Xiwaboré, chieftain of the Tugo Paru: "Songs, stories and ceremonial representations are like paths in the forest. To the right and left are the thorns, beasts and the dark, but the words go through right to the end" (Crocker 1967, p. 314). But if that is so, we might wonder why is it that many educators have banished fairy tales and myths from school and are vehemently against using them in education, their argument being that they cultivate the irrational and keep the pupils in a magic, unreal world that is incompatible with adult life and the most important principle of reality.

The answer lies in the historical cultural repression and prejudice toward the imagination, the subjective, and the irrational. Recalling a fairy tale, a legend, or a myth to illustrate a teaching can be highly structuring to show themes that would otherwise be unattractive and difficult to memorize.

I will never forget my science teacher stressing the importance of oxygen above all other gases by using the story of the ugly duckling. I still remember the illustration that my biology teacher used for the deformations of science through the Frankenstein story.

Dreams also bring forth images that can be used profitably in teaching. It can be very productive for pupils and teachers to tell dreams that may have to do with the class, the subject, and/or the teacher so as to create a symbolic atmosphere that is propitious to the pedagogic use of the imagination. It is not a matter of interpreting dreams or revealing the intimate thoughts of students, which should be avoided at all costs. The images of dreams are used to illustrate significant pedagogic situations. In the second class of a course I gave for teachers on creativity, I asked the participants if they had dreamed about the course. (The first class had been a general artistic, philosophical, and psychological introduction.) One teacher said that she had dreamt that the class had been infested with lice. She and other colleagues had so many lice running all over their heads that it looked like an ant race. After we had laughed at the oddity of the dream, we tried to associate it as a function of the group Self. One colleague associated it with the lice that many of her young pupils have and that the teachers are always warning the pupils' mothers to look for (free association). Another, using the amplification method, considered that the lice are bloodsuckers, which could mean that the many ideas presented in the first class were sucking the energy from their heads. I made use of the image to recall the main ideas exposed at the first class, which we were to integrate during the course "so that they would not stick there like lice" (autonomous ideas). "Was anyone left with a lice after the last class?" I asked. "Well, it wasn't a lice; it was actually a lice and a half!" one student answered. "It was when you associated art and science in the Renaissance as an expression of the cultural imagination." And so it went on. The image was so significant that it helped us to elaborate the ideas all the way through to the end of the course. The symbol amused us and helped us to elaborate teaching. Dreams are the poetry of the night and are an inexhaustible source of the Self's imagination; when used in teaching, they can greatly enrich education, especially dreams that speak clearly of the teacher-pupil relationship, the material studied, the school, or the class's reactions to teaching situations.

The way in which parents and educators convey the symbolic source contained in legends, fairy tales, myths, and dreams to children and adults depends basically on their relation with the symbols of culture and with life itself. Parents and teachers most recommended to teach using symbolic material are sensitive persons with the ability to open themselves up to elaborate the rational and emotional meanings of symbols. Merely rational opening is treacherous inasmuch as it keeps the door closed to the basic characteristics of symbols. Merely emotional opening runs the same risk. The opening has to be both rational and emotional, since in this way it accompanies the pupils' psychic reactions in the experience of symbols. Such parents and teachers can support the full exercise of infantile and adult imagination in the process of elaboration that constitutes symbolic education.

A five-year-old boy was sent by the psychological coordinator of his school to psychotherapy because he said in class that he often woke up at night in fear. A child psychiatrist consulted by the family had diagnosed night fright and prescribed clomipramine. After reading the medicine instructions, the parents decided to take him to the recommended psychologist, who interviewed the child and then tested him with the CAT (Children Apperception Test). The child emphasized fear situations and at the same time was very anxious to protect the therapist from being afraid. An interview with the parents revealed that the father had suffered from phobia and obsessive symptoms in his youth. He had decided to "teach" his son not to feel fear by telling him terrible bedtime stories of brave heroes and horrible dragons every night to make him brave and fearless. No doubt, this was related to the boy's nightmares and the person who most needed psychological counseling was the father. To have maintained the medication without the symbolic elaboration of the boy's fear within the individual and the family Selves would have been a gross error.

The process of symbolic education is initiatory, but not hermetic. It is initiatory because teaching is inseparable from life and emotion but it is not hermetic because it is not secret. Clearly this is an old path in the culture and work of educators. The main message is that only symbolic living in education accumulates experience and through time forms—*Deo concedente,* as the alchemists say—the creative, intellectual, emotional, and ethical pedagogic maturity necessary to practice it. It is a matter of training educators who, in their daily activity and in their own way of working, become students of human life and culture and elaborate them critically along with their pupils. This professional training requires the creative development of a teacher who is at the same time priest, scientist, artist, and politician, with some distance from faculty chairs, campaign platforms, and altars, and who wishes simply to dedicate himself or herself to the curiosity, vitality, and intimacy of the pupils so that together they may learn, with love and mutual experience, the marvelous exercise of knowing how to be (Furlanetto 1997).

## The Return of Imagination in Leading-edge Technology

As mentioned earlier, by seizing the power of the university in the late eighteenth century, science repudiated faith and, along with it, the subjective and the imagination. One historic fact eloquently represents that repudiation.

In 1778, two doctors arrived in Paris who were to become famous the world over: Philippe Pinel, who separated the insane from criminals, and Franz Anton Mesmer, who discovered "animal magnetism", known to us today as hypnotism. It might be said that Pinel brought pathological imagination in the form of hallucination to be studied by science and that Mesmer brought the scientific study of the subjective capacity of normal imagination through hypnotism. The death of Voltaire (1694–1778) in the same year as their arrival is a significant occurrence (synchronicity), for the philosopher was one of the great symbols of the crowning of reason in the Enlightenment, which ended by repudiating subjectivity and imagination together with religion (Zilboorg and Henry 1941).

Pinel's struggled to have mental pathology recognized as the condition of psychic disease, that is, a disease of the imagination. Mesmer's creativity in discovering the suggestive power of creative imagination was disregarded together with his sensationalist vanity which made him appear to be a charlatan. In the century that followed, the application of what Mesmer described as animal magnetism was gradually recognized as hypnotism and later, through the libido and psychic energy, as the reality of conscious and unconscious imagination.

Science's relation with animal magnetism was one of the most meaningful chapters in the history of imagination in the West. Mesmer carried out *séances* in the salons of Paris and hypnotized many people in front of mirrors with his "magnetizing wand", making them experience emotions and altered states of consciousness artificially created by suggestion. In 1784, the Academy of Sciences in Paris appointed a committee led by Jean Sylvain Bailly, who besides being a famous doctor had also been mayor of Paris. The other commissioners included Benjamin Franklin, Antoine Lavoisier, and Joseph-Ignace Guillotin. They were to examine the work of Charles d'Eslon, a disciple of Mesmer, and they unanimously concluded that:

> Imagination without magnetism produces convulsions and that magnetism without imagination produces nothing ... that such [magnetic fluid] does not exist and therefore cannot be useful ... that the violent effects seen in public result from the imagination which is set into action ... that the repeated excitement of the imagination may prove harmful ... any public magnetic treatment cannot but have at length very harmful results. (Zilboorg and Henry 1941, p. 345)

The guillotine invented by Guillotin is a bizarre symbol of the subjective-objective dissociation expressed in the mind-body polarity, which did not spare even the members of this commission. Nine years later, Bailly was guillotined, and one year after that, it was Lavoisier's turn. Pinel himself was lucky to escape the same fate (ibid.). What this committee did not realize was the extraordinary effect of the imagination on the emotions, which was to become famous through hypnotism during the nineteenth century. Thus, imagination flourished in psychology through Freud's discovery of the transference to which Jung gave an archetypal base.

However, for ninety-eight years, the Academy of Sciences in Paris resisted studying hypnotism. A century after Mesmer, in 1882, Jean-Martin Charcot (1845–1893) succeeded in having the academy accept his work on hypnotism, and it is possible that this concession was only granted because the paper included the gross error of reducing hypnotic imagination to pathology. Charcot claimed that hypnosis only worked on hysterical patients. Hippolyte Bernheim had thoroughly demonstrated that normal people may also be hypnotized, but the academy did not accept his paper (Zilboorg and Henry 1941).

The prejudice against the imagination continued. I have already pointed out that Joseph Breuer's great discovery in Anna O.'s hysterical phobia of water (see the beginning of this chapter) was the creative action of the imagination in producing symptoms via the conscious-unconscious polarity. I drew attention to how this discovery was reduced to the unconscious by psychoanalysis, which also greatly reduced the creative imagination of the psyche to childhood, sexuality, and pathology.

We may consider the discovery of the imagination, the cornerstone of modern psychology. In spite of having reduced it to pathological symptoms it was through the imagination that Freud discovered psychic reality. For him, until 1887, hysteria and obsessive neurosis were caused by sexual traumas lived literally in childhood. After having published these basic ideas, he discovered that many stories told by hysterical patients were lies; they had been based in fantasies. Freud's scientific world, formed in the Viennese positivist school of the great Helmholtz, suffered an enormous impact. Freud thought of abandoning medicine. However, the light of his genius sparked in the abyss of his deception to show him that the root of those symptoms and lies was the imagination, the true essence of psychic reality.

> When this etiology [the sexual traumas] disappeared by the very weight of its improbability and of the contradictions of undeniable circumstances, the immediate result was accompanied by an appalling and impotent surprise. The analysis had gone through the right path to the sexual traumas and yet, they were not true. The reality under my feet disappeared. In that moment, I would have abandoned everything, as had my dear antecessor Breuer, when he came to this unfortunate discovery. I persevered, perhaps, because I had no other choice. Finally, came the reflection that one should not give in to despair because of being frustrated in one's own expectations. If hysterics can attribute their symptoms to fictitious trauma *this fact means that they create these scenes in their fantasy* and psychic reality must be taken into consideration side by side with common reality. (Freud 1914, pp. 27–28; italics added)

Although Jung, like Freud, also reduced the concepts of the archetype and of creative imagination to the unconscious, he can be credited with having the genius to root the imagination archetypally in the normal psyche (Jung 2009). This was no easy task; in order to do so, Jung had to stand up to the psychiatric tradition that, in his day and unfortunately even in ours, often reduces the visions of creative imagination to pathology, mainly to psychotic hallucination. As we know, psychotic hallucination consists of the invasion of consciousness by contents of the imagination dissociated from the ego and with sense perception characteristics of reality. In the hallucination of a psychotic patient, the terrible witch appears "in flesh and blood", with all the characteristics of reality.

Jung developed creative imagination based on the images of his fantasies and dreams, which led him to develop the method of active imagination that is nowadays practiced by many types of psychologists. However, as a psychiatrist, Jung could not fail to clash with the reduction of creative imagination to psychosis that existed in his time. In his *Memories* he tells us:

> Around the autumn of 1913, the pressure that I had felt until then seemed to shift to the outside as if something were hovering in the air. Indeed, the atmosphere struck me as more somber than before. It did not appear to be a psychic situation, but rather a concrete reality. This impression became more and more intense. In the month of October, on a trip by myself I was all of a sudden taken by a vision: I saw a huge wave covering all the countries in the septentrional plateau situated between the North Sea and the Alps. The waves stretched from England to Russia and the coasts of the North Sea almost all the way to the Alps. When they reached Switzerland I saw the mountains rise up higher and higher as if to protect our country. An awful catastrophe had just taken place. I saw hurling yellow waves, the floating debris of the works of civilization and the death of countless human beings. The sea turned into a torrent of blood. This vision lasted about an hour. Perturbed and nauseated, I was ashamed of my weakness . . . I wondered whether these visions had to do with some revolution, but the images were not clear. So I reached the conclusion that the visions were about me and I supposed I was being threatened by a psychosis. The thought of the possibility of a war did not occur to me. (1961, pp. 175–76)

Jung was doubtless a great intuitive, whose capacity for creative imagination included the structuring function of a medium, which is present in all of us to a certain degree. However, he himself and many psychiatrists, including Jungians, even today believe that he had psychotic crises on this and other occasions. From my long clinical experience, I am quite sure that Jung was not psychotic. There is no doubt that in many cases it is hard to separate creative from pathological imagination, especially when it includes elements of sense perception. In such cases, many psychiatrists do not hesitate in diagnosing imagination or visions as psychotic hallucination. These psychiatrists tend to pathologize imagination for lack of the psychological experience of creative imagination acquired during analysis.

Jung's *Red Book* (2009), recently published, has thoroughly amplified this question by including paintings and writings of his imagination during that critical period which lasted from 1913 to 1930. There we see the representation of Jung's exuberant imagination and practice of active imagination. Considering the limitations psychiatry had at that time and even today in differentiating normal from pathological imagination, we can understand why he himself feared that his visions could be psychotic hallucinations.

Leading-edge technology today provides us with virtual reality or artificial imagination with strong sense perception elements that appear as normal hallucination. If you travel to Epcot Center, in Florida, and spend a couple of hours experiencing virtual reality, you will have no doubts that modern technology allows anyone to experience normal hallucinatory imagination. We buy a ticket, enter a booth, and sit down on a chair with special audio-visual equipment. A film begins, and we participate in it. We enter an abyss and an ocean ... it is raining, the wind blows, we think we are sinking and drowning. We go into tunnels and duck to avoid objects that come at us. We sweat, scream, our hearts beat fast and our breathing speeds up. There is no doubt that we are experiencing a discharge of adrenaline. This does not mean that many people, when they experience normal imagination with strong sense perception elements, cannot suffer a psychotic crisis, especially those who bear hereditary or psychodynamic components that predispose them to psychosis.

The lights are turned on, and we see that we have not left our seat, and yet we can swear that everything we experienced was absolutely real and true. We experienced an artificial hallucination within the imagination, helped by our spring-loaded seat; if we put on equipment with cutaneous sense perception, like gloves, we will feel in the body what we have just seen and heard without our chair having to move. We thought that the progress of technology would distance us even more from subjective reality, but on the contrary, we see that leading-edge technology came to enable us to rediscover the imagination in such an intense and revolutionary way, that all we have to do is put on the proper equipment and press a button to experience imagination as normal hallucination, as long as we have the necessary psychological resistance to stand it without becoming psychotic. Where is this new phase of the imagination going to lead and how can it be used in education?

## Imagination, Hallucination and Virtual Reality

To close this book and its final chapter on the importance of the imagination, I want to call attention to computerized normal hallucinatory imagination in life, culture, and education. I think it is meaningful to draw attention to this new awakening of the imagination in modern societies favored by leading-edge technology. Computerized imagination is its most fantastic innovation, and it will revolutionize normal cultural life and education. I am referring to virtual reality, or rather, computerized normal hallucinatory imagination.

The scientific imagination of Teilhard de Chardin, one of the pillars of this book, conceived the noosphere as the layer of communication that increasingly integrates planetary consciousness. The Internet and global positioning systems (GPS) express this unification and show us two aspects in which the noosphere enormously amplifies our nervous system, which generates it. In the first place, not being uniquely centralized, it cannot be easily blocked, whereas a small needle inserted into the respiratory center of our medulla oblongata paralyzes life. Second, the structural expansion of the system is boundless, while the human nervous system, as we see in cases of paralysis, once formed, becomes relatively incapable of producing neurons to extend or renew itself anatomically. It is true that sound areas and functions can substitute for those that have been injured, but this is always a relative solution. Axons and mainly dendrites are liable to change and grow but not the whole nerve cell. The Internet is by definition unlimited. The users, transmitters, and receivers can multiply practically without limits. They can occupy the whole planet through chips inserted in fish and fowl and in rockets and robots sent to outer space.

In the area of verbal and numerical communication alone, this globalization of communication is already extraordinarily significant in expanding the interaction of knowledge and relationship. Nonetheless this gigantic transformation of verbal and numerical communication is just a part of what is expected to come. Computation is going much farther, for it is entering not only verbal and numerical transmission but also the imaginal and sense perception dimensions of the right cerebral hemisphere, the limbic and the autonomous nervous system. This means an extension in quantity but also a great change in quality. Computerized transmission has gone beyond the rational barrier and is already acting in the experiential, emotional, and unconscious world through virtual reality, which is the technological power of turning imagination into reality, that is, acquiring the capacity to produce normal hallucination. In this way leading-edge technology will have access to the transcendent function of imagination of the symbolic elaboration process of the Self, with a mobilizing power that knows no bounds. In psychiatric terms this means that we are passing through the barrier traditionally established between normality and psychosis in the dimension of imagination. This is more than the equivalent of going beyond the speed of sound in aviation. This passing through occurs when the limits of the natural use of imagination are transcended and we enter into the territory of hallucination, which is the sense perception eruption of the imagination in consciousness beyond the natural control of the ego. In the human nervous system, this corresponds roughly to the technological expansion of consciousness in order to mobilize the limbic and the vegetative nervous system where normally most of our emotional and hormonal system functions unconsciously and is therefore relatively inaccessible to the ego.

On the level of graphic computation, this new world of creativity goes from videogames to the programming of the separation of the stages of a rocket in outward space. In joining together verbal, numerical, imaginal, and sense perception communication, a world of creativity has opened that will have access to human experiences in all their psychological, conscious, and unconscious complexity. We see how our children are fascinated today by videogames. In the future we shall see all humanity fascinated, commercializing and experiencing computerized hallucinatory imagination. Meanwhile, videogames, information, and sales of existing products are the great attraction of planetary intercommunication. This is just the start. Besides all this, in the era that is beginning, the emotional and existential center of this communication will be occupied by the exchange and commercialization of artificial experiences imagined for all sorts of human needs. This is the use of the imagination on the level of hallucination for the optional commercialization of the most varied experiences of the deep and intimate reality of the soul. It is difficult for us to have a more exact notion of what will happen with ideologies and cultural values, with the psychic reality known today as normal (without normal hallucination), and with how each human being will live when this comes to happen. The use of lysergic acid diethylamide in the 1960s gave us an idea of what this can be. All we know is that it is not far away and that it is likely to occur on a large scale very soon. We can affirm that living daily with artificial hallucination is perhaps the moot gigantic step of postmodernism.

Let us imagine that a child in northeastern Brazil is born with a heart complication that only a surgeon in southern China, who is attending a cardiology meeting in Rome, knows how to handle with a new technique. The child is operated on in the hospital in Brazil by the Chinese surgeon who remained in Rome. The telerobotic operation is attended by anyone who wants to, all over the world. The following day, in several places around the world, surgeons prepare to operate on similar cases with the new technique. The immense distance between the surgeon and the patient is something that impresses us so much that it may blur an even more extraordinary fact in this miraculous scenario—that the surgeon operated with gloves supplied by sensors that enabled him to touch the child's heart valves and test their consistency. Seeing the heart from afar on the video, the surgeon was also able to experience the sensorial reality of its valves through the sensors on his gloves. This is still fantasy, but the operation has already been performed on animals (José Salomão Schwartzman, personal communication, 1996) and even on human beings (*Folha de S.Paulo,* February 10, 1996). The door has been opened to virtual reality, that is, to computerized normal hallucinatory imagination on the objective and subjective levels: on the objective level because the valve was touched only through the imagination; on the subjective because we can experience such hallucinations without any objective reality whatsoever.

## Computerized Normal Hallucinatory Imagination and Drug Trafficking

The billions of dollars spent to repress the frightening growth of drug trafficking and the fight against the criminal powers of the international drug racket until now have not been enough to curb them. The fascination the users have for the drug experience defeats this immense, sophisticated police organization because what people want is an altered state of consciousness that goes beyond materialism and activates the imagination. Amid all the spiritual impoverishment of materialistic modern society, drugs appear as "the big thrill", capable of animating an uninteresting life by generating strong emotional sensations, even at the terrible risk of addiction. Computerized normal hallucinatory imagination is capable not only of altering the state of consciousness without chemicals, but also of directing the imagination toward specific experiences chosen by the consumer and incredibly cheaper and more fascinating than the effect of drugs. The market will have the next say. The popular use of artificial hallucination may defeat the international drug racket in a very surprising way—by depriving illegal drugs of their *raison d'être*.

### Computerized Normal Hallucinatory Imagination and the Experience of Culture and Education

Let us imagine a working-class family. After dinner, they wash the dishes and then prepare for fascinating experiences. Each family member picks a disc or searches the Internet, looking for the latest experience with the new generation of videogames which include artificial hallucination. One of them watches a thrilling soccer game, playing goalkeeper; another dances and then has sex with a favorite actor or actress; another takes part in a bison hunt as an American Indian; another parades as a Dior model; and another joins Jesus at the Last Supper. Tired of chasing bison, one of the boys changes his videogame to experience his death at Pompeii, covered by the ashes of Mount Vesuvius. As imagination has no end, and nor do videos with artificial hallucination, perhaps the most spectacular experience it will afford is living with those who have died. Imagine an orphanage, for instance, where for a few hours every day the children turn on the artificial hallucination device to be cuddled by their parents. What is to happen to individual and social life on the planet with this kind of experience available? How many will grow away from everyday life and even go mad? Will artificially established emotional dependencies arise and what will be the extent of their normal and pathological consequences? We will know only in the future. There is no doubt, however, that the interest and participation in culture of all time will undergo an essential change whose consequences are today difficult to imagine.

Of course, education in the future, like all cultural activities, will be unthinkable without computerized normal hallucinatory imagination. It is also obvious that this is an expressive technique perfected to the highest degree.

On using expressive techniques today as much as possible to construct learning symbolically, Jungian symbolic education will not only be preparing the educator of the future but also educating culture to exercise and live with this passionate technological use of the imagination, which will be the highest degree of symbolic teaching that we can conceive of today.

*Diagram 2*

# PEDAGOGIC SELF

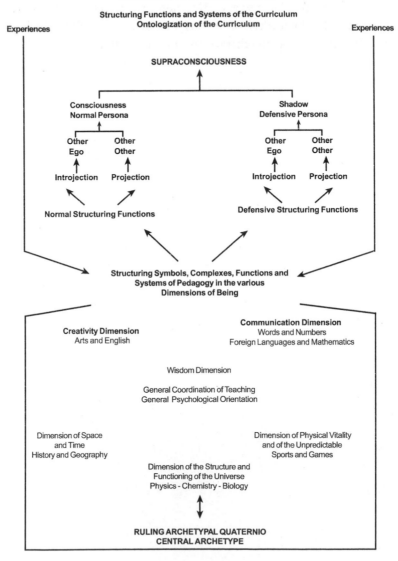

**Elaboration System of Symbolic Education**

**Structuring Functions and Systems of the Curriculum
Ontologization of the Curriculum**

Experiences                                                                 Experiences

**SUPRACONSCIOUSNESS**

**Consciousness
Normal Persona**

**Shadow
Defensive Persona**

Other        Other
Ego          Other

Other        Other
Ego          Other

Introjection   Projection

Introjection   Projection

**Normal Structuring Functions**

**Defensive Structuring Functions**

**Structuring Symbols, Complexes, Functions and
Systems of Pedagogy in the various
Dimensions of Being**

**Creativity Dimension**
Arts and English

**Communication Dimension**
Words and Numbers
Foreign Languages and Mathematics

Wisdom Dimension

General Coordination of Teaching
General Psychological Orientation

Dimension of Space
and Time
History and Geography

Dimension of Physical Vitality
and of the Unpredictable
Sports and Games

Dimension of the Structure and
Functioning of the Universe
Physics - Chemistry - Biology

**RULING ARCHETYPAL QUATERNIO
CENTRAL ARCHETYPE**

Diagram 3

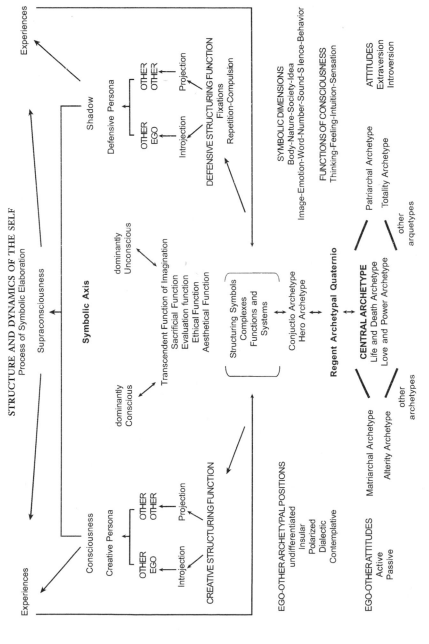

STRUCTURE AND DYNAMICS OF THE SELF
Process of Symbolic Elaboration

Experiences

Supraconsciousness

**Symbolic Axis**

Shadow

Defensive Persona

OTHER  OTHER  OTHER
OTHER  EGO
Introjection  Projection

DEFENSIVE STRUCTURING FUNCTION
Fixations
Repetition-Compulsion

dominantly Unconscious

Transcendent Function of Imagination
Sacrificial Function
Evaluation function
Ethical Function
Aesthetical Function

dominantly Conscious

Structuring Symbols
Complexes
Functions and
Systems

Conjuctio Archetype
Hero Archetype

**Regent Archetypal Quaternio**

SYMBOLIC DIMENSIONS
Body-Nature-Society-Idea
Image-Emotion-Word-Number-Sound-S lence-Behavior

FUNCTIONS OF CONSCIOUSNESS
Thinking-Feeling-Intuition-Sensation

Patriarchal Archetype

Totality Archetype

other
arquetypes

**CENTRAL ARCHETYPE**
Life and Death Archetype
Love and Power Archetype

ATTITUDES
Extraversion
Introversion

Matriarchal Archetype

Alterity Archetype

other
archetypes

EGO-OTHER ARCHETYPAL POSITIONS
undifferentiated
Insular
Polarized
Dialectic
Contemplative

Consciousness

Creative Persona

OTHER  OTHER  OTHER
OTHER  EGO
Introjection  Projection

CREATIVE STRUCTURING FUNCTION

Experiences

EGO-OTHER ATTITUDES
Active
Passive

# Bibliographic References

ADLER, Gerhard (1960). *The Living Symbol.* New York: Pantheon Books.

ALVARENGA, Maria Zélia (1991). Transference relationship and structuring of consciousness. *Junguiana: Journal of Brazilian Society for Analytical Psychology*, 9:114–145.

AVALON, Arthur (1918). *The Serpent Power.* Madras: Vasanta Press, 1958.

BACHOFEN, J. J. (1967). *Myth, Religion and Mother Right: Selected Writings of J. J. Bachofen.* Princeton: Princeton University Press, 1973.

BAIR, Deirdre (2003). *Jung: A Biography.* Boston: Little, Brown and Co.

BERRY, Patricia (1984). Echo and beauty. *Spring.* Dallas: Spring Publications, 1984, 49–56.

BOLEN, Jean S. (1984). *Goddesses in Everywoman.* New York: HarperCollins.

BREUER, Joseph (1893). *The case of Anna O.* In Sigmund Freud, SE, vol. 2. Rio de Janeiro: Ed. Imago, 1974, 63–90.

BUSTOS, Dalmiro (1979). *New Developments in Psychodrama.* São Paulo: Ed. Ática, 1987.

BUSTOS, Elena Noseda; DE ESPINOSA, Graciela Bustos; RIMOLI, Dinah; DE SANGIÁCOMO, Raquel Brocchi (1980). Pedagogic psychodrama. In Dalmiro Bustos, et al., *Psychodrama.* São Paulo: Summus Ed., 1982.

BYINGTON, Carlos Amadeu Botelho (1965). *Genuineness as Duality in Unity.* Analyst' Diploma Thesis at the C. G. Jung Institute, Zürich.

BYINGTON, Carlos Amadeu Botelho (1982a). A mythological theory of history. *Journal Vozes,* 76(8): 599–610.

――― (1982b). The symbolic richness of football. *Journal Psicologia Atual,* 25: 20-32.

――― (1983). A symbolic theory of history: The Christian myth as the main structuring symbol of the alterity pattern in Western culture. *Junguiana: Journal of Brazilian Society for Analytical Psychology,* 1: 120–177.

――― (1984). The concept of the therapeutic Self and the interaction of the creative and the defensive transference within the transference quaternio. *Junguiana: Journal of Brazilian Society for Analytical Psychology,* 3: 5–18.

――― (1985). Amadeus: The psychology of envy and its function in the creative process. *Junguiana: Journal of Brazilian Society for Analytical Psychology,* 3: 81–120.

――― (1986). The pathological shadow of the Western cultural Self. *Tenth International Congress of Analytical Psychology,* Mary A. Mattoon, ed. Einseideln, Switzerland: Daimon, 1987, pp. 301–316.

――― (1987a). *The Development of Personality: Symbols and Archetypes.* São Paulo: Ed. Ática, 1987.

――― (1987b). Symbolic science: epistemology and archetype. A holistic approach to objective and esoteric knowledge. *Junguiana: Journal of Brazilian Society for Analytical Psychology,* 5: 5–24.

――― (1988a). *The Four Symbolic Dimensions of the Personality.* São Paulo: Ed. Ática, 1988.

――― (1988b). Adolescence and the interaction of individual, familiar, cultural and cosmic Self. *Junguiana: Journal of Brazilian Society for Analytical Psychology,* 6: 47–118.

――― (1988c). *Persona and Shadow.* São Paulo: Ed. Ática, 1988.

――― (1990a). Polarities, reductionism and the five archetypal positions of consciousness. *Junguiana: Journal of Brazilian Society for Analytical Psychology,* 8: 7–42.

――― (1990b). The creative and defensive structures in music therapy. Opening lecture of the IV World Congress of Music Therapy. Rio de Janeiro, 1990.

――― (1990c). Symbolic science: epistemology and archetype. In Dênis M. S. Brandão and Roberto Cremai, eds. *The New Holistic Paradigm.* São Paulo: Ed. Summus, 1991.

――― (1991a). Preface to the portuguese translation of Malleus Maleficarum: *The Witches' Hammer* by Kramer, Heinrich and Sprenger, James (1484). Rio de Janeiro: Ed. Rosa dos Tempos–Record.

BYINGTON, Carlos Amadeu Botelho(1991b). The psychic reality of the dream dimension. *Junguiana: Journal of Brazilian Society for Analytical Psychology*, 9: 74–87.

———(1991c). Mnemosyne's punishment: archetype and education. Opening lecture of the I Group Congress of High Schools of São Paulo.

——— (1992a). Workshop on symbolic constructivism illustrated by the myth of Genesis in the II Group Congress of High Schools of São Paulo.

——— (1992b). Democracy and the archetype of alterity. *Junguiana: Journal of Brazilian Society for Analytical Psychology*, 10: 90–107.

——— (1992c). Symbolic psychodynamic of psychoses. Psychiatry Department of University of São Paulo. São Paulo: Ed. Litografia Mattavelli.

——— (1993a). An evaluation of expressive techniques by Jungian symbolic psychology. *Junguiana: Journal of Brazilian Society for Analytical Psychology*, 11: 134–49.

——— (1993b). Workshop on narcissism-echoism in the teacher-student relationship. III Group Congress of High Schools of São Paulo.

——— (1993c). The initiation of the Virgin Mary by Mary Magdalene: An interpretation of St. John's Gospel. Lecture in Uni-Rio University, Rio de Janeiro.

——— (1995). Academic scientific research in the perspective of symbolic psychology. In Ivani Fazenda, ed., *Research in Education and the Transformations of Knowledge*. São Paulo: Ed. Papirus, 2nd edition, 1997.

——— (1996). The archetype of life and death. *Junguiana: Journal of Brazilian Society for Analytical Psychology*, 14: 92–115; revised in 2002.

——— (2000). The archetype of alterity and the Latin-American process of humanization. Second Latin-American Congress of Jungian Psychology. Rio de Janeiro, June 21–24.

——— (2002a). *Creative Envy—The Rescue of One of Civilization's Major Forces*. Wilmette, Ill: Chiron Publications, 2003.

——— (2002b). The senses as structuring functions of consciousness: A contribution of Jungian symbolic psychology. *Junguiana: Journal of Brazilian Society for Analytical Psychology*, 20: 7–15.

——— (2006a). *Jungian Symbolic Psychopathology*. São Paulo: Linear B, 2006.

——— (2006b). Jealousy. *Journal Psique Ciência e Vida*. 1(3):46–51.

——— (2008). *Jungian Symbolic Psychology*. Wilmette, Ill.: Chiron Publications, forthcoming.

CAPRA, Fritjof (1982). *The Turning Point*. São Paulo: Ed. Cultrix, 1993.

CONDE, Cecília (1978). Meaning and function of music in education. Research Project of Education through Art in the Brazilian Society. Rio de Janeiro, 1978.

CORRÊA PINTO, Gustavo Alberto, and Alayde Mutzenbecher, trans. (1982). *I Ching: The Book of Changes*. São Paulo: Ed. Pensamento.

CROCKER, Jon Christopher (1967). The social organization of Eastern Bororo. Cambridge: Harvard University, Ph.D. Dissertation.

DE MACEDO, Lino (1993). Constructivism and pedagogic practice. Lecture in Fundação do Desenvolvimento da Educação (FDE) in collaboration with Valquíria dos Santos. São Paulo.

DE ROLA, Klossowski Stanilas (1988). *The Golden Game*. New York: George Braziller.

DESCARTES, R. (1637). Discours de la méthode pour bien conduire sa raison, et chercher la vérité dans les sciences [Discourse on the method of rightly conducting reason to seek truth in science]. *in Descartes, Oeuvres et Lettres*. Paris: Bibliothéque da la Pléiade, Gallimard, 1953.

DÉSOILLE, R. (1961). *Theorie et Pratique du Rêve Éveillé Dirigé*. Genéve: Mont-Blanc.

ECO, Umberto (1980). *The Name of the Rose*. New York: Knopf, 2006.

EINSTEIN, A. (1930). *The World as I See It*. New York: Philosophical Library, 1979.

ELIADE, Mircea (1954). *Yoga, Immortality and Freedom*. Princeton: Princeton University Press, 1969.

ENGELS, Friedrich (1884). *The Origins of the Family, Private Property and the State*. Rio de Janeiro: Civilização Brasileira, 1977.

FRAZER, James (1890). *The Golden Bough*. Abridged edition. New York: Macmillan, 1922.

FREIRE, Paulo (1970). *Pedagogy of the Oppressed*. New York: Herder and Herder.

FREUD, Sigmund (1900). *The Interpretation of Dreams*. SE, vols. 4 and 5. Rio de Janeiro: Ed. Imago, 1972.

——— (1909). *A Case of Obsessive Neurosis*. SE, vol. 10. Rio de Janeiro: Ed. Imago, 1969.

——— (1911). *The Formulation of Two Principles of Mental Functioning*. SE, vol. 12. Rio de Janeiro: Ed. Imago, 1969.

——— (1913). *Totem and Tabu*. SE, vol. 13. Rio de Janeiro: Ed.Imago, 1974.

———(1914). *The History of the Psychoanalytic Movement*. SE, vol. 14. Rio de Janeiro: Ed. Imago, 1969.

——— (1917). *Transference*. SE, vol. 16. Rio de Janeiro: Ed. Imago, 1976.

FREUD, Sigmund (1921). *Psychoanalysis and Telepathy*. SE, vol. 18. Rio de Janeiro: Ed. Imago, 1976.

_____ (1929). *Civilization and its Discontents*. SE, vol. 21. Rio de Janeiro: Ed. Imago, 1974.

FURLANETTO, Ecleide Cunico (1986). A symbolic interpretation of school. Thesis in Education, Catholic University, São Paulo.

────── (1997). Interdisciplinary formation of teachers in the perspective of Jungian symbolic psychology. Dissertation, Catholic University, São Paulo.

GALIÁS, Iraci (1989). Teaching-learning, a polarity in symbolic development. *Junguiana: Journal of Brazilian Society for Analytical Psychology*, 7: 89–100.

GARCIA, Antonio C. (1983). The virgin and the wounded healer. Analyst Diploma Thesis. Brazilian Society of Analytical Psychology, São Paulo.

GARDNER, Howard (1983). *Structures of the Mind: A Theory of Multiple Intelligences*. Porto Alegre: Artes Médicas Sul, 1994.

GOLEMAN, Daniel (1995). *Emotional Intelligence*. Rio de Janeiro: Ed. Objetiva, 1995.

GRIMALDI MOREIRA, Sueli (1986). *The Pedagogic Relationship from the Consulting Room to the Classroom: An Anthropological Investigation*. Volume 12, Coleção Espaço. São Paulo: Ed. Loyola, 1989.

GUERRA, Maria Helena Ribeiro Mandacarú (1988). Encounter: Dialectical Interpersonal Relationship as Symbol of Totality. Master's dissertation. Institute of Psychology, University of São Paulo.

────── (2001). The loving Relationship in its Pre and Post-Personal Polarity. *Journal Jung and Body (Jung&Corpo)*, 1: 81-92.

GRINBERG, Luiz Paulo (2003). *Jung and the Creative Man*. São Paulo: FTD.

GUGGENBÜHL-CRAIG, Adolph (1971). *Power in the Helping Professions*. Texas: Spring Publications.

HAWKES, Jacquetta (1963). *History of Mankind: Cultural and Scientific Development*. New York: Harper and Row.

HEIDEGGER, Martin (1927). *Being and Time*. New York: Harper, 1962.

HERMES TRISMEGISTUS (II to IV Cent). *Corpus Hermeticum: Discurso de Iniciação*. São Paulo: Ed. Hemus, 1974. English edition: Brian P. Copenhaver, ed. *Hermetica: The Greek Corpus Hermeticum and the Latin Asclepius*. Cambridge, U.K.: Cambridge University Press, 1995.

JACOBY, Mario (1991). *Shame and the Origins of Self Esteem*. London: Routledge and Kegan Paul, 1994.

JUNG, C. G. (1921). Psychological Types. CW, vol. 6. New Jersey: Princeton Int. University Press, 1989.

_____ (1933). *The Real and the Surreal.* In CW, vol. 7. New Jersey: Princeton Int. University Press, 1960.

────── (1934). *The Practical use of Dream-Analysis.* In CW, vol. 16. New Jersey: Princeton Int. University Press, 1954.

────── (1935). *The Relations Between the Ego and the Unconscious,* 2nd edition. In CW, vol. 7. New Jersey: Princeton Int. University Press, 1953.

────── (1943). *On the Psychology of the Unconscious.* In CW, vol. 7. New Jersey: Princeton Int. University Press, 1953.

────── (1944). *Psychology and Alchemy.* CW, vol. 12. New Jersey: Princeton Int. University Press, 1953.

────── (1946). *The Psychology of Transference.* CW, vol. 16. New Jersey: Princeton Int. University Press, 1954.

────── (1948). *A Psychological Approach to the Dogma of Trinity.* CW, vol. 11. New Jersey: Princeton Int. University Press, 1958.

────── (1950). *Aion.* CW, vol. 9ii. New Jersey: Princeton Int. University Press, 1959.

────── (1952). *Synchronicity: An acausal Connecting Principle.* CW, vol. 8. New Jersey: Princeton Int. University Press, 1960.

────── (1954a). *On the Nature of the Psyche.* CW, vol. 8. New Jersey: Princeton Int. University Press, 1960.

────── (1954b). *Psychological Aspects of the Mother Archetype.* CW, vol. 9i. New Jersey: Princeton Int. University Press, 1959.

────── (1955–56). *Mysterium Coniunctionis.* CW, vol. 14. New Jersey: Princeton Int. University Press, 1963.

────── (1957). *Commentary on The Secret of the Golden Flower.* CW, vol. 13. New Jersey: Princeton Int. University Press, 1967.

────── (1958). *The Transcendent Function.* CW, vol. 8. New Jersey: Princeton Int. University Press, 1960.

────── (1961). *Memories, Dreams, Reflections.* New York: Random House. Portuguese edition published Rio de Janeiro: Ed. Nova Fronteira, 1975.

────── (1964). *Man and His Symbols.* New York: Doubleday & Company Inc..

────── (1913-1930). *The Red Book.* New York: W. W. Norton, 2009.

KANDEL, Eric R.; J. H. SCHWARTZ, and JESSEL, T. M. (2000). *Principles of Neural Science,* 4th edition. New York: McGraw-Hill.

KANT, Emanuel (1781). *The Critique of Pure Reason.* Rio de Janeiro: Tecnoprint (Edições de Ouro), Coleção Universidades, 1971.

KARDEC, Allan (1861). *The Book of Mediums.* São Paulo: Ed. Pensamento, 2002.

KAUFMAN, Arthur (1991). *Pedagogic Theatre.* São Paulo: Ed. Ágora.

KLEIN, Melanie (1946). Notes on some schizoid mechanisms. In Melanie Klein, Paula Heimann, Susan Isaacs, and Joan Riviere, *Developments in Psychoanalysis.* London: Karnac Books, 1989.

KOHUT, H. (1988). *Self and Narcissism.* Rio de Janeiro: Ed. Zahar.

KRAMER, Heinrich, and SPRENGER, James (1484). *Malleus Maleficarum— The Witches' Hammer.* Rio de Janeiro: Ed. Rosa dos Tempos, 1991.

Lao-Tzu (nd). *Tao Tè Ching.* English translation by H. G. Ostwald. Köln: Eugen Diederichs Verlag, 1978.

LEAKEY, Richard E. (1977). *Origins.* New York: Dutton.

LEVI-STRAUSS, Claude (1958). *Anthropologie Structurale.* Paris: Libraire Plon. English edition: *Structural Anthropology.* Chicago: University of Chicago Press, 1983.

———(1962). *La Pensée Sauvage.* Paris: Ed. Plon. English edition: *The Savage Mind.* Chicago: University of Chicago Press, 1968.

LOVELOCK, James E. (1979). *Gaia: A New Look at Life on Earth.* Oxford: Oxford University Press, 2000.

MAY, Rollo (1975). *The Courage to Create.* New York: W. W. Norton.

MOCCIO, Fidel (1980). *Workshop of Expressive Techniques.* Buenos Aires: Ed. Paidos, 1980.

MONTELLANO, Raquel Maria Porto (1996). Narcissism: Considerations today. *Junguiana: Journal of Brazilian Society for Analytical Psychology,*14: 64–69.

NEUMANN, Erich (1948). *Depth Psychology and a New Ethic.* New York: Putnam's and Sons.

———(1949). T*he Origins and History of Consciousness.* New York: Routledge and Kegan Paul, 1954.

———(1955). *The Child.* New York: Putnam's and Sons, 1970.

NOVOA, Antonio; CAVACO, Maria Helena, and HAMELINE Daniel (1991). *Profession: Teacher.* Porto: Porto Editora, Coleção Ciências da Educação.

PENTEADO, José Roberto Whitaker (1997). *Lobato's Sons.* Rio de Janeiro: Ed. Dunya.

PIAGET, Jean (1926). *The Language and Thought of the Child.* New York: Humanities Press, 1959.

_____ (1963). *La Construction du Réel chez L'Enfant.* 3 ème ed. Neuchatel: Delachaux et Niestte.

———— (1964). *Symbol Formation in Childhood: Imitation, Game and Dream, Image and Representation.* Rio de Janeiro: Zahar Eds., 1978.

———— (1967). *The Psychology of Intelligence.* Rio de Janeiro: Zahar Eds, 1977.

RAMOS, Denise Gimenez (1990). *A Psique do Coração* [*The Psyche of the Heart*], 2nd ed. São Paulo: Cultrix.

SAIZ LAUREIRO, Mario E. (1986). Symbolicity and temporality. *Junguiana: Journal of Brazilian Society for Analytical Psychology,* 4: 79–98.

———— (1989). La Psicologia Simbólica di Carlos Byington in *Psicologia Analítica Contemporanea.* Milan: Studi Bompiani, pp. 53-118 .

SALVADOR, César Coll (1994). *School Learning and the Construction of Knowledge.* Porto Alegre: Ed. Artes Médicas.

SILVEIRA, Nise (1981). *Images of the Unconscious.* Rio de Janeiro: Alhambra.

SOLMS, Mark, and TURNBULL, Oliver (2002). *The Brain and the Inner World.* New York: Other Press.

SPITZ, René, and CODLINER, Godfrey W. (1966). *First Year of Life: A Psychoanalytic Study of Normal and Deviant Development of Object Relations.* New York: Int. Universities Press.

*State of the World.* Transforming Cultures: From Consumerism to Sustainability. (2010).Worldwatch Institute. Washington, D.C.

STEIN, Murray (1976). *On narcissism. Spring.* New York: Spring Publications, 1976, pp. 23–53.

———— (1993). *Solar Conscience, Lunar Conscience.* Wilmette, Ill.: Chiron Publications.

TEILHARD DE CHARDIN, Pierre (1947). *Le Phenomène Humain.* Paris: Edition du Seuil, 1955. English edition : *The Phenomenon of Man.* New York: HarperCollins, 2008.

———— (1950). *Man's Place in Nature.* New York: HarperCollins, 2000.

TILLICH, Paul (1952). *The Courage to Be.* New Haven, Conn.: Yale University Press, 1955.

VARGAS, Milton (1987). Preface to *From Alchemy to Chemistry* by Ana Maria A. Goldfarb. São Paulo: Ed. Nova Estela, EDUSP.

VIDAL, Lux (1977). *Death and Life in a Brazilian Indian Society.* São Paulo: Ed. Hucitec.

VILLARES DE FREITAS, Laura (1990). The archetype of the master-pupil. *Junguiana: Journal of Brazilian Society for Analytical Psychology*, 8: 72–98.

VON BERTALANFFY, Ludwig (1968). *General Systems Theory.* New York: Bazillen.

VON FRANZ, Marie-Louise (1980). *On Divination and Synchronicity: The Psychology of Meaningful Chance.* Toronto: Inner City Books.

——— and HILLMAN, James (1971). *Jung's Typology.* New York: Spring.

VYGOTSKY, L .S. (1960). *The Social Formation of the Mind.* São Paulo: Martins Fontes Ed., 1989.

WAHBA, Liliana Liviano. 1996. *Camile Claudel: Creativity and Madness* (Criação e Loucura). Rio de Janeiro: Record/Rosa dos Tempos.

WATZLAWICK, Paul; BAVELAS, Janet Beavin and JACKSON, Don D. (1967). *The Pragmatics of Human Communication.* New York: W. W. Norton, 1967.

WICKES, Frances (1927). *The Inner World of Childhood: A Study in Analytical Psychology.* New York: P. Appleton & Co.

WHITEHEAD, Alfred North (1929). *Process and Reality: An Essay in Cosmology.* Cambridge, UK: Cambridge University Press.

WHITMONT, Edward C. (1969). *The Symbolic Quest.* Pinceton: Princeton University Press, 1979.

WILHELM, Richard, trans. (1923). *I Ching: The Book of Changes.* Rendered into English by Cary F. Baynes (1951). London: Routledge and Kegan Paul Ltd., 1960.

WINNICOTT, Donald W. (1965). *The Maturational Processes and the Facilitating Environment.* London: Hogarth Press.

ZILBOORG, Gregory, and HENRY, George W. ( 1941). *A History of Medical Psychology.* New York: W. W..Norton & Co., Inc.

## Films

*Dead Poets' Society* (1989). Directed by Peter Weir. Distributed by Touchstone Pictures.

*Forrest Gump* (1994). Directed by Robert Zemeckis. Distributed by Paramount Pictures.

*Freedom Writers* (2007). Directed by Richard La Gravenese. Distributed by Paramount Pictures.

*Instinct* (1999). Directed by Jon Turteltaub. Distributed by Touchstone Pictures- Spyglass Entretainment.

This book is printed on demand and digital system corresponds
consumption of 14.3 trees reforested under ISO 14001.
ALWAYS RECYCLE.

www.linearb.com.br
Tel.(11)3812-2817